Britain Votes: The 2024 General Election

Edited by Alistair Clark, Louise Thompson and Stuart Wilks-Heeg

in association with the Hansard Society

OXFORD
UNIVERSITY PRESS

Great Clarendon Street, Oxford OX2 6DP
United Kingdom

Oxford University Press is a department of the University of Oxford.
It furthers the University's objective of excellence in research, scholarship,
and education by publishing worldwide. Oxford is a registered trade mark
of Oxford University Press in the UK and in certain other countries.

© The Hansard Society, 2025

The moral rights of the authors have been asserted.

All rights reserved. No part of this publication may be reproduced, stored
in a retrieval system, transmitted, used for text and data mining, or used
for training artificial intelligence, in any form or by any means, without the
prior permission in writing of Oxford University Press, or as expressly
permitted by law, by licence or under terms agreed with the appropriate
reprographics rights organization. Enquiries concerning reproduction
outside the scope of the above should be sent to the Rights Department,
Oxford University Press, at the address above.

You must not circulate this work in any other form
and you must impose this same condition on any acquirer.

Published in the United States of America by Oxford University Press
198 Madison Avenue, New York, NY 10016, United States of America

British Library Cataloguing in Publication Data

Data available

ISBN 9780197903414

Typeset by Newgen Knowledge Works Pvt. Ltd, Chennai, India.
Printed in Great Britain by Bell & Bain Ltd, Glasgow, UK

The manufacturer's authorized representative in the EU for product safety
is Oxford University Press España S.A. of Parque Empresarial San Fernando de Henares, Avenida de Castilla, 2 – 28830 Madrid (www.oup.es/en
or product.safety@oup.com). OUP España S.A. also acts as importer into
Spain of products made by the manufacturer.

CONTENTS

v   Acknowledgements
vi   Contributors and Editors
vii   List of Tables
viii   List of Figures

Introduction

1   Introduction: A record-breaking election
Alistair Clark, Louise Thompson and Stuart Wilks-Heeg

The Results and Election Context

9   The results: How Britain voted in 2024
Hannah Bunting

30   The electoral system: All a question of geography
John Curtice

Political Parties

48   'Come, Armageddon, come': The Conservatives
Sam Power, Paul Webb and Tim Bale

65   The Labour Party under Keir Starmer: Plotting the route to a shallow landslide
Eunice Goes

94   Yellow fever returns: The 2024 Liberal Democrat campaign
David Cutts and Andrew Russell

110   Voices from the edge make breakthrough in British politics: The Greens, Reform UK, and independents
Lynn Bennie and Anders Widfeldt

Territorial Dimensions

128   Shifting sands: Sources of voter volatility in the 2024 UK General Election in Scotland
Ailsa Henderson and James Mitchell

148 The 2024 UK General Election in Wales
Jac M. Larner and Richard Wyn Jones

162 Northern Ireland: Sinn Féin completes a hat-trick
Jonathan Tonge and Stuart Wilks-Heeg

Campaign Themes

182 Party finance: Labour exploits its advantage
Justin Fisher

205 The first TikTok election? Social media, generative AI, and data-driven campaigning in the 2024 UK General Election
Filip Biały and Rachel Gibson

220 There may be trouble ahead: Women's representation, voters, and issues in the 2024 election campaign
Emily Harmer and Rosalynd Southern

236 Ethnic minority voters and the 2024 General Election
Nicole S. Martin

254 Tax, trip-ups, and transgressions: Reporting the 2024 UK General Election
David Deacon, David Smith and Dominic Wring

272 Breweries, bricklaying, and bungee jumping: Understanding the 2024 campaign trail
Alia Middleton and David Cutts

287 An inexperienced parliament
Philip Cowley

Conclusion

300 Conclusion: A time to take stock
Stuart Wilks-Heeg, Alistair Clark and Louise Thompson

Acknowledgements

Britain is fortunate to have a vibrant and active community of electoral scholars, without which this volume (and its predecessors), could not have been pulled together so quickly. As editors, we are fortunate to have been able to work with such a high-profile group of electoral experts. We are grateful for their enthusiastic contributions to this latest in the *Britain Votes* series.

To research British elections is to build on foundations constructed over many decades by earlier generations of psephologists. Since the last *Britain Votes* volume, three significant British psephologists have passed away. It seems appropriate here to briefly acknowledge the debt the study of British elections owes them.

Sir David Butler was one of the originators of the British Election Study and contributed numerous volumes to the Nuffield British General Election series. He was also Chairman of the Hansard Society, which publishes *Parliamentary Affairs* and the *Britain Votes* series, from 1994-2001. Prof. Ron Johnston brought the study of electoral geography to the fore, and was noted for his work on Britain's electoral system, boundary changes and commissions, and the effects of local candidate spending on constituency results. Prof. David Denver published numerous editions of his popular textbook on British voting behaviour, thereby introducing students to the joys of studying elections. He was noted for his work on Scottish local elections, for developing research into constituency campaigning, and was a long-time contributor to this *Britain Votes* series. They are all missed. The study of British elections would have been very different without their contributions.

Alistair, Louise and Stuart would like to thank their families for their forbearance as this volume was brought together. In the Clark household, the 2024 General Election at least led to one primary school pupil being interested in what it all meant. In the Thompson household, the children were forgiven for not knowing there was an election happening as no campaign literature was received at all despite being in a marginal seat. In the Wilks-Heeg household, the number of parliamentary electors quadrupled from the 2019 General Election, which at least added some family excitement to voting in the safest seat in the country.

Alistair Clark, Louise Thompson and Stuart Wilks-Heeg
April 2025

Britain Votes 2024

List of Contributors

Tim Bale	Professor of Politics at Queen Mary University of London.
Lynn Bennie	Reader in Politics at the University of Aberdeen.
Filip Bialy	Assistant Professor at Adam Mickiewicz University Poznań and Research Associate at the University of Manchester.
Hannah Bunting	Senior Lecturer in Quantitative British Politics and Co-Director of The Elections Centre at the University of Exeter.
Alistair Clark	Professor of Political Science at Newcastle University.
Philip Cowley	Professor of Politics at Queen Mary University of London.
John Curtice	Professor of Politics at Strathclyde University, and Senior Fellow at the National Centre for Social Research and 'The UK in a Changing Europe.'
David Cutts	Professor of Political Science at the University of Birmingham.
David Deacon	Professor of Communication and Media Analysis at Loughborough University.
Justin Fisher	Professor of Political Science and Director of Brunel Public Policy at Brunel University of London.
Rachel Gibson	Professor of Politics at the University of Manchester.
Eunice Goes	Professor of Politics at Richmond, The American University in London.
Emily Harmer	Senior Lecturer in Media at the University of Liverpool.
Ailsa Henderson	Professor of Political Science at the University of Edinburgh.
Jac Larner	Lecturer in Political Science at Cardiff University's Wales Governance Centre.
Nicole Martin	Lecturer in Politics at the University of Manchester.
Alia Middleton	Senior Lecturer in Politics at the University of Surrey.
James Mitchell	Professor of Public Policy at the University of Edinburgh.
Sam Power	Lecturer in Politics at the University of Bristol.
Andrew Russell	Professor of Politics at the University of Liverpool.
David Smith	Lecturer in Media and Communication at the University of Leicester.
Rosalynd Southern	Senior Lecturer in Political Communication at the University of Liverpool.
Louise Thompson	Senior Lecturer in Politics at the University of Manchester.
Jonathan Tonge	Professor of Politics at the University of Liverpool.
Paul Webb	Professor of Politics at the University of Sussex.
Anders Widfeldt	Senior Lecturer in Politics at the University of Aberdeen.
Stuart Wilks-Heeg	Professor of Politics at the University of Liverpool.
Dominic Wring	Professor of Political Communication at Loughborough University.
Richard Wyn Jones	Professor and Director of Cardiff University's Wales Governance Centre.

List of Tables

1.1 Total number of councillors for each party after the local elections, with net gains/losses in parentheses
1.2 Seat projections per party in MRP polls during the campaign
1.3 The results of the 2024 General Election for each party compared with the 2019 notional result (Great Britain only)
1.4 Smallest winning majorities and biggest majorities overturned
1.5 Best constituency vote share performances by each party
1.6 Highest and lowest turnouts in Great Britain
1.A1 2024 Vote share models
1.A2 Vote share change 2024-2019 models
2.1 The 2024 UK General Election result (with change from 2019 notional results)
2.2 Impact on seats of uniform swing from Conservative to Labour after 2019 election
2.3 Actual outcome in seats compared with uniform movement scenarios
2.4 Mean change in share of vote 2019–24 by Conservative share of vote 2019-24
2.5 Mean change in % share of vote 2019–24 by type of contest
2.6 Standard deviation of geographical distribution of party support 1974–2024
2.7 Distribution of the two-party vote, 1955–2024
2.8 Measures of two-party bias 1955–2024
2.9. Impact on seats of uniform swing from Labour to Conservative after 2024 election
3.1 Involvement in election campaign activities by party members
3.2 Time committed to campaign activities by party members, 2024
3.3 Logistic regression model of Conservative vote 2024
4.1 Labour's performance in the Red Wall 2005-24
4.2 Seats Labour won thanks to Reform UK
4.A1 Labour's offensive campaign
5.1 Summary of Liberal Democrat general election performance 1992-2024
5.2 2024 Liberal Democrat performance: National and regional breakdown (English regions)
5.3 2024 Liberal Democrat performance by incumbency and seat type
5.4 2024 Liberal Democrat performance by historical legacy and new target seats
6.1 Votes and seats for the Greens in general and EU elections 1974-2024
6.2 Votes and seats for UKIP and successor parties in general and EU elections 1999-2024
6.3 Seats won by the Greens and Reform UK at the 2024 General Election
6.4 Socio-demographic profile of voters (%)
6.5 Most important issue facing the country among voters (%)
6.6 Seats won by independents in the 2024 General Election

7.1 UK General Election 2024 results in Scotland
7.2 Vote switching in 2024
7.3 Perceived and actual difference between party supporters
7.4 Support for policy options by party vote, 2024, %
8.1 UK General Election result in Wales, 2024 (change from 2019)
8.2 Westminster election results in Wales, 1979-2024, vote share (seats)
9.1 The Northern Ireland General Election result 2024
9.2 Northern Ireland constituency results, Westminster Election 2024
9.3 Party constituency placings
9.4 Party votes by self-declared religious affiliation of voters, 2024 Northern Ireland Westminster Election (%)
9.5 Constituency outcomes by religion and vote shares by pro-Northern Ireland (NI) in the UK versus pro-United Ireland (UI) candidates, Northern Ireland election 2024
10.1 Source of election period declared cash donations and levels of declared non-cash donations
10.2 Timing of weekly declared cash and non-cash donations
12.1 Candidate gender by party, 2019 and 2024
12.2 Woman MPs by party after the 2024 General Election
13.1 Ethnic diversity in constituencies in different regions
13.2 Voter eligibility and registration by ethnicity
13.3 Average change in vote share in constituencies according to ethnic diversity
14.1 Proportion of news presence of political parties across all news media 2001-24
14.2 Top 10 issues in the 2024 and 2019 media campaigns
14.3 Issue balance per TV channel—top ten themes
14.4 Quotation time in news items only
14.5 Daily newspapers' 2024 partisanship with circulations (hard copy in 000s) (with 2019 equivalent partisanships and circulations in brackets)
16.1 Parliamentary experience of MPs, 2024

List of Figures

1.1 Vote share by region 2019 and 2024
1.2 Constituency majorities over 30 years of general elections
1.3 Effective number of parties at the constituency level over 30 years of general elections
1.4 Constituency turnout over 30 years of elections
1.5 2024 party vote share explained by constituency demographics
1.6 Change in party vote share 2019-24 explained by constituency demographics
3.1 How well is Boris Johnson doing as Prime Minister?
3.2 How well is Rishi Sunak doing as Prime Minister?
3.3 Which political party would be best at handling the economy?
3.4 Do you think the Conservative Party is trustworthy or untrustworthy, competent or incompetent?
4.1 How patriotic is Keir Starmer?
4.2 Top issues for voters
4.3 Voting intentions
4.4 Which party is best at handling asylum and immigration?
4.5 Which party is best at handling the economy?
5.1 Liberal Democrat gains in Conservative-Liberal Democrat battlegrounds by 2019 notional marginality
6.1 Voting intentions in six months before General Election
6.2 Greens and Reform UK in the countries and regions of the UK (% vote)
7.1 Pedersen Volatility Index 2024 Scotland
7.2 Types of constituency contest 2017-24
7.3 What voters wanted from the 2024 UK General Election
7.4 Constitutional preferences by party vote, 2024
8.1 Satisfaction with government over time
8.2 Proportion of respondents who thought the UK Government has done a bad job of Brexit, by 2024 vote
9.1 Roman Catholic population (%) by constituency and vote share for nationalist parties (%), Northern Ireland 2024 General Election
9.2 Protestant population (%) by constituency and vote share for unionist parties (%), Northern Ireland 2024 General Election
9.3 Unionist, Nationalist and 'Others' bloc votes, Northern Ireland general elections 2001-24
10.1 Central party income 1989-2023
10.2 Labour income as a percentage of Conservative income 1989-2023

10.3 Central party expenditure 1989-2023
10.4 Central party expenditure as a percentage of income 1989-2023
10.5 Number of declared cash donations 2010 Q3 to 2024 Q2
10.6 Declared cash donations 2020 Q3 to 2024 Q2
12.1 The General Election recalled vote by gender
12.2 The 2024 General Election recalled vote for the Conservative and Labour parties by gender and age
14.1 Labour and Conservative TV share, press share, and vote share 2001-24
14.2 Proportion of positive to negative coverage of political parties by newspaper title
15.1 2024 party leader visits by electoral competitiveness
15.2 2024 weekly leader visits by electoral competitiveness
15.3 2024 Campaign trail: policy-themed visits (%)

Introduction: A record-breaking election

Alistair Clark[1], Louise Thompson[2], and Stuart Wilks-Heeg[3,*]

[1] School of Geography, Politics and Sociology, Newcastle University, Newcastle upon Tyne, NE1 7RU, UK
[2] Department of Politics, University of Manchester, Arthur Lewis Building, Oxford Road, Manchester, M13 9PL, UK
[3] Department of Politics, University of Liverpool, 8-11 Abercromby Square, Liverpool, L69 7ZA, UK

*Correspondence: swilks@liverpool.ac.uk

Britain Votes 2019 concluded, somewhat bravely, that 'for Labour to win an overall majority at the next election would be remarkable but not impossible' (Tonge, Wilks-Heeg, and Thompson 2020: 298). The prospect of a Labour landslide was not even remotely hinted at. Yet, this is the outcome we seek to document and explain in *Britain Votes 2024*.

On one level, the explanation is straightforward. First, the Conservatives squandered enormous reserves of political capital as they struggled with a series of crises under three unpopular prime ministers. For all his campaigning talents, Boris Johnson proved inept at governing, especially during a pandemic. Caught in a web of dishonesty surrounding the 'partygate' revelations in late 2021, his departure became inevitable. He was one of the last to realize it, only announcing his resignation on 7th July 2022 after sixty-two government ministers had resigned. Two months later, Liz Truss became Prime Minister, yet within weeks, her personal ratings were below Johnson's at his nadir (Fiedler 2022). The fallout from the mini-budget on 23rd September did most of the damage. Having become the most unpopular Prime Minister on record, Truss announced her resignation on 20th October, 6 days after dismissing her Chancellor, Kwasi Kwarteng. On 25th October, Rishi Sunak was hurriedly appointed as the fifth Conservative Prime Minister in 6 years. He inherited the problems his predecessors had failed to tackle: a stagnant economy, rising inflation, widespread industrial action, record National Health Service (NHS) waiting times and escalating public disquiet over immigration. By early 2023, Sunak's personal ratings had gone the same way as

Johnson's and Truss's, amid multiple failures to reset the agenda (Ipsos 2023). No dent was made in the twenty-point Labour poll lead that had opened up in Autumn 2022.

Second, under Keir Starmer, Labour became electable again. In response to the crushing defeat under Jeremy Corbyn in 2019, Starmer's reshaping of Labour was rapid and ruthless (and seemingly at odds with what he had suggested during the party leadership contest). Labour's poll ratings improved, overtaking the Conservatives in the wake of partygate, and remaining ahead through to election day. Starmer's personal ratings were tepid, at best. But he consistently polled better than any Conservative leader from late 2021 onwards. Polling evidence accumulated that Labour were a government-in-waiting, with voters indicating that they preferred Labour over the Conservatives on all key issues (Ipsos 2024). By early 2024, all that really remained was a guessing game about when Sunak would deem the least-worst time to call a general election.

Of course, there is much more to the 2024 General Election than Conservative collapse and Labour recovery. A striking feature of the 2024 contest was the number of electoral records it established. Taken together, these paint a picture of remarkable volatility. The turnaround from an eighty-seat majority for one party to a majority of 174 for another was unprecedented.[1] The 11% swing from the Conservatives to Labour is the highest in the post-war era. With only 121 Members of Parliament (MPs), the Conservatives were reduced to their lowest-ever level of parliamentary representation, beating the previous record set in 1906. Yet, the scale of movement between the two main parties is only half the story. Electoral volatility from 2019 to 2024, as measured by the Pedersen Index (20.3), was the highest since 1945 and probably ever. The same is true of disproportionality, as measured by the Gallagher Index (23.6). The gap between the Effective Number of Parties as measured by votes (4.8) and as measured by seats (2.2) was also at a record high. Put another way, the two main parties received their lowest combined share of the vote under universal suffrage (see Bennie and Widfeldt, this volume) resulting in twelve parties taking their seats in the House of Commons, nine of whom had more than three MPs (plus six independents, the most at any election since 1945). Finally, as Philip Cowley notes in his chapter, 52% of MPs elected in 2024 are new to the Commons, another post-war record, while the 350 departures from the Commons arising from the election (resignations and defeats) is higher than at any election this side of the First World War.

There were far-reaching changes to the UK's legal and institutional framework prior to the election. The Fixed-term Parliaments Act 2011 was repealed by the

---

[1] Figures for Labour's majority in 2024 vary between 172 and 174, depending on the method of calculation, and these variations are reflected in this volume. The BBC's results used the figure of 174, which counts the Speaker, Lindsay Hoyle, as a Labour MP.

Dissolution and Calling of Parliament Act 2022. The calling of an early general election once again became a matter for the prime minister, not parliament, as a royal prerogative power. The Elections Act 2022 introduced a slew of changes to the legal framework for elections. The controversial requirement for all voters at UK-wide elections to show voter identification at polling stations (already in place in Northern Ireland since the mid-1980s) overshadowed its numerous other provisions. These included the removal of the fifteen-year limit on voting rights for UK citizens living abroad, new restrictions on postal and proxy voting, provisions for ministerial direction of the Electoral Commission and requirements for imprints on digital campaign materials indicating who was responsible for them. In a separate piece of legislation, the Ballot Secrecy Act 2023 sought to address concerns about family members unduly influencing voting in polling stations.

Legal changes impacting on election spending and donations to political parties were also made in November 2023, via secondary legislation. The caps on campaign spending by parties nationally and candidates locally were raised, to take account of inflation. Equivalent changes were made to the monetary threshold at which donations had to be declared by political parties.

Finally, the election was also fought on a new set of constituency boundaries, as required by the Parliamentary Constituencies Act 2020. These were the first boundary changes since 2010, after reviews completed in 2013 and 2018 failed to receive parliamentary approval. Under the new rules, all but five island constituencies were required to have electorates within 5% of the mean, resulting in 90% of existing constituencies being redrawn to varying degrees. While Northern Ireland retained eighteen constituencies, Scotland lost two bringing its number of seats to fifty-seven. Wales experienced a reduction of eight seats bringing its total to thirty-two. England gained ten seats as a consequence, bringing its total to 543. The boundary changes necessitated a reliance on 'notional' models of those new seats for parties' campaign strategising and the eventual post-election analysis (see Rallings and Thrasher 2024).

Some observers saw these reforms as advantaging the Conservatives. Claims of rigging by the governing party were, however, well wide of the mark. Despite suggestions that lack of photographic voter identification would disproportionately impact Labour voters, and evidence that the identification requirements prevented a small minority from voting in 2024, it is unlikely that the change had any clear partisan effect. Similarly, if there was a master plan to enfranchise up to 2.3 million, presumed Conservative-voting, British ex-patriots, it failed spectacularly. Only 191,338 overseas electors registered in 2024, fewer than in 2019. Accusations that donation and election spending limits were raised to benefit the Conservatives fall down against the reality that Labour raised more than the Conservatives and outspent them comprehensively. The boundary changes, drawn up by the independent Boundary Commissions, would have tilted things slightly in the Conservatives' favour, had voting patterns remained as they were in 2019. However, as John Curtice demonstrates in this volume, the distribution of electoral support for the parties changed radically. Revised boundaries might have mattered in 2015 or 2017, when margins were narrow. They were essentially irrelevant in the context of Labour landslide.

The campaign failed to inspire. The election was announced by Sunak in the pouring rain, weather which barely stopped through to polling day. The TV debates were widely derided and viewing figures were down on previous elections. Tory campaign gaffes were a constant theme, garnering more attention than any detailed discussion of key issues. The most serious gaffe was arguably a betting scandal, involving multiple cases of Conservative candidates and staff betting on the date of the general election. The most damaging for Sunak personally was, without a doubt, his decision to leave the D-Day commemorations early to conduct an interview with ITV (McKiernan 2024). High-profile Conservative policies, like a plan to restore national service, did not move the dial for them. Neither did their attacks on Labour's tax plans, which became a major point of focus in the final weeks. Starmer played it safe, repeating the same lines, notably that he was the son of a toolmaker. Davey did the opposite, quite literally embracing danger on the campaign trail. The entry of Nigel Farage for Reform UK caused much angst for the Conservatives. The proliferation of multilevel regression with poststratification (MRP) estimates of the election outcome became a major talking point, amid speculation about the prospect of a near-total Conservative wipeout. Once the polls had closed, the exit poll mostly surprised viewers for suggesting Labour's majority would be just under that achieved in 1997 (which was ultimately correct) and for hinting at an unexpectedly high level of Reform UK representation (which ultimately was not).

As the results came in, the geographical spread of the Labour victory rapidly became clear. The map turned red in places it had never before. Wilks-Heeg's law that Labour win a general election if you can walk from the Humber to the Mersey without leaving a Labour constituency was very clearly met. Indeed, there are many 'red routes' now available for this psephological variant of Wainwright's Coast to Coast. Rather more remarkably, the new electoral map permits travel from the Bristol Channel to the Thames Estuary without entering a Conservative-held constituency, or even from the Solent to the Menai Strait, albeit via a scenic route. Football fans will find it particularly easy to avoid spending time in Conservative constituencies, if they are so inclined. Only one of the ninety two teams in the top four levels of English football, Bromley, now plays its home games in a Conservative-held seat. Starmer's regular use of lower league football grounds as campaign stops seemed to pay off, at least symbolically, as Alia Middleton and David Cutts highlight in their chapter on the campaign trail.

Introduction: A record-breaking election   5

1. Overview of the volume

This collection follows the format of its predecessor volumes. It analyses the results of the 2024 General Election and the rival party campaigns, as well as territorial variations in party competition and election outcomes. It provides expert insight into important campaign themes, including women's representation, ethnic minority voters, social and mainstream media, party finance and the nature of the campaign trail.

The first section examines the results in detail. Hannah Bunting sets out the magnitude of Labour's victory and dissects its characteristics. As she notes, opinion polls and MRPs foretold the outcome, albeit with a degree of error that was perhaps inevitable given volatility in the electorate. As Bunting highlights, 2024 was an election in which competence mattered greatly, but trust in politicians was at a record low. A splintering of party support and low turnout were key consequences of an electorate indicating clearly who they did not want but showing no agreement on who they did want. These same dynamics are considered by John Curtice in his account of how the electoral system operated in 2024. Superficially, first-past-the-post delivered a clear swing of the pendulum and replaced an unpopular single-party government with its primary rival. Among the many electoral records set in the election was that for disproportionality, with Labour winning almost two-thirds of the seats on one-third of the votes. As Curtice shows, shifts in electoral geography are key to understanding this outcome. In particular, Labour's vote became more evenly, and more efficiently, distributed in 2024.

Given these overall outcomes, the second section of the book turns to consider the campaigns of the political parties. Sam Power, Paul Webb and Tim Bale begin by asking how the Conservatives lost their grip on power so spectacularly, given the predominant assumption after 2019 that they were virtually guaranteed a further term. They document a litany of shortcomings that collectively undermined the scope for the Conservatives to present themselves as a credible party of government. A gaffe-riddled campaign, which many party activists seemed reluctant to participate in, failed to change that perception. By contrast, Eunice Goes documents how Labour's highly efficient campaign enabled it to recover from its electoral nadir of 2019. She sets out how Labour's campaign aimed to show that the party had turned its back on the Corbyn era, expose the failures of Conservative governments and convince voters to see Labour as a competent and credible alternative. The party succeeded in attracting enough of its target voters in the places it needed to win, even if its well-funded campaign was 'gloriously boring', with transformative policy proposals sacrificed for a strict focus on electoral strategy.

While a Labour landslide was expected, the Liberal Democrats winning a record seventy-two seats was not. David Cutts and Andrew Russell suggest that this success owed much to good fortune, notably the chaotic collapse of the

Conservatives, but that it was also the result of smart campaigning under a new leader, Sir Ed Davey. Cutts and Russell note that the Liberal Democrats prospered by opposing the Conservatives, a task made far easier by widespread public anger at the ruling party. The party's focus on maximizing seats, not votes, paid dividends, enabling it to win 11.1% of parliamentary contests on 12.2% of the votes. Another striking feature of the 2024 General Election was the vote share gained by parties other than the main three. Lynn Bennie and Anders Widfeldt examine the commonalities and contrasts in the campaigns of the Greens and Reform UK. As they note, these are very different parties, whose voter bases are almost mirror-images of each other. They ran highly contrasting campaigns; the Greens targeting four seats highly effectively, while Reform UK took a more scattergun 'all-out' strategy. Both took votes from the major parties while facing common challenges under first-past-the-post. The success of six independent candidates further underlines the challenges posed to the mainstream parties by a fragmented political sphere.

The third section of the book turns to the unique nature of the electoral contests in Scotland, Wales and Northern Ireland. Ailsa Henderson and James Mitchell examine the Scottish results demonstrating that, behind the headline of extensive Labour gains from the SNP, there is a more complex picture of multilevel volatility. Labour made thirty-six gains, on a vote share of 35%, benefitting from a context in which voters in Scotland prioritized the removal of a Conservative government at Westminster rather than constitutional issues. However, Henderson and Mitchell stress that there are good reasons to question whether Labour's recovery in Scotland is sustainable, not least because support for independence has not waned.

Similar questions apply to the apparent reassertion of Labour dominance in Wales, where the party won twenty-seven out of thirty-two seats. As Jac Larner and Richard Wyn-Jones show, this was not quite the triumph it may seem. Labour's vote share in Wales fell to 37.5% and its electoral success owed much to the weakness of its opponents, notably the Conservatives, whose representation was wiped out entirely. Meanwhile, Plaid Cymru, the most effective challenger to Labour, won four seats on a record national vote share of 14.8%, but made little impact outside of its Welsh-speaking heartlands. In Northern Ireland, by contrast, the results were most notable for the reshuffling of party support within the Unionist bloc. Notwithstanding recent demographic change, Jonathan Tonge and Stuart Wilks-Heeg find no evidence that Northern Ireland's electoral divide is thawing. On one side, Sinn Fein cemented its place as the leading Nationalist party while, on the other, divides among Unionists split the vote, costing the Democratic Unionist Party (DUP) three seats. Alliance remains unable to mobilize the growing numbers who identify with neither bloc.

The final section of the book examines a range of other themes relating to the election campaign. In the first of these, Justin Fisher provides a detailed assessment of party finance. Fisher sets out significant legislative changes in party election finance passed ahead of the election, before going on to demonstrate that these did not benefit the governing party. Indeed, in 2024, the financial advantage swung back to Labour, a situation last seen under Blair. Digital campaigning, one area in which Labour's financial advantage was evident, is the focus of the chapter by Filip Biały and Rachel Gibson. They point to huge spending differentials on digital, with Labour committing £6.1m to the Conservatives' £2.1m. Yet, despite much talk about the use of artificial intelligence and the role of TikTok, there were limited new developments in digital campaigning and more voters were still reached via traditional methods.

Emily Harmer and Rosalynd Southern examine the gender dimensions of the campaign. They note that most parties adopted policies specifically to target women and the election saw the return of the first House of Commons that was 40% female. However, they also found that male politicians dominated media coverage, especially in the final stages of the campaign. Meanwhile, Nicole Martin looks at ethnic minority voters in the 2024 election, underlining the growing competition to gain the support of this increasingly heterogeneous group, now comprising 14% of the electorate. Labour's lower than expected vote share was significantly impacted by ethnic minority voters either staying at home or opting for other parties or independents.

David Deacon, David Smith and Dominic Wring assess the role of the media in the election campaign noting that, despite structural change in the media ecosystem, legacy media remain central. Their detailed content analysis of reporting highlights a two-party squeeze in media coverage at odds with the multi-party outcome. Deacon et al. highlight that GB News is a particular outlier in several ways, paying almost zero attention to smaller parties other than Reform UK. A staple of modern media coverage of elections is coverage of leaders' constituency visits. Alia Middleton and David Cutts undertake a detailed mapping of leadership tours and their significance. While the electoral effects of leaders' visits are likely modest, they tell us much about the rival parties' campaign strategies. Sunak's travel itinerary reflected a defensive campaign; Starmer's an expansionist one. As Middleton and Cutts note, it was Davey's stunts that 'stole the show', securing the party visibility and enabling it to cut through on its key campaign issues.

The 2024 election saw 350 parliamentary careers ended, or at least interrupted, because of sitting MPs either standing down or being defeated. As Philip Cowley discusses, this turnover has ushered in a hugely inexperienced parliament. Just over one-half of MPs are entirely new to the Commons, while less than one-quarter have at least a decade's experience. Meanwhile, Cowley notes, the fragmented opposition, comprising 121 Conservatives alongside 118 other MPs, will bring significant challenges to the functioning of parliament.

In our conclusion to the volume, we reflect in more detail on an election that was notable both for its classic 'kick the rascals out' valence qualities and for its exceptional levels of volatility. We also highlight several issues which have arguably gone under the radar, ranging from turnout decline to increased disproportionality, that pose important challenges for British electoral democracy in the years ahead. The UK has a multi-party system struggling to get out and the consequences of this for the next general election are exceptionally hard to predict.

References

Fiedler, T. (2022) 'Liz Truss Now the Least Popular UK Prime Minister in the History of Polling', *Politico*, https://www.politico.eu/article/uk-liz-truss-tories-least-popular-pm/, accessed 16 Jan. 2025.

Ipsos (2023) 'Majority of Britons Hold Unfavourable Opinion of Rishi Sunak', https://www.ipsos.com/en-uk/majority-of-britons-hold-an-unfavourable-opinion-of-rishi-sunak, accessed 16 Jan. 2025.

Ipsos (2024) 'British Public More Likely to Think Labour has the Best Policies on the Issues That Matter Most to Them', https://www.ipsos.com/en-uk/british-public-more-likely-think-labour-has-best-policies-issues-matter-most-them, accessed 16 Jan. 2025.

McKiernan, J. (2024) 'PM Apologises for Leaving D Day commemorations Early', *BBC News*, https://www.bbc.co.uk/news/articles/c722zv2myjro, accessed 16 Jan. 2025.

Rallings, C. and Thrasher, M. (2024) 'Guide to the New Parliamentary Constituencies 2024', *BBC, ITV News, Sky News, PA Media*, https://www.electionscentre.co.uk/wp-content/uploads/2024/05/Guide-to-the-New-Parliamentary-Constituencies.pdf, accessed 16 Jan. 2025.

Tonge, J., Wilks-Heeg, S. and Thompson, L. (2020) 'Conclusion: The BBC and the Election: Boris, Brexit and Corbyn', in: J. Tonge, S. Wilks-Heeg and L. Thompson (eds.) *Britain Votes: The 2019 General Election*, pp. 288–99. Oxford: Oxford University Press.

The results: How Britain voted in 2024

Hannah Bunting*

The Elections Centre, University of Exeter, Clayden Building, Streatham Rise, Exeter, EX4 4PE, UK

*Correspondence: h.bunting@exeter.ac.uk

With the repeal of the Fixed-Term Parliaments Act in 2022, the power to call a general election returned to the Prime Minister. The latest possible date was 28th January 2025, and speculation around its timing had been mounting. One criticism of the UK's lack of fixed terms is that it often benefits the governing party, prompting political pundits to try and calculate the optimal moment for the Conservatives to hold the contest. Most believed it would be November. However, Rishi Sunak surprised the nation, and even his own party, by calling the election on the 22nd May, setting polling day for 4th July 2024—the first July general election since 1945. Although he made the announcement around 5pm, news of an imminent speech had been circulating for much of the day. This gave protesters time to organize musical demonstrations, though it was not enough time for Sunak to check the weather and bring an umbrella. Standing in the rain, with 'Things Can Only Get Better' playing in the background, the Prime Minister did not look like he held the advantage.

1. The story between elections

The previous general election in December 2019 saw the Conservatives, under Boris Johnson, win a sizable eighty-seat majority. The global coronavirus pandemic hit just a few months later, forcing the government to impose strict lockdown rules across the UK. Parliament itself had to adapt, introducing remote voting for the first time in the earlier months, and the government enacted a range of restrictive measures, including fines to ensure public compliance. Citizens were barred from gathering, could only leave their homes for one hour a day, and businesses and schools were forced to close unless deemed essential. Britons looked to their government to guide them through this time of crisis.

© The Author(s) 2025. Published by Oxford University Press on behalf of the Hansard Society. All rights reserved. For commercial re-use, please contact reprints@oup.com for reprints and translation rights for reprints. All other permissions can be obtained through our RightsLink service via the Permissions link on the article page on our site—for further information please contact journals.permissions@oup.com.

This resulted in a temporary boost for the Conservatives and Johnson in both party support and approval ratings. Although Sir Keir Starmer replaced Jeremy Corbyn as Leader of the Opposition in April 2020, Labour's support did not change significantly at first.

In November 2021, after all Covid-19 restrictions were lifted, a breaking news story revealed that some Ministers and civil servants had not followed lockdown rules while they were in force. Dubbed 'Partygate', the scandal quickly grew in both scope and significance. The Metropolitan Police ultimately issued 126 fines to eighty-three people, including Boris Johnson and then-Chancellor Rishi Sunak, after investigating twelve gatherings in and around Downing Street. The public outcry to this and other scandals was reflected in Conservative polling numbers, which declined sharply by around ten points over a six-month period. By April 2022 calls for Johnson's resignation mounted. Allegations that he had deliberately misled parliament were referred to the Privileges Committee, further eroding his credibility and stirring party infighting. Meanwhile, Starmer and Deputy Leader Angela Rayner faced their own investigation by Durham Police for sharing a meal with their campaign team during a May 2021 by-election. While Johnson's charges were upheld, Starmer and Rayner were cleared. Nonetheless, the damage to trust in politicians had already been done. A report by Ipsos MORI revealed that only 9% of people trusted politicians to tell the truth—the lowest figure ever recorded and the worst of any profession surveyed.

Johnson's leadership became increasingly untenable. In June 2022, he narrowly survived a Conservative Party vote of no confidence, with 41% of his MPs voting against him. As the scandals continued to mount, so did ministerial resignations. By 7th July, an unprecedented sixty-two ministers had resigned, and Johnson was forced to step down. By this time Labour had overtaken the Conservatives in the polls, a lead the governing party ultimately never regained. The ensuing leadership contest saw Liz Truss, MP for South West Norfolk, and Rishi Sunak, MP for Richmond and Northallerton, emerge as the final contenders. Truss won the party membership vote and became Prime Minister on 6th September 2022. However, a series of economic policies she enacted caused the pound to plummet and mortgage rates to skyrocket. After just forty-five days in office, Truss resigned, becoming the shortest-serving British Prime Minister in history. On 25th October 2022, Rishi Sunak walked into Downing Street as the new Prime Minister. Labour were twenty points ahead in the polls.

The 2019–24 Parliament saw twenty-three by-elections, nine of which were triggered by scandals—both unusually high figures in what was largely a record-breaking set of contests. The first was a rare case of the governing party gaining a seat from the opposition, when the Conservatives won

Hartlepool in May 2021. Yet the tides soon turned against the Conservatives. Just a month later, the Liberal Democrats overturned a Conservative majority of 29.1% in Chesham and Amersham. Of the fourteen by-election seats that were defended by the Conservatives, eleven were lost. The average swing for those losses was 23.1 points. Three of the by-elections set new records for the largest Conservative majorities overturned: first in Shropshire North in December 2021 (40.6%), then in Tiverton and Honiton in June 2022 (40.7%), and finally in Tamworth in October 2023 (42.6%). Turnout during this period was historically low, averaging just 38.9%.

The mood of the electorate was further reflected in the four sets of local elections held between December 2019 and July 2024. These elections followed a similar pattern to the by-elections. Due to Covid-19 the 2020 local elections were postponed for a year, making 2021 a bumper year for local election contests. Held six months before the Partygate scandal broke, and on the same day as the Hartlepool by-election, the local elections saw Labour losing control of eight councils and losing 328 councillors. The Conservatives were the biggest beneficiaries, resulting in their best performance since 2008. It was also a good result for the Greens, who took seats from both main parties. Yet in following years, it was the Conservatives who haemorrhaged councillors. In 2023, Labour became the largest party of local government for the first time in two decades. This was despite a marked fragmentation of votes as both the Liberal Democrats and Greens continued to make gains. It was also in spite of low participation, with turnout averaging less than a third in the latter two years. The local elections held just a few weeks before the general election announcement saw the rise of the independents and others. More than 60% of the gains were made by parties other than Labour, with councils such as Oldham opting for local independents over established parties. Reform UK achieved an average vote share of more than 14% in the seats they contested, yet only won two (Table 1.1).

Table 1.1. Total number of councillors for each party after the local elections, with net gains/losses in parentheses

	2021	2022	2023	2024
Conservatives	7,562 (+234)	7,081 (−482)	5,686 (−1,059)	5,183 (−473)
Labour	5,849 (−328)	6,017 (+113)	6,495 (+578)	6,581 (+186)
Liberal Democrats	2,487 (+5)	2,697 (+208)	2,983 (+432)	3,101 (+104)
Green	462 (+88)	570 (+100)	776 (+231)	835 (+74)
Independents and Others	2,981 (+4)	3,006 (+61)	2,051 (−182)	2,915 (+109)
Average turnout	**35.8%**	**34.9%**	**33.1%**	**32.0%**

Source: The Elections Centre.

2. Candidates, predictions, and the campaign period

Whilst the National Equivalent Vote share in local elections, using the assumption of a uniform national swing, suggested Labour were some way off a parliamentary majority, polling consistently predicted Starmer would win a landslide. The projections were numerous and not always consistent. Dr Mark Pack's PollBase recorded thirty publicly released voting intention (VI) polls during the six-week campaign, an average of five polls a week, from thirteen different polling companies. They provided a snapshot of projected vote shares for each party. The campaign was dominated by reports of multilevel regression with post-stratification (MRP) polls. These gave a seat estimation for each party based on modelling that combines survey and demographic data. At least seventeen MRPs were released, by a smaller subset of pollsters.

Estimations were generated for seven parties plus 'others', in part because the 2024 election saw a record 4,379 candidates standing across Britain. This exceeded the previous high of 4,093 in 2010. 90% of seats had candidates from each of the five well-known parties—Conservative, Labour, Liberal Democrat, Green and Reform UK—and the SNP and Plaid Cymru contested all seats in Scotland and Wales respectively. There were a further 1,064 candidates from local parties such as the South Devon Alliance, other parties like UKIP, or those standing as independents. Every constituency had at least five candidates on the ballot; nearly half had eight or more.

At the start of the campaign, the Conservatives had still not selected candidates in more than 100 seats. There were also many MPs who chose to stand down ahead of the election, a total of 132 for all parties. Nearly two-thirds of those were Conservatives and included eight announcements made after the election was called. This included Michael Gove on 24th May 2024, who had been in parliament since 2005 and was a prominent feature of the several Conservative governments since 2010. Labour were much better prepared, with candidates ready for almost every seat. Another surprise announcement came when Nigel Farage revealed he would stand in Clacton for the Reform UK party and replace Richard Tice as their leader. This was Farage's eighth attempt to win a parliamentary seat. He had originally said he would be focussing on supporting Trump in the US election in November 2024, but the early calling of the UK general election seemed to change his mind.

The numerous parties and unexpected developments were reflected in the opinion polling. On the day the election was called, Labour were twenty-five points ahead of the Conservatives in voting intention polls, and the consensus was that this would narrow. However, on the eve of polling day, while Labour had declined five points, all changes for other parties were within the three-point margin of error. That is, while there had been fluctuations throughout the campaign, they largely returned to the predicted vote share they began with.

The biggest range of possibilities was in the MRP projections. Labour and the Conservatives saw a ninety-eight and seventy-three-seat range of plausible outcomes across polling companies throughout the campaign period respectively. This declined with the size of the party but remained large proportional to the number of expected seats. According to some estimates, the Conservatives were facing the possibility of becoming the third party, whilst Reform UK could gain either zero or seven seats; Labour's most favourable estimate in an MRP poll saw them projected to win nearly 80% of all constituencies (Table 1.2).

These wide variations in seat estimates were largely due to voter volatility—people frequently switching their party support between elections or even between individual polls. In addition, a significant proportion of respondents remained undecided and fewer people were confident about whether they would vote at all. The election was also being fought on new constituency boundaries. Just sixty-five seats had no change in their composition meaning almost every seat's baseline was an estimated 'notional' result compiled by Colin Rallings and Michael Thrasher.[1] Pollsters had to navigate these exceptional factors when making their projections.

The MRP polls also released detailed seat-by-seat estimates, projecting that nearly a quarter of all constituencies (151 out of 632) had forecasted winning margins of less than 5%. This was almost three times higher than the actual number of marginals in 2019. Even slight variations in polling data or adjustments in methodology could result in different outcomes for these marginal seats, substantially altering overall seat projections. They also eliminated the concept of 'safe' Conservative seats as no constituency featured a 100% probability that the Conservative candidate would win—even the Prime Minister's seat saw Rishi

Table 1.2. Seat projections per party in MRP polls during the campaign

	Average seat projection	Minimum seat projection	Maximum seat projection	Seat projection range
Conservatives	95	53	126	73
Labour	452	418	516	98
Liberal Democrats	59	38	72	34
Greens	2	0	4	4
Reform UK	3	0	7	7
SNP	17	8	29	21
Plaid Cymru	3	0	4	4

[1] Available at: https://www.electionscentre.co.uk/wp-content/uploads/2024/05/Guide-to-the-New-Parliamentary-Constituencies.pdf

Sunak allocated a 20% probability he would lose. Therefore, whilst it may have appeared that the result was a foregone conclusion in favour of Labour, there was widespread uncertainty in the range of outcomes and what this would mean for each party.

3. The national result

The general election results showed that polling had overestimated Labour's performance while underestimating the relative success of both the Conservatives and Liberal Democrats. Still, it was a landslide victory for Keir Starmer's party who won a 174-seat majority, and a crushing defeat for the Conservatives. Down more than twenty points on 2019, and securing less than a quarter of all votes, the Conservatives came away with the fewest seats in their history since 1832. A record number of cabinet members were unseated. Notable figures from the previous 14 years of government failed to be re-elected, such as Liz Truss, Jacob Rees-Mogg, and Johnny Mercer, who all lost their seats to Labour candidates. In total, they lost more than 67% of their MPs. It was a dramatic departure from their period in power (Table 1.3).

Labour were able to secure their third-largest victory in terms of seats, on the lowest vote share of a winning party in modern times. On an increase of just 1.7 percentage points in national vote share, they won 211 seats more than suggested by the 2019 notional results. This election tested the boundaries of the first-past-the-post system. The party with the biggest rise in vote share was Reform UK. Their share increased sixfold on the Brexit Party's 2019 result. However, it should

Table 1.3. The results of the 2024 General Election for each party compared with the 2019 notional result (Great Britain only)

	Number of seats	Seats change	Vote share	Share change
Conservative	121	−251	24.4%	−20.4%
Labour	412	+211	34.6%	+1.7%
Liberal Democrat	72	+64	12.6%	+0.7%
Green	4	+3	6.9%	+4.1%
Reform UK	5	+5	14.7%	+12.6%
SNP	9	−39	2.6%	−1.3%
Plaid Cymru	4	+2	0.7%	+0.2%
Independents	5	+5	3.6%	+2%

Source: House of Commons Library (2024 results) and Rallings and Thrasher (2019 notionals).
Note: The Speaker is included in Labour's 2024 total.

be noted that they fielded nearly twice as many candidates in 2024 as there was no longer an informal electoral pact between Leave-supporting parties. In 2019, the Brexit Party opted not to field candidates in more than 300 seats to avoid splitting the Leave-supporting vote where the Conservatives were capable of winning. Four and a half years later, all five of Reform UK's seats were gains from the Conservatives, including Nigel Farage's win in Clacton. The Liberal Democrats had a similar success, winning eight times as many seats as the previous election and returning their highest number of MPs since 1923. They did this on a vote share increase of less than a percentage point and a 2.1% lower vote share than Reform UK. The Greens also doubled their vote share and gained more representation, unseating Labour Shadow Cabinet Member Thangam Debbonaire in Bristol Central where they had been doing well in local council contests. Each of the parties that made gains took the majority of their seats from the Conservatives.

In Scotland, the SNP lost seats at almost the same rate the Conservatives did in England and Wales. They achieved 30% of the Scottish vote, down 15 points from 2019. It was their worst performance since 2010. Losing more than 80% of their seats, most of which were gained by Labour, the SNP were no longer the third largest party in the UK. Plaid Cymru had their representation halved by the notional results in Wales when the number of constituencies in the nation fell from 40 to 32, but returned four MPs on a small increase in share. There were also five independent MPs elected in England, all of which were gains from the Labour party. This included Jeremy Corbyn, who was barred from running as a Labour candidate in the Islington seat he has represented for more than forty years.

3.1 Regional results

Labour's support grew more in Scotland than in any other region/nation, but that was also where it was lowest in 2019. However Labour did not increase their vote share everywhere. In London, Wales, and the North West—all areas of traditionally strong Labour support—they declined by up to 5.2 percentage points, a clear indication of how the party had chosen to target its resources in areas where it needed to make gains. Labour achieved the highest vote share in eight of the eleven regions, leaving the East of England, South East, and South West as the only places the Conservatives remain the party with the most votes. The scale of the Conservatives' success in 2019 meant they were able to drop 26.5 points (from 57.1% to 30.6%) in the East of England and still come out on top. This was also due to fragmentation of the vote, particularly in the two Southern regions where success was split between Labour and the Liberal Democrats—the Conservatives dropped nearly twenty-five points in the South West, but there was less than half a percentage point difference between the rates achieved by Labour and the Liberal Democrats in second and third place (Fig. 1.1).

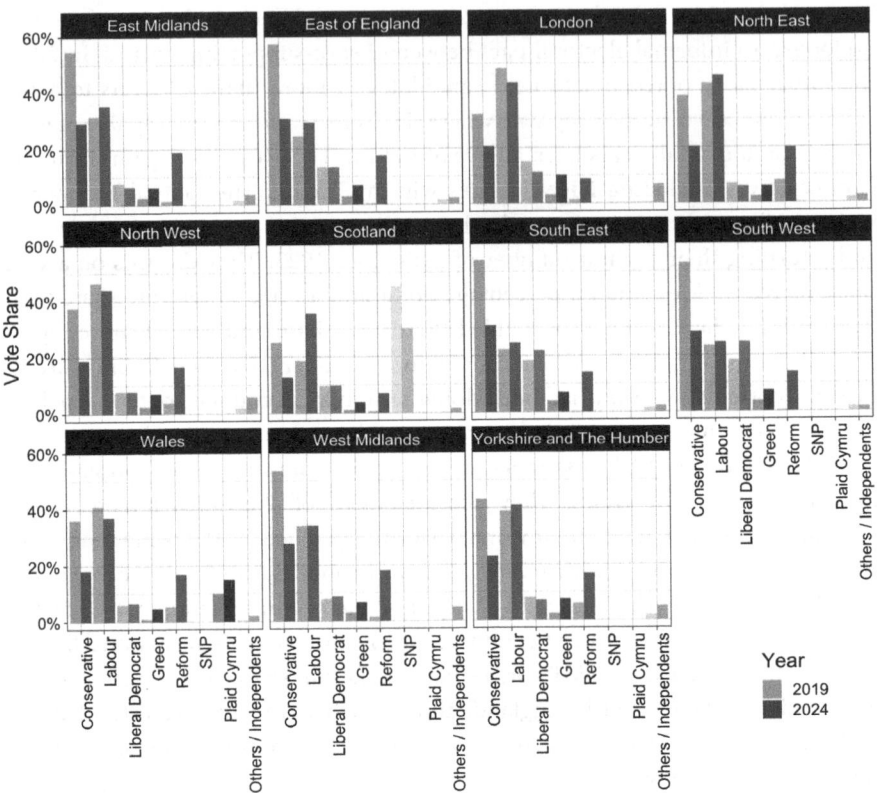

Figure 1.1. Vote share by region 2019 and 2024

Reform UK's performance is compared to that of the Brexit Party in 2019. 2024 was the best performance of any party Nigel Farage has led into a general election. This time, they received more than one in ten of all votes cast in every region in England and Wales apart from London. Reform UK's highest share was in the North East, where they were just 0.4% behind the Conservatives and therefore narrowly fell short of becoming the second party of the region. Their worst result, outside of Scotland and London, was in the South West, once home to UKIP's headquarters.

The removal of Brexit from the electoral agenda also impacted the Liberal Democrats' results, having been the party of Remain in 2019. Their support fell in four regions and stayed the same in a further four, meaning they achieved their best ever election result by improving in only three regions. 72% of Liberal Democrat seats come from just two regions—the South West and South East—where they won more than a fifth of all votes. Their biggest fall was in London, down nearly four points on 2019, yet they still doubled their seat tally in the capital from three to six. The East Midlands and the North East are the only regions with no Liberal Democrat representation.

The Green Party's four seats were accompanied by a rise in vote share across all parts of Britain. They achieved at least 6% of the vote in English regions and almost quadrupled their share (from 1% to 3.9%) in both Wales and Scotland. London was their best-performing region, where 1 in 10 voters opted for the Greens—three times the proportion that supported them in 2019. Whilst this perhaps sounds modest, a small party making gains in an FPTP electoral system is noteworthy, particularly in a year that returns a landslide majority for a newly incoming major party. The rise of Reform UK, the Greens, independents and others across the country was the driving factor for Labour to win the election on such a small percentage of the overall vote. They are discussed further by Lynn Bennie and Anders Widfeldt in this volume.

4. Electoral competitiveness in 2024

Patterns of competition between parties made it a more competitive election, despite it looking the opposite at first glance of the seat tallies. Labour overwhelmingly won the most seats, but they did so on small margins. Looking across thirty years of general elections in Britain, as in Figs 1.2 and 1.3, shows 2024 to be an

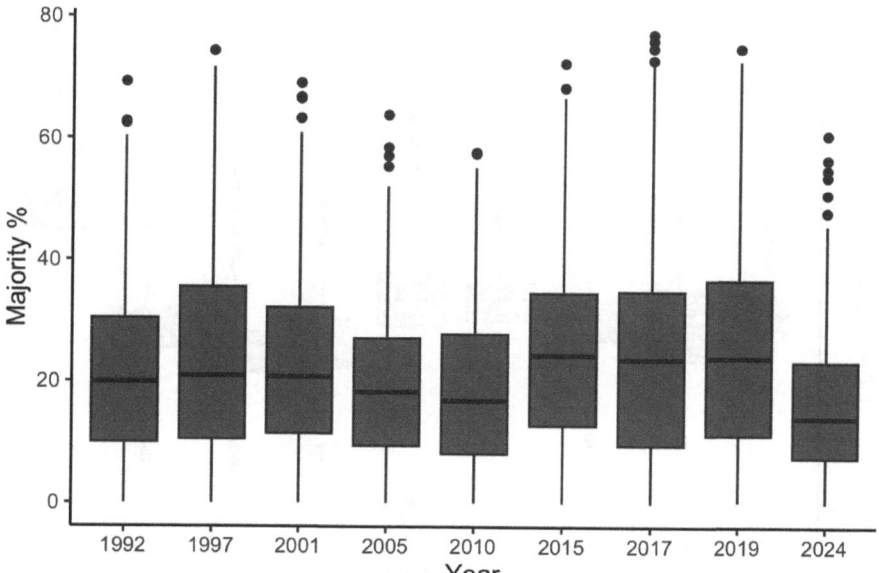

Figure 1.2. Constituency majorities over 30 years of general elections

unusual year. The median constituency majority is now 14.3%, much lower than the 23.9% figure in 2019, and half of all majorities were in the 7.6%–23.3% range. The closest comparable year is 2010 which produced a hung parliament result. These marginal results are due to the scale of change at this election. In 2019, the Conservatives won lots of seats with larger majorities, in part due to facing no opposition from ideologically similar parties after the Brexit Party decided not to field candidates in a swathe of seats, meaning a sizeable swing was needed to gain the seat from them in 2024. Moreover, each extra candidate that stands—and wins votes—makes the available margin smaller. This was a change election with multiple parties, so those winning majorities were narrower.

Fig. 1.3 shows the effective number of electoral parties (ENEP) at the constituency level. This measure quantifies the number of parties that had a substantive impact on the result in a constituency. It is also a measure of competitiveness because it shows how evenly spread the votes were across multiple candidates—if voters predominantly opted for one party, the ENEP is low; if several parties received equal proportions of the vote, the ENEP is high. A constituency can have the same number of candidates yet a different ENEP score. For instance, Liverpool Walton had six candidates on the ballot but an ENEP of 1.89 because Labour won more than 70% of all votes. Whereas Torridge and Tavistock also had six candidates, but its ENEP is 4.24 as the Conservatives got 31.5% of the votes, followed by Liberal Democrats with 23.8%, Labour with 21.2%, and Reform UK winning 18% of votes. Multiple parties were electorally effective in the Devon seat (Torridge and Tavistock), but only one

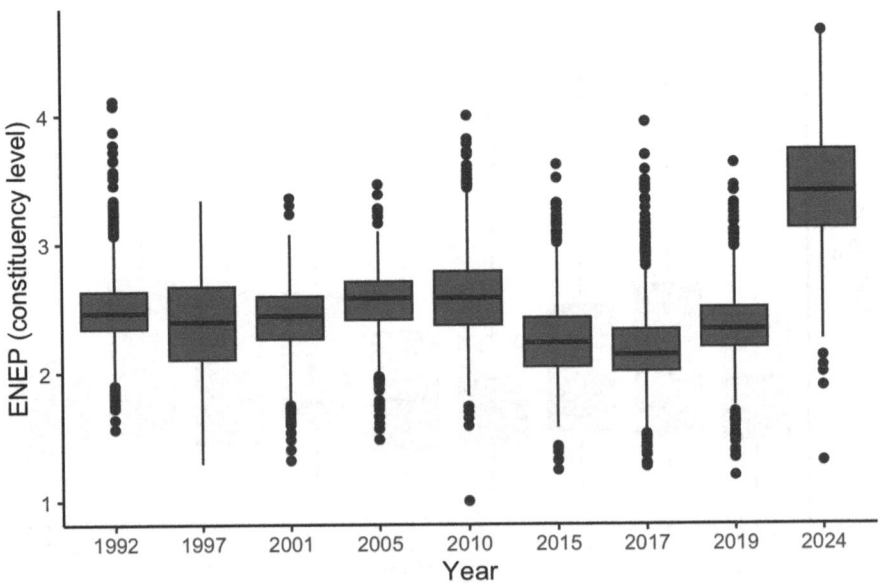

Figure 1.3. Effective number of parties at the constituency level over 30 years of general elections

was in the North West (Liverpool Walton) example. When there were fewer parties in Britain, these types of competitive seats were illustrated via the number of 'three-way marginals' where the distance between the first-placed party and the third-placed party was less than twenty points. In 2019, there were seventeen three-way marginals; in 2024 there are more than 100. This ENEP measure is therefore a more comprehensive way of demonstrating the differences in party competition across constituencies.

The median average ENEP, represented by the black line inside the box, is much higher for 2024 than in any other year. This tells us that there were few areas where the electorate clearly preferred one party over all others. More than 75% of constituencies had at least three effective parties. The average was 3.4 in 2024, compared to 2.4 across all other years. On a scale of 1–5, an increase of a fifth is not insignificant. It tells us the party system fragmented, and suggests that the electorate have diverse ideas about the representatives they want to see in parliament. The constituency with the highest ENEP was Montgomeryshire and Glyndŵr at 4.9, where Labour gained the seat from the Conservatives but on a vote share of just 29.3%. This is closely followed by South West Norfolk at 4.7 and 26.7% Labour vote share. Both are two of the three seats Labour won with less than 30% of the vote.

Some seats were won by just a handful of votes, signifying fierce competition in the constituency. There were twelve where the winner was victorious on a margin of less than 200 votes and eighteen on less than a percentage point. Similar to the predictions made by pollsters, 112 were won with a majority less than 5%, almost twice the number with the same margin in 2019. Most were Labour gains, however some were instances where the Conservatives managed to hold on. At the other end of the scale, there were also substantial majorities overturned. Two of Reform UK's seats were the result of large Conservative majorities collapsing and voters switching directly from Sunak's to Farage's party. Nineteen seats saw a majority of at least 40% overturned, more than three-quarters of which were gains from the Conservatives (Table 1.4).

The extent of the Conservative collapse becomes clearer when looking not just at the seats they won but the vote shares they received. The highest constituency share of the vote for the Conservatives was 53.3%, in all others they received less than half of votes. Their eighth-best performance was a seat they lost to Labour, Middlesborough South and East Cleveland, where they achieved 42.7% of the result but Labour got 43%. As a comparison, in 2019 they won at least half the votes in 288 constituencies and their highest share was 76.5%. In 2024, the Greens placed higher than the Conservatives in seventy-eight seats. Reform UK placed higher than them in 140 seats.

Some of this reduced vote share is a function of fragmentation as Labour's landslide was won with just seventy constituencies where they took at least 50% of the votes, down from 122 in 2019, which was their worst performance in eighty-four

Table 1.4. Smallest winning majorities and biggest majorities overturned

	Narrowest wins			Biggest majorities overturned		
	Constituency	2024 Majority	Result	Constituency	2019 Majority	Result
1	Hendon	15 (0.04%)	Lab gain from Con	Boston & Skegness	60.9%	Reform UK gain from Con
2	Poole	18 (0.04%)	Lab gain from Con	Clacton	56.3%	Reform UK gain from Con
3	Basildon & Billericay	20 (0.05%)	Con hold	South West Norfolk	50.3%	Lab gain from Con
4	North West Cambridgeshire	39 (0.08%)	Con hold	Islington North	48.7%	Ind gain from Lab
5	Central Devon	61 (0.11%)	Lab gain from Con	Birmingham Perry Barr	47.6%	Ind gain from Lab

years. The Liberal Democrats more than tripled the number of seats where they won a majority of votes, from five in 2019 to eighteen in 2024. Tim Farron's seat of Westmorland and Lonsdale was their best performance, winning 62.7% of the vote. Leader Ed Davey's seat was their thirteenth-highest vote share. Reform UK and the Greens also improved. In 2019, the Brexit party came second in just two seats and failed to return an MP. At this contest, Reform UK came second in ninety-eight constituencies. Green candidates placed second in forty seats, whereas last time it was just one. This also means that they won Waveney Valley after coming third at the last election and North Herefordshire after coming fourth in 2019. As new entrants, the Workers Party of Britain came second in three constituencies. The SNP came second in all the Scottish seats they did not win, but Plaid Cymru only placed second in four Welsh constituencies (Table 1.5).

5. Turnout

Across Britain, turnout dropped by 7.8 percentage points to 59.8%. This was the second-lowest post-war turnout, and only slightly above the record low in 2001. The drop in participation was experienced almost everywhere. However, the boundary changes make it difficult to directly compare turnout between 2019 and 2024 at the constituency level. Wales had the most dramatic decline, at 10.3 percentage points lower, followed by London, where it fell by 9.1 percentage points. There were 58 constituencies where less than half of all registered voters cast a ballot. This compares to just one in 2019. Three-quarters of constituencies in 2024 had a turnout that was lower than the median 2019 rate of 67.7%. All seats—apart

Table 1.5. Best constituency vote share performances by each party

	Constituency	Vote share	Place	Constituency	Vote share	Place	Constituency	Vote share	Place	Constituency	Vote share	Place
	Conservative			*Labour*			*Liberal Democrat*			*Green*		
1	Harrow East	53.3%	1st	Liverpool Walton	70.6%	1st	Westmorland & Lonsdale	62.7%	1st	Bristol Central	56.6%	1st
2	Richmond & Northallerton	47.5%	1st	Bootle	68.7%	1st	St Albans	56.6%	1st	Brighton Pavilion	55%	1st
3	Stone, Great Wyrley & Penkridge	46.5%	1st	Knowsley	67.3%	1st	Twickenham	56.3%	1st	North Herefordshire	43.2%	1st
4	Ruislip, Northwood & Pinner	45.4%	1st	Liverpool West Derby	66.6%	1st	Orkney and Shetland	55.1%	1st	Waveney Valley	41.7%	1st
5	Hertsmere	44.7%	1st	Liverpool Riverside	61.9%	1st	North East Fife	54.7%	1st	Bristol East	30.7%	2nd
	Reform UK			*SNP*			*Plaid Cymru*			*Others/Independents*		
1	Clacton	46.2%	1st	Angus & Perthshire Glens	40.4%	1st	Dwyfor Meirionnydd	53.9%	1st	Islington North	49.3%	1st
2	Ashfield	42.9%	1st	Dundee Central	40%	1st	Ceredigion Preseli	46.9%	1st	Blackburn	46.5%	1st
3	Boston & Skegness	38.4%	1st	Perth & Kinross-shire	37.8%	1st	Caerfyrddin	34%	1st	Dewsbury & Batley	41.1%	1st
4	Great Yarmouth	35.3%	1st	Glenrothes & Mid Fife	36.1%	2nd	Ynys Môn	32.5%	1st	Bradford West	40.2%	2nd
5	Barnsley South	33.2%	2nd	Arbroath & Broughty Ferry	35.3%	1st	Llanelli	23.3%	3rd	Birmingham Perry Barr	38.1%	1st

from Harpenden and Berkhamsted, which saw the highest turnout—had at least a quarter of the electorate stay home. Recent evidence suggests that this may be due to the greater number of parties and increase in the number of citizens that are unsure of who to vote for; the complex choice environment makes the decision more difficult and ultimately leads to fewer people participating in the election (Bunting 2024). In particular, working-class citizens are voting at lower rates than those who are middle class (Heath and Serra 2024) (Fig. 1.4 and Table 1.6).

Constituencies that elected Green and Liberal Democrat MPs had the highest turnouts, related to the fact that they also tend to be home to higher educated and

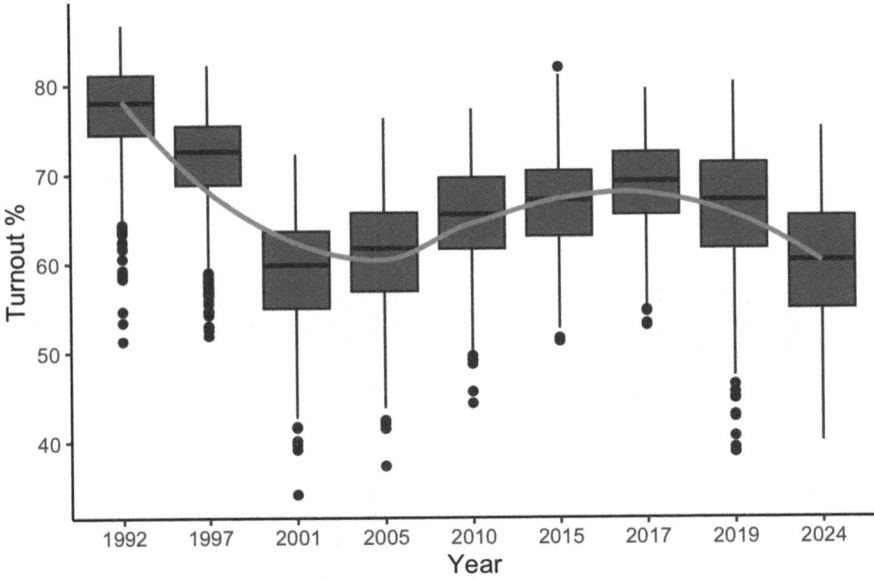

Figure 1.4. Constituency turnout over 30 years of elections

Table 1.6. Highest and lowest turnouts in Great Britain

	Highest turnout		Lowest turnout	
	Constituency	Turnout	Constituency	Turnout
1	Harpenden & Berkhamsted	75.2%	Manchester Rusholme	39.9%
2	Rushcliffe	72.9%	Leeds South	41.7%
3	Winchester	72.9%	Kingston upon Hull East	42.2%
4	Esher & Walton	72.8%	Blaenau Gwent & Rhymney	42.7%
5	Chesham & Amersham	72.7%	Tipton & Wednesbury	42.9%

Source: House of Commons Library.

more affluent citizens. Seats won by Labour had the third lowest turnout (placing sixth out of nine winning parties). These were ethnically diverse areas with an above-average number of people who are economically active. Areas that elected Reform UK and independent candidates had the lowest participation rates and were typically places with more people experiencing deprivation. However, Reform UK won in areas with a high proportion of White residents, and independents typically gained seats with more than half the population identifying as an ethnic minority. These aggregate statistics suggest that Labour was backed by workers, the Greens and Liberal Democrats by the most affluent, and either Reform UK or independents were the choices for ethnically homogenous areas.

6. Demographics

Patterns of party support have been less clearly related to demographics in recent years, particularly since the 'electoral shock' of the Brexit referendum. Voting behaviour has become driven more by identity. However, economic security and government performance are still important predictors of party success or failure and can explain whether voters opted for main parties or smaller parties. The proliferation of candidates and parties at this election makes this one of the first opportunities to explore how different demographics voted in a general election of this type. Figs 1.5 and 1.6 show unstandardized coefficient results from a series of ordinary least squares (OLS) regression model using demographics to first explain

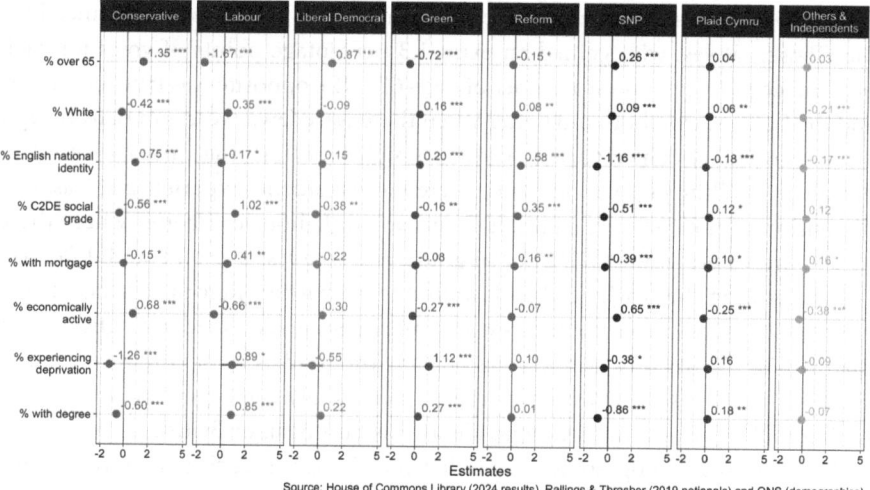

Figure 1.5. 2024 party vote share explained by constituency demographics

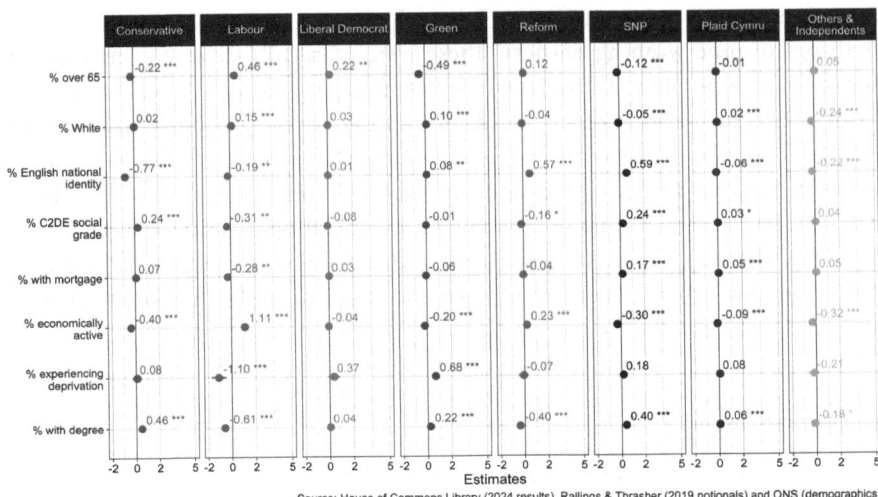

Figure 1.6. Change in party vote share 2019–24 explained by constituency demographics

each party's vote share, and then the change in their vote share compared to 2019. They assess how the percentage of each demographic in a constituency impacted the parties' performance. In Fig. 1.5, positive numbers mean a party's vote share increased as the proportion of that demographic did, whereas negative numbers mean it decreased. Full results with model fit statistics are displayed in Tables 1.A1 and 1.A2 of the appendix.

A greater presence of older voters in a seat meant the Conservatives and Liberal Democrats achieved a higher vote share. This was more pronounced for the Conservatives, who gained an extra 1.3 percentage points of votes for each percentage point rise in the number of over-65s. The opposite was true for Labour and the Greens, who both did better when there were fewer voters of pension age. These two left-of-centre parties were also higher performing in seats with predominantly White populations, and where more residents experience at least one dimension of the Index of Multiple Deprivation. Labour did better where there were more voters in the C2DE social grade, and to a lesser extent so did Reform UK, suggesting the working class favoured these parties. Reform UK also had a higher vote share in constituencies where more people identified as English rather than British, Scottish or another nationality. The models imply these voters also preferred the Conservatives and, perhaps interestingly, the Green Party who have traditionally appealed to those who identify as European or British.

Fig. 1.6 uses demographics to predict the change in each party's vote share. Positive numbers indicate an increase in vote share—or for the Conservatives and SNP who did not rise in vote share anywhere, a less substantial drop—and negative numbers represent a decrease in vote share or a sharper fall in their proportion of votes. For the Liberal Democrats, the only demographic that explained their change in vote share was the proportion of over 65s, an increase in which meant they did better in a constituency. Others and independents' vote share rose in areas with fewer people of White ethnicity and who identify with English as their nationality.

Education has been a key driver of political choice in the last decades, particularly since the expansion of university attendance. Labour vote share was higher in areas where more people hold a degree, but they also suffered more substantial drops in these places. This suggests that areas with more educated voters opted for a different party compared to 2019, yet these were still seats where Labour did well. Most of these were constituencies where 2019 Labour and Conservative voters instead chose the Greens or others and independents this time. Seats such as Bethnal Green and Stepney in London was a Labour hold, but their majority reduced from 63% in 2019 to just 3.62% in 2024. 42% of voters hold a degree here, much higher than the 34% constituency average, and the Labour vote dropped by 39 percentage points. Most of this went to the independent candidate but some also to the Green party. The opposite was true for the Conservatives who did worse in higher educated areas, but their vote share did not fall as sharply.

The rise in mortgage interest rates was a significant feature of the post-Covid-19 political narrative for the Conservative government. Along with inflation and rising energy prices, it was a key contributor to the cost of living crisis. The Conservatives did worse in areas with a high proportion of mortgage holders but this did not explain their vote share change. It only impacted Labour's change in shares, which fell more in constituencies where lots of people have mortgages, even though these areas generally preferred Labour. These seats were also slightly more likely to opt for Reform UK but it does not explain Farage's party's change in vote share. Its lack of explanatory power is perhaps surprising on first glance. However, the most common tenure across the UK is owning a home without a mortgage, meaning the number of people the interest rate increase affected is limited. The wider cost of living is probably a better predictor of party support but this is difficult to capture with demographic data and needs further research.

Change in Plaid Cymru's vote share was not substantially affected by demographics, however they did better where fewer people identified as English. Scotland has few citizens who identify as English, but it was a predictor of SNP vote share and its changes in vote share. The Angus and Perthshire Glens constituency was one of three SNP holds with a relatively high proportion of those choosing English as their national identity. The Scottish party still achieved 40% of votes here in 2024, falling only 9.98 percentage points compared to their average drop of more than fifteen points. It is an area that has supported the SNP for a long time. Labour, the Liberal Democrats and Reform UK all rose in vote share in this seat. The SNP also did better where there were fewer graduates and more residents of pension age. They did worse where there was a higher proportion of citizens in the C2DE social grade but better where more people are economically active, meaning those people who are not considered out of the workforce for reasons such as illness or homemaking. As with most elections, the dimensions of competition and patterns of support were different in Scotland and Wales compared to England. These are explored further by Henderson and Mitchell and Larner and Wyn Jones below.

7. Explanation

The Conservatives had been in power for fourteen years with five different leaders, so it was expected that this would be a change election. What was less anticipated was the number of factors that would change. It was the first time since 2015 that a government had served close to a full term in office, as both 2017 and 2019 were snap elections largely caused by Brexit. Parties, voters, and the components of British politics shifted substantially over that entire term. The withdrawal from the European Union, the pandemic, and a set of scandals finally put to bed the dominance that the in-out referendum had over the previous eight years. Though many people still wanted to discuss Brexit, its significance faded in 2024.

Instead, it was competence and trust on the agenda. Partygate damaged the reputation of politicians, particularly in the wake of a global health crisis, which could have been an opportunity to regain some of the trust declines seen in recent decades. That bounce was only temporary and instead compounded a series of perceived betrayals in the public's eyes—a divisive Brexit, followed by scandals, on top of crumbling public services and rising inflation. The electorate were dissatisfied with the Conservatives, the signs were there in local and by-election results, but the polling reflected the uncertainty in how this would pan out for a general election.

There was a marked increase in the number of candidates and the vote fragmented. The UK is now a multiparty system with majoritarian electoral rules. The UK has an uncertain electorate with diverse preferences. The large proportion of people who did not vote might indicate a feeling that politics does not work for them or they are unsure how to make it work for them. Not only does this impact the mandate of the Labour government, but it also means small changes in turnout could substantially alter results in the future. These are perhaps factors that Keir Starmer will want to think about before the next contest, whenever that may be. One thing this election has affirmed is that while the results might produce a stable government—a 174-seat majority for Labour this time and an eighty-seat Conservative majority last time—under the surface and throughout the British population, there is plenty of instability. Ultimately, the Conservatives may never have held the advantage and would have lost whatever they had done. The extent of the rejection from the electorate was nevertheless sobering. The public knew who they did not want, but the vote shares showed they did not uniformly agree on who they wanted to govern them.

Acknowledgements

This contribution uses data from multiple sources. Thanks are extended to The Elections Centre, The House of Commons Library, The Office for National Statistics (ONS), the Sky News Poll Tracker, Dr Mark Pack's Pollbase and Rallings and Thrasher.

Funding

None declared.

References

Bunting, H. (2024) 'Individual Electoral Competitiveness: Undecided Voters, Complex Choice Environments and Lower Turnout', *Electoral Studies*, 92: 102866.

Heath, O., and Serra, L. (2024) 'The True Class Divide in British Politics Is Not Which Party People Choose, But Whether They Vote at All', *The Conversation*, https://theconversation.com/the-true-class-divide-in-british-politics-is-not-which-party-people-choose-but-whether-they-vote-at-all-240645, accessed 5 Aug. 2025.

Appendix

Table 1.A1. 2024 Vote share models

	Con (1)	Lab (2)	LibDem (3)	Green (4)	Reform UK (5)	SNP (6)	PC (7)	Oth/Ind (8)
% with degree	−0.605***	0.850***	0.225	0.267***	0.007	−0.861***	0.183**	−0.066
	(0.094)	(0.162)	(0.174)	(0.067)	(0.069)	(0.067)	(0.062)	(0.095)
% experiencing deprivation	−1.263***	0.891*	−0.547	1.123***	0.104	−0.378*	0.160	−0.090
	(0.251)	(0.435)	(0.466)	(0.178)	(0.184)	(0.179)	(0.167)	(0.254)
% economically active	0.678***	−0.660***	0.295+	−0.269***	−0.067	0.650***	−0.246***	−0.381***
	(0.081)	(0.141)	(0.151)	(0.058)	(0.060)	(0.058)	(0.054)	(0.082)
% with mortgage	−0.146*	0.415**	−0.215	−0.084	0.157**	−0.386***	0.103*	0.157*
	(0.074)	(0.129)	(0.138)	(0.053)	(0.055)	(0.053)	(0.049)	(0.075)
% C2DE social grade	−0.559***	1.021***	−0.384**	−0.159**	0.353***	−0.515***	0.120*	0.122
	(0.078)	(0.135)	(0.144)	(0.055)	(0.057)	(0.055)	(0.051)	(0.079)
% English national identity	0.746***	−0.168*	0.146+	0.204***	0.577***	−1.159***	−0.178***	−0.169***
	(0.047)	(0.082)	(0.088)	(0.034)	(0.035)	(0.034)	(0.031)	(0.048)
% White	−0.417***	0.349***	−0.091	0.157***	0.075**	0.085***	0.055**	−0.214***
	(0.031)	(0.055)	(0.058)	(0.022)	(0.023)	(0.022)	(0.021)	(0.032)
% over 65	1.347***	−1.671***	0.872***	−0.725***	−0.152*	0.259***	0.044	0.026
	(0.081)	(0.141)	(0.151)	(0.058)	(0.060)	(0.058)	(0.054)	(0.082)
Num.Obs	632	632	632	632	632	632	632	632
R^2 Adj.	0.688	0.438	0.288	0.377	0.619	0.760	0.105	0.322

***$P < .001$, **$P < .01$, *$P < .05$, +$P < .1$

Table 1.A2. Vote share change 2024–2019 models

	Con (1)	Lab (2)	LibDem (3)	Green (4)	Reform UK (5)	SNP (6)	PC (7)	Oth/Ind (8)
% with degree	0.463***	−0.610***	0.043	0.221***	−0.402***	0.401***	0.064***	−0.179*
	(0.075)	(0.117)	(0.096)	(0.052)	(0.076)	(0.037)	(0.019)	(0.085)
% experiencing deprivation	0.079	−1.102***	0.367	0.679***	−0.073	0.177+	0.084	−0.211
	(0.202)	(0.313)	(0.257)	(0.139)	(0.205)	(0.098)	(0.052)	(0.227)
% economically active	−0.397***	1.111***	−0.041	−0.195***	0.230***	−0.297***	−0.094***	−0.316***
	(0.066)	(0.102)	(0.083)	(0.045)	(0.066)	(0.032)	(0.017)	(0.074)
% with mortgage	0.067	−0.280**	0.032	−0.062	−0.035	0.171***	0.053***	0.054
	(0.060)	(0.093)	(0.076)	(0.041)	(0.060)	(0.029)	(0.015)	(0.067)
% C2DE social grade	0.242***	−0.314**	−0.081	−0.009	−0.156*	0.243***	0.034*	0.040
	(0.063)	(0.097)	(0.079)	(0.043)	(0.063)	(0.030)	(0.016)	(0.070)
% English national identity	−0.771***	−0.190**	0.012	0.077**	0.567***	0.586***	−0.064***	−0.217***
	(0.038)	(0.059)	(0.048)	(0.026)	(0.039)	(0.019)	(0.010)	(0.043)
% White	0.020	0.150***	0.034	0.096***	−0.039	−0.048***	0.023***	−0.238***
	(0.025)	(0.039)	(0.032)	(0.017)	(0.026)	(0.012)	(0.006)	(0.029)
% over 65	−0.221***	0.457***	0.220**	−0.486***	0.115+	−0.122***	−0.011	0.049
	(0.066)	(0.102)	(0.083)	(0.045)	(0.066)	(0.032)	(0.017)	(0.074)
Num.Obs	632	632	632	632	632	632	632	632
R^2 Adj.	0.670	0.510	0.078	0.366	0.520	0.721	0.116	0.396

***P < .001, **P < .01, *P < .05, +*P* < .1

The electoral system: All a question of geography

John Curtice*

School of Government and Public Policy, University of Strathclyde, 16 Richmond Street, Glasgow, G1 1XQ, UK

*Correspondence: J.Curtice@strath.ac.uk

The outcome of the 2024 election (see Table 2.1) broke many a psephological record. The Conservatives sunk to their smallest-ever share of the Britain-wide vote (24.4%) and lowest-ever tally of seats (121, twenty fewer than the 141 the party won in Great Britain in 1906). Labour secured an overall majority while winning just 34.7% of the vote across Great Britain (and 33.8% across the whole of the UK). Never before had a party secured an overall majority on so low a share of the vote, let alone one as big as 174—the previous low was the 36.1% of the vote (35.2% across the UK) that delivered Labour a majority of sixty-six in 2005. Meanwhile, the Liberal Democrats secured their highest tally of seats (seventy-two) since 1923 (when the then Liberal Party won 158 seats) even though, at 12.6%, the party's share of the vote was lower than at all elections between February 1974 and 2010. At the same time, in England a record total of fourteen candidates standing either for other parties or as an independent secured election, beating the previous record of eight in 1918. Indeed, despite a sharp fall in the Scottish National Party's representation (from forty-eight to nine), the success of the Liberal Democrats and other smaller parties ensured that as many as 117 third-party MPs were elected across the UK as a whole, also the highest number since 1923.

Yet curiously, at 2.24, the effective number of parliamentary parties statistic is now lower than after any election since 2005 (Laakso and Taagepera 1979). The figure is heavily influenced by Labour's dominance of the Commons. Indeed, the effective number of parties in terms of votes reached an all-time high of 4.76. The difference between the two statistics arises because the country's single-member

© The Author(s) 2025. Published by Oxford University Press on behalf of the Hansard Society. All rights reserved. For commercial re-use, please contact reprints@oup.com for reprints and translation rights for reprints. All other permissions can be obtained through our RightsLink service via the Permissions link on the article page on our site—for further information please contact journals.permissions@oup.com.

Table 2.1. The 2024 UK General Election result (with change from 2019 notional results)

	GB		UK				
	Vote share (%)	Change in vote share	Vote share (%)	Change in vote share	No. of seats	Seat share (%)	Change in seats[a]
Labour	34.7	+1.7	33.8	+1.6	412	63.4	+211
Conservative	24.4	−20.4	23.7	−19.9	121	18.6	−251
Reform UK	14.7	+12.6	14.3	+12.3	5	0.8	+5
Liberal Democrat	12.6	+0.8	12.2	+0.7	72	11.1	+64
Greens	6.9	+4.1	6.7	+4.0	4	0.6	+3
SNP	2.5	−1.5	2.5	−1.4	9	1.4	−39
Plaid Cymru	0.7	+0.2	0.7	+0.2	4	0.6	+2
Independents	1.9	+1.1	2.0	+1.4	6	0.9	+6
Others	1.6	+1.2	4.1	+1.1	17	2.6	−1
Turnout	59.8	−7.7	59.7	−7.6			

For Reform UK change in vote share is as compared with the Brexit Party in 2019. The Speaker is included in the Labour tally throughout.
[a]Change in seats is as compared with estimated outcome of the 2019 election on the new parliamentary boundaries introduced in 2024 (Rallings and Thrasher 2024).
Source: Baker et al., (2020); Cracknell and Baker (2024); Rallings and Thrasher (2024).

plurality system delivered its most disproportional result yet, as measured both by the Loosemore-Hanby (29.6) and the Gallagher indices of disproportionality (23.6) (Loosemore and Hanby 1971; Gallagher 1991). Indeed, the result is one of the most disproportional recorded anywhere in a democratic election (Gallagher 2024).

There is therefore much to unpack about how Britain's electoral system operated in 2024. Why did Labour secure well over 60% of the seats on barely more than one-third of the vote? How were the Liberal Democrats, hitherto the party that had lost out most and most often from the system, suddenly able to secure almost their proportionate share of the seats? And what are the implications of such an unprecedented outcome for the debate about electoral reform?

We have to start with a crucial observation. Under the single-member plurality electoral system, the outcome of an election in terms of seats depends not only on the level of support the parties secure but also on how their support is distributed geographically across constituencies (Gudgin and Taylor 1979). This insight leads to two possible approaches to addressing our questions. The first is to examine whether the outcome was the product of the geography of party support bequeathed by the 2019 election—and thus, perhaps, while unprecedented was not surprising—or whether it reflected significant changes in the geography of party support that favoured, in particular, Labour and the Liberal Democrats while disadvantaging the Conservatives.

The second approach we can take is to bear in mind that, for its advocates at least, the single-member plurality system is not meant to be a proportional system. Rather it is regarded as one that is deliberately and systematically disproportional, not least because it exaggerates the lead of the first party over the second party in terms of votes into a much bigger lead in terms of seats. This claim came to be formulated in the 1950s as a 'cube law', which states that if the vote for the two largest parties is divided between them in the ratio A:B, the seats they win will be shared in the ratio $A^3:B^3$ (Butler 1951; Kendall and Stuart 1951). This in effect means that at outcomes where support for the two largest parties is close to 50:50, a one percentage point increase in a party's share of the two-party vote will result in a three-point increase in its share of the seats. This exaggerative relationship, it is argued, helps ensure the winning party will nearly always succeed in winning an overall majority, especially because a second attribute of the system is that it makes it difficult for smaller, third parties to win seats. Thanks to these two features the system enables the electorate to choose between alternative governments, facilitates voters' ability to hold governments to account, and avoids the formation of government being left to coalition deals between the parties (Norton 1997; Bingham Powell 2000; Renwick 2011). However, as we will discover, whether or not the single member plurality system works in this way also depends on the geography of party support.

1. The legacy of 2019

One of the staples of electoral analysis in the UK is to calculate what the outcome of the next election would be if there were any particular 'swing', that is, movement of votes, from Conservative to Labour or *vice versa*. In so doing the simplifying assumption is made that the level of support for all other parties (together with the turnout) remains the same as it was at the last election. Table 2.2 shows the result of this calculation following the 2019 election—but taking into account a redrawing of the country's constituency map following a parliamentary boundary review during the last parliament. The figures are based (as is all the analysis here of the changes in party support since 2019) on estimates produced for the media of what the outcome of the 2019 election would have been if the new boundaries had already been in place (Rallings and Thrasher 2024).

The first row of the table, where it is assumed that the vote totals for Conservative and Labour are the same as in 2019, indicates that, if the new boundaries had been in place on that occasion, the outcome would likely have been an overall Conservative majority of ninety-four, a little higher than the actual outcome of

Table 2.2. Impact on seats of uniform swing from Conservative to Labour after 2019 election

Swing to Con	Con %	Lab %	Con lead	Con seats	Lab seats	Other seats	Majority
0.0	44.7	33.0	11.7	372	201	77	Con 94
−4.1	40.6	37.1	3.5	327	240	83	Con 4
−4.2	40.5	37.2	3.3	325	241	84	None
−5.85	38.85	38.85	0.0	307	257	86	None
−8.3	36.4	41.1	−4.9	280	282	88	None
−12.6	32.1	45.6	−13.5	238	325	87	None
−12.7	32.0	45.7	−13.7	237	326	87	Lab +2
−16.2	28.5	49.2	−20.7	190	373	87	Lab +96

Source: Author's calculations. % vote figures are for Great Britain. Seat tallies are for all of the UK.

eighty. In other words, the boundary review that took place after the 2019 election was slightly favourable to the Conservatives, a point to which we will return later.

Even though the boundary review only had a minimal impact, the table reveals that, if the geography of party support remained as it was in 2019, the electoral system was set to treat the Conservatives much more favourably than Labour. The Conservatives would still have an overall majority if their lead in votes over Labour fell to only three and a half points. Labour, in contrast, would require a voting lead over their principal rivals of nearly fourteen points just to secure an overall majority of two. Although an even split of Conservative and Labour support would have resulted in a hung parliament in which neither party would have an overall majority, the Conservatives would win fifty more seats than Labour. Meanwhile, for Labour to succeed in replicating the Conservatives' majority of ninety-six, the party would need a voting lead of nearly twenty-one points, compared with the one of just under twelve points the Conservatives secured in 2019.

In short, the electoral geography bequeathed by the 2019 election potentially made it very difficult for Labour to win an overall majority of any kind, let alone one of 174. While the eleven-point lead the party actually secured over the Conservatives would have been enough to make it the largest in the Commons, it would, under the assumptions used in calculating Table 2.2, have left it well short of a majority. Indeed, this remains the case if we undertake a further calculation in which we estimate what the outcome of the 2024 election would have been if the rises and falls in all the parties' shares of the vote (including that of the Liberal Democrats and all the other third parties) had been the same everywhere. As Table 2.3 shows, irrespective of whether we assume every party's vote rises or falls in line with its share of the vote across Britain as a whole or, alternatively, in line with the change in its share of the vote in the relevant UK nation, the result would have been a hung parliament in which Labour would have been at least a

Table 2.3. Actual outcome in seats compared with uniform movement scenarios

	Uniform GB movement	Uniform movement in England/Scotland/Wales	Actual result
Conservative	240	249	121
Labour	302	323	412
Liberal Democrat	32	35	72
SNP/PC	56	21	13
Reform	1	3	5
Green	1	1	4
Others	18	18	23

Uniform GB movement: Assumes every party's share of the vote rises and falls everywhere since 2019 in line with the change in its overall share of the vote across Great Britain. Uniform movement in England/Scotland/Wales: Assumes every party's share of the vote rises and falls since 2019 in line with the change in its overall share of the vote in England, Scotland or Wales, as appropriate.
Source: Author's calculations.

little short of an overall majority. Meanwhile, the Conservatives would have won twice as many seats as the 121 they actually secured, while the Liberal Democrats would have won just half the total of seventy-two that they won. Evidently, there must have been a significant change in the geography of party support for the outcome of the 2024 election to have been record-breaking in the many ways in which it proved to be.

Indeed, there was. To some degree this was arithmetically inevitable. There were as many as sixty-nine seats where the Conservatives did not win as much as 20.4% of the vote in 2019, meaning that in these seats it was impossible for the party's vote to fall by the 20.4 points by which it fell across Britain as a whole. Consequently, to some extent at least the party's share of the vote had to fall more heavily in seats where the party was previously stronger. Meanwhile, in 2019, Reform UK's predecessor, the Brexit Party, did not contest seats that were being defended at that election by the Conservative party, and thus in most seats being defended by the Conservatives this time whatever share of the vote Reform UK won would represent an increase on zero.

Table 2.4 shows that, in practice, there was a strong and consistent relationship between the share of the vote won by the Conservatives in 2019 and the mean percentage point fall in their support as compared with 2019. Indeed, at thirty points, the average fall in Conservative support in seats where the party won more than 60% of the vote in 2019 was more than three times the 9.4 point fall in constituencies where the party had less than 25% last time around. As Table 2.4 also shows, much of the difference is associated with a systematically bigger increase in support for Reform UK in constituencies where the Conservatives were previously

Table 2.4. Mean change in share of vote 2019–24 by Conservative share of vote 2019

Conservative % share 2019	Mean change in % share of vote 2019–24				
	Conservative	Labour	Liberal Democrat	Reform UK	Green
Less than 25	−9.4	−3.2	−1.3	+5.7	+7.8
25–35	−15.7	−2.4	−0.5	+9.7	+5.7
35–45	−18.7	+0.8	−0.6	+11.5	+5.1
45–55	−21.6	+3.5	+1.1	+13.6	+3.5
55–60	−26.1	+5.0	+2.6	+16.4	+2.2
More than 60	−30.0	+6.4	+0.2	+20.4	+2.6
All seats	−20.6	+1.9	+0.3	+13.2	+4.3

In the case of the Conservatives, Labour, and the Liberal Democrats, figure is based on seats where the party was also represented in (at least in part of) the constituency in 2019 and 2024. In the case of Reform UK and the Greens figure is based on all seats fought by the party in 2024 irrespective of whether or not it contested the constituency in 2019. In the case of Reform UK change is calculated as compared with the Brexit Party's share of the vote in 2019.
Source: Author's calculations.

strongest, though Labour and, to a lesser degree, the Liberal Democrats performed somewhat better in such seats too.

This pattern was clearly disadvantageous for the Conservatives. It meant that in the over 200 seats where the party won more than 55% of the vote in 2019, it was losing many a seat that, if the decline in its support had been stemmed at little more than twenty points, it might have been able to defend successfully. Meanwhile, this pattern was compounded by a second one, whereby some voters demonstrated a propensity to vote tactically for whichever of Labour or the Liberal Democrats appeared to be better placed to defeat the Conservatives locally. As Table 2.5 shows, Labour's vote increased on average by six points in seats where the party had been second to the Conservatives in 2019, whereas the party did little more than hold its own in constituencies where the Liberal Democrats had been second to the government party. Conversely, the Liberal Democrats' share of the vote increased on average by nine points where the party started off in second place to the Conservatives, whereas its vote fell back somewhat in constituencies where Labour occupied second place. In other words, in many a seat the Conservatives' ability to retain their status as the local incumbents was made even more difficult because their principal challengers locally were able to advance despite rarely doing so elsewhere—giving the tally of both Labour and Liberal Democrat seats a significant boost.

Meanwhile, in Labour's case, two other patterns are also worthy of note. First, the party performed much more strongly in Scotland (a 16.7-point increase in its share of the vote) than elsewhere in Britain. As a result, it was able to win thirty-six

Table 2.5. Mean change in % share of vote 2019–24 by type of contest

Type of contest	Mean change in % share of vote 2019–24				
	Conservative	Labour	Liberal Democrat	Reform UK	Green
Con/Lab	−26.2	+6.1	−1.6	+17.6	+3.1
Con/LD	−23.6	+0.1	+9.1	+12.9	+2.0
Lab held	−14.1	−7.2	−1.0	+9.2	+7.1
SNP held	−12.7	+18.3	−0.6	+6.3	+3.7
All other	−15.7	+4.7	+2.9	+9.8	+4.0
All seats	−20.6	+1.9	+0.3	+13.2	+4.3

Con/Lab: Seats won by Conservatives in 2019 where Labour were second. Con/LD: Seats won by Conservatives in 2019 where Liberal Democrats were second. Lab held: All seats won by Labour in 2019. SNP held: All seats won by SNP in 2019. All other: All other seats not otherwise defined.
See also note to Table 2.4.
Source: Author's calculations.

seats previously held by the SNP. Second, Labour's vote actually fell back in seats that it was trying to defend—on average by seven points. This happened partly because of a relatively poor performance in Wales (where the party provides the country's devolved government and its share of the overall vote fell by 3.9 points) and partly because, in the wake of the Israeli-Gaza conflict, of some very heavy losses in seats where a large proportion of the population identify as Muslim (the party's vote fell on average by twenty-three points in seats where more than 20% regard themselves as Muslim). However, because of the weak performance of their principal opponents, the reverses in heavily Muslim constituencies only cost the party seven seats, five of them to independents standing on a pro-Palestinian platform. For the most part, Labour's loss of support in constituencies it was trying to defend simply meant the party was 'wasting' fewer votes piling up large majorities in safe seats. It largely only gained votes where it could make a difference to the outcome.

So, both Labour and the Conservatives typically recorded their worst performances (in terms of the change in their share of the vote) in constituencies where they were previously strongest. This means that in both cases their support became more evenly spread across constituencies (see Table 2.6). Indeed, at 13.9, the standard deviation in Labour's share of the vote across constituencies was by far the lowest it has been at any election since February 1974 (the first post-war election at which the Liberal Democrats fought most of the seats). Meanwhile at 10.7, the equivalent statistic for the Conservatives fell heavily from the figure that pertained in 2019 and was the lowest it has been at any election since October 1974. In contrast, the tactical voting it enjoyed in seats where the party was challenging the Conservatives meant the Liberal Democrats' vote typically increased

Table 2.6. Standard deviation of geographical distribution of party support 1974–2024

	Conservative	Labour	Liberal Democrat
1974 (Feb)	10.5	15.7	7.8
1974 (Oct)	12.1	15.2	8.3
1979	12.4	16.0	8.2
1983	13.2	15.7	7.3
1987	14.5	17.8	8.9
1992	14.0	17.8	10.1
1997	12.2	17.9	10.9
2001	13.1	16.6	11.0
2005	14.0	15.1	10.4
2010	14.6	15.9	10.4
2015	16.9	16.5	8.4
2017	15.9	17.7	8.8
2019	17.0	17.5	10.0
2024	10.7	13.9	13.2

Source: Author's calculations.

most where it was previously strongest. As a result, the party's support became more geographically concentrated; the standard deviation of its support across constituencies rose from 10.0 in 2019 to a record high of 13.2. This was a remarkable change for a party whose support has historically been much more evenly spread than that of its two principal rivals.

2. The cube law

At first glance this marked change in the geography of party support helped ensure that the single-member plurality system came close to meeting the expectations of the cube law. In the 533 seats won by either Labour or the Conservatives, Labour won 61.7% of the vote for the two parties combined (hitherto the 'two-party vote'), while the Conservatives won the remaining 38.3%. If we cube these two figures, we obtain a ratio between them of 80.7% to 19.3%, and therefore Labour would be expected to win 80.7%, that is, 430 of the 533 seats. In practice, Labour won 412, just eighteen seats short of that target. It appears that, in this respect at least, the electoral system came close to operating in the manner that its advocates suggest.

Geography is crucial to the operation of the cube law. Writing in the early 1950s, two statisticians demonstrated that, in practice, the expectations of the law would be met if the Conservative (or Labour) share of the two-party vote across constituencies was approximately normal with a standard deviation of 13.7 (Kendall and Stuart 1951). Furthermore, they showed that, at the time they were writing, this condition was close to being met, except that the distribution was a little flatter than that of a normal distribution (a feature reflected in a slightly negative kurtosis) (see also Butler 1951; Gudgin and Taylor 1979; Taagepera and Shugart 1989). As a result, as Table 2.7 shows, in the 1950s and 1960s there were slightly fewer—but only slightly fewer—marginal seats than the tally of 180 (or 30% of the total) that would be generated by a normal distribution of the two-party vote across 600 constituencies with a standard deviation of 13.7. By marginal seats we mean those where, were the two-party vote evenly divided nationally, the share of that vote secured by the winner would (assuming an unchanged geography) be less than 55%.

Table 2.7. Distribution of the two-party vote, 1955–2024

Election	Marginals		Two-party vote	
	No.	%	Standard deviation	Kurtosis
1955	166	27.2	13.5	−0.25
1959	157	25.7	13.8	−0.29
1964	166	27.3	14.1	−0.45
1966	155	25.6	13.8	−0.46
1970	149	24.5	14.3	−0.27
1974 (Feb)	119	19.9	16.1	−0.68
1974 (Oct)	98	16.4	16.8	−0.82
1979	108	17.8	16.9	−0.87
1983	80	13.2	20.0	−1.05
1987	87	14.4	21.4	−1.03
1992	98	16.1	20.2	−1.03
1997	114	19.6	18.1	−0.85
2001	114	19.7	18.3	−0.82
2005	104	18.8	19.7	−0.96
2010	85	15.0	22.2	−1.08
2015	74	13.1	21.7	−1.19
2017	89	15.3	18.6	−0.89
2019	88	15.5	20.3	−0.69
2024	104	19.5	17.0	−0.62

Marginal Seat: Seat where Conservative share of two-party vote − (overall Conservative share of two-party vote −50%) lies within the range 45%–55%.
Two-party vote: Votes cast for Conservative and Labour combined.
Table based only on seats won by Conservative or Labour at that election and contested by both parties.
Source: Curtice (2020) and author's calculations.

However, a growing geographical polarization of Conservative and Labour support meant that by the 1970s the standard deviation of the two-party vote had increased and the number of marginal seats had fallen (see Table 2.7) (Curtice and Steed 1982, 1986). By the time of the 1983 election, there were just eighty seats that could be classified as marginal, a feature that helped ensure that, despite winning just 39% of the two-party vote, Labour still managed to win 34% of the seats won by Conservative or Labour when, under the cube law the party would have won just 21%. Meanwhile, although as Table 2.7 shows there has been some variation in the number of marginal seats since then, hitherto the geographical variation in Conservative and Labour support has remained too big for the electoral system to be producing results in conformity with the cube law (Curtice 2009).

However, as we have seen, the geographical variation in both the Conservative and Labour share of the total vote became less marked in 2024. Consequently, we would anticipate that the standard deviation of the two-party vote will have fallen too. Indeed, this proves to be the case (see Table 2.7). The figure has fallen to its lowest level since 1979, while the kurtosis (that is, the peakedness of the middle of the distribution) is now less negative than at any election since 1970. As a result, nearly one in five (19.5%) of the seats won by Conservative or Labour are now marginal, close to the highest proportion at any point during the last fifty years. However, with a standard deviation of 17.0 and a negative kurtosis, Table 2.7 also suggests the geographical distribution of the two-party vote still fails to meet fully the preconditions that have to be satisfied for the division of seats between Conservative and Labour to be in accordance with the cube law.

Why then was Labour's tally of seats not far below the total generated by the cube law? In truth there are two different ways in which the single-member plurality system can exaggerate the lead of the winning party over their principal opponents. The first is through systematic exaggeration, that is, a level of disproportionality that would occur irrespective of which party is in the lead. It is that exaggeration the cube law summarizes. The second, however, is that the system treats either the Conservatives or Labour more favourably than its principal opponents for any given division of the vote between them.

There are two main reasons why single-member plurality might treat one of the two main parties more favourably than the other (Gudgin and Taylor 1979; Johnston 1979). The first is difference in the size of the constituencies that they win. If one of the parties is more successful than the other in winning seats with fewer voters—either because the registered electorate is lower or because turnout is not so high—this will translate into it winning more seats for any given share of the overall national vote. The second possibility is that one party's vote is more efficiently distributed, that is, that it either wins fewer seats by large majorities or loses fewer seats narrowly. Such a distribution means that more of that party's vote contributes to the election of an MP rather than being 'wasted' on piling up large leads or failing to win seats.

Table 2.8 uses two simple measures of these potential sources of bias (Soper and Rydon 1958). The first is the difference between the mean share of the two-party vote across constituencies won by the Conservatives and their overall share.

Table 2.8. Measures of two-party bias 1955–2024

Election	Conservative % two-party vote		
	Mean – Overall	Median – Mean	Median – Overall
1955	+0.3	+0.6	+0.9
1959	+0.4	+0.8	+1.2
1964	+0.1	+0.4	+0.5
1966	−0.3	+0.2	−0.1
1970	−0.9	+0.8	−0.1
1970 (NT)	−0.1	+0.5	+0.4
1974 (Feb)	−0.1	−0.5	−0.5
1974 (Oct)	−0.3	+1.4	+1.1
1979	−0.7	−0.5	−1.2
1979 (NT)	−0.1	+0.9	+0.9
1983	−0.5	+1.7	+1.2
1987	−0.8	+1.4	+0.6
1992	−1.2	−0.0	−1.2
1992 (NT)	−0.2	−0.7	−0.9
1997	−0.4	−1.6	−2.0
2001	−1.4	−1.5	−2.9
2001 (NT)	−1.1	−1.4	−2.5
2005	−2.1	−1.1	−3.2
2005 (NT)	−1.5	−1.0	−2.5
2010	−1.3	−0.8	−2.1
2015	−1.6	+2.1	+0.5
2017	−0.4	+0.6	+0.2
2019	−0.5	+2.0	+1.5
2019 (NT)	−0.3	+3.2	+2.9
2024	−0.3	−0.1	−0.4

NT: Notional results based on estimates of what the outcome would have been if that election had been fought on the new constituency boundaries that were introduced at the subsequent election. The 2001 redistribution (together with a reduction in the number of seats) was confined to Scotland, while the 2005 one only occurred in England and Wales.
Two-party vote: Votes cast for Conservative and Labour combined.
Figures based on all seats in Great Britain. Northern Ireland excluded.
Source: Curtice (2020) and author's calculations.

If a party tends to secure a higher share of the vote in constituencies with fewer voters, its mean share of the vote will be higher than its overall share. The second measure is the difference between the Conservatives' share of the two-party vote in the median constituency and its mean share across constituencies. If a party's vote is more efficiently distributed, its share of the vote in the constituency in the very middle of the distribution of support across constituencies will be higher than its mean share. This is because the median, unlike the mean, is not unduly inflated if a party wins some seats by unusually large majorities.

The table reveals that the electoral system has often been biased in one direction or the other in its treatment of the two largest parties. So far as differences in the sizes of constituencies are concerned, it has typically been biased towards Labour. This is because turnout has tended to be lower in the predominantly urban seats the party wins, while population movement from the cities to suburban and rural seats has meant that between each boundary review a gap has typically gradually opened up between the average (declining) electorate in Labour-held seats and that in (growing) constituencies won by the Conservatives (Champion 2005; Rossiter, Johnston, and Pattie 2009). In contrast, the direction and size of the second source of bias generated by differences in the efficiency of the two parties' support has been more variable. During the fifties and sixties, it typically favoured the Conservatives because Labour piled up large majorities in some industrial seats, most notably those dominated by coal mining (Butler 1951). But during the nineties and noughties, it was Labour's vote that was more efficiently distributed, not least because in 1997, as in 2024, the Conservatives lost ground more heavily in places where they were previously strongest, while Labour benefited from tactical voting in marginal Conservative seats (Curtice and Steed 1997). However, in 2015 the pendulum swung back in the Conservatives' favour thanks to an above average performance in marginal seats and the party's success in gaining as many as twenty-seven seats from the Liberal Democrats.

Although the constituency boundaries were redrawn for this election, there was only a small fall in the extent to which the first source of bias advantaged Labour. This was the consequence of two developments. First, over the last decade or so the tendency for people to move out of the cities and into suburban and rural areas largely came to a halt and in some instances, most notably London, was reversed (Champion 2016; Department for Environment, Food and Rural Affairs 2021). Second, the Conservatives' success in 2017 and 2019 in winning a number of traditionally Labour but Leave-inclined constituencies (the so-called 'Red Wall') meant the party gained some seats with smaller constituencies that were adversely affected by the boundary review (Curtice 2020). As a result, at 2,470, the difference between Conservative and Labour-held seats in their average electorate in 2019 was actually less than in 2015. Meanwhile, that remaining gap was eliminated by the boundary review—indeed it left the average Labour seat in

2019 with just 194 more registered voters, a difference that slipped to eighty-three by the time registration for the 2024 election was finalized.

However, turnout continues to be lower in seats where Labour are strongest. Indeed, the gap widened in 2024. Turnout in 2024 in the average seat that had been won by Labour in 2019 was just 54.4%, 9.7 points down on 2019. In contrast, in seats that had been won by the Conservatives in 2019, turnout was 62.7%, down 6.5 points. As a result, 5,739 more votes were cast in the average constituency won by the Conservatives this time around than were counted in seats won by Labour, slightly up on the equivalent figure of 5,498 in 2019. Although the boundary commissioners succeeded in equalizing the electorates of Conservative and Labour seats, Labour still profited from differences in the level of turnout.

The boundary review did, however, prove to be advantageous to the Conservatives in respect of the efficiency of their support. Compared with the old constituencies, it left the Conservatives with slightly more seats that were marginal and Labour with somewhat more that were very safe. As a result, the Conservatives went into the 2024 election with an even more favourable electoral geography than in 2019. However, as we have already seen, Labour's vote often fell heavily in constituencies it was defending, a pattern that ensured that in 2024 the party wasted fewer votes by piling up large majorities. If in 2019 the two parties had had the same share of the two-party vote across the country as a whole, Labour would have won fifty-six seats with more than 80% of the two-party vote, while the Conservatives would have won just eighteen. In 2024, the equivalent figures were fifteen and seventeen, respectively.

There is, however, another important potential source of bias that is not adequately captured by the statistics in Table 2.8. This is a difference in the extent to which the two parties waste votes in seats won by third parties. As we have seen, the Conservatives lost sixty-six seats to the Liberal Democrats, while Labour captured thirty-six from the SNP. This ensured that what was already a tendency in 2019 for the Conservatives to waste more votes than Labour in seats won by third parties became more marked in 2024. On average, the Conservatives won 24.4% of the vote in seats won by third parties, whereas Labour secured 13.9%, a difference of 10.5 points and more than double the equivalent figure of 5.1 points in 2019. Votes for the Conservatives in seats won by third parties represented as much as 19.4% of the party's total vote, whereas the equivalent figure for Labour was just 6.6%.

As a result, although Table 2.8 suggests there was only a modest bias to Labour in 2024, in practice it proved to be rather more than that. This is illustrated in Table 2.9, which undertakes for the results of the 2024 election the same calculation as we performed in Table 2.9 for the outcome of the 2019 election (on the new boundaries). It shows that, on the assumption of an unchanged geography, the Conservatives would need to be nearly five points ahead of Labour in the overall national vote before they would become the largest party in the House of Commons. If the party had the same share of the vote as Labour, it would have as many as ninety-eight fewer seats. Meanwhile, the Conservatives would have to be just over eleven points ahead of their principal opponents to secure an overall majority, whereas for Labour a lead of little more than one point would be sufficient.

So, although there has been some reduction in the geographical polarization of Conservative and Labour support, the fact that the outcome of the election apparently came close to fulfilling the requirements of the cube law also owed a great deal to the fact that, in sharp contrast to 2019, the system treated Labour more favourably than the Conservatives. Despite Labour's large majority, the system still cannot necessarily be relied upon to exaggerate the lead of the winning party over the second party to the degree required to ensure that the winner secures an overall majority—or indeed even to be sure that the party with most votes secures the most seats. For, as Table 2.9 shows, on the current electoral geography and levels of third-party support, any outcome between a Labour lead of one point and a Conservative lead of eleven, that is, a range of twelve points, would result in a hung parliament. That is a not insubstantial range, albeit one somewhat below the equivalent spread of seventeen points in 2019 (see Table 2.9).

3. Third parties

Not least of the reasons, of course, why this is the case is that however well the system exaggerates the lead of the largest party over the second party, the possibility that a hung parliament might arise is increased the greater the number of seats won by third parties. Indeed, as noted earlier, a crucial second leg of the traditional defence of the single-member plurality electoral system is that it reinforces a system of alternating majority government by making it difficult for third

Table 2.9. Impact on seats of uniform swing from Labour to Conservative after 2024 election

Swing to Con	Con %	Lab %	Con lead	Con seats	Lab seats	Other seats	Majority
0.0	24.4	34.7	−10.3	121	412	117	Lab 176
4.6	29.0	30.1	−1.1	207	330	113	Lab 10
4.7	29.1	30.0	−0.9	214	325	111	None
5.15	29.55	29.55	0.0	222	320	108	None
7.65	32.0	27.1	4.9	274	273	103	None
10.5	34.9	24.2	10.9	325	223	102	None
10.6	35.0	24.1	11.1	327	221	102	Con 4
14.65	39.05	20.05	19.0	413	146	91	Con 178

Source: Author's calculations. % vote figures are for Great Britain. Seat tallies are for all of the UK.

parties to win seats—and in so doing discourages voters from voting for smaller parties in the first place (Duverger 1954; Blais and Carty 1991). However, this feature was notably absent from the outcome of the 2024 election. Not only did third parties and independents win over one in six (18%) of all the seats in the House of Commons, but, at 42.5%, the share of the vote across the UK won by third parties was the highest since 1922, that is, since the first election at which Labour became the principal competitors to the Conservatives. Although, as noted earlier, the Liberal Democrats did not perform especially well in terms of votes, the 14.7% vote won in Great Britain by Reform UK was the highest ever recorded for a party other than the Conservatives, Labour or the Liberal Democrats. At the same time, the Greens' 6.9% of the vote was their highest-ever percentage share.

Yet, in contrast to the success achieved by the Liberal Democrats, the electoral system was relatively successful at denying representation to both Reform UK and the Greens. In truth, the single-member plurality system only has a marked tendency to give third parties little reward if their vote is geographically evenly spread. Even quite small parties, such as Plaid Cymru in Wales and parties in Northern Ireland, can secure something close to a proportionate share of seats if their vote is geographically concentrated (Gudgin and Taylor 1979). This time the same was also true of the Liberal Democrats thanks to a heavy concentration of their support in seats where the party was an effective challenger to the beleaguered Conservatives—on average the party won 37.9% of the vote in seats where it shared first and second place with the Conservatives in 2019, but only 7.4% elsewhere (see also Table 2.6).

However, support for both Reform UK and the Greens was relatively evenly spread. In the case of the former the standard deviation of the party's support across constituencies was 6.7, lower than that for the Liberal Democrats at any election since 1974 (see Table 2.6), while in the case of the Greens, it was just 5.4. Consequently, neither party enjoyed anything like the success of the Liberal Democrats. That said, Reform UK's vote was a little less evenly spread than was UKIP's at the height of that party's success in 2015 (a standard deviation of 6.2). Meanwhile, because the party's support rose rather more in constituencies where it was previously strongest, support for the Greens was also more varied than in 2019 (a standard deviation of 3.1). Both patterns help explain why Reform UK were able to win more than the one seat UKIP secured in 2015 and the Greens more than the single seat in Brighton that the party had made their own since 2010.

Although the SNP's support is confined to Scotland, within that country its support is quite evenly spread. That had long been disadvantageous for the party in its attempt to win seats—until in 2015 it won nearly 50% of the vote in Scotland and thus came first in fifty-six of the fifty-nine seats that then existed north of the border. However, because this time the party was outpolled by Labour, the relatively even spread of its support became a disadvantage once more. Indeed, at 5.0, the standard deviation of its support was slightly down on the 5.7 figure registered in 2019. Consequently, the party retained just nine seats, rather fewer than the seventeen it would have won if the rises and falls in party support in Scotland had been the same everywhere, an outcome that would also have represented the party's proportionate share.

4. Conclusion

At first glance, the UK's electoral system was remarkably successful in 2024 in delivering what is often claimed for it—an ability to provide a system of alternating majoritarian government. The electorate were able to secure the removal of an incumbent government that had widely become unpopular and have it replaced by its principal opponents armed with a safe overall majority. Indeed, after the hung parliaments of 2010 and 2017 and the small majority of 2015, the outcome in 2024 together with that in 2019 would appear to signify a return to business as normal.

Yet, in truth, what the 2024 election underlined was the heavily contingent character of the relationship between seats and votes under the single-member plurality system. The geography of party support changed dramatically—and consequently so also did the relationship between seats and votes. True, in part this changed geography resulted in some restoration of one of the key foundations of the system, that is, its ability to exaggerate in terms of seats the lead of the largest party over the second party in terms of votes. However, Labour's success—much like that of the Conservatives in 2019—was also founded on an electoral geography that ensured the system benefitted Labour more than its principal opponents. Meanwhile, the highly contingent character of the system's ability to keep third parties out of the Commons was heavily underlined. After having long been treated relatively harshly by the system, a newly geographically concentrated vote enabled the Liberal Democrats to secure their biggest Commons representation for over a century. At the same time, however, two other third parties, including one that outpolled the Liberal Democrats, found it much more difficult to secure seats because their vote was geographically more evenly spread.

Of course, for anyone who feels that the aim of a parliamentary election should be to produce a representative assembly of legislators rather than the election of a government, the highly disproportional outcome of the 2024 election will simply have reinforced their existing doubts about its suitability as a method for electing MPs. Others, perhaps, might conclude that while it might have been appropriate to use a system that facilitates alternating majority government when the winning party normally secured well over 40% of the vote, a threshold of acceptable disproportionality has been crossed when the winner secures a very large majority with barely more than a third of the vote. Yet others might ask whether the fact a record number of 14 different parties were able to win at least one seat means the system is proving ineffective anyway at insulating Britain from the supposed risks of multi-party politics.

However, whatever, the merits of these arguments, the real question posed by the outcome of the 2024 election is whether it is democratically defensible to use an electoral system under which the geography of party support can seemingly play as important a role as the national popularity of the parties in determining the shape of parliamentary representation. Still, with Labour now ensconced in power by the system with a majority of 174, there will presumably now, despite the party conference's decision in 2022 to back proportional representation, be plenty of time to contemplate the answer.

Funding

This research was conducted while the author was funded by the Economic and Social Research Council as a Senior Fellow of 'The UK in a Changing Europe' (Grant number ES/X005798/1).

References

Baker, C., Cracknell, R., and Uberoi, E. (2020) General Election 2019: results and analysis. London: House of Commons Library Briefing Paper CBP8749. https://commonslibrary.parliament.uk/research-briefings/cbp-8749/, accessed 25 July 2024.

Bingham Powell, G., Jr. (2000) *Elections as Instruments of Democracy: Majoritarian and Proportional Visions*. New Haven: Yale University Press.

Blais, A., and Carty, R. (1991) 'The Psychological Impact of Electoral Laws: Measuring Duverger's Elusive Factor', *British Journal of Political Science*, 21: 79–93.

Butler, D. (1951) 'An Examination of the Results', in: H. Nicholas (ed.) *The British General Election of 1950*, pp. 306–33. Basingstoke: Macmillan.

Champion, A. (2005) 'Population Movement within the UK', in: R. Chappell (ed.) *Focus on People and Migration*, pp. 91–114. London: Palgrave Macmillan.

Champion, A. (2016) 'Internal Migration and the Spatial Distribution of the Population', in: A. Champion and J. Falkingham (eds) *Population Change in the United Kingdom*, pp. 125–41. London: Rowman and Littlefield.

Cracknell, R. and Baker, C. (2024) General election 2024 results, House of Commons Library Research Briefing CBP 10009. https://commonslibrary.parliament.uk/research-briefings/cbp-10009/, accessed 25 July 2024.

Curtice, J. (2009) 'Neither Representative nor Accountable: First Past the Post in Britain', in: B. Grofman, A. Blais, and S. Bowler (eds) *Duverger's Law of Plurality Voting*, pp. 27–46. New York: Springer.

Curtice, J. (2020) 'A Return to 'Normality' at Last? How the Electoral System Worked in 2019', *Parliamentary Affairs*, 73: 29–47.

Curtice, J., and Steed, M. (1982) 'Electoral Choice and the Production of Government: The Changing Operation of the Electoral System in the UK Since 1955', *British Journal of Political Science*, 12: 249–98.

Curtice, J., and Steed, M. (1986) 'Proportionality and Exaggeration in the British Electoral System', *Electoral Studies*, 5: 209–28.

Curtice, J., and Steed, M. (1997), 'Appendix 2: the Results Analysed', in: D. Butler and D. Kavanagh (eds) *The British General Election of 1997*, pp. 295–325. Basingstoke: Macmillan.

Department for Environment, Food and Rural Affairs (2021) 'Rural Population and Migration', https://www.gov.uk/government/statistics/rural-population-and-migration/rural-population-and-migration, accessed 1 Nov. 2024.

Duverger, M. (1954) *Political Parties: Their Organisation and Activity in the Modern State*. London: Methuen.

Gallagher, M. (1991) 'Proportionality, Disproportionality and Electoral Systems', *Electoral Studies*, 10: 33–51.

Gallagher, M. (2024) 'Election Indices', https://www.tcd.ie/Political_Science/about/people/michael_gallagher/ElSystems/Docts/ElectionIndices.pdf, accessed 30 Oct. 2024.

Gudgin, G., and Taylor, P. (1979) *Seats, Votes and the Spatial Organisation of Elections*. London: Pion.

Johnston, R. (1979) *Political, Electoral and Spatial Systems*. Oxford: Clarendon Press.

Kendall, M., and Stuart, A. (1951) 'The Law of Cubic Proportions in Election Results', *British Journal of Sociology*, 1: 183–97.

Laakso, M., and Taagepera, R. (1979) '"Effective" Number of Parties: A Measure with Application to Western Europe', *CPS*, 12: 3–27.

Loosemore, J., and Hanby, V. (1971) 'The Theoretical Limits of Maximum Distortion: Some Analytic Expressions for Electoral Systems', *British Journal of Political Science*, 1: 467–77.

Norton, P. (1997) 'The Case for First Past the Post', *Representation*, 34: 84–8.

Rallings, C., and Thrasher, M. (2024), *Guide to the New Parliamentary Constituencies*. London: *BBC, ITV News, Sky News, PA Media*, https://www.electionscentre.co.uk/wp-content/uploads/2024/05/Guide-to-the-New-Parliamentary-Constituencies.pdf, accessed 10 Oct. 2024.

Renwick, A. (2011) *A Citizens' Guide to Electoral Reform*. London: Biteback.

Rossiter, D., Johnston, R., and Pattie, C. (2009) *The Boundary Commissions: Redrawing the UK's Map of Parliamentary Constituencies*. Manchester: Manchester University Press.

Soper, C., and Rydon, J. (1958) 'Under-Representation and Electoral Prediction', *Australian Journal of Politics and History*, 4: 94–106.

Taagepera, R., and Shugart, M. (1989) *Seats and Votes: The Effects and Determinants of Electoral Systems*. New Haven: Yale University Press.

'Come, Armageddon, come'[1]: The Conservatives

Sam Power[1,*], Paul Webb[2], and Tim Bale[3]

[1]School of Sociology, Politics and International Studies, University of Bristol, 11 Priory Road, Bristol, BS8 1TU, UK
[2]School of Law, Politics and Sociology, Freeman Centre, University of Sussex, Brighton, BN1 9QE, UK
[3]School of Politics and International Relations, Queen Mary University of London, 1 Westfield Way, Bethnal Green, London, E1 4PD, UK

*Correspondence: s.power@bristol.ac.uk

In May 2021, the Conservatives took Hartlepool from Labour on a swing of sixteen percentage points—the biggest towards an incumbent governing party in a by-election in the post-war era—prompting Keir Starmer, Leader of the Opposition, to wonder whether he should resign after just a year or so in post (Halliday 2021; Baldwin 2024). Five months later—as we entered conference season, and with the first round of a vaccine rollout nearly complete—the UK's national newspapers seemed convinced that the Conservatives would be in government for at least the foreseeable future. 'Boris Johnson eyes another decade in power', read *The Times*, quoting an unnamed cabinet minister boasting that he wanted 'to go on for longer than Thatcher' (Swinford and Wright 2021). And, a month later, on 6th October, Chief Political Commentator at *The Sunday Times*, Tim Shipman (2021), suggested that Johnson 'now squats like a giant toad across British politics', going on to ask '[W]here does Labour find a gap?'

Cut to Partygate, to Sue Gray's report, to the Chris Pincher allegations that eventually did for Johnson. Cut to Liz Truss, a disastrous mini-budget, and a lettuce with googly-eyes that simply refused to rot before her forty-nine days in office were up. Cut to Rishi Sunak on the Downing Street steps promising a government of 'integrity, professionalism and accountability at every level'. Cut to Rishi Sunak back on

---

[1]Lyrics by Morrissey (1988).

© The Author(s) 2025. Published by Oxford University Press on behalf of the Hansard Society. All rights reserved. For commercial re-use, please contact reprints@oup.com for reprints and translation rights for reprints. All other permissions can be obtained through our RightsLink service via the Permissions link on the article page on our site—for further information please contact journals.permissions@oup.com.

the Downing Street steps, in the pouring rain, surprising almost everyone—except a select few who just happened to have a flutter on it—sending the UK to the polls. And, after the rain, the deluge: Labour on 411 seats (up 211); the Liberal Democrats on seventy-two (up sixty-four); the Conservatives on just 121 (down 251).

It was, in terms of both seats and votes, a historic low for the Conservatives. Eleven cabinet ministers were defenestrated, and Liz Truss became the first former PM to lose a seat in nearly 100 years. And yet, amongst all this, one was left with a feeling as both the exit poll dropped—and then the actual results began to flood in—that almost all the parties (barring, perhaps, the SNP), would have taken the outcome if presented to them when the polls opened. Labour had gained a stonking majority from a historic low in 2019 (see Tonge et al., 2020; Ford et al., 2021). The Liberal Democrats had won more seats than ever. Reform UK and the Greens bagged five and four seats, respectively. And, relative to some of the truly catastrophic polling the Conservatives were seeing during the campaign, escaping with more than 100 seats came as something of a relief.

So how did we get here? How did we go from a result in 2019 that many saw as 'tantamount to Labour's last rites' (Power, Bale, and Webb 2020: 79) to it rising, phoenix-like, from the ashes just four-and-a-half years later?

1. Where did it all go wrong? The long campaign

In the edited collection *How Tory Governments Die*, Anthony Seldon identifies nine factors that have been evident in the failure of Conservative governments to retain power (Seldon 1997). They are

- A negative image of the party leader.
- Confusion over policy direction.
- Manifest internal disunity.
- Organization in the country in disarray.
- Depleted party finance.
- Hostile intellectual and press climate.
- Loss of confidence in the electorate in economic management.
- Strength of feeling of time for a change.
- A revived and credible opposition.

There is a credible case to be made that each of these factors was apparent in the lead-up to (and during) the 2024 election. There was an undoubted—and unprecedented—*negative image of the party leader(s)*. If we look at the three leaders of the Conservative Party over the 2019–24 electoral cycle, they all ended up in a similar place. Christmas Day 2019 saw Boris Johnson enjoying a relative honeymoon for prime ministerial approval with 47% of people telling YouGov he was doing well as Prime Minister, as opposed to 41% who thought he was doing badly. However,

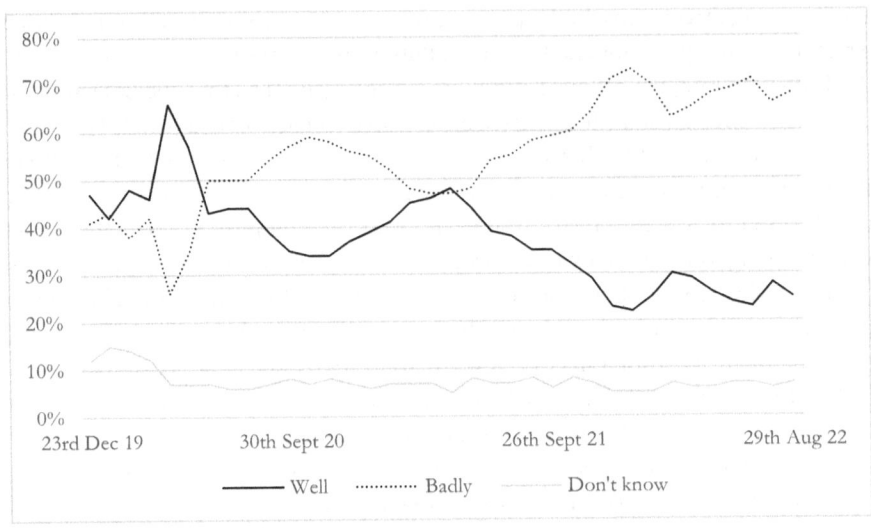

Source: YouGov, 2022.

Figure 3.1. How well is Boris Johnson doing as Prime Minister?

by the time he was replaced as PM two-and-a-half years later his approval rating had fallen to just 25% while his negative rating had risen to 68%, leaving him forty-three points in arrears (see Fig. 3.1).

Rishi Sunak, for his part, enjoyed a far shorter honeymoon than Johnson. When he assumed the premiership in the Autumn of 2022, some 45% 'didn't know' whether Sunak was doing a good job, compared with 28% who thought he was doing well, and 27% who thought he was performing poorly. By the election less than two years later, his positive ratings had fallen to just 20%, with 72% of respondents replying in the negative—a net approval rating of −52 (see Fig. 3.2).

As for Liz Truss, she wasn't long enough in the job to make it worthwhile tracking any change.

1.1 As go the leaders, so too the party

It was not, of course, just the leaders who were struggling to impress the public. By the time Sunak assumed office in November 2022, the Conservative Party had fallen to its lowest level of approval since Ipsos started (regularly) asking whether they were liked in 2007 (Ipsos 2022). The question was whether Sunak could pull the Conservatives up? Or would he instead find himself dragged down to their level? The answer? Emphatically the latter.

This was largely because of the second and third factors pointed to by Seldon— *confusion over policy direction* and *manifest internal disunity*. In part, that was a

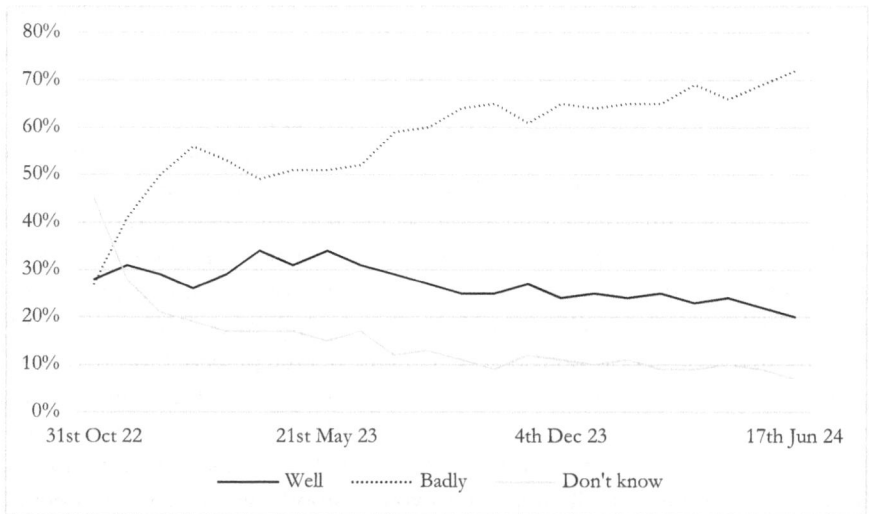

Figure 3.2. How well is Rishi Sunak doing as Prime Minister?

product of the 'fragile and fissiparous coalition of support' (Power, Bale, and Webb 2020: 79) that the party had pulled together in order to win in 2019, but it was made worse by a series of policy own goals, most obviously the mess the Sunak team got into over immigration, and particularly the Rwanda policy designed to act as a deterrent to those migrants (declared 'illegal' by the government) making the perilous journey across the English Channel in order to claim asylum in the UK. Setting aside moral qualms about whether a liberal democracy ought to be spending a great deal of time and money working with regimes that have—to put it mildly—a questionable human rights record (see Wrong 2021), the politics of the scheme became a huge problem for the Conservatives, and for Sunak in particular.

Internally, Rwanda strained collective cabinet responsibility. To pick just a few examples, Home Secretary James Cleverly appeared on the morning news rounds in November 2023 to deny he had called the policy 'batshit' (BBC 2023), and a clip of his aide James Sunderland describing it as 'crap' to Conservative supporters was uncovered during the election campaign itself (Culbertson 2024). All the while its continued failure—owing to both British and continental court decisions—to produce any forced deportation flights was used as a stick with which to beat Sunak by MPs on the right of the party. It also allowed frontbenchers laying the groundwork for future leadership campaigns to make hay, most obviously Robert Jenrick, who resigned as immigration minister because further reforms 'didn't go far enough' to halt the 'merry-go-round of legal challenges which risk paralyzing the scheme' (Morton 2023). It also caused significant disquiet amongst the more liberal wing of the Conservatives, particularly those who were worried that the government's evident desperation to see 'flights take off' might lead it to pursue withdrawal from the European Convention on Human Rights.

But if Rwanda managed to aggravate both 'One Nation Tories' and their more populist, right-wing colleagues who thought either that it failed to go far enough or else that it was bound to fail owing to Sunak's original (and imagined) sin of never really being a true right winger, it also harmed the party externally. Conservative splits signalled to the public a party in disarray. Moreover, it risked repelling the more socially progressive elements of the Tory voting shires, who were already showing signs at local elections that they might well be prepared to vote Liberal Democrat. At the very same time its (some would say inevitable) failure handed issue ownership of migration to Reform UK, who, if only it could bag itself a charismatic leader capable of channelling the resentment of more socially conservative (and overwhelmingly Brexit-supporting) voters, stood a good chance of hoovering up another tranche of the 2019 Conservative electorate.

1.2 As go the leaders, so too the infrastructure

Going into the election the Conservatives were not necessarily in the financial doldrums, although that accounts neither for the dire state of their fundraising during the campaign itself (see below and Fisher in this volume). Nor the fact that, of the £36.4m they received in donations in the nine months prior to the election, £15.2m (i.e. just over 40%) came from the wealthy businessman Frank Hester, which, after details emerged of some of his less than savoury views, turned out to have considerable reputational disadvantages (Zeffman and Morton 2024). In terms of wider infrastructure, MP for Mid-Norfolk George Freeman lamented that 'Labour were the beneficiaries of a Chernobyl-style meltdown…on any measure you choose – electoral, financial, administrative, or cultural – the Party is damaged. If we were a company we would have just suffered a massive shareholder revolt, share price and sales collapse, with customers and investors abandoning us…[W]e are politically bust' (Freeman 2024).

If we look to the press, and whether they were openly hostile, the answer is likely much less than in 1997. Whilst *The Sun* and *The Financial Times,* for example, plumped for Labour for the first time since 2005, *The Times* endorsed no party (see Deacon et al., this volume). And whilst traditional stalwarts like the *Daily Mail* and *Telegraph* backed the Tories, again this was broadly as an encouragement to tactically vote to keep Labour from power. More damaging over the Conservative five-year term for some, was that the press was not quite hostile enough. Instead, the 'well-documented pro-Tory bias of much of the print media' was 'killing it with kindness' (Elledge 2023). Rather than being a useful check on Conservative excesses, in almost any policy area one could open the pages of right-leaning broadsheets or tabloids and find a political commentator or editorial (or sometimes both) that would defend them to the hilt, often in a manner well out of step with popular opinion. After the surprising Conservative majority in 2015, after Brexit, after Trump, even after Johnson's 2019 victory, a common refrain (indeed taunt) from the right was to remind progressives that 'Twitter isn't Britain'. Neither, it seems, were the Conservatives' friends in the press.

1.3 As goes the party, so too the voters

We come, then, to the final three, Seldon-style failures of the long campaign: the *loss of confidence in the electorate in economic management*, the *strength of feeling of time for a change*, and a *revived and credible opposition*. The former was surely the most damaging and stems largely from the disastrous Truss/Kwarteng 'mini-budget' of October 2022. Indeed, before that point, and despite a precipitous decline from a 'rally round the flag' Covid-19 bounce that accompanied the vaccine rollout, the Conservatives were ahead of, or tied with, Labour on measures of economic competence. Afterwards, however, we saw a Black Wednesday-esque fall from which the Conservatives did not recover (see Fig. 3.3).

Alongside dire poll ratings for economic management, measures of trust and overall competence also caused increasing problems for the Conservatives. This was largely because of one event—partygate. Fig. 3.4 outlines two YouGov

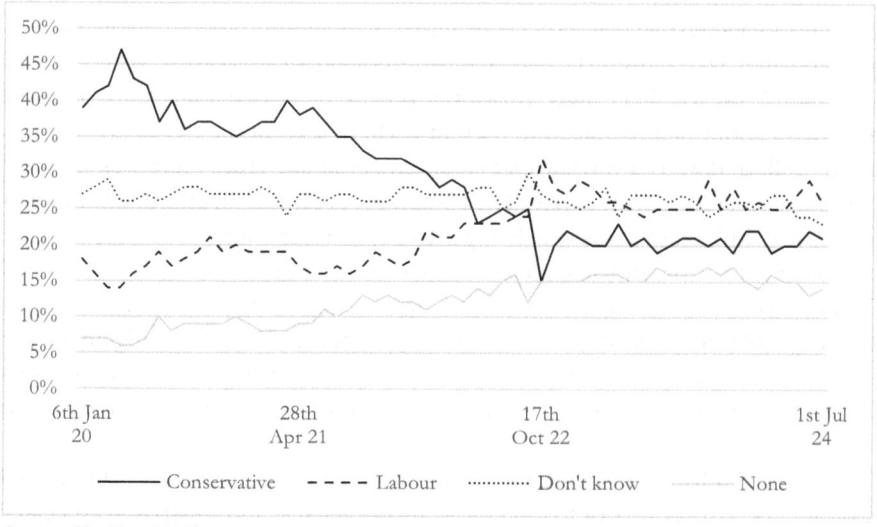

Source: YouGov, 2024b.

Figure 3.3. Which political party would be best at handling the economy?

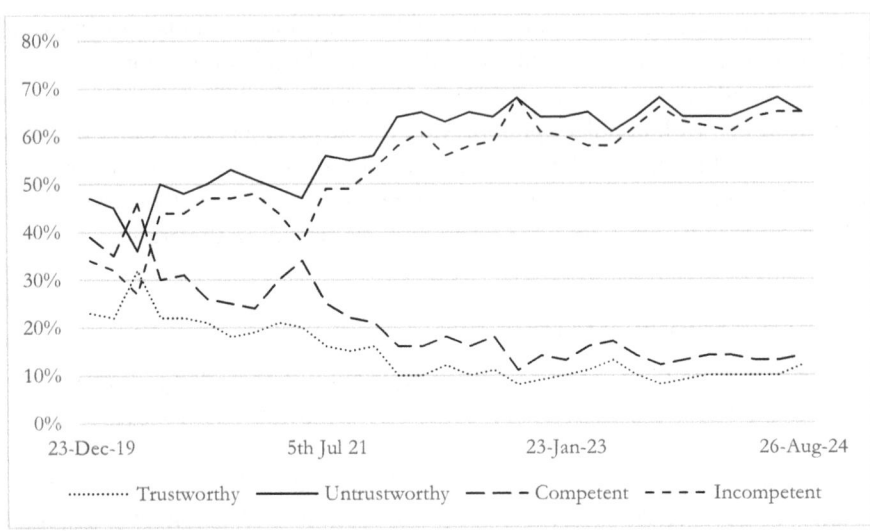

Source: YouGov, 2024c; 2024d.

Figure 3.4. Do you think the Conservative party is trustworthy or untrustworthy, competent or incompetent?

measures on trust and competence and shows that, even taking into account the fact that the British public rarely credits political parties with being trustworthy or competent, the drop was as stark as it was rapid.

This led to an overwhelming sense that it was time for a change, given rocket boosters by tactical voting (especially among Labour and Liberal Democrat supporters) that was 'extremely effective in removing Conservative MPs' (Labour Together 2024; see also Calver 2024). But this in turn owed a fair amount to the fact that Labour had managed to present itself, at least in the two years running up to polling day, as a *revived and credible opposition*. True, there was no great groundswell of support for Keir Starmer and his party that in effect blew away its main rival. But Labour was widely regarded, as it never really was under Corbyn, as a viable, realistic and safe alternative (see Goes, this volume). As Channel 4 Political Editor Gary Gibbon put it on election night, they were the recipients of a landslide, sure, but it was a loveless one (Gibbon 2024). This judgement was confirmed in that Labour only won 34% of the vote in the general election. That said, in a hypothetical head-to-head with the Conservatives that number jumped to 61% (Walker 2024).

Leading up to the campaign itself, then, we can see all nine of Seldon's factors at play. A toxic mix of Conservative incompetence and mistrust—especially over issues of sleaze, the economy, and immigration—coupled with the sheer volatility of the British electorate meaning that voters were much less likely to stick with them or give Sunak and his colleagues the benefit of the doubt at the tail end of a fourteen-year reign. They therefore started the campaign in a position of extraordinary weakness, trailing in the polls and seemingly so doomed that only by playing an absolute blinder could they hope to avoid what looked like being unprecedented losses.

2. Where did it all go wrong? The short campaign

As metaphors go, Rishi Sunak announcing that the country would go to the polls in the pouring rain whilst the strains of D:Ream's 'Things Can Only Get Better' could be heard echoing around Downing Street, was rather on the nose. Nevertheless, it did speak to a genuine weakness in the Sunak team that would recur again and again during the campaign itself.

Firstly, it hammered home the perception that his otherworldly wealth left him out of touch. What immediately sprang to mind was one of the legion of valedictory pieces that were written during the final season of HBO's Emmy winning TV show *Succession* whose writing team had to employ a 'super rich consultant, whose job was to explain what it was like to be a billionaire', the first lesson being 'rich people don't wear coats…they move seamlessly from their cars to their jets to their buildings' (Prichett 2023). If this seems a little unfair, it does recall Sunak's inability to use a contactless card machine in a photo-op when buying petrol as the Chancellor. Or, to quote a participant from a Labour Together-run focus group, he 'hasn't got a clue, and to be that out of touch is frightening, he's never going to understand the working-class mentality' (Labour Together 2024).

Secondly, and in a question that was raised more than once during the campaign, it also made one wonder just who it was that was advising him. This was made acutely apparent at any number of stages, but began with the Conservatives' first big policy announcement, bringing back national service. True, it achieved its aim of grabbing attention and at least suggesting that the party hadn't run out of ideas and still knew where its core vote was. But it generated more laughter than enthusiasm among the audience of the campaign's first televised debate. That said, the occasion nevertheless proved something of a success for Sunak, who (by sheer force of repetition if nothing else) managed to set the media agenda for two or three days with a much-disputed claim (which a flat-footed Starmer failed to counter early enough) that Labour's economic plans would cost working families £2,000 ('you name it, Labour will tax it').

As the polls had Sunak coming out marginally on top in the first head-to-head debate with Starmer (Sky News 2024), it seemed the Conservative campaign had a bit of wind in its sails—enough wind to power the PM over the Channel for commemorations marking the 80th anniversary of D-Day in good spirits.

Unfortunately, it was also breezy enough to get him back home before the event was finished—much to the outrage (confected or otherwise) of the other parties and some of his own supporters. Sunak was forced to apologize for his mistake and Conservative insiders variously described it as 'disastrous', the 'stupidest of stupid ideas', and, more bluntly, 'a fuck-up'—before comparing it unkindly to other major campaign blunders such as Gordon Brown's 'bigoted woman' jibe in 2010 and Theresa May's 'dementia tax' fiasco in 2017 (Parker et al., 2024). More worryingly, it spoke to what some of them claimed was the dysfunctional relationship in the Conservative campaign team between its manager (and the mastermind behind Johnson's 2019 victory) Isaac Levido, and close Sunak aides such as his Chief of Staff Liam Booth-Smith, communications chief Nerissa Chesterfield, and political secretary James Forsyth (Mason et al., 2024). Though *The Sunday Times* reported that all four were present when Sunak's timetable was decided, so all culpable, party insiders seemed happy to brief (anonymously of course) that this, to quote one of them, was the 'worst operation I have ever seen. From the Prime Minister down, there is a combination of arrogance and sheer incompetence' (Shipman 2024).

And for those who would wager it could not get much worse for Sunak, a second story was about to shake the Conservative campaign—one that by all accounts did its prospects more damage than D-Day, reinforcing, as it did, pre-existing prejudices about Tory greed and sleaze. On 12th June the *Guardian* reported that Craig Williams, the Parliamentary Private Secretary to Sunak, had placed a bet that the election would take place in July. Subsequently, a police constable from the Royalty and Specialist Protection Command, as well as Conservative Party campaign director Tony Lee and his wife Laura Saunders, were also reported as being under investigation by the Gambling Commission. The story snowballed. The situation was not helped, first, by eagle-eyed observers noting that CCHQ (Conservative Campaign Headquarters) had posted, and then subsequently pulled, an advert that warned the public not to 'bet' on Labour (Gibbons 2024) and, second, by Starmer (in contrast to Sunak, who took his time to do the same thing over 'gamblegate') then summarily suspending a candidate who had bet on himself to lose his constituency race. It was a move which seemed to signal not only that he had greater control of his party, but also that he cared more about probity and standards in public life.

Yet for all that, it was surely the re-introduction of Nigel Farage to the political scene that represented the greatest blow to the Conservatives' campaign – and one they could do next to nothing about. Not only did Reform UK pick off disaffected voters from elements of the right wholly dissatisfied with a party that had lost its grip on immigration and, as former leadership contender Andrea Leadsom put it on election night, was perceived to be 'too woke'. It also re-activated internal disquiet over Sunak's decision to call the election early in the first place. Many, after all, had hoped that an October date would mean Farage would be occupied across the pond helping his 'friend' Donald Trump to regain the White House. Worse, Farage's entry into the campaign drew the media's attention away from the Conservatives' attacks on Labour, while the immediate boost it provided to Reform UK's poll ratings (widely assumed to come at the expense of the Conservatives rather than Labour or the Liberal Democrats) kicked off speculation that it might actually overtake the Conservatives. This, in turn, along with multiple companies producing MRP (multilevel regression and post-stratification) polls that allowed anxious candidates to check the supposed state of play in the constituencies they themselves were fighting, only served to further depress an already demoralized bunch of activists.

Meanwhile, the media were reporting that the Conservatives had become reliant on paid-for leaflet delivery services due to a 'chronic lack of volunteers', alongside a 'shrinking and ageing membership' and 'a calamitous fall in the number of Conservative councillors' (Walker 2024). Research seems to bear out the picture they painted. A post-election survey of members of the five major GB-wide parties found that Tory members were the least active (see Table 3.1). Out of a set of ten possible campaign activities, their average level of engagement was lowest, compared to (in descending order) Labour, Liberal Democrats, Greens, and Reform UK. Further, Table 3.2 reveals that Tory members were the least likely to have devoted more than forty hours of their time to campaigning and the most likely to have done nothing at all.

Table 3.1. Involvement in election campaign activities by party members

	Conservative	**Labour**	**Lib Dem**	**Green**	**Reform**
Poster	25	66	51	50	44
Leaflet	47	50	59	41	34
Meeting	31	29	28	25	30
Canvassed	29	30	31	20	21
Candidate	1	2	4	6	3
Committee	11	6	13	11	2
Drove	4	4	2	1	3
Donated	37	51	60	52	58
SM post	18	29	20	35	39
SM share	45	57	48	67	71
Mean	25	32	32	31	31

Note: All figures are percentages of sample indicating that they participated in these campaign activities.
Source: Data from Party Members Project Survey 2024 (Queen Mary University of London and University of Sussex). SM, social media.

Table 3.2. Time committed to campaign activities by party members, 2024

	Conservative	Labour	Lib Dem	Green	Reform
None	56	43	36	49	35
Up to 5 h	17	24	24	26	22
From 6 to 10 h	7	10	8	8	8
From 11 to 20 h	4	6	8	4	9
From 21 to 30 h	3	3	5	2	7
From 31 to 40 h	2	2	3	1	3
More than 40 h	7	9	15	7	10
Don't know	3	3	2	3	6
Total	99	100	101	100	100
Sample number	1067	1003	894	732	570

Note: All figures are percentages, unless otherwise stated. Rounding errors account for totals that vary from 100.
Source: Data from Party Members Project Survey 2024 (Queen Mary University of London & University of Sussex).

But it wasn't just human resources that were a problem for the Conservatives. Money was too. An analysis of pre-poll donation reports since they started being collected in 2001 showed not only that the Conservatives were beaten by Labour by some margin, but that 2024 was comfortably their worst short campaign ever as far as their fundraising was concerned (Halford et al., 2024; Fisher, this volume). Donors have long had numerous motivations for giving to political parties, be they ideological, to invest in a party in the expectation of a return, or simply because they like going to events (see Francia et al., 2003; McMenamin and Power 2023). The overarching sense of doom, it seems, led to many Conservative donors, like many Conservative voters, deciding to simply sit this one out. One regular donor who kept his hand in his pocket had noted that 'any self-respecting businessperson conducts due diligence before an investment decision. Time will tell whether smart money will back Mr Sunak' (Fisher 2024). Evidently it did not.

For all the drawbacks and disadvantages they suffered, however, the Conservatives do seem to have regained some ground during the campaign, with the final results somewhere between the kindest polls and the altogether more apocalyptic ones. This may well have been as a result of quite deliberate campaign messaging from CCHQ around a 'supermajority'—the idea that Conservative supporters should come out and vote for the party in order to avoid a Labour government with so many seats at Westminster that it could practically do whatever it wanted. Certainly, there was some evidence in both internal and external polling of a slight hardening of, and even a small uptick in, Conservative support in the final few days of the campaign, albeit nowhere near enough to save them from what was still a truly terrible result. It was also, by the time Sunak announced he was going to the country, practically inevitable. If 2017 was the campaign in which, for the Conservatives, everything that could go wrong did go wrong, then the same could be said of 2024 but with bells on. In truth, however, the Conservatives had lost the election long before the starting gun was ever fired.

3. The factors that drove individual voter decisions to vote Tory (or not)

Explaining exactly why someone decides to vote one way or another is always complex but the clues are there if you look hard enough. Table 3.3 reports the results of a multivariate model that combines attitudinal and demographic factors. There are few surprises here. The more right-wing, socially authoritarian or opposed to European integration a respondent was, the more likely they were to vote Conservative rather than for another party. The more they liked Sunak but disliked Starmer or Farage, the greater the likelihood of a Conservative vote. A positive view of the UK's economic performance over the previous five years increased the chances of supporting the party, although a positive view of *prospective* economic performance meant a lower likelihood of favouring the Conservatives, presumably because those anticipating that a Labour victory would bring an economic upturn were less likely to vote Conservative. A negative view of immigration drove down the odds on voting Conservative, while a strong sense of Englishness had the opposite effect. Interestingly, contact with Tory campaigners during the election seems to have made an elector more likely to vote for the party, suggesting that the inability of the party to mobilise much activity on the part of its members may well have harmed it. Finally, the demographic factors are largely non-significant in the model, although it does show that being in the lower C2DE social bracket increased the likelihood of a Conservative vote, thus confirming the reversal of traditional class voting patterns that were so apparent in 2019.

4. Reports of a death greatly exaggerated? Or perhaps not

We finished our chapter analysing the Conservative victory (and almighty Labour defeat) in 2019 by asking the question 'Must the Conservatives win?' We then presented a roll-call of the now classic election post-mortems that failed to stand the test of time that include, but are not limited to, *Must Labour Lose?* (Abrams and Rose 1960), *Labour's Last Chance* (Heath et al., 1992), and *The Strange Death of Tory England* (Wheatcroft 2005). The lesson is clearly to never count a political party out, nor assume that a landslide will assure it an extended period of electoral dominance. This is particularly true in an era of increased voter volatility and in an environment when partisan loyalty means less than it once did.

Table 3.3. Logistic regression model of Conservative vote 2024

	B	SE	Sig	Exp(B)
Left-right scale	0.173	0.032	<.001	1.188
Authority/liberty scale	0.151	0.037	<.001	1.163
European Integration scale	0.073	0.025	.003	1.076
Like/dislike: Rishi Sunak	0.544	0.030	<.001	1.724
Like/dislike: Keir Starmer	−0.173	0.031	<.001	0.841
Like/dislike: Ed Davey	−0.035	0.030	.243	0.965
Like/dislike: Nigel Farage	−0.134	0.023	<.001	0.875
Expected general economic situation in this country (12 months)	−0.128	0.069	.065	0.880
General economic retrospective evaluation	0.253	0.064	<.001	1.288
Allow more or fewer immigrants	−0.074	0.032	.021	0.929
Conservatives contacted in last 4 weeks	0.812	0.147	<.001	2.253
English identity scale	0.111	0.035	.002	1.117
Age	0.003	0.005	.543	1.003
ABC1 (1)	−0.281	0.138	.041	0.755
Sector (1)	−0.072	0.126	.568	0.930
Housing			.138	
Housing (1)	−0.322	0.222	.146	0.725
Housing (2)	−0.418	0.286	.144	0.658
Gender (1)	0.085	0.128	.506	1.089
Constant	−5.833	0.516	<.001	0.003

Nagelkerke R^2 = 0.580, N = 3456.
Notes: Dependent variable: 1 = voted Conservative, 0 = voted other party. Independent variables: Left-right—multi-item scale constructed by BES team, 0 = left-wing, 10 = right-wing; Authority/liberty scale—multi-item scale constructed by BES team, 0 = libertarian, 10 = authoritarian; European Integration scale—0 = fully unite with EU, 10 = fully protect our independence; Like/dislike Sunak, etc, - 0 = strongly dislike, 10 = strongly like; Expected economic situation—1 = will get a lot worse ... 5 = will get a lot better; General economic retrospective evaluation—1 = got a lot worse ... 5 = got a lot better; Conservatives contacted in last 4 weeks—1 = did make contact, 0 = did not make contact; English identity scale—1 = not at all English ... 7 = very strongly English; Age in years; ABC1 – 1 = ABC1, 2 = C2DE; Sector—1 = private sector employee, 2 (reference category) = public/charitable sector employee; Graduate—1 = graduate, 0(reference category) = non-graduate; Housing—1 = owner (with or without mortgage), 2 = private sector tenant; 3 (reference category) = local authority/housing association tenant; Gender—1 = male, 2 (reference category) = female.
Source: Data from BES 2019, wave 29a.

Moreover, Labour has had a tough start to their time in office. They have inherited a mess in almost every area, but particularly as it relates to the economic state of the UK, a creaking NHS, and a crisis of political trust. On taking office they had to deal with full prisons, riots following the Southport attacks, and increased blowback over the means-testing of the Winter Fuel Allowance. This was all before Starmer, and his front bench, were embroiled in a rolling scandal about the extent to which they accepted free gifts as donations in-kind. And, indeed, long before Donald Trump secured a second term in office and enacted a tariff plan which has caused, put lightly, further economic insecurity.

That Labour's move from opposition to the government proved a bumpy one should boost the Conservatives' morale. Indeed, it may even engender a degree of complacency (Bale 2024), but a question remains as to whether discontent with Labour will end up benefiting them directly. Trust in a party is hard won but easily lost, and even if voters turn against Labour in 2028–9, there is an open question as to whether they will be ready to vote Conservative, rather than, say, Liberal Democrat or Green or (for many Conservatives, their ultimate nightmare) Reform UK.

Indeed, it seems much more likely that the first few years of opposition will be taken up not with being an effective party of opposition but fighting internal battles—particularly when it comes to how to deal with the threat that Reform UK poses. It has become a received wisdom amongst some elements of the party that they lost because they were 'not Conservative enough', and that the only way to rectify this is by some kind of electoral pact or institutional merger with Farage's outfit. This is almost certainly the wrong diagnosis of the wrong disease. In fact, a study conducted by *More in Common* showed that had Farage not been Reform UK's leader—and had Reform agreed not to compete with Tory MPs as they did in 2019—the Conservatives would probably only have held on to forty more seats (More in Common 2024). Winning 161 seats—whilst admittedly an improvement on 121—still does not a majority (or minority) government make. Moreover, any kind of deal risks a downside, not least the number of more liberal Tory supporters that might be lost as a result (and perhaps forever) to the Liberal Democrats—a party that some would see as posing an even greater threat to the prospects of a Conservative recovery.

The picture for the Conservatives, then, looks bleak in the immediate aftermath of the 2024 election. The electoral coalition Boris Johnson and friends patched together in 2019 has fractured. It is hard to see a way in which they can pull them back together in a manner that pleases each (or any) side. To stand any chance of doing so they need to think fast about how it all went so wrong. In short, it's time—and not for the first time (Ashcroft 2005)—for the party to wake up and smell the coffee.

Funding

The party members survey provided as a part of the Party Members Project funded by Queen Mary University of London.

References

Abrams, M., and Rose, R. (1960) *Must Labour Lose?* Harmondsworth: Penguin.

Ashcroft, M. (2005) *Smell the Coffee: A Wakeup Call for the Conservative Party*. London: Politico's.

Baldwin, T. (2024) *Keir Starmer: The Biography*. London: William Collins.

Bale, T. (2024, 26 September) 'Labour Is Struggling, But There Are Four Reasons Conservatives Cannot Be Complacent', *The Conversation*, https://conservativehome.com/2024/09/26/tim-bale-labour-is-struggling-but-there-are-four-reasons-conservatives-cannot-be-complacent/, accessed 9 Oct. 2024.

BBC (2023, 16 November) 'James Cleverley Does Not Deny Privately Ridiculing Rwanda Policy', *BBC News*, https://www.bbc.co.uk/news/av/uk-politics-67440137, accessed 23 Sep. 2024.

Calver, T. (2024, 3 July) 'How Tactical Voting Threatens the Tories in the General Election', *The Times*, https://www.thetimes.com/article/3d72e281-0eef-4b77-a4d0-02ae084fe9c5, accessed 23 Sep. 2024.

Culbertson, A. (2024, 23 June) 'Home Secretary James Cleverly Says Aide Who Called Rwanda Policy 'Crap' Did It for 'Dramatic Effect', *Sky News*, https://news.sky.com/story/home-secretary-james-cleverly-says-aide-who-called-rwanda-policy-crap-did-it-for-dramatic-effect-13157451, accessed 24 Sep. 2024.

Elledge, J. (2023, 11 February) 'Right-Wing Newspapers Are Killing the Tories with Kindness', *The New Statesman*, https://www.newstatesman.com/comment/2023/02/right-wing-newspapers-killing-tories-with-kindness, accessed 24 Sep. 2024.

Fisher, L. (2024, 4 June) 'Trio of Tory Donors Decide Against Funding Election Campaign', *The Financial Times*, https://www.ft.com/content/86ea7334-0860-4dde-86a6-373061fba2e4, accessed 25 Sep. 2024.

Ford, R., et al. (2021) *The British General Election of 2019*. Basingstoke: Palgrave MacMillan.

Francia, P. L., et al. (2003) *The Financiers of Congressional Elections: Investors, Ideologues and Intimates*. New York: Columbia University Press.

Freeman, G. (2024, 6 August) 'George Freeman: Our country Isn't Broken. But Our Party Is', *ConservativeHome*, https://conservativehome.com/2024/08/06/george-freeman-our-country-isnt-broken-but-our-party-is/, accessed 24 Sep. 2024.

Gibbon, G. (2024, 5 July) 'Labour Wins Massive Majority – But Is This a Loveless Landslide?', *Channel 4 News*, https://www.channel4.com/news/labour-wins-massive-majority-but-is-this-a-loveless-landslide, accessed 24 Sep. 2024.

Gibbons, A. (2024, 20 June) 'Tories Delete Ad Telling Public Not to 'Bet' on Labour Amid Election Gambling Row', *The Telegraph*, https://www.telegraph.co.uk/politics/2024/06/20/conservative-party-labour-party-x-gambling-commission/, accessed 24 Sep. 2024.

Halford, E., et al. (2024, 7 July) *The Times*, https://www.thetimes.com/uk/politics/article/how-tory-donations-dwindled-in-run-up-to-the-general-election-8j9dffb0f, accessed 24 Feb. 2025.

Halliday, J. (2021, 7 May) 'Labour Crashes to Humiliating Byelection Defeat in Hartlepool', *The Guardian*, https://www.theguardian.com/politics/2021/may/07/hartlepool-byelection-result-labour-starmer-conservatives, accessed 23 Sep. 2024.

Heath, A., et al. (1992) *Labour's Last Chance? The 1992 Election and Beyond*. Aldershot: Dartmouth Publishing.

Ipsos (2022, 21 November) 'Rishi Sunak Much More Liked Than the Conservative Party', *Ipsos*, https://www.ipsos.com/en-uk/rishi-sunak-much-more-liked-conservative-party, accessed 23 Sep. 2024.

Labour Together (2024, 20 September) 'How Labour Won', *Labour Together*, https://www.labourtogether.uk/how-labour-won-2024-report, accessed 27 Oct. 2024.

Mason, R., et al. (2024, 7 June) 'D-Day Was the Final Straw': Sunak's Blunders Ignite Tory Party Fury', *The Guardian*, https://www.theguardian.com/politics/article/2024/jun/07/d-day-was-the-final-straw-sunaks-blunders-ignite-tory-party-fury, accessed 24 Sep. 2024.

McMenamin, I., and Power, S. (2023) 'What Motivates Business to Donate to Politics? A Framework and an Empirical Application', *Interest Groups and Advocacy*, 12: 272-96.

More in Common (2024, 15 July) 'Change Pending: the Path to the 2024 General Election and Beyond', *UCL Policy Lab*, https://www.ucl.ac.uk/policy-lab/sites/policy_lab/files/ucl_policy_lab_change_pending.pdf, accessed 24 Sep. 2024.

Morrissey (1988) *Everyday Is Like Sunday, from the Album Viva Hate*. London: HMV.

Morton, B. (2023, 6 December) 'Robert Jenrick Resigns as Immigration Minister Over Rwanda Legislation', *BBC News*, https://www.bbc.co.uk/news/uk-politics-67640833, accessed 27 Oct. 2024.

Parker, G., Fisher, L., and Uddin, R. (2024, 7 June) '"The Stupidest of Stupid Ideas": Rishi Sunak's D-Day Snub Sparks Tory Outrage', *Financial Times*, https://www.ft.com/content/0596349e-2b33-4a84-a16b-002fdeb4bf12, accessed 24 Sep. 2024.

Power, S., Bale, T., and Webb, P. (2020) 'Mistake Overturned, so I Call It a Lesson Learned: The Conservatives', in: J. Tonge, S. Wilks-Heeg, and L. Thompson (eds), *Britain Votes: The 2019 General Election*, pp. 65–83. Oxford: Oxford University Press.

Prichett, G. (2023, 30 May) 'Succession, the Inside Story: Could a Few Scruffy Brits Write a Glossy, High-End New York Drama? Yes and No', *The Guardian*, https://www.theguardian.com/commentisfree/2023/may/30/succession-inside-story-brits-write-new-york-drama-tv-series-final-season-spoilers, accessed 27 Oct. 2024.

Seldon, A. (1997) *How Tory Governments Die: The Tory Party in Power, 1783-1997*. London: Harper Collins.

Shipman, T. (2021, 6 October) *X*, https://x.com/ShippersUnbound/status/1445711840378511360?lang=en-GB, accessed 23 Sep 2024.

Shipman, T. (2024, 8 June) 'Infighting on the Beaches: Behind the Scenes of the D-Day Debacle', *The Times*, https://www.thetimes.com/uk/politics/article/infighting-on-the-beaches-behind-the-scenes-of-the-d-day-debacle-6rlvt8nr6, accessed 24 Sep. 2024.

Sky News (2024, 5 June) 'Rishi Sunak Came Out Fighting and Just About Shaded First TV Debate', *Sky News*, https://news.sky.com/story/rishi-sunak-came-out-fighting-and-just-about-shaded-first-starmer-debate-but-it-probably-wont-work-in-the-election-13148058, accessed 27 Oct. 2024.

Swinford, S., and Wright, O. (2021, 11 September) 'Boris Johnson Eyes Another Decade in Power', *The Times*, https://www.thetimes.com/uk/politics/article/boris-johnson-eyes-another-decade-in-power-jp0chz9xl, accessed 23 Sep. 2024.

Tonge, J., Wilks-Heeg, S. and Thompson, L. eds (2020) *Britain Votes: The 2019 General Election*. Oxford: Oxford University Press.

Walker, B. (2024, 9 August) 'The End of Keir Starmer's Honeymoon: Love for the Party Matters Little with a Majority Like This', *New Statesman*, https://www.newstatesman.com/politics/polling/2024/08/the-end-of-keir-starmers-honeymoon, accessed 24 Sep. 2024.

Walker, P. (2024, 13 June) 'Conservative Grassroots Campaign in 'Disarray', Say Insiders', *The Guardian*, https://www.theguardian.com/politics/article/2024/jun/13/conservatives-grassroots-uk-election-campaign, accessed 24 Sep. 2024.

Wheatcroft, G. (2005) *The Strange Death of Tory England*. London: Allen Lane.

Wrong, M. (2021) *Do Not Disturb: The Story of a Political Murder and an African Regime Gone Bad*. London: HarperCollins.

YouGov (2022, 29 August) 'How Well Is Boris Johnson Doing as Prime Minister?', *YouGov*, https://yougov.co.uk/topics/politics/trackers/boris-johnson-approval-rating, accessed 23 Sep. 2024.

YouGov (2024a, 17 June) 'How Well Is Rishi Sunak Doing as Prime Minister?', *YouGov*, https://yougov.co.uk/topics/politics/trackers/rishi-sunak-prime-minister-approval, accessed 23 Sep. 2024.

YouGov (2024b, 9 September) 'Which Political Party Do You Think Would Be Best at Handling the Economy?', *YouGov*, https://yougov.co.uk/topics/politics/trackers/which-political-party-would-be-the-best-at-handling-the-economy, accessed 24 Sep. 2024.

YouGov (2024c, 26 August) 'Is the Conservative Party Trustworthy or Untrustworthy?', *YouGov*, https://yougov.co.uk/topics/politics/trackers/is-the-conservative-trustworthy-or-untrustworthy, accessed 24 Sep. 2024.

YouGov (2024d, 26 August) 'Is the Conservative Party Competent or Incompetent?' *YouGov*, https://yougov.co.uk/topics/politics/trackers/is-the-conservative-party-competent-or-incompetent, accessed 24 Sep. 2024.

Zeffman, H. and Morton, B.(2024) 'Tories accepted donation from Hester after Abbott row', *BBC News*, https://www.bbc.co.uk/news/articles/c900138vek4o, accessed 7 April 2025.

The Labour Party under Keir Starmer: Plotting the route to a shallow landslide

Eunice Goes*

Department of Social Sciences and Humanities, Richmond, The American University in London, Building 12, 566 Chiswick Park, Chiswick High Road, London, W4 5AN, UK

*Correspondence: eunice.goes@richmond.ac.uk

When it felt safe to celebrate in public Labour's largest landslide victory since 1997, Keir Starmer and his wife drove down to Tate Modern in the early hours of Friday 5th July, where Labour was holding its victory party. Looking relieved and happy, the Labour leader turned to the audience composed largely of party officials, MPs, advisers and a few journalists, and shouted: 'We did it!' (BBC News 2024).

Starmer's joy is understandable. In little more than four years, he turned around the electoral fortunes of the Labour Party, winning 411 seats on 33.7% of the vote (Cracknell and Baker 2024: 11). In 2024, Labour recovered from its worst defeat since 1935 and was just eight seats away from replicating New Labour's landslide of 1997. If in 2019 Labour lost seats everywhere in Britain, in 2024, Labour won seats everywhere, albeit on a shallow vote share. It is worth remembering that in 2019, Labour lost on 32.1% of the vote, electing only 202 MPs. These results suggest that Labour's electoral strategy was very efficient at winning seats where it needed to and contrasted with the one adopted in 2019 when the party won large majorities in urban areas while becoming less competitive in marginal constituencies (Furlong and Jennings 2024: 75).

This contribution argues that Labour's electoral triumph can be explained by voter fatigue with fourteen years of Conservative governments, but it is above all the result of a successful strategy that was carefully plotted by Starmer's team. This was a strategy which prioritized evaluations of competence over ideological coherence, and which focussed on winning back the support of voters who had deserted Labour in 2019 and on capturing the support of a fair share of

© The Author(s) 2025. Published by Oxford University Press on behalf of the Hansard Society. All rights reserved. For commercial re-use, please contact reprints@oup.com for reprints and translation rights for reprints. All other permissions can be obtained through our RightsLink service via the Permissions link on the article page on our site—for further information please contact journals.permissions@oup.com.

stability-craving Conservative voters while taking for granted the support of core Labour supporters in England's urban centres. It starts by analysing the nature and purpose of Starmer's political and electoral strategy and how it was deployed in the electoral campaign. Next, it outlines Labour's results across the country and assesses the party's strategy through the lens of valence theory. Finally, it identifies the challenges Labour faces to maintain its fragile electoral coalition until the next general election.

1. The political and electoral strategy

Labour's path to power was carefully planned in the early days of Keir Starmer's leadership. In truth, some of the groundwork had been done before the 2019 General Election, when Starmer was plotting his bid for the leadership of the party. His team, heavily supported by the think-tank Labour Together, had amassed extensive survey data and focus group material offering a fine-grained diagnosis of Labour's electoral vulnerabilities which had become glaringly visible following the 2019 General Election. At this election, the party not only did not make any gains where it needed to but it lost dozens of seats in Labour's traditional strongholds in the Midlands, North of England, and Scotland. These losses posed an existential threat to the party.

Starmer, who was elected Labour leader in April 2020, understood that to turn around Labour's electoral fortunes, the party had to win back those seats (especially in the Midlands and North of England, which became known as the Red Wall). This was not a trick that the party could pull off that easily. As Table 4.1[1] shows, support for the party in these seats had been eroding since 2005 (see also Sobolewska and Ford 2020). Moreover, the voters that Labour lost in 2019 in the so-called Red Wall had different priorities and values from those of younger voters in England's urban centres. But Table 4.1 shows that Starmer's strategy worked: in many of these seats, Labour registered a very modest growth in the vote share, but it was sufficient to win them in 2024.

If the task seemed insurmountable at the time, Starmer seemed undaunted. As he said in his acceptance speech 'we've got a mountain to climb. But we will climb it' (Starmer 2020). In his resolve, Starmer assembled a team of advisers who had a

---

[1] Some of these constituencies were abolished and others were merged with others because of changes to constituency boundaries. Doncaster East and Isle of Axholme incorporates the former Don Valley constituency; the constituency of Leigh and Atherton incorporates the former seat of Leigh; Newton Aycliffe and Spennymoor incorporates the former constituency of Sedgefield; and the seat of Whitehaven and Workington incorporates the former constituency of Workington; and Stockton South became Stockton West; Dewsbury and Batley was only Dewsbury until 2005; Cleethorpes was a single constituency until it merged with Great Grimsby. The electoral results were collated from House of Commons reports of the 2005, 2010, 2015, 2017, 2019, and 2024 elections.

Table 4.1. Labour's performance in the Red Wall 2005-24

Constituency/Labour Share of the Vote	2005	2010	2015	2017	2019	2024
Ashfield	48.6	33.7	41	42.6	24.4	29
Barrow and Furness	47.6	48.1	42.2	47.5	39.3	43.9
Bassetlaw	56.6	50.5	48.6	52.6	27.5	41.2
Bishop Auckland	50	39	41.4	48.1	35.9	42.1
Blackpool South	50.5	41.1	41.8	50.3	38.3	48.1
Blyth Valley/Blyth and Ashington	55	44.5	46.3	55.9	40.9	49.6
Birmingham Northfield	49.6	40.3	41.6	53.2	42.5	39.6
Bolsover	65.2	50	51.2	51.9	35.9	40.5
Bolton North East	45.7	45.9	43	50.6	44.5	37.3
Bradford South	49	41.3	43.4	54.5	46.3	35.8
Bury South	50.4	40.4	45.1	53.3	43	45.6
Burnley	38.6	31.3	37.6	46.7	36.9	31.7
Chesterfield	40.4	39	47.9	54.8	40.2	46.5
Coventry North West	48.2	42.8	41	54	43.8	46.9
Coventry South	45.8	41.8	42.3	55	43.4	47.6
Darlington	52.4	39.4	42.9	50.6	40.5	39.2
Dewsbury and Batley	41	32.2	41.8	51	43.7	22.9
Doncaster East and Isle of Axholme	52.7	37.9	46.2	53	35.2	38.6
Dudley (former Dudley South)	45.3	33	32.6	36.2	25.3	34.1
Gedling	46.1	41.1	42.3	51.9	44.1	47.8
Great Grimsby and Cleethorpes	47.1	32.7	39.8	49.4	32.7	41.9
Halifax	41.8	37.4	40	52.8	46.3	35.1
Heywood and Middleton North	49.8	40.1	43.1	53.3	41.7	40.6
Hyndburn	46	41.1	42.1	53.4	41.5	33.5
Leigh and Atherton	63.3	48	53.9	56.2	41.1	48.5
Newcastle–under-Lyme	45.4	38	47.2	48.2	35.9	40.4
Newton Aycliffe and Spennymoor	58.9	45.1	47.2	53.4	36.3	46.2
North Durham	64.1	50.5	54.9	59.9	44.2	39.8
Normanton and Hemsworth	51.2	48.2	54.9	59.5	37.9	47.5
Oldham East and Saddleworth	41.4	31.9	39.4	54.5	43.5	35.2
Penistone and Stocksbridge	(did not exist)	37.8	42	45.8	33.3	43.6
Redcar	51.4	42.3	43.9	55.5	37.4	41
Rother Valley	55.4	40.9	43.6	48.1	32.1	38.5

Table 4.1. Labour's performance in the Red Wall 2005-24

Constituency/Labour Share of the Vote	2005	2010	2015	2017	2019	2024
Scunthorpe	53.1	39.5	41.7	52	36.7	39.7
Stoke-on-Trent Central	52.9	38.8	39.3	51.5	43.3	42.4
Stockton West	47.8	38.3	37	48.5	41.1	37.5
Wakefield and Rothwell	43.3	39.3	40.3		39.8	43.7
West Bromwich (former West Bromwich East)	55.6	46.5	50.2	49.7	42.3	46.2
Whitehaven and Workington	50.5	45	42.3	51.1	39.3	53

Source: House of Commons (2005, 2011, 2015, 2019, 2020); Cracknell and Baker (2024).

plan. Morgan McSweeney, who had run Starmer's leadership campaign and who plotted Labour's path to power, had a simple strategy. The 'project', as McSweeney explained to a journalist, was 'to return Labour to the service of working people, to become once again the natural vehicle for their hopes and aspirations' (McTague 2024).

McSweeney's understanding of Labour's electoral priorities was shared by three other key advisers who joined Starmer's team at different times. One of them was Claire Ainsley, the author of a book on the new working-class and Executive Director of Policy until 2022; the second was the pollster Deborah Mattinson who was Head of Strategy until the 2024 General Election; and the third was the former Royal Society researcher Alan Lockey, who became Starmer's speech-writer in 2022.

While there was a common thread uniting the thinking of these three key advisers, there were slight differences of emphasis in their interpretations about what Labour's electoral strategy should entail. For example, in her book on the new working-class, Ainsley argued that to be electorally successful, parties like Labour should follow a public values-based policy agenda, which reflects the values of the voters who compose the new and more ethnically diverse and feminine working-class (2018: 3). To win the support of these voters, Labour needed to develop an agenda rooted in the values of family, fairness, hard work, decency, and patriotism (Ainsley 2018: 153).

Mattinson conveyed a similar message in her book on the Red Wall (2020) and throughout her work for Starmer. In a strategy note, she told Starmer that Labour needed to win the support of what she called 'hero voters' who were middle aged and older skilled manual and administrative workers, who tended to live in towns, were often economically insecure Brexit supporters who cared about family and country but who 'had lost faith in politics' (Mattinson 2020: 19-23). Lockey agreed with many of these recommendations and added that Starmer should not forget the aspirational middle-classes living in traditional Conservative seats (Lockey 2021b).

These advisers also agreed on how the message should be delivered. While Ainsley argued that this message should be articulated in a language of 'ordinariness' (2018: 39), Mattinson recommended a rhetoric which resonated with the aspirations of those voters (Mattinson quoted in Baldwin 2024: 319). Above all, the party should avoid references to abstract concepts or make promises that sounded too ambitious. As Lockey put it, Starmer should 'resist siren calls' to do 'the traditional "vision thing"' (Lockey 2020) because British politics 'is more rooted in competing class interests than in a contest of philosophical ideas' (Lockey 2021a).

These perspectives shaped Labour's political, electoral, and communication strategies which privileged moral language and eschewed ideological categorizations (Goes 2021a). Very early on in Starmer's leadership, the party made clear that it was focussing on winning the support of these 'hero voters'—referred to as 'working people' by Labour's frontbenchers—if it was going to win the next election. Starmer himself made that clear in a speech when he said that 'The Labour Party will only restore hope in the country, if we once again become the natural vehicle for working people' (Starmer 2023).

Later, these 'hero voters' morphed into the concept of 'Stevenage Woman', an archetypal voter identified by the think-tank Labour Together as the key to Labour's electoral success. Roughly matching (though not entirely in terms of age) Ainsley and Mattinson's assumptions about the demographic profile of Labour's 'hero voters', 'Stevenage Woman' is a voter who lives in towns and in suburbs, is young, hard-working but struggling with the rising cost of living, holds socially conservative values but supports a more interventionist state in the economy, had voted Conservative in 2019 but was leaning towards Labour (Labour Together 2023: 6).

Having identified Labour's target voters, the party, led by the astute McSweeney, developed a political strategy which was deployed in three stages. In the first stage, Starmer had to show to voters that Labour had turned the page on the Corbyn era. The second stage of the campaign was about exposing the failures of the Conservative government and stage three involved convincing voters that Labour was competent and had a credible programme.

McSweeney's plan was executed with military precision. Turning the page on the Corbyn era meant demonstrating that the party was patriotic, responsible with the public finances, and tough on crime and immigration. The first step in that process involved the marginalization of the left of the party (including Jeremy Corbyn who was suspended from the party following his response to the Equality and Human Rights Commission report on Labour's antisemitism and was expelled weeks before the general election). McSweeney also made sure that the rules to elect future party leaders were changed to prevent the future election of left-wing candidates, and that parliamentary or local candidates associated with the left were deselected.

Finally, this first stage involved demonstrating patriotic values by wrapping the party in the Union Jack (Goes 2021b). Within six months, the Union Jack was ubiquitous in the party's communications strategy featuring as a background, beside lecterns, behind desks, in posters, and even as banners on the social media profiles of MPs and party officials. As Fig. 4.1 shows, this strategy worked. By the time of the 2024 General Election, 57% of voters thought Starmer was 'very' or 'fairly' patriotic (More in Common 2024b).

The second stage of McSweeney's strategy was relatively easy to develop. As the contribution by Bale, Webb, and Watts in this volume shows, Labour did not need to do much. The Conservative Party provided plenty of ammunition to Starmer's team. From the illegal parties in Downing Street during Covid-19, to the then Prime Minister Liz Truss's Growth Plan (popularly known as the 'mini-budget') announced in the Autumn of 2022, to the rise of inflation and interest rates Labour had plenty of material to work with. Similarly in Scotland, the collapse of the Scottish National Party (SNP), following Nicola Sturgeon's resignation from the leadership of the party in early 2023, helped Labour to appear credible in contrast with its opponents' visible incompetence.

2. Bring on "Mr Competent"

But showing that the Conservatives and the SNP were incompetent was not enough. Labour needed to be trusted by voters. To win voters' trust, Labour developed a political agenda that sought simultaneously to put an end to what Starmer

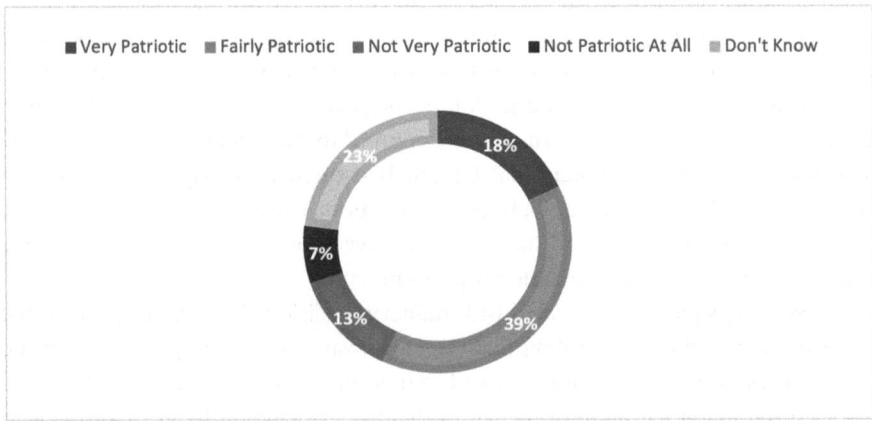

Figure 4.1. How patriotic is Keir Starmer?
Source: More in Common (2024b).

defined as 'sticking-plaster politics' with a programme that simultaneously promised to deliver prosperity for working people and reassured voters with credible but modest proposals. This was a difficult message to deliver because a transformative agenda is not necessarily compatible with a programme that prioritizes a concept of competence that privileges caution.

Labour's economic agenda was built around Rachel Reeves's ideas of 'securonomics' which prioritized 'economic strength and resilience' and 'securing the finances of working people', as well as 'good jobs, decent pay, strong public services' (Reeves 2023). Labour's securonomics had three main planks: the first plank was the Green Prosperity Plan, designed to turn the UK into a 'clean energy superpower' by investing 28 billion pounds annually in the green transition. The second plank of Labour's agenda was the New Deal for Working People, which was designed to strengthen workers' rights. The third plank of Labour's agenda was about the devolution of power to local authorities and reforms to urban planning with a view to unleash investment in housing. In tandem with this economic plan, Labour also promised a law and order agenda that prioritized crime reduction and immigration controls.

By 2023, Labour adopted the concept of 'mission economy' developed by the economist Mariana Mazzucato (2021) and which sought to combine ambition with reassuring technocratic language. As such, Labour proposed 'Five Missions' which included: securing the highest sustained growth of the G7 group of rich countries; turning Britain into a clean energy superpower; building a National Health Service (NHS) fit for the future; making Britain's streets safe; breaking down barriers for opportunity at every stage (Labour Party 2023).

But this balancing act between transformative policy goals and a reassuring electoral strategy became more difficult to maintain as the election approached. The drive to reassure voters—reported in the media as the 'Ming Vase strategy'—took precedence over the transformative agenda. Indeed, Labour started to backtrack on its more ambitious promises because it was afraid of Conservative attacks on its alleged profligacy (Pike 2024: 109). After accusing the Conservative government of 'maxing-out the nation's credit card' (Starmer and Reeves 2024), the party announced a series of U-turns that aimed to demonstrate that Labour would be a competent manager of the economy.

The most visible U-turn affected the Green Prosperity Plan. Instead of investing 28 billion pounds annually in the green transition, as it had promised initially, Labour was only committing 23.7 billion pounds over a parliamentary term (Starmer and Reeves 2024). Scaling down this programme was justified on the grounds of meeting Reeves's fiscal rules which committed a Labour government to meeting day-to-day costs with tax revenues and reducing debt by the fifth year of the forecast.

To show that Labour would not 'play fast and loose with people's money', as Reeves liked to put it (2024), the party backtracked on the provision of universal free childcare and free school meals. Controversially, the party also announced that it would keep the two-child benefit cap on universal credit. But Labour was not only planning to be cautious with public spending; it also promised not to raise income and corporation tax and Value Added Tax (VAT) rates. If these policy commitments were designed to show that Labour would be a competent manager of public finances, they raised questions about the party's ability to deliver its ambitious plans to change the country.

A few weeks before the Prime Minister announced the election date, Starmer presented Labour's 'First Steps for Change'. The purpose of this launch was to remind voters that the party's programme promised to deliver a 'decade of national renewal', but the modesty of its First Steps—delivering economic stability, cutting NHS waiting times, launching a New Border Security Command, cracking down on antisocial behaviour and recruiting 6,500 new teachers—emphasized the message that a Labour government would not make unfunded pledges. And it was the promise of these modest First Steps that Labour made to the country when the election date was announced on 22nd May.

3. A 'gloriously boring' campaign

Shortly after a rain-drenched Prime Minister Rishi Sunak announced the election date outside the front door of 10 Downing Street, Keir Starmer kick-started Labour's campaign from a wood-panelled room decorated with two large Union Jacks and a lectern that displayed the word 'Change'. The message was clear: a vote for Labour was a vote for change and security. As Starmer's sleek launch showed, Labour was ready for the campaign, thanks in part to a 25 million pound warchest (Progrund 2024a).

The state of Labour's readiness was also shown when candidates from 150 battleground seats published tailor-made videos on social media platforms as the Prime Minister announced the election date to the nation (Francis 2024). This move had been possible because Labour's deputy campaign manager Hollie Ridley made sure that candidates in every marginal seat were equipped with 'break in case of emergency' packs containing posters, leaflets, garden boards, and digital adverts (Pogrund 2024a).

This sleek launch set the tone for Labour's six week electoral campaign which was not flashy but disciplined and gaffe-free. The discipline meant that apart from Keir Starmer, only a few frontbenchers—notably Wes Streeting, Rachel Reeves, Bridget Phillipson, Pat McFadden, Jonathan Ashworth, and Darren Jones—were allowed to speak to broadcasters. This resulted in what a Labour adviser defined as a 'gloriously boring' campaign in an interview with *The House* magazine (Rodgers 2024).

Its purpose was to turn the election into a referendum on the Conservative government. But to maintain the focus on the flaws of the Conservatives, Labour had to avoid doing anything that could undermine Labour's two-digit poll lead. Hence, Labour's campaign theme—Change—was vaguely defined. Indeed, 'change' meant a change from the mismanagement and instability of the Conservative governments.

From the start, Labour showed it was fighting an offensive campaign (the results of which can be seen in Appendix 4.1). Apart from defending Labour's 201 seats, the party had identified 233 battleground constituencies which included seats once thought unwinnable (Green 2024). The offensive campaign was largely successful as Labour only lost thirty-two of the battleground seats.

As Alia Middleton and David Cutts show in their contribution to this volume, Starmer played a key role in this offensive campaign. The Labour leader campaigned across the country, visiting a large number of Conservative-held seats. His first visit was to Gillingham and Rainham, a Conservative seat since 2005 and which Labour won in 2024. With an eye to the Scottish battleground, Starmer also visited Scotland several times, including on the last day of the campaign. He also ventured into seats the party had few chances of winning (especially in Scotland), and into safe Conservative territory like Aldershot which Labour won. But if some of Starmer's visits were wide bets on the electoral lottery, the party tended not to waste resources on unwinnable seats.

On the third week of the campaign, Labour launched its manifesto in a carefully choreographed event at the Co-Operative Headquarters in Manchester. The launch started with interventions by the CEO of the Iceland supermarket chain Richard Walker, and by a string of voters who represented key policy areas for Labour's campaign. 'Daniel' from London spoke of the challenges his family faced living in an overcrowded flat; 'Nathaniel' a teacher who had been diagnosed with terminal cancer addressed voters' concerns with NHS waiting lists; and the eighteen-year-old A-level student 'Holly' spoke of Starmer's promise of 'a better future, and greater equality and prosperity for all of us' (Mason 2024).

Following these introductions, Starmer used his intervention to say that Labour had 'given up on being a party of protest' and wanted 'to be a party of power' (2024a). The manifesto launch was hailed as a very sleek and professional event by most of the news media. Indeed, Labour won the endorsement of *The Times*, the *Financial Times* and *The Economist* which had not endorsed Labour in the previous three general elections.

In terms of content, Labour's manifesto, simply entitled *Change*, did not contain any new policy proposals and was designed to offer a message of technocratic reassurance (Labour Party 2024). The document revisited Labour's missions and its 'first steps for change' and insisted on the themes of fiscal prudence, economic stability, and security. Crucially, as Fig. 4.2 shows, Labour's manifesto roughly matched voters' most important issues at stake in the election.

Labour's digital campaign, led by Tom Lillywhite, was also successful, partly reflecting the generous resources—10 million pounds—devoted to it (Asthana 2024: 276). These resources enabled Labour to dominate the digital space with 'channel-native content' by promoting user engagement and community building on social media platforms like Facebook, YouTube, Instagram, and TikTok. On WhatsApp, Labour's efforts were less successful. Clipped videos of Starmer's comments about Bangladesh being a safe place to which asylum-seekers could be returned, were quickly shared on WhatsApp and undermined the party's standing amongst Muslim voters (Scott 2024).

There were other setbacks in Labour's campaign. Perhaps the most damaging was the row about the potential deselection of Diane Abbott, the MP for Hackney North and Stoke Newington. Abbott had been suspended from the party in 2023 following the publication of an article where she wrote that Jewish and Roma people had not suffered racism. Party officials close to McSweeney told *The Times* that Abbott would have the whip restored but would be blocked from standing as a candidate for that seat. Predictably this leak backfired. The story dominated the news agenda for three days and pressure from frontbenchers like Angela Rayner and Blairite grandees like John McTernan led to a change of tactic. The party eventually announced that it was up to Abbott to decide whether she would fight for her seat at the election. Her answer was a resounding yes.

But these setbacks, as well as Starmer's lacklustre performance in the different televised debates, had little effect over the party's polling lead. In truth, Labour was also helped by the disastrous Conservative campaign (see Bale, Webb, and Watts in this volume). The only moment when the Conservative campaign threatened Labour's poll lead was when Conservative frontbenchers started to warn voters

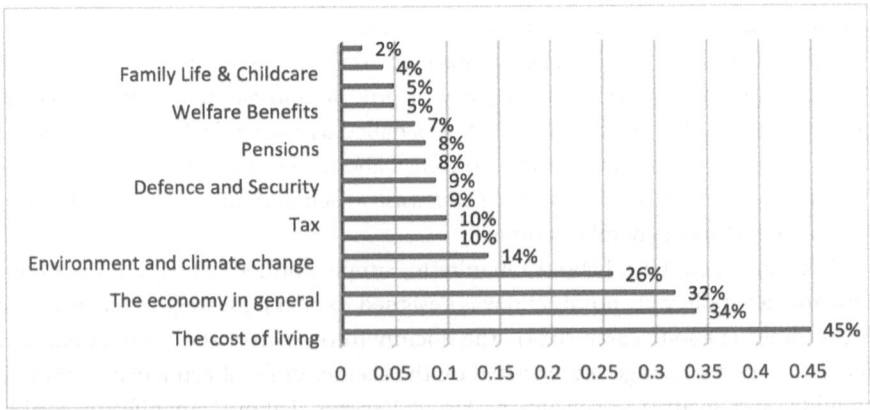

Figure 4.2. Top issues for voters.
Source: YouGov (2024g).

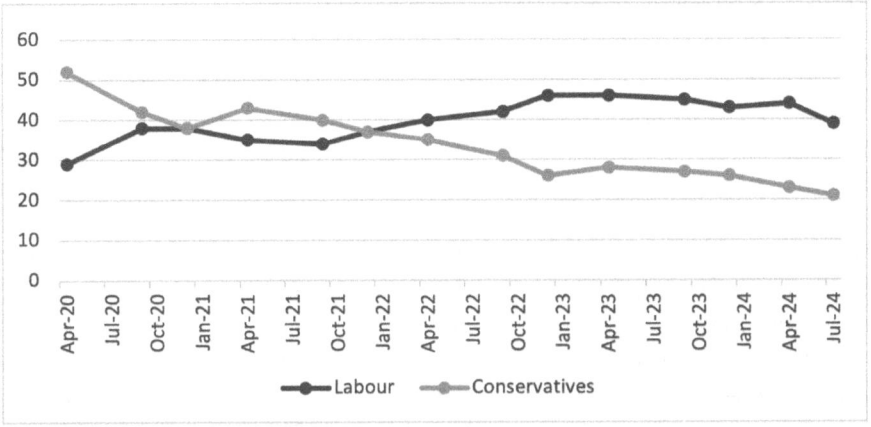

Figure 4.3. Voting intentions.
Source: YouGov (2024a).

about the dangers of a Labour 'supermajority'. Understandably, Labour strategists feared that this message could encourage many voters to stay at home.

But these were mere hiccups. For the six weeks of the campaign, Labour maintained the eighteen to twenty points lead over the Conservatives, that is, the same poll lead the party had maintained since the Autumn of 2022 as Fig. 4.3 shows. If anything, Labour's sleek but unshowy campaign and fatigue with fourteen years of Conservative governments persuaded many voters that it was time for change.

4. Labour results: a shallow landslide

Labour's victory was a true landslide that swept several Conservative cabinet ministers (namely Penny Mordaunt and Grant Shapps), a former Prime Minister (Liz Truss), as well as high-profile MPs like Jacob Rees-Mogg from their seats. Crucially, Labour was also able to win thirty-six out of the thirty-eight Red Wall seats it had targeted (Ashfield elected a Reform UK MP and Dewsbury elected an independent) (Focaldata 2024). More surprisingly, Labour won a string of safe Conservative seats, namely Altrincham and Sale West, Chipping Barnet, Ashford, Swindon, Weston-Super-Mare, Stevenage, Derbyshire Dales, Dartford, Aylesbury and Aldershot (known as the home of the British army). The party also recovered Nuneaton, a marginal seat which Labour lost in 2015.

Interestingly, and as Table 4.2 shows, Labour won eighteen Conservative seats because Reform UK candidates were also standing. In Scotland, Labour recovered its position as the largest party, winning thirty-seven seats (thirty-six seats more than in 2019), while in Wales, Labour won twenty-seven of the thirty-two seats, albeit on a lower share of the vote.

Table 4.2. Seats Labour won thanks to Reform UK

Constituency	Labour	Conservative	Reform
Sittingbourne and Sheppey	29.1	28.2	25.6
Dudley	34.1	28.8	26.4
South West Norfolk	26.7	25.3	22.5
Lowestoft	34.6	29.8	24.7
Cannock Chase	36.5	29.2	26.9
North Warwickshire and Bedworth	36	30.6	26.1
Stoke-on-Trent South	34.7	33.2	21.6
North West Cambridgeshire	33.3	33.2	19.7
Chatham & Aylesford	33.5	28.6	24.5
Dartford	24.6	31.9	21.4
Portsmouth North	34.8	33	20.4
Redditch	34.9	33.1	20.1
Lichfield	35.1	33.4	19.8
North West Leicestershire	34.7	32.7	19.9
Bexleyheath and Crayford	36.2	31.2	22.7
Stoke-on-Trent Central	42.4	17.6	24.2
Stoke-on-Trent North	40.3	26.3	24.4
Penistone and Stocksbridge	43.6	23.7	21.4

Source: Cracknell and Baker (2024).

Starmer's success at transforming Labour into a party of government was visible in the demographic groups it managed to attract. Labour was the most supported party amongst all voters below the age of fifty-nine, that is, all working-age voters. Interestingly, Labour lost support among the under-forties (Focaldata 2024). In terms of gender, Labour was equally popular among female and male voters: 35% of women and 34% of men voted Labour. Labour continued to lead among ethnic minority voters; however, this lead fell by 18% from 2019 (Ipsos 2024c). The decline in support among ethnic minority was especially felt in constituencies with large Muslim populations.

Unsurprisingly, Labour did well among university graduates, attracting 42% of support among this group (McDonnell 2024). Labour was also the most voted party among students and among those working or not working, while the Conservatives were more popular among retirees (YouGov 2024f). Labour also received the largest support among voters who have a mortgage or live in rented accommodation (YouGov 2024f).

But Labour also suffered a few shocks at this election. Two Labour frontbenchers lost their seats. Thangam Debonnaire lost the seat of Bristol Central to the co-chair of the Green Party, Carla Denyer, while Jonathan Ashworth lost his seat of Leicester South to the independent candidate Shockat Adam. Labour lost five other seats to independent candidates, including in Islington North where the Labour candidate was defeated by the independent Jeremy Corbyn. The election of four Green MPs and of six independents suggests that Labour lost votes from its left flank: only 49% of left-wing voters voted Labour; the Greens on the other hand won the support of 20% of this group.

In addition, some Labour frontbenchers are now defending razor-thin majorities. For example, Wes Streeting who represents Ilford North, is sitting on a majority of 528 votes; Shabana Mahmood won the seat of Birmingham Ladywood with a majority of 3,421 votes. Even Keir Starmer saw his majority in the super safe seat of Holborn and St Pancras go down from 22,766 in 2019 to 11,576. More worrying for Labour, in eighty-nine seats, including in the seats represented by the frontbenchers Angela Rayner, Yvette Cooper and Bridget Phillipson, Reform UK, which elected five MPs, came a close second.

In short, and as the vote share of 33.7% suggests, Labour's landslide has shallow foundations. The party's focus on 'Stevenage woman' was only partly successful. If many of Labour's new voters fall into the category of 'working people', only 13% of them had voted Conservative in 2019 and 23% voted Leave at the referendum on membership of the European Union (EU) (YouGov 2024f).

5. A valence election

The results of the 2024 General Election show that Labour's political and electoral strategies were extremely successful. As we saw earlier, in the wake of Labour's catastrophic defeat in 2019, Starmer's team realized that the party's return to power was predicated on abandoning the ideological radicalism of Corbyn and on adopting an approach that converged with the views and concerns of the average voter. For Labour, the average voter was someone who lived in towns and suburban areas of the country, who worked but was struggling with the cost of living, who mistrusted politicians, valued a more interventionist state, and held socially conservative views. Labour also understood that following the turmoil of the Brexit battles voters aspired to calmer politics. But Starmer wanted also to distinguish Labour from the Conservative Party, and 'competence' was the indicator that he chose. By making this choice, Labour turned the 2024 General Election into a valence election.

By positioning Labour close to the Conservatives on issues like tax and spend, immigration, and law and order, the party shifted the ground of electoral competition from ideology to evaluations of competence. Starmer also avoided ideological references and dressed Labour's 'change' message in either ordinary or technocratic language. Finally, Labour's frontbench never missed an opportunity to accuse the government of 'maxing-out the nation's credit card' and of 'losing control' of the country's borders, two key issues to voters.

With this approach, Starmer was testing Donald J. Stokes's adage of valence theory, according to which voters respond to the framing of political parties and to the cues offered by the direction of the political debate at the time of the election (Stokes 1963: 373; see also Green and Jennings 2017: 8). It turns out he was both lucky and skilful in that venture. After all, parties may try to frame the election around the issue of competence, but they are not always successful in that pursuit. As Green, and Jennings explained, 'valence voting occurs when major events heighten the relevance of competence' (Green and Jennings 2017: 11). Thus, for competence to become the main issue at the election, 'high-salience performance shocks' or 'high-salience events' must have preceded it (Green and Jennings 2017: 221).

The years that preceded the election were rich in 'high-salience performance shocks' and 'high-salience events'. The turmoil caused by the negotiations to leave the EU, the 2020 pandemic, the chaos associated with the premiership of Boris Johnson, Russia's invasion of Ukraine, the rise in energy prices and inflation, Liz Truss's mini-budget, the death of Queen Elizabeth II, and long NHS waiting lists were both 'high-salience events' and 'high-performance shocks' which heightened the relevance of competence for the voters who were choosing a new government in 2024. In Scotland, Labour was helped by the SNP's collapse, a development which is explained with great clarity by Ailsa Henderson and James Mitchell in this volume.

Starmer made the most of these high-performance and high-salience shocks. In a move that was repeated hundreds of times from 2020, the Labour leader contrasted the chaos and incompetence of Conservative rule with the common sense of Labour's proposals. In an interesting twist, Starmer routinely accused the Conservatives of being the ideological party, that is the party that pursued 'trickle-down economics' that didn't 'work' and of proposing a 'Jeremy Corbyn-style manifesto where anything you want can go in it' (Starmer quoted in Whannel 2024).

Interestingly, as Fig. 4.3 shows, Labour's twenty-point poll lead became visible in September of 2022, shortly after Liz Truss and her Chancellor Kwasi Kwarteng presented the 'mini-budget'. From that period onwards, Labour maintained a 15%-20% poll lead ahead of the Conservative Party. As Figs 4.4 and 4.5 illustrate, until the 'mini-budget' the Conservatives were the most trusted party at managing the economy (see also Ipsos 2022) and controlling immigration (YouGov 2024b), but after 2022, the Conservative Party was no longer the most trusted party on those issues. Just before the election, 69% of the public claimed to be unsatisfied or dissatisfied? with the way the Conservative government was dealing with immigration (Ipsos 2024b).

Crucially, voters' evaluations of competence focussed more on the Conservative government than on Labour. This is so because voters tend to prioritize the assessment of the performance of incumbents over the promises of opposition parties (Fortunato and Stevenson 2013: 474). In truth, voters' evaluation of opposition parties tends to rely more on party identification (Green and Jennings 2017: 176).

The Labour Party   79

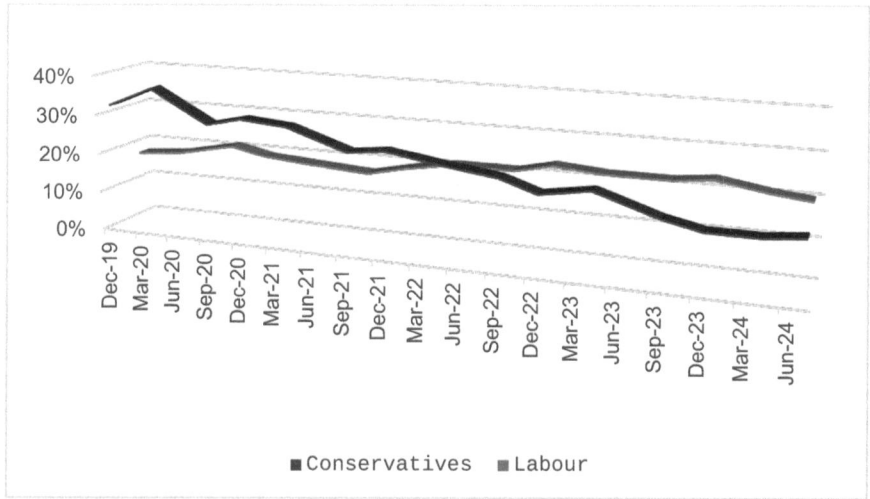

Source: YouGov, 2024b.

Figure 4.4. Which party is best at handling asylum and immigration?
Source: YouGov, (2024b).

As voters started to evaluate negatively the incumbent Conservative government, they gave more positive scores to the Labour Party in their evaluations of the party's competence to manage the economy, public services and control immigration. As Fig. 4.5 shows, as the Conservative government lost the trust of voters, Labour started to score higher poll ratings, though those leads were, and remained, modest until the election. As Fig. 4.5 shows, voters trusted Labour more than the Conservatives to manage the economy, though not by a huge margin (YouGov 2024c).

Voters' evaluations of the competence of party leaders contributed too to the overall picture of dissatisfaction with the Conservative government. Opinion polls show that voters changed their minds about who would make the best Prime Minister. If in 2022, Sunak performed better on that score, two years later Starmer was ahead, but this was because voters changed their minds about Sunak. In reality, voters' perception of Starmer's competence only changed slightly between 2022 and 2024 (YouGov 2024h).

Polling conducted after the election suggests that voters accepted Labour's framing of the election around the issue of competence. Polling by More in Common shows that 'voters were more likely to say they backed the party at this election they saw as the most competent, rather than whose policies they preferred' (More in Common 2024b: 14). Similarly, polling from YouGov conducted just before the election showed that for 48% of voters, the main reason to vote Labour was to 'get the Tories out', only 5% said the main reason was 'agreeing with their policies', and only 2% identified as Labour voters (YouGov 2024d). Polling

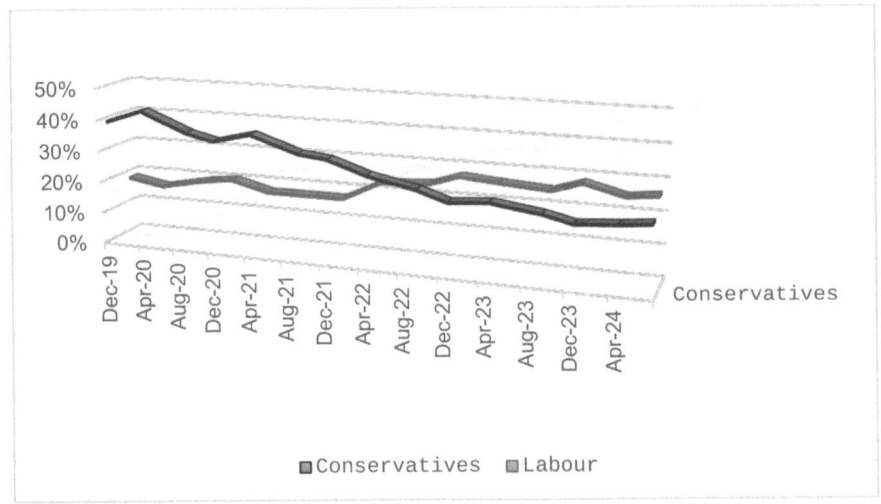

Source: YouGov, 2024b.

Figure 4.5. Which party is best at handling the economy?
Source: YouGov, (2024b).

and focus group work conducted by Labour Together reached similar conclusions: 41% voted Labour because 'the country needed change' (Labour Together 2024).

Voters were not entirely convinced by Starmer's competence credentials. If he outperformed the Prime Minister Rishi Sunak, only 35% of voters agreed that Starmer would make the best Prime Minister. In another poll, the Labour leader outperformed Sunak on a range of attributes but only 40% of voters saw him as competent, 49% thought he was untrustworthy and 52% saw him as indecisive (YouGov 2024h). Tellingly, polling from Ipsos/Mori revealed there were low levels of trust in the Labour Party in the months leading to the election: only 31% thought that Labour was 'fit to govern' and only 24% thought that the party had 'a good team of leaders' (Ipsos 2024a). Labour Together found similar levels of trust in Labour. Their polling shows that only 9% of voters chose Labour because they trusted Labour over other parties (2024).

The fact that for so many voters the main reason to vote Labour was to vote out the Conservative government suggests that Labour's support is fragile, and that the party's coalition of supporters is, as the report for More in Common concluded, 'a much broader and a less ideologically cohesive coalition than in 2019' and which can be summarized as a 'coalition of valence' and 'not a coalition of ideology' (More in Common/UCL Lab 2024a: 8).

In short, Labour's decision to fight the 2024 election on valence issues was astute as it enabled the party to address its electoral vulnerabilities quickly, beat an increasingly unpopular government, and win the necessary seats to control a comfortable majority. However, the election results and the survey data on how the public rates Labour on a range of competence indicators illustrated in Figs 4.4

and 4.5 also show that the party's landslide does not reflect voters' enthusiasm for its agenda. The low turnout, the modest vote share, and Starmer's personal ratings in opinion polls suggest that Labour cannot rest on its laurels if it wants to win a second parliamentary term.

6. The challenges of shallow victories

The sun had just started to shine the moment Keir Starmer, accompanied by his wife Victoria, walked to Downing Street for the first time as the UK's new Prime Minister. They were surrounded by exhausted but jubilant party workers, advisers, and activists who obediently waived their Welsh, Scottish, and Union Jack flags to the TV cameras, celebrating Labour's first victory since 2005.

But if the jubilant scenes on the steps of Downing Street the morning after the election were a justifiably joyful celebration of Labour's victory, Starmer's first speech as Prime Minister suggested that not only was he already thinking of the next election, but that he was planning to win it again on a competence ticket. In his speech on the steps of Downing Street, Starmer spoke of Labour's 'clear mandate' for change but he also promised to lead a government 'unburdened by doctrine' (Starmer 2024b).

As the new Prime Minister familiarized himself with the nooks and crannies of Number 10 Downing Street, his advisers were briefing the weekend papers about the task ahead. With some bravado, Starmer's advisers said that the party was now after Reform UK voters (Pogrund 2024b). To that end, the party was putting in place a strategy that aimed to address voters' concerns with immigration, crime, and the NHS and to deliver the promises contained in the party's manifesto (Pogrund 2024b). But this strategy is not risk-free, as it can alienate progressive voters who in the 2024 election discovered there are left-wing alternatives to Labour. To win, Labour needs to keep on board its fragile coalition of voters and widen it. But Labour's cautious manifesto and challenging economic and geopolitical circumstances are not likely to deliver the economic growth and widespread prosperity that voters are expecting. The problem is that voters are impatient for change. Several opinion polls conducted after the election show that most voters are disappointed with the performance of the Labour government (Ipsos 2024d). This suggests that to win again in 2029, the Labour government needs to store the Ming Vase in a safe place and start to deliver tangible improvements to voters' lives.

Appendix Table 4.A1. Labour's offensive campaign

Offensive Battleground Seats	Gain/Loss	Vote Share
Aberdeen North	Loss	30.30%
Aberdeen South	Loss	24.70%
Aberdeenshire North and Moray East	Loss	10.10%
Airdrie and Shotts	Gain	51.50%
Aldershot	Gain	40.70%
Alloa and Grangemouth	Gain	43.80%
Altrincham and Sale West	Gain	40.40%
Amber Valley	Gain	37%
Angus and Perthshire Glens	Loss	14.40%
Arbroath and Broughty Ferry	Loss	33.40%
Argyll, Bute and South Lochaber	Loss	19.15%
Ashfield	Loss	29%
Ayr, Carrick and Cumnock	Gain	36.50%
Banbury	Gain	38.30%
Bangor and Aberconwy	Gain	33.60%
Barrow and Furness	Gain	43.90%
Basingstoke	Gain	42.70%
Bassetlaw	Gain	41.20%
Bathgate and Linlithgow	Gain	47%
Beckenham and Penge	Hold	49.30%
Berwickshire, Roxburgh, and Selkirk	Loss	13.60%
Bexleyheath and Crayford	Gain	36.20%
Birmingham Northfield	Hold	39.60%
Bishop Auckland	Gain	42.10%
Blackpool North and Fleetwood	Gain	40%
Blackpool South	Gain	48.10%
Bolsover	Gain	40.50%
Bolton North East	Gain	37.30%
Bolton West	Gain	38.90%
Bournemouth East	Gain	40.80%
Bournemouth West	Gain	36.40%

Offensive Battleground Seats	Gain/Loss	Vote Share
Brecon, Radnor and Cwm Tawe	Loss	21.30%
Brighton Pavilion	Loss	27.60%
Broxtowe	Gain	40.90%
Buckingham and Bletchley	Gain	36.90%
Burnley	Gain	31.70%
Burton and Uttoxeter	Gain	35.60%
Bury North	Gain	43.10%
Bury South	Gain	45.60%
Caerfyrddin	Loss	24.10%
Caithness, Sutherland and Easter Ross	Loss	7.40%
Calder Valley	Gain	44.40%
Camborne and Redruth	Gain	40.50%
Carlisle	Gain	39.40%
Central Ayrshire	Gain	43.70%
Ceredigion Preseli	Loss	11.60%
Chelsea and Fulham	Gain	39.40%
Chingford and Woodford Green	Loss	25.80%
Chipping Barnet	Gain	42.40%
Cities of London and Westminster	Gain	39%
Clwyd East	Gain	38.70%
Clwyd North	Gain	35.50%
Coatbridge and Bellshill	Gain	49.80%
Colchester	Gain	41.90%
Colne Valley	Gain	41%
Corby and East Northamptonshire	Gain	42.40%
Cowdenbeath and Kirkcaldy	Gain	45.70%
Crawley	Gain	38.20%
Crewe and Nantwich	Gain	44.10%
Croydon South	Loss	35.30%
Cumbernauld and Kirkintilloch	Gain	45.20%
Dagenham and Rainham	Hold	42.60%

Offensive Battleground Seats	Gain/Loss	Vote Share
Darlington	Gain	39.20%
Derby North	Gain	45.50%
Derbyshire Dales	Gain	34.60%
Doncaster East and the Isle of Axholme	Gain	38.60%
Dover and Deal	Gain	39.60%
Dudley	Hold	34.10%
Dumfries and Galloway	Loss	25.70%
Dumfriesshire, Clydesdale and Tweeddale	Loss	22.90%
Dundee Central	Loss	38.30%
Dunfermline and Dollar	Gain	45.70%
Dunstable and Leighton Buzzard	Gain	32.50%
Earley and Woodley	Gain	39.70%
East Kilbride and Strathaven	Gain	48.60%
East Renfrewshire	Gain	43.70%
East Thanet	Gain	39.90%
East Worthing and Shoreham	Gain	45.10%
Edinburgh East and Musselburgh	Gain	41.20%
Edinburgh North and Leith	Gain	42.10%
Edinburgh South West	Gain	40.90%
Edinburgh West	Loss	15%
Eltham and Chislehurst	Gain	44%
Erewash	Gain	40.10%
Falkirk	Gain	43.00%
Filton and Bradley Stoke	Gain	45.50%
Finchley and Golders Green	Gain	44.30%
Forest of Dean	Gain	34%
Gedling	Gain	47.80%
Gillingham and Rainham	Gain	37.80%
Glasgow East	Gain	43.90%

Offensive Battleground Seats	Gain/Loss	Vote Share
Glasgow North	Gain	42.20%
Glasgow North East	Gain	45.90%
Glasgow South	Gain	41.80%
Glasgow South West	Gain	43.60%
Glasgow West	Gain	46.70%
Glenrothes and Mid Fife	Gain	44.30%
Gloucester	Gain	36.10%
Gordon and Buchan	Loss	10.75%
Gravesham	Gain	38.50%
Great Grimsby and Cleethorpes	Gain	41.90%
Great Yarmouth	Loss	31.80%
Halesowen	Gain	38.90%
Hamilton and Clyde Valley	Gain	49.90%
Harlow	Gain	37.60%
Harrow East	Loss	28.90%
Hartlepool	Hold	46.20%
Hastings and Rye	Gain	41.60%
Hemel Hempstead	Gain	38.20%
Hexham	Gain	38.40%
Hendon	Gain	46.30%
High Peak	Gain	45.80%
Hitchin	Gain	43.90%
Huddersfield	Hold	37.60%
Hyndburn	Gain	33.50%
Inverclyde and Renfrewshire	Gain	46.95%
Inverness, Sky, and West Ross-Shire	Loss	13.00%
Ipswich	Gain	43.30%
Isle of Wight East	Loss	18.40%
Isle of Wight West	Gain	38.60%
Keighley and Ilkley	Loss	36.70%
Kensington and Bayswater	Hold	40.60%

Offensive Battleground Seats	Gain/Loss	Vote Share
Kettering	Gain	35.90%
Kilmarnock and Loudoun	Gain	44.90%
Kingston upon Hull West and Haltemprice	Gain	46.80%
Lancaster and Wyre	Gain	44.90%
Leeds South West and Morley	Gain	44%
Leigh and Atherton	Gain	48.50%
Lincoln	Gain	43.80%
Livingston	Gain	40.90%
Lothian East	Gain	49%
Loughborough	Gain	40.80%
Lowestoft	Gain	34.60%
Macclesfield	Gain	46.70%
Mansfield	Gain	39.10%
Mid and South Pembrokeshire	Gain	35.40%
Mid Cheshire	Gain	44.50%
Mid Derbyshire	Gain	36.50%
Mid Dunbartonshire	Loss	20.80%
Middlesbrough South and East Cleveland	Gain	43.30%
Midlothian	Gain	46.55%
Milton Keynes Central	Gain	43.30%
Milton Keynes North	Gain	42%
Monmouthshire	Gain	41.30%
Moray West, Nairn and Strathspey	Loss	17.70%
Morecambe and Lunesdale	Gain	40.80%
Motherwell, Wishaw and Carluke	Gain	49.10%
Na h-Eileanan an Iar	Gain	49.50%
Newcastle-under-Lyme	Gain	40.40%
Newton Aycliffe and Spennymoor	Gain	46.20%
North Ayrshire and Arran	Gain	39.80%
North East Derbyshire	Gain	38.40%

Offensive Battleground Seats	Gain/Loss	Vote Share
North East Fife	Loss	9.40%
North East Somerset and Hanham	Gain	40.60%
North Northumberland	Gain	36.60%
North Warwickshire and Bedworth	Gain	36%
North West Leicestershire	Gain	34.70%
Northampton North	Gain	43.50%
Northampton South	Gain	38.50%
Norwich North	Gain	45.40%
Nuneaton	Gain	36.90%
Ossett and Denby Dale	Gain	39.30%
Paisley and Renfrewshire North	Gain	47.10%
Paisley and Renfrewshire South	Gain	47.40%
Pendle and Clitheroe	Gain	34.50%
Penistone and Stocksbridge	Gain	43.60%
Penrith and Solway	Gain	40.60%
Perth and Kinross-shire	Loss	37.80%
Peterborough	Gain	32%
Plymouth Moor View	Gain	41.20%
Portsmouth North	Gain	34.80%
Reading West and Mid Berkshire	Gain	35%
Redcar	Gain	41%
Redditch	Gain	34.90%
Rochdale	Hold	32.80%
Rochester and Strood	Gain	36.20%
Rossendale and Darwen	Gain	40.90%
Rother Valley	Gain	38.55%
Rugby	Gain	39.90%
Rushcliffe	Gain	43.80%
Rutherglen	Gain	50.50%
Scarborough and Whitby	Gain	40.20%
Scunthorpe	Gain	39.70%

Offensive Battleground Seats	Gain/Loss	Vote Share
Selby	Gain	46.30%
Sherwood Forest	Gain	38.70%
Shipley	Gain	45%
Shrewsbury	Gain	44.50%
Slough	Hold	33.90%
South Derbyshire	Gain	38.80%
South Ribble	Gain	42.50%
Southampton Itchen	Gain	41.50%
Southend East and Rochford	Gain	38.80%
Southend West and Leigh	Gain	35.60%
Southport	Gain	38.30%
Spen Valley	Gain	39.20%
Stafford	Gain	40.30%
Stevenage	Gain	41.40%
Stirling and Strathallan	Gain	33.90%
Stockton West	Loss	37.50%
Stoke-on-Trent Central	Gain	42.40%
Stoke-on-Trent North	Gain	40.30%
Stoke-on-Trent South	Gain	34.70%
Stourbridge	Gain	38.50%
Stroud	Gain	46.40%
Swindon North	Gain	40.60%
Swindon South	Gain	48.40%
Tamworth	Gain	35%
Telford	Gain	44.70%
Thurrock	Gain	42.70%
Tipton and Wednesbury	Gain	36.90%
Truro and Falmouth	Gain	41.30%
Uxbridge and South Ruislip	Gain	36.20%
Vale of Glamorgan	Gain	38.70%
Wakefield and Rothwell	Gain	43.70%
Walsall and Bloxwich	Gain	33.60%

Offensive Battleground Seats	Gain/Loss	Vote Share
Warrington South	Hold	46.80%
Watford	Gain	35.30%
Wellingborough and Rushden	Gain	40.30%
Welwyn Hatfield	Gain	41%
West Aberdeenshire and Kincardine	Loss	13.10%
West Bromwich	Gain	46.20%
West Dunbartonshire	Gain	48.80%
Weston-super-Mare	Gain	38.50%
Whitehaven and Workington	Gain	53%
Wimbledon	Gain	21.30%
Wolverhampton North East	Gain	42.90%
Wolverhampton West	Gain	44.30%
Worcester	Gain	40.50%
Worthing West	Gain	40.20%
Wrexham	Gain	39.20%
Wycombe	Gain	35.90%
Ynys Môn	Loss	23.40%
York Outer	Gain	45.30%

Source: House of Commons (2024).

Acknowledgements

I am very grateful for the help of my friend and colleague Dr Jane Norris in converting my figures into high-resolution files.

References

Ainsley, C. (2018) *The New Working Class: How To Win Hearts, Minds and Voters*. Bristol: Policy Press.

Asthana, A. (2024) *Taken as Red: How Labour Won Big and the Tories Crashed the Party*. London: Harper Collins.

Baldwin, T. (2024) *Keir Starmer: The Biography*. London: William Collins.

BBC News (2024) '"We Did It! Change Begins Now" – Starmer's Victory Speech', *BBC News*, https://www.bbc.co.uk/news/videos/czrj3zd0g48o, accessed 5 July 2024.

Cracknell, R., and Baker C. (2024) *General Election 2024 Results*. House of Commons Library Research Briefing, https://researchbriefings.files.parliament.uk/documents/CBP-10009/CBP-10009.pdf, accessed 7 Aug. 2025.

Focaldata (2024) 'How Britain Voted 2024', https://www.focaldata.com/blog/how-britain-voted-2024, accessed 6 July 2024.

Fortunato, D., and Stevenson, R. T. (2013) 'Perceptions of Partisan Ideologies: The Effect of Coalition Participation', *American Journal of Political Science*, 57: 459–77.

Francis, G. (2024) 'How a Modern Digital Strategy Helped Labour Deliver a Landslide', *Formative*, https://www.formativecontent.com/blog-detail/how-a-modern-digital-strategy-helped-labour-deliver-a-landslide-2, accessed 5 July 2024.

Furlong, J., and Jennings, W. (2024) *The Changing Electoral Map of England and Wales*. Oxford: Oxford University Press.

Goes, E. (2021a) 'The Labour Party Under Keir Starmer: Thanks, But No 'Isms', Please!'. *The Political Quarterly*, 92: 176–83.

Goes, E. (2021b) 'Wrapped Up in the Union Jack: Labour's Patriotic Turn'. *Renewal*, 29: 49–59.

Green, D. (2024) 'Revealed: The 250 Seats Labour Calls "Battlegrounds"- Full List and Map'. *Labourlist*, https://labourlist.org/2024/06/labour-battleground-areas-full-list-general-election-2024/, accessed 7 June 2024.

Green, J., and Jennings, W. (2017) *The Politics of Competence: Parties, Public Opinion and Voters*. Cambridge: Cambridge University Press.

House of Commons (2005) *General Election 2005 Final Edition*. Research Paper 05/33, 17 May 2005. London: House of Commons Library.

House of Commons. (2011) *General Election 2010 Final Edition*. Research Paper 10/36, 2 February 2011. London: House of Commons Library.

House of Commons. (2015) *General Election 2015 Briefing Paper*. Number CBP7186, 28 July 2015. London: House of Commons Library.

House of Commons. (2019) *General Elections 2017: Results and Analysis*, Second Edition. Briefing Paper CBP 7979, 29 January 2019. London: House of Commons Library.

House of Commons. (2020) *General Elections 2019: Results and Analysis*, 2nd edn. London: House of Commons Library.

Ipsos (2022) 'Conservatives No Longer Most Trusted to Grow Britain's Economy', https://www.ipsos.com/en-uk/conservatives-no-longer-most-trusted-grow-britains-economy, accessed 19 Dec. 2024.

Ipsos (2024a) 'Trends – Political Parties', https://www.ipsos.com/en-uk/uk-opinion-polls/trends-political-parties#partyimagetrends, accessed 11 Mar. 2024.

Ipsos (2024b) 'Dissatisfaction With Government on Immigration at Highest Level Since 2015', https://www.ipsos.com/en-uk/immigration-tracker-march-2024, accessed 25 March 2024.

Ipsos (2024c) 'How Britain Voted in the 2024 Election', https://www.ipsos.com/en-uk/how-britain-voted-in-the-2024-election, accessed 26 July 2024.

Ipsos (2024d) 'Half of Britons Disappointed In Labour Government So Far – Including 1 in 4 Labour Voters', 20 September, https://www.cfr.org/blog/chinas-public-image-actually-getting-worse, accessed 18 Nov. 2024.

Labour Party (2023) *Five Missions For a Better Britain: A 'Mission-Driven' Government To End 'Sticking Plaster' Politics*. Newcastle: Labour Party, https://labour.org.uk/wp-content/uploads/2023/02/5-Missions-for-a-Better-Britain.pdf, accessed 5 Aug. 2025.

Labour Party (2024) 'Change: Labour Party Manifesto 2024'. London: Labour Party, https://labour.org.uk/wp-content/uploads/2024/06/Labour-Party-manifesto-2024.pdf, accessed 5 Aug. 2025.

Labour Together (2023) *'Red Shift: Labour's Path to Power'*. London: Labour Together, https://static1.squarespace.com/static/64f707cf512076037f612f60/t/6502d87070a60a6a39fefe87/1694685302745/Red±Shift±±Labour%27s±Path±to±Power.pdf, accessed 23 April 2023.

Labour Together (2024) *'How Labour Won'*, https://www.labourtogether.uk/how-labour-won-2024-report, accessed 18 Sept. 2024.

Lockey, A. (2020) 'If He Wants to Make an Impact, Starmer Must Resist the "Vision Thing"', CapX, 21 September, https://capx.co/if-he-wants-to-make-an-impact-starmer-must-resist-the-vision-thing/, accessed 9 May 2024.

Lockey, A. (2021a) 'Why Labour is Losing the Working-Class', CapX, https://capx.co/why-labour-is-losing-the-working-class/, accessed 12 May 2024.

Lockey, A. (2021b) 'What Should Keir Say?', September, https://lockey-alan.medium.com/what-should-keir-say-5a282872948b, accessed 9 May 2024.

Mason, R. (2024) 'Change and Growth: Five Key Takeaways From the Labour Manifesto Launch'. *The Guardian*, 13 June 2024, https://www.theguardian.com/politics/article/2024/jun/13/change-and-growth-five-key-takeaways-from-the-labour-manifesto-launch?CMP=Share_iOSApp_Other, accessed 5 Aug. 2025.

Mattinson, D. (2020) *Beyond the Red Wall: Why Labour Lost, How the Conservatives Won and What Will Happen Next?* London: Biteback Publishing.

Mazzucato, M. (2021) *Mission Economy: A Moonshot Guide to Changing Capitalism*. London: Penguin Books.

McDonnell, A. (2024) 'How Britain Voted in the 2024 General Election', *YouGov*, 8 July, https://yougov.co.uk/politics/articles/49978-how-britain-voted-in-the-2024-general-election, accessed 8 July 2024.

McTague, T. (2024) 'The Kingmaker in Labour Who's Ensuring that Starmer is No Heir to Blair', *The Times*, 10 May, https://www.thetimes.com/comment/columnists/article/the-kingmaker-in-labour-whos-ensuring-keir-is-no-heir-to-blair-gp5lvfj9d, accessed 12 May 2024.

More in Common/UCL Policy Lab (2024a) 'Change Pending: The Path to the 2024 General Election and Beyond', https://www.moreincommon.org.uk/media/e3in12zd/change-pending.pdf, accessed 10 July 2024.

More in Common. (2024b) 'Wheelbarrow Politics: Can Labour Keep Its Coalition on Track?', https://www.moreincommon.org.uk/media/vgqamgwj/8_lpc-coalition-deck-1.pdf, accessed 23 Sept. 2024.

Pike, K. (2024) *Getting Over New Labour*. Newcastle upon Tyne: Agenda Publishing.

Pogrund, G. (2024a) 'Rewrites, God Jokes, and the Diane Dilemma: Inside Labour's War Room', *The Times*, 26 May, https://www.thetimes.com/uk/politics/article/rewrites-god-jokes-and-the-diane-dilemma-inside-labours-war-room-m60529pbv, accessed 8 July 2024.

Pogrund, G. (2024b) 'Labour Celebrated Election Success – Now They're Targeting Reform', *The Sunday Times*, 7 July, https://www.thetimes.com/uk/politics/article/how-labour-celebrated-election-success-and-why-theyre-now-targeting-reform-b2f7rcpqr, accessed 8 July 2024.

Reeves, R. (2023) 'Securonomics', Speech to the Peterson Institute, Washington D.C, 24 May 2023, https://labour.org.uk/updates/press-releases/rachel-reeves-securonomics/, accessed 20 May 2024.

Reeves, R. (2024) 'No One Is Going to Give a Box of Matches Back to the Arsonists Who Burnt the House Down', *Daily Mail*, 24 May, https://www.dailymail.co.uk/debate/article-13457721/Shadow-Chancellor-Rachel-Reeves-Britain-Labour-money.html, accessed 15 Nov. 2024.

Rodgers, S. (2024) '"Gloriously Boring": How Ruthlessly Efficient Labour Machine Won the Election', *The House Magazine*, 6 July, https://www.politicshome.com/thehouse/article/gloriously-boring-keir-starmer-won-2024-general-election, accessed 8 July 2024.

Scott, G. (2024) 'The Army of Digital Sleeper Agents Who Propelled Labour to Power', *The Times*, 5 August, https://www.thetimes.com/uk/politics/article/the-army-of-digital-sleeper-agents-who-propelled-labour-to-power-69f5vv0hd, accessed 8 Aug. 2024.

Sobolewska, M., and Ford, R. (2020) *Brexitland*. Cambridge: Cambridge University Press.

Starmer, K. (2020) 'Victory Speech', 4 April 2020, https://www.politicshome.com/news/article/read-in-full-sir-keir-starmers-victory-speech-after-being-named-new-labour-leader, accessed 4 April 2024.

Starmer, K. (2023) 'Speech to Progressive Britain', 18 March 2023, https://www.youtube.com/watch?v=ocm3mRqZKxo, accessed 7 July 2024.

Starmer, K. (2024a) 'Address at Manifesto Launch', https://labour.org.uk/updates/press-releases/keir-starmer-launches-change-labours-general-election-manifesto/, accessed 13 June 2024.

Starmer, K. (2024b) 'First Speech as Prime Minister', https://www.gov.uk/government/speeches/keir-starmers-first-speech-as-prime-minister-5-july-2024, accessed 5 July 2024.

Starmer, K., and Reeves, R. (2024) 'Circumstances Have Changed, Our Ambitions Have Not. That's What You Need to Know About Our Green Plan', *The Guardian*, 8 February, https://www.theguardian.com/commentisfree/2024/feb/08/labour-28bn-green-prosperity-plan-keir-starmer-rachel-reeves, accessed 20 March 2024.

Stokes, D. E. (1963) 'Spatial Models of Party Competition', *The American Political Science Review*, 57: 368–77.

Whannel, K. (2024) 'Starmer Accuses Sunak of 'Jeremy Corbyn-Style' Manifesto', *BBC News*, 11 June, https://www.bbc.co.uk/news/articles/c1dd7m3zjxzo, accessed 7 July 2024.

YouGov. (2024a) 'Voting Intentions: Monthly Tracker' https://yougov.co.uk/topics/politics/trackers/voting-intention, accessed 9 Aug. 2024.

YouGov. (2024b) 'Which Political Party Would Be Best at Handling Asylum and Immigration? Monthly Tracker', https://yougov.co.uk/topics/politics/trackers/which-political-party-would-be-the-best-at-handling-asylum-and-immigration, accessed 9 Aug. 2024.

YouGov. (2024c) 'Which Political Party Would Be Better at Handling the Economy?', https://yougov.co.uk/topics/politics/trackers/which-political-party-would-be-the-best-at-handling-the-economy, accessed 9 Aug. 2024.

YouGov. (2024d) 'Why Are Britons Voting Labour? 03 July 2024', https://yougov.co.uk/politics/articles/49947-why-are-britons-voting-labour, accessed 8 July 2024.

YouGov. (2024e) 'How Britain Voted in the 2024 General Election', https://yougov.co.uk/politics/articles/49978-how-britain-voted-in-the-2024-general-election, accessed 8 July 2024.

YouGov. (2024f) 'Sunak vs Starmer: How Have Attitudes Changed Since the PM Took Office', https://yougov.co.uk/politics/articles/48452-sunak-vs-starmer-2024-how-have-attitudes-changed-since-the-pm-took-office, accessed 8 July 2024.

YouGov. (2024g) 'General Election 2024: What Are The Most Important Issues For Voters?', https://yougov.co.uk/politics/articles/49594-general-election-2024-what-are-the-most-important-issues-for-voters, accessed 1 June 2024.

YouGov. (2024h) 'General Election 2024: How Are Sunak and Starmer Performing on Key Attributes', https://yougov.co.uk/politics/articles/49884-general-election-2024-how-are-sunak-and-starmer-performing-on-key-attributes, accessed 30 June 2024.

Yellow fever returns: The 2024 Liberal Democrat campaign

David Cutts[1,*] and Andrew Russell[2]

[1]Department of Political Science and International Studies, School of Government and Society, College of Social Sciences, University of Birmingham, Edgbaston, Birmingham, B15 2TT, UK
[2]Department of Politics, University of Liverpool, 8-11 Abercromby Square, Liverpool, L697WZ, UK

*Correspondence: D.Cutts@bham.ac.uk

2024 proved to be a historic election for the Liberal Democrats. After flirting with electoral extinction after the 2010–5 coalition and getting their political and electoral strategy so badly wrong in 2019, the Liberal Democrats spent a decade in the backwaters of British politics. Facing perennial structural barriers, public uncertainty about their political pitch, little media airtime and with new redistricted seats notionally reducing their parliamentary representation further, the prospects for a significant electoral surge seemed unlikely.

Yet just five years on from the disaster of 2019, the Liberal Democrats made history. Winning seventy-two seats, the party secured their largest haul in more than 100 years of Liberal history despite only marginally increasing their vote share from 2019. So how did the Liberal Democrats overcome persistent and longstanding issues to surpass pre-election expectations? What was the party's political and electoral strategy and how vital was it in securing their historic success? And how significant were party campaign tactics and targeted activism in determining the Liberal Democrats historic seat haul? We examine what happened and why and assess whether the party's unprecedented triumph could be a platform for even greater success or whether 2024 masked a fragility in support that might be severely exposed in the future.

1. The Liberal Democrats' post-2019 renaissance

As a third force in two-party politics, the Liberal Democrats do not control their own destiny but rely on the misfortune of key rivals in order to flourish

(Cutts, Russell, and Townsley 2023). When Boris Johnson won a landslide election in 2019, few envisaged that the Conservatives' term in office would be so turbulent, chaotic, and crisis-ridden. For five years under three different Prime Ministers, numerous scandals, sleaze, and bare incompetence, at times the Conservatives appeared unmanageable as a party and unfit to govern.

As public anger towards the Conservatives grew, the Liberal Democrats abandoned equidistance between the main two parties and positioned themselves as part of an anti-Conservative alternative. Aiming to attract disillusioned Conservatives, the party's decision also reflected Labour's transition to the centre ground under new leader Sir Keir Starmer. Labour's transformation was a crucial driver of the Liberal Democrats' revival. In 2019, the Liberal Democrats struggled to convert wavering Conservative Remain voters in Conservative-Liberal Democrat battlegrounds who were sceptical of any Corbyn-led administration. By repositioning Labour, Starmer increasingly appeared a credible economic option and with voters no longer fearing a Labour government, Liberal Democrat prospects improved. Starmer's abandonment of Corbyn's policies helped neutralize the political discourse around the 2010–5 coalition's legacy and detoxified the Liberal Democrat brand, giving Labour voters the green light to lend tactical votes to the Liberal Democrats where necessary to rout the Conservatives (Cutts, Russell, and Townsley 2023).

Despite reliance on their competitors to prosper, the Liberal Democrats also need to be a viable and credible alternative to take maximum advantage when their rivals hit hard times. Agency is fundamental to this and crucially, the leadership of Sir Ed Davey was vital for the Liberal Democrats' renaissance. Davey's technocratic style proved quietly effective at rebuilding the party internally and compared favourably with Johnson and Truss among sizeable sections of the electorate who valued sound judgment and expertise on serious issues (Cutts, Russell, and Townsley 2023). His personal backstory—caring for a terminally ill mother as a teenager and now as a father to a disabled son—gave him and his party the platform to highlight the lack of investment in social care and stand up for carers' issues. This issue became the centrepiece of the Liberal Democrat campaign, enabling Davey to speak personally about health and social care and resonate with public discontent with the Conservatives' record during the cost of living crisis.

While Davey made few mistakes he also proved to be a fortunate leader. During Johnson's tenure, three historic by-election wins in short succession epitomized the Conservatives' malaise while simultaneously kick-starting the Liberal Democrats' revival. A swing of 25% from Conservative to Liberal Democrat in Chesham and Amersham was surpassed a few months later by a 34% swing to win North Shropshire and a 30% swing in Tiverton and Honiton where the party overturned a 24,000 Tory majority. Each by-election revealed how Johnson's 2019 coalition of voters was unravelling and how the Liberal Democrats could exploit the

Conservative collapse. Chesham and Amersham exemplified the types of places where the Liberal Democrats had made progress since 2017—solidly Remain and a large number of graduates—although the high levels of home ownership and fewer professionals suggested that the Liberal Democrats post-2019 appeal was widening. Winning North Shropshire and Tiverton and Honiton, two traditional Conservative seats that voted Leave in 2016, made a bigger statement. The Brexit realignment 'Leave bloc' which propelled Johnson to a 2019 landslide was increasingly fragile. Furthermore, Davey's repositioning of the party on 'Brexit'— ruling out reapplying to join the EU while he remained leader—had started to defuse 'Leave' voters' concerns in key battlegrounds against the Conservatives. The by-election victories showcased the Liberal Democrats' ability to secure borrowed support from Labour and win over disaffected Conservatives. Changing the Conservative leader did little to nullify the Liberal Democrat threat. Further by-election success in Glastonbury and Somerton allowed Davey to hail his party as the dominant force against the Conservatives in South West England.

However, during January 2024, the legacy of coalition came back to haunt the Liberal Democrats. A four part ITV drama *Mr Bates versus the Post Office* told the real life scandal of how the Post Office wrongly accused 3,500 sub-postmasters and prosecuted 900 of them for theft and fraud related offences based on evidence from the faulty Horizon IT system and how Alan Bates, a postmaster and leading campaigner, exposed the Post Office cover-up. A letter emerged that Davey, who had been Post Office minister during the first two years of the coalition government, had refused to meet Bates, prompting widespread criticism. Davey responded by saying 'he felt regret' but defended his role. His failure to apologize (asked 10 times in an ITV interview but he refused to do so) proved to be a serious misstep with Conservative opponents calling on him to resign. It wasn't until a few weeks later that Davey apologized for 'not seeing through the Post Office' and taking five months to meet Bates (The Guardian 2024). With Davey not required to give evidence to the Post Office inquiry until after the election, he was able to deflect any further probing questions. While it did not have any long-lasting damage on Davey or the party it reiterated just how easy agency failings could derail the Liberal Democrats.

2. The political and electoral strategy

Credibility remained pivotal to any Liberal Democrat success at the ballot box. Heading into 2024, the Liberal Democrats were second in ninety-eight seats, eighty-five of which were Conservative-held. Two of the three key battlegrounds against the SNP contained Liberal Democrat incumbents who under the new boundaries were notionally second. Elsewhere, the Liberal Democrats were second to Labour in only ten seats and Sheffield Hallam seemed their only real prospect of success. With Conservative prospects looking increasingly dire, the Liberal Democrats adopted highly aggressive targeting strategies in Conservative-held battleground seats. This was ambitious and brought into play the thirty seats where the Liberal Democrats were 20% or less behind the incumbent, of which twenty-four were held by the Conservatives. To make deep inroads though, the party needed to target the thirty-one Conservative seats where the party were up to 30% behind, of which only twenty-five were credible targets given they were in second place. Beyond this, seats such as Chichester, Maidenhead, and Witney, where there was increasing internal optimism, seemed like indulgent fantasies rather than viable targets given that the Liberal Democrats had little or no history of success in these seats at Westminster elections.

The party's electoral strategy concentrated on winning specific seats rather than broadly accumulating vote share. The targeting approach was reminiscent of the Ashdown-Kennedy (and Rennard) era, as the party sought to advance across the Home Counties and commuter belt outside London while simultaneously winning back traditional seats in the South West and extending its presence into Dorset and Hampshire. The key goal was to get the campaign right on the ground in the places that mattered. In these seats, the party prioritized the selection of high-profile and experienced candidates, some of whom ran previously, as early in the electoral cycle as possible. The aim was to build momentum at the local level, one election at a time, and use this as the platform for parliamentary success. Those selected as target seats would have a track record of two or more years of intensive activism and were chosen by the centre early on to receive heavily focussed support and extra resources in order to equip local teams with skills and capabilities to run continuous targeted campaigns. Target seats had to fulfil criteria to get central backing but party strategists invested early in officially 'promising areas'. They aided ground activity through digital innovations, new centrally designed templates for leaflets and target letters and a variety of other developments to ease local administrative costs.

Central to the electoral strategy was exploiting national issues that mattered locally and ensuring that the salient message was tailored to voters in the right places. At the national level, the party's manifesto commitment to invest £9.8 billion on the NHS and social care (including free personal care in England, reforming the carer's allowance, faster cancer treatment and more GPs) was deliberately wrapped around the personal experiences of Davey in order to help him and the party cut through with the public. The goal was to gain credibility on the issue and hope that it would appeal to strategic Labour supporters and encourage them to lend the Liberal Democrats their vote where they were facing the Conservatives. Other policies and measures to ease the 'cost of living crisis', tripling the early years pupil premium and scrapping the two-child benefit cap also strategically helped the party target Labour supporters in these battleground seats. The party's proposals to tackle sewage dumping featured prominently reflecting long running high profile local campaigns over the electoral cycle in a number of target seats. Sewage dumping by water companies was deemed a 'cut through' issue locally with 'lifelong Conservatives' and the party's proposals of a 'sewage tax' on water company profits, a ban on company executive bonuses and a new tougher regulator (Clean Water Authority) had significant public support on the ground.

The Liberal Democrats needed to build a coalition of support to succeed. Motivating its core vote would be the easy part, but switching 'lifelong Conservatives' required specific tactics and tailored policy messages according to the local nature of the seat. National messages mattered but building local trust between these voters and the prospective candidate was vital. Credibility was also the key to maximize tactical switching. Traditional Labour supporters needed to know that the Liberal Democrats were the only credible competitor to the Conservatives, so while the national picture mattered, it was the day-to-day ground activism constructed over a sustained period that allowed the Liberal Democrats to borrow as much transactional support as possible. As polling day neared numerous MRP polls providing estimates of constituency results encouraged predictions that the Liberal Democrats would get in excess of fifty seats. YouGov even claimed the final figure would be an incredible seventy-two seats (YouGov 2024a).

3. The electoral outcome

In the 2024 General Election the combined Conservative and Labour vote share plummeted to 57.4%, the lowest combined vote share in any UK election since the extension of the franchise in 1918. The election was a triumph for smaller parties, particularly Reform UK who secured an unprecedented five seats, more than four million votes and 14.3% of the overall vote, and the Greens who increased their vote by four percentage points and won a historic four seats. The Scottish National Party (SNP) also bore the brunt of an incumbent backlash losing thirty-nine seats and fifteen percentage points compared to 2019. Meanwhile, with seventy-two MPs (a net gain of sixty-four), the Liberal Democrats moved out of the category of small parties. Three key features stood out from the Liberal Democrats' electoral performance in 2024: the proportionality between party representation and vote; the continuing unevenness in party support and representation between and within regions; and the growing North-South divide in the geography of the party's votes and seats. The Liberal Democrats polled slightly over 3.5 million votes, a drop of around 200,000 from 2019 and only marginally increased vote share by 0.7 percentage points to 12.2% (Table 5.1). Yet with 11.1% of the representatives in Westminster, the Liberal Democrats had emphatically overcome a structural barrier that had restricted their electoral progress for generations by becoming a

Table 5.1. Summary of Liberal Democrat general election performance 1992–2024

LD	1992	1997	2001	2005	2010	2015	2017	2019	2024
Votes (000)	5,999	5,243	4,814	5,985	6,836	2,416	2,372	3,696	3,519
% UK Vote	17.8%	16.8%	18.3%	22.0%	23.0%	7.9%	7.4%	11.5%	12.2%
Seats Won	20	46	52	62	57	8	12	11	72
% Seats Won	3.2%	7.0%	7.9%	9.6%	8.8%	1.2%	1.8%	1.7%	11.4%
Votes:Seats[a]	1.12	2.74	2.84	2.82	2.48	1.01	1.62	0.96	5.90
Lost Deposits	11/632	13/639	1/639	1/626	0/631	341/631	375/629	136/611	229/630

[a]Votes:Seats ratio derived from dividing LD seats won by LD share of the vote. In 1992, the Liberal Democrats stood in 632 constituencies; and in 2017 they stood in 629. In 2019, the party only stood in 611 seats following their pact with Plaid Cymru and the Greens. *Note*: These are UK-wide vote share percentages so differ slightly from the GB-only figures where in 2024 the party secured 12.6% of the vote.

party, if not the only party, whose representation was broadly in line to its overall vote. Despite the improvement in the Liberal Democrats' vote share from 2019 it was around eleven percentage points lower than it had been in 2010 and was worse than any Liberal performance between the era of Jeremy Thorpe and the coalition.

Despite winning an additional four seats in Scotland and securing representation in Wales for the first time since 2015, all but seven of the seventy-two Liberal Democrat seats are English. Alongside the notionally held Orkney and Shetland and Edinburgh West, the party comfortably gained the seats they held in 2019—Caithness, Sutherland and Easter Ross and North-East Fife. The Liberal Democrats also regained the new version of ex-leader Jo Swinson's seat in Mid Dunbartonshire. Perhaps the most emotional victory for many Liberal Democrat activists saw the party regaining the late Charles Kennedy's old Highland seat of Inverness, Skye, and West Ross-shire. These successes though papered-over obvious frailties in the Liberal Democrat Scottish vote. Aside from these six seats, the Liberal Democrats only recorded double digit percentage vote shares in three other Scottish seats, losing its deposit in thirty. In Wales, the Liberal Democrats won their key target seat of Brecon, Radnor, and Cwm Tawe albeit with less than 30% of the overall vote but secured distant second places in only two other constituencies and actually only saved their deposit in eleven of the thirty-two seats.

Across England, the post-2010 North-South divide in Liberal Democrat support and seats remains evident. In 2024, the Liberal Democrats only increased their 2019 vote share in three of the nine regions (see Table 5.2). In the South West, the Liberal Democrats saw a 6.5 percentage point increase in support and gained twenty-one seats. To put this in perspective, the 2005 Liberal Democrats won sixty-two seats but captured only sixteen South West constituencies despite receiving nearly eight points more in the region than in 2024. In 2010, the party polled ten percentage points more in the South West but captured seven fewer seats. If anything though, the 2024 Liberal Democrats were most efficient in the South East, where with roughly 22% of the vote, an increase of 3.5 points on five years ago, the Liberal Democrats won an unprecedented twenty-four seats. Again, the difference was the translation of votes to seats. In 2010, when the party secured five percentage points more in the South East, the Liberal Democrats could only muster four seats.

Elsewhere, Liberal Democrat support remained around the national average in the Eastern region and the party were rewarded with six additional seats compared to five years ago. In London, party support fell by nearly four points reflecting a hangover from 2019 when prominent figures from both Labour and the Conservatives switched to the party and unsuccessfully stood in a number of London seats. Nonetheless, the party still picked up their three key targets—Carshalton and Wallington, Sutton and Cheam and Wimbledon—and easily held their incumbent seats.

Across the English North and Midlands, four of the five regions saw a decline in Liberal Democrat support but again the party scored their key target bullseyes

Table 5.2. 2024 Liberal Democrat performance: National and regional breakdown (English regions)

National & Regional	2024 % LD Vote	% Change ± 19–24	Seats 2024	Seats 2019	Change 19–24
Country					
UK	12.2	+0.7	72/650	8/650	+64
England	13.2	+0.8	65/543	6/533	+59
Scotland	9.7	+0.2	6/57	2/59	+4
Wales	6.5	+0.5	1/32	0/40	+1
Region					
East Midlands	6.4	−1.4	0/47	0/46	0
Eastern	13.2	−0.2	7/61	1/58	+6
London	11.0	−3.9	6/75	3/73	+3
North East	5.9	−0.9	0/27	0/29	0
North West	7.8	−0.0	3/73	0/75	+3
South East	21.9	+3.6	24/91	1/84	+23
South West	24.7	+6.5	22/58	1/55	+21
West Midlands	8.8	+1.0	2/57	0/59	+2
Yorkshire & The Humber	7.1	−0.9	1/54	0/54	+1

Note: 2019 seats are based on notional results for the new 2024 boundaries. % Change ± 19–24 is rounded to one decimal place.

winning West Midlands and Yorkshire seats for the first time since 2015. In the North West, the party won Tim Farron's redistricted Westmoreland and Lonsdale (a notional Conservative seat) and their two top targets Cheadle and Hazel Grove. Nevertheless, the overall picture remains fairly bleak. In 2024, Liberal Democrat support increased in only 235 constituencies. Two-thirds of seats across the North of England and more than 70% of seats in the Midlands saw a drop in Liberal Democrat support. Outside of the six seats won by the Liberal Democrats across the North and the Midlands, the party recorded more than 25% of the vote in only two other seats. The party increased their number of lost deposits by ninety-three compared to 2019. Of the 178 lost deposits in England, nearly 75% were in the North and the Midlands. In the North East, the Liberal Democrats lost deposits in roughly 60% of seats and half of the constituencies in the rest of the North of England. The North-South gap in Liberal Democrat support remains stark—more than 70% of Liberal Democrat seats won and 75% of newly gained seats are located in South East and South West England. In 2017 and 2019, it polled around 64% of its national vote in the South whereas in 2024 the comparable figure was 68%. Simply put, the Liberal Democrats are increasingly a party of the South of England (Cutts, Russell, and Townsley 2023).

3.1 The constituency battleground

Table 5.3 examines the Liberal Democrats' 2024 performance by seat type. Since 2015, the personal standing of the incumbent had helped the Liberal Democrats maintain a presence in Westminster. In 2019, where the Liberal Democrats retained incumbent candidates, party support was 1.6 points higher than in all Liberal Democrat-held seats. In 2024, across the eight notional Liberal Democrat incumbent seats, party support increased on average by two points. There was some unevenness as Liberal Democrat support fell in three of the eight seats—offset by large shifts in support towards the party in both Scottish seats. Support for Liberal Democrat incumbents in England actually fell on average by 1.1 points indicating that it may have reached its ceiling.

Credibility continues to matter. Five years ago, support in non-held seats increased by more than four points. Given the significant gains made, it is perhaps unsurprising that Liberal Democrat support in non-held seats continued its upward trajectory in 2024. However, in those seats where the Liberal Democrats neither held nor occupied second place going into the 2024 election, party support fell. Moreover, ruthlessly efficient targeting came at a cost. The floor of the Liberal Democrat vote seems to be on a downward spiral. In more than 80% of parliamentary seats the party cease to be competitive. This growing 'competitiveness gap' has long term consequences for any future electoral growth. Simply put, despite

Table 5.3. 2024 Liberal Democrat performance by incumbency and seat type

Seats	2024 % LD Vote	2019 % LD Vote	Change ± 19–24
Incumbency			
LD 2019 Incumbent Seats (8)	52.2	50.1	+2.1
LD Non-Held Seats (622)	11.3	10.9	+0.4
Seat Type (LDs Second Place in 2019)			
LD All Second Place (98)	35.1	27.8	+7.3
Con-LD Seats (85)	37.0	27.9	+9.1
Lab-LD Seats (10)	15.2	23.5	−8.3
SNP-LD Seats (3)	48.8	35.9	+12.9
LDs Neither Incumbent or Second (524)	6.8	7.8	−1.0
2024 LD Seats Gained			
LD All 2024 Seats Gained (64)	44.0	30.4	+13.6
Con-LD Seats (60)	43.8	30.4	+13.4

Note: Incumbent seats are based on 2019 notional votes because of boundary changes. The 2019 Incumbent seats were—Bath, Edinburgh West, Kingston and Surbiton, Orkney and Shetland, Oxford West and Abingdon, Richmond Park, St Albans and Twickenham. All incumbent candidates ran again in 2024. The Liberal Democrats stood in 630 seats (did not stand in Chorley and Manchester Rusholme).

a post-war record number of seats, there remain significant structural challenges facing the party.

In 2019, tactical unwind of the Liberal Democrat vote had not only stopped but reversed, although the scale was modest and uneven (Cutts and Russell 2020). As Table 5.3 shows, while 2024 Liberal Democrat support rose by more than seven percentage points across all seats where it was in second place, in the eighty-five seats where it was second to the Conservatives, it increased by more than nine points. Across these eighty-five seats, the change in Labour support from 2019, on average, actually increased by 0.6 points. Again there was considerable unevenness. Of the sixty-four gains in 2024, sixty were won from the Conservatives.[1] In these seats, the Liberal Democrat vote increased by more than 13 percentage points, including large increases in three of the four seats won in by elections. Nonetheless, a further four of the sixty seats gained from the Conservatives in England and Wales recorded twenty point plus increases in Liberal Democrat support—Chichester, Harpenden and Berkhamsted, Tewkesbury and Westmoreland

---

[1] Of those eighty-five seats where the party were second to the Conservatives in 2019, the Liberal Democrats won fifty-eight of them, Labour won one (Finchley and Golders Green) and the Conservatives the remaining twenty-six. Where the Liberal Democrats were second to the SNP, the Liberal Democrats won all three seats.

and Lonsdale. Conservative support in these sixty seats declined by an average of more than 24 percentage points, greater than the overall drop in UK Conservative support. Moreover, the Liberal Democrats were also aided by an average drop of 2.5 points in Labour support across these sixty seats. Yet in thirteen of these seats the Labour vote actually increased while in another seven seats the Labour vote fell by less than one percentage point. Nevertheless, there was a significant negative correlation (−0.81*) between the change in Liberal Democrat and Labour vote share from 2019 to 2024 which implies, across these sixty seats gained, as Liberal Democrat vote change increased, Labour vote change decreased. It therefore seems evident that Liberal Democrat success in these key battleground seats was in part driven by centre-left tactical switchers (including Greens whose support increased less in these seats) lending their vote to the party best placed to defeat the incumbent Conservatives.

Strikingly, the Liberal Democrats only failed to win three seats—Godalming and Ash, Farnham and Bordon, and Romsey and Southampton North—where the party was 30% or less behind the incumbent Conservatives going into the election. Before the 2024 election there were a further nineteen Conservative-Liberal Democrat battlegrounds where the party was between 30 and 35% behind the Conservatives. Remarkably, the Liberal Democrats managed to win half of these seats and success extended beyond this with unprecedented victories in Chichester, Stratford on Avon and Tewkesbury (see Fig. 5.1 below).

3.2 Uniting old and new geographies

If the Liberal Democrats were to return to the levels of Westminster representation of the pre-coalition era, the party had to unite old and new geographies of support and ruthlessly convert votes into seats. Table 5.4 examines Liberal Democrat performance in seats where the party had a historical legacy and new geographies of potential support in the so-called 'Blue Wall'. Our evidence suggests that Liberal Democrat success in 2024 was partially driven by a recovery in its historical strongholds. The party saw a sizeable uptick in support in its legacy seats albeit from a low base. Of the twenty-two legacy seats, eight now have Liberal Democrat MPs, with victories in old non-conformist seats such as North Cornwall, North Devon and Inverness, Skye and West Ross-shire spearheading the revival. However, the largest surge was in 'breakthrough seats' (where the party won for the first time in 1997) with the Liberal Democrats, on average, increasing their vote by 5.5 percentage points to roughly 40% across the twenty-three seats. Crucially though, the party converted these votes into seats. It now holds eighteen of these twenty-three seats, with thirteen gains in the 2024 election. Moreover, the Liberal Democrats were successful in thirty-two of the fifty-seven seats won by Clegg in 2010. In summary, forty-one of the seventy-two seats that the Liberal Democrats won in

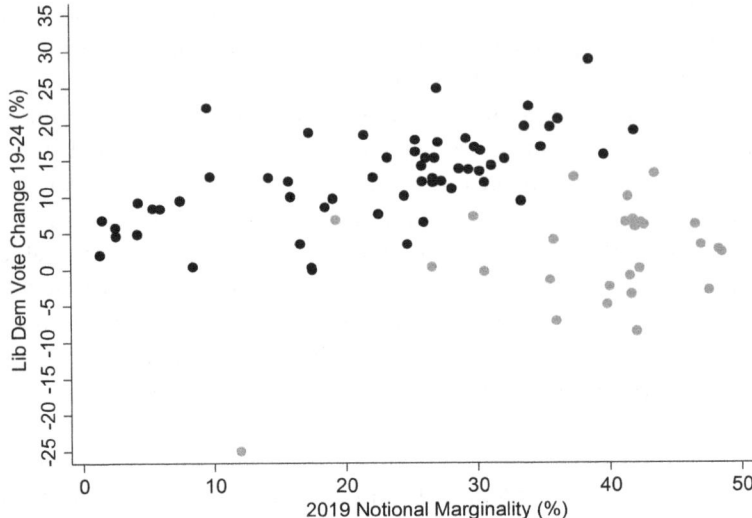

Figure 5.1. Liberal Democrat gains in Conservative-Liberal Democrat battlegrounds by 2019 notional marginality.
Note: 2024 seats won by the Liberal Democrats (coded Black) in Conservative-Liberal Democrat battlegrounds by marginality.

Table 5.4. 2024 Liberal Democrat performance by historical legacy and new target seats

Seats	2024 % LD Vote	2019 % LD Vote	Change ± 19–24
Historical Legacy			
LD Legacy Seats (22)	22.4	18.1	+4.3
LD Heartland Seats (12)	26.4	23.8	+2.6
LD Breakthrough 1997 Seats (23)	39.8	34.3	+5.5
All LD Pre-Coalition 2010 Seats (57)	31.5	26.4	+5.1
New Target Seats			
Blue Wall (25)	31.7	27.2	+4.5

Note: Liberal Democrat legacy seats are those constituencies where the party was successful between 1955 and October 1974. Heartland seats are those new seats that the party won between 1979 and 1992 (they do not include legacy seats). Heartland seats also include Portsmouth South won in a by-election in 1984 but was subsequently lost in 1987 but regained in 1997.

2024 had, at one point in time from the mid-1950s to 2019, Liberal representation. Winning again where it had a legacy of Westminster representation proved pivotal to the Liberal Democrats record seat return in 2024.

The scale of the Liberal Democrats' success, however, meant that the party won thirty-one Westminster seats, at the expense of the Conservatives, where they had never triumphed before. Since the late 2010s, the changing socio-demographics in traditional Conservative seats across the South of England had facilitated

Labour, and particularly Liberal Democrat, development of new geographies of support. Conservative woes between 2019–24 further exposed fault lines in the Tory vote and made these 'Blue wall' seats increasingly vulnerable.[2] In the end, the Conservatives only managed to hold onto four of these twenty-five 'Blue wall' seats with the Liberal Democrats picking up fifteen and, increasing their vote by an average of 4.5 points.

The remaining sixteen seats gained from the Conservatives, however, did not fit this 'Blue wall' profile. Many have elderly populations, larger numbers of retirees and relatively high levels of home ownership, mirroring the characteristics of its old strongholds. Crucially, eleven of the sixteen new non-Blue Wall seats voted Leave in the 2016 EU referendum. Since 2016, the Liberal Democrats' inability to compete in Leave seats, some of which was self-inflicted, had hurt the party in many of its traditional strongholds (Cutts and Russell 2020). Yet while 2019 was labelled the 'Brexit election', 2024 was emphatically not as only 8% of UK voters felt that Brexit was one of the top issues at the election (YouGov 2024b). As such, in those seats where the electorate saw them as the main competitors to the Conservatives, Liberal Democrat support surged irrespective of whether they were Remain areas, evenly balanced or strong Leave seats. To emphasize this, twenty-nine of the sixty-four Liberal Democrat gains were in Leave seats, of which twelve were constituencies where support for Brexit was greater than 55%. The Brexit status of the seat did not appear to harm the party's chances of success. As a consequence, the Liberal Democrats were able to unite old and new geographies, which combined archetypal 'Blue Wall' Remain areas with growing numbers of educated young professionals but also Leave seats with sizeable numbers of older people and retirees, many of which were near to areas of historic Liberal strength.

4. Why it went right

4.1 The Davey factor

Increasingly Liberal Democrat leaders matter in elections. In the battle for airtime during an election campaign, where both the main protagonists failed to ignite the electorate, Ed Davey prospered. Through a series of media-friendly stunts, from bungee jumping and paddle boarding, to flying down a slip 'n' slide, the leader's antics drew widespread attention. While political opponents and some media commentators questioned the appropriateness of the stunts, they gave Davey and the party exposure they craved. Crucially each stunt was followed by a serious message, carefully choreographed to match voter concerns in specific seats and

---

[2] See Cutts, Russell, and Townsley (2023) for a classification of Blue Wall seats.

matched to Liberal Democrat policy fixes. The strategy was not foolproof; a day at Thorpe Park for a manifesto launch which would have gained media attention automatically seemed a misstep but generally, the tactic worked. Evidence suggests that while voters were divided on Davey's campaigning style, more were supportive than found it unfavourable (YouGov 2024c). Despite a willingness to be lampooned Davey largely avoided campaign mistakes while he came across as normal and relatable which for sizeable numbers of the electorate contrasted positively with his opponents.

Party strategists were keen to present Davey's personal story and experiences and unite these with the party's flagship policies on health and social care. The goal was to present Davey as a warrior for neglected causes and voices. Widely praised, the party's election broadcast—'Ed's Story'—depicted Davey's life as a carer. Emotional and thought provoking, it successfully portrayed Davey as sincere and decent while simultaneously reinforcing the party as the 'voice for carers'. Of the main party leaders Davey was the only one to improve his net approval ratings over the campaign and significantly outperformed the campaign effectiveness of previous Liberal Democrat leaders Farron and Swinson. A political gamble paid off primarily because the Liberal Democrats got the communication right, not only on the diagnosis, but, on the issues that mattered to people, also the cure.

4.2 The campaign

In 2019, the party's electoral strategy centred on opposing Brexit. Five years later with equidistance abandoned, the party's goal was much simpler—to oppose the Conservatives. In preparation for the 2024 election, the party went back to basics in order to establish local credibility—constructing a local campaign infrastructure early on in the electoral cycle to engage in continuous campaigning outside election time. This familiar formula was supported by the hiring of an extensive network of field campaigners with many appointed early in the electoral cycle. Money was found to 'beef up' the national campaign team while strenuous efforts were made to improve coordination between the digital, traditional and local campaign teams to avoid a repeat of the logistical and message quality issues that marred the 2019 campaign. Under the new Liberal Democrat campaign guru, Dave McCobb, fresh from orchestrating by-election successes, a renewed emphasis was placed on community grassroots activism and a 'door knocking culture' alongside upgrades in digital activism to get personalized messages across to voters. In simple terms, the party was better prepared, had spent resources wisely well in advance of the election to support teams in the field and had instilled a cohesive joined-up campaign strategy to derive high-quality data which it then used ruthlessly to target messages to voters that mattered. The election marked the return of the fabled Liberal Democrat campaign machine.

4.3 Riding a wave of good fortune?

For all the Liberal Democrats did right, it is undeniable that their success owed more to Conservative collapse than their own endeavours. The Conservative vote declined more where it was previously strong which accounts for the above average drop in support in longstanding traditional Liberal strongholds. One possible explanation is that the Liberal Democrats benefited from 'lifelong Conservatives' staying at home rather than switching their loyalty. The evidence is mixed. Overall turnout declined by 7.5 points between 2019 and 2024. In all Conservative incumbent seats, the turnout decline was, on average, 6.5 percentage points but across the sixty Conservative-held seats which the Liberal Democrats gained, turnout actually fell by 5.5 points. Only in twenty-three of the sixty seats gained did turnout fall by more than the average across all Conservative incumbent seats (6.5 points). Interestingly, 70% of these seats voted Leave and more than 60% were located in the South West of England. And only seven of these were where the Liberal Democrats had no previous track record of success in Westminster elections. In order to win back some of its traditional strongholds, particularly in the South West, the Liberal Democrats were aided by some Conservative abstentions.

In 2019, the Liberal Democrats' prospects of winning seats off the Conservatives was dealt a blow when the Brexit party decided not to stand in Conservative-held seats. Five years later, not only had the agreement broken down but Nigel Farage had entered the fray. On average, Reform UK did not advance as strongly in Conservative-Liberal Democrat battlegrounds compared to other seats. It polled 12.4% across the sixty seats gained by the Liberal Democrats in 2024, around two points lower than what Reform UK polled overall in the election. Yet in those Leave seats gained by the Liberal Democrats, Reform UK secured 14.5%, which was comparable to its average vote across all seats. In twenty-seven of these sixty seats gained, the Reform UK vote was greater than the margin of victory, of which fourteen voted Leave in 2016. Post-polling day individual data also suggests that 23% of 2019 Conservative voters who voted switched to Reform UK while only 10% went to the Liberal Democrats (YouGov 2024d). The Conservatives seemingly held onto far more of their 2019 Remain supporters than Leave voters, albeit the former was smaller and perhaps more loyal from the outset. So while the Liberal Democrats switched more 2019 Conservative voters in these key battlegrounds than elsewhere, their ability to translate votes into seats was aided by Reform UK winning over Leave voters, particularly in those Leave areas that went Liberal Democrat. Looking forward to the next election, where the Liberal Democrats are defending against the Conservatives, the data does suggest that there is more Labour vote to tactically squeeze in a number of these Liberal Democrat gains which could somewhat offset any potential switch back from Reform UK to the Conservatives. In fifteen of the sixty Liberal Democrat gains against the Conservatives, for instance, Labour polled higher than Reform UK. Safe to say that the electoral picture is complicated but one should not automatically assume if the Conservatives pick up at the expense of Reform UK that the Liberal Democrats will fall away easily.

5. Conclusion

The 2024 election will forever be etched in Liberal folklore. It came after a period of severe hardship for the party with many important battles lost and at times their political future in the balance. The Conservative collapse after fourteen years in power undoubtedly opened the door for them. They rode a wave of good fortune—a growing consensus that Labour was ready for power—but not attractive enough to encourage much direct Tory-Labour switching—and sizeable numbers of Conservative voters willing to protest by voting Reform UK. Yet it would be completely wrong to ignore the fact that while the Liberal Democrats had a 'helping hand' they were in a position to grab it. The party was a different beast from 2019. The communication and presentation of policies was slick, precise and tailored to specific sets of voters. The campaign machine of folklore, relatively limp recently, was muscular again and Davey surpassed the expectations of many. For all the stunts and silliness, there was a serious point that cut through. Using Davey's own personal experiences, the Liberal Democrats were able to cultivate issue identity around social care which sets them apart from other parties. The Liberal Democrats now need to show that their word on these and other issues is backed up by actions. With seventy-two MPs in Parliament, they will get the publicity and airtime that they have so longed for to achieve these goals. They need to make best use of it. Now they have the opportunity to carve a distinctive political identity which the wider public understands.

The downside of their 2024 success is that is that the Liberal Democrats now have fewer and much harder offensive opportunities. They are now second in only twenty-seven seats, ten of which are Conservative-held and if they could not be won in 2024 they might be an impossible task thereafter. Offensively, the temptation will be to target Labour seats, given it is easier for them to position themselves against the incumbent government. However, this will require intensive local rebuilds to win back credibility and a shift in strategy where the goal is about driving up vote share as much as targeting specific seats. The likelihood is that the next election will be about the Liberal Democrats defending the gains from 2024. This arguably matters for Labour as much as the Liberal Democrats. Keeping the Conservatives at bay in the seventy-two Liberal Democrat seats makes another Labour administration more likely. On the Liberal Democrat side, retaining good relations with Labour and distinguishing themselves enough to retain and gain tactical support from Labour supporters should be the aim. For Labour, it will be in their interest to ensure that the Liberal Democrats can claim some wins so they can sell to voters that trusted them this time that voting Liberal Democrat can make a difference. How a non-aggression pact develops (or not) may be the key to the next election. Notwithstanding this, history tells us (leaving aside the self-infliction of going into coalition) that when the Liberal Democrats win a parliamentary seat, they are difficult to budge. In 2024 the Liberal Democrats ceased to be a backmarker and once again became a frontrunner. They are unlikely to let other parties pass them by without a fight.

References

Cutts, D., and Russell, A. (2020) 'Relevant Again but Still Unpopular? The Liberal Democrats' 2019 Election Campaign', in: J. Tonge, C. L. Bandeira, and S. Wilks-Hegg (eds) *Britain Votes 2019*. Oxford: Oxford University Press.

Cutts, D., Russell, A., and Townsley, J. H. (2023) *The Liberal Democrats: From Hope to Despair to Where*. Manchester: Manchester University Press.

The Guardian (2024) 'Horizon Scandal: Ed Davey Sorry He 'Did Not See Through the Post Office Lies'', https://www.theguardian.com/uk-news/2024/feb/01/ed-davey-apologises-for-his-role-in-post-office-horizon-scandal, accessed 7 Aug. 2024.

YouGov (2024a) 'Final YouGov MRP Shows Labour on Course for Historic Election Victory', https://yougov.co.uk/politics/articles/49950-final-yougov-mrp-shows-labour-on-course-for-historic-election-victory, accessed 10 Aug. 2024.

YouGov (2024b) 'General Election 2024: What Are the Most Important Issues for Voters?', https://yougov.co.uk/politics/articles/49594-general-election-2024-what-are-the-most-important-issues-for-voters, accessed 15 Jul. 2024.

YouGov (2024c) 'How Well Did Ed Davey's Campaign Go Down', https://yougov.co.uk/politics/articles/49958-how-well-did-ed-daveys-campaign-go-down, accessed 8 Aug. 2024.

YouGov (2024d) 'How Britain Voted in the 2024 General Election', https://yougov.co.uk/politics/articles/49978-how-britain-voted-in-the-2024-general-election, accessed 9 Aug. 2024.

Voices from the edge make breakthrough in British politics: The Greens, Reform UK, and independents

Lynn Bennie*, and Anders Widfeldt

Politics and International Relations, School of Social Science, University of Aberdeen, Dunbar Street, Aberdeen, AB24 3QY, UK

*Correspondence: l.bennie@abdn.ac.uk

The General Election of 2024 saw a significant breakthrough for smaller parties. During the campaign, the political commentator Laura Kuenssberg (2024) observed that 'voices from the edge' were 'making big parties nervous'. In the end, the two main parties received less than 60% of the vote for the first time since universal suffrage, and the spread of parliamentary seats amongst other parties was broader than ever before. Six independents, five Reform UK candidates and four Greens became MPs, contributing to this parliamentary diversity. Nigel Farage became an MP at the eighth attempt, the Greens quadrupled their seats, and the Labour party's perceived position on the Israel-Hamas conflict cost it a handful of seats to independents. The 2015 General Election saw a rise in the number of votes going to parties other than Conservative or Labour, but support for the two main parties rallied thereafter. In 2024, the pendulum of support again swung away from the big two, to an even greater extent.

In the theoretical literature there is debate over what constitutes a small party, and the critical factors which aid such a party's development (Copus et al., 2009). The Greens and Reform UK are now the biggest of the small parties in Britain, based on their electoral performance and influence on the political agenda. In this contribution, we aim to explain the small party breakthrough of 2024 and assess where this leaves British politics. The analysis is centred on the Greens and Reform UK, but we also consider the independents elected. We address the ideological and policy character of the Greens and Reform UK and examine why the General Election of 2024 proved successful for these parties. We argue that the single-member plurality electoral system is a major obstacle to further progress in Britain's state-wide parliamentary arena, but that comparative experiences of similar parties across Europe suggest a process of 'normalisation' may be taking place, whereby green and radical right parties become regular actors in modern parliamentary systems.

1. What kind of parties are the Greens and Reform UK?

The Greens and Reform UK are very different parties. The Greens were founded in England in 1973, the first European green party to stand in a national election, but they existed on the periphery of politics for decades. Other European states presented green parties with much more favourable opportunities to influence and enter governments (Müller-Rommel, and Poguntke 2002). The Greens in Scotland and Northern Ireland became organisationally separate in 1990 but maintained strong links with the Green Party of England and Wales (GPEW). The internal organisation broadly reflects the party's ideals of decentralisation and democracy. The membership is important in the party's practice and identity, not least because members provide income. At the same time, members tend not to be very active (Bennie, Mitchell, and Johns 2024), and the need for conventional leadership is now accepted. The GPEW has had formal leaders since 2008, previously 'speakers' and 'conveners', who perform public-facing roles. Other key ideas and policies revolve around environmental sustainability, challenging traditional conceptions of economic growth. The Greens have become more clearly left of centre with a focus on social justice, equality and radical democracy. This is combined with a socially liberal outlook involving the protection of minority rights. The party has moved beyond suggestions that it is 'single-issue', concerned only about the environment, although it arguably remains a 'niche' party (Dennison 2020).

When Caroline Lucas won the seat of Brighton Pavilion in 2010, becoming the party's first MP, the Greens were becoming more widely *perceived* as a party of the left. A series of co-leaders took the party firmly in the direction of anti-austerity and pro-EU politics. The 2024 manifesto was confirmation of the party's green-red-liberal character, with promises to tax and spend to tackle poverty and declining public services, and to make rapid progress on renewable energy (Green Party 2024). Specific policies included reaching net zero by 2040, 'phasing-out' nuclear energy, a wealth tax, nationalisation of rail and energy companies, banning domestic flights for journeys that would take under three hours by train, the removal of market structures from the NHS and legislation to allow assisted dying.

Reform UK can be treated as successor to the UK Independence Party (UKIP), even though the latter still exists. UKIP, formed in 1993, was often dismissed as a single-issue anti-EU party, but soon developed a range of policies which could be likened to EU- and immigration-critical parties elsewhere in Europe (Widfeldt and Brandenburg 2018). Internal divisions culminated in 2019 when Nigel Farage and his supporters left to form the Brexit party, renamed Reform UK in 2021. The party became a 'guard dog' against re-entry into the EU, also focussing on issues such as immigration, climate scepticism and resistance to what it views as 'woke' policies on, for example, transgender rights. The organisation of Reform UK is distinct from other parties. On its formation the Brexit party registered as a limited company, a status it retained when the party name was changed in 2021. Nigel Farage owned 53% of the shares. It was possible to register with the party as a supporter or member, but there was little membership influence (Dewsnip 2024).

The classification of Reform UK is a somewhat delicate issue. In March 2024 the then leader Richard Tice forced the BBC into an apology for referring to the party as 'far right'. Such epithets, claimed Tice, are 'defamatory' and 'libellous' (Quinn and Dodd 2024). However, far right can be used as an umbrella term, with extreme right and radical right as its two main subsets. The former are anti-democratic, while the latter work within parliamentary democracy (Mudde 2019). Reform UK fits into a broader European family of radical right parties working within democratic structures.

In the 2024 General Election manifesto, titled 'Our Contract with You', Reform UK wanted to reduce 'nonessential immigration' to zero and raise the National Insurance rate to 20% for foreign workers (Reform UK 2024a). Pledges also included zero tolerance policing and mandatory life sentences for repeated serious offences. The manifesto contained economic reforms which could be summarised as right-leaning, including tax cuts and private alternatives to the NHS. There were populist claims of corruption in government and 'an out-of-touch, London-centric elite'.

2. Electoral impact pre-2024

The Greens first made their presence known in British politics by winning nearly 15% of the vote in the 1989 European parliamentary elections. From 1999, when a form of proportional representation was introduced, the Greens began to win seats in the European Parliament. This contrasts with their difficulty penetrating the Westminster system. In general elections, the Greens were a very minor party for much of their existence (Table 6.1). The single-member plurality voting system makes votes for challenger parties 'wasted' in most constituencies, which largely explains why the Greens were less successful than many of their European counterparts. However, with increased professionalisation, targeting of campaign resources to build on local support and a high-profile candidate, Caroline Lucas

Table 6.1. Votes and seats for the Greens in general and EU elections 1974–2024

General elections UK

	Votes	Vote %	Seats	Seat %
1974 (F)	4,576	0.0	0	–
1974 (O)	1,996	0.0	0	–
1979	39,918	0.1	0	–
1983	54,299	0.2	0	–
1987	89,753	0.3	0	–
1992	170,047	0.5	0	–
1997	63,991	0.2	0	–
2001	166,477	0.6	0	–
2005	283,414	1.0	0	–
2010	285,612	1.0	1	0.2
2015	1,157,630	3.8	1	0.2
2017	525,666	1.6	1	0.2
2019	865,707	2.7	1	0.2
2024	1,944, 501	6.7	4	0.6

European parliament elections UK

	Votes	Vote %	Seats	Seat %
1979	17,953	0.1	0	-
1984	73,025	0.5	0	-
1989	2,299,287	14.5	0	-
1994	494,561	3.1	0	-
1999	625,378	5.8	2	2.4
2004	1,033,093	6.1	2	2.6
2009	1,319,509	8.4	2	2.8
2014	1,255,573	7.7	3	4.1
2019	2,023,380	12.7	7	9.6

Note: The party was founded as 'People', changed its name to the Ecology Party in 1975 and to the Green Party in 1985. Figures are UK-wide.
Source: House of Commons Library (https://commonslibrary.parliament.uk/research-briefings/).

took Brighton Pavilion from Labour in 2010. In 2015, the Greens received more than 1 million votes in a general election for the first time.

When competing in elections based on proportional representation, the Greens have made more of an impact, sometimes surpassing Pedersen's (1982) 'threshold of relevance'. Greens in Scotland, for example, have had continuous representation in the Scottish Parliament, and entered a cooperation agreement with the SNP (2021–4), co-leaders Patrick Harvie and Lorna Slater serving as government ministers. In Wales, the Greens have yet to enter the devolved parliament, but in the London Assembly they have had two or three seats since the first election in 2000.

Green influence on local government in England has steadily grown, even though councillors are elected via first-past-the-post. Local government elections in May 2024 saw 812 Green councillors elected, a rise of seventy-four, and Greens became the biggest party on Bristol City Council. As of 2024, the Greens have entered over thirty council coalitions. Before the 2024 General Election, then, the party had some local and regional relevance, but still only one representative in the House of Commons.

Similarly, the UK has not been fertile ground for radical right parties. As seen in Table 6.2, UKIP entered the EU Parliament in 1999, and its vote and seat share then grew. Ironically, the party benefited from the proportional system used in EU elections. UKIP was the biggest UK party in the 2014 election to the EU Parliament, a feat repeated by the Brexit party in 2019. Like the Greens, though,

Table 6.2. Votes and seats for UKIP and successor parties in general and EU elections 1999-2024

General elections UK

	Party	Votes	Vote %	Seats	Seat %
2001	UKIP	390,575	1.5	0	0
2005	UKIP	605,173	2.2	0	0
2010	UKIP	919,486	3.1	0	0
2015	UKIP	3,881,099	12.5	1	0.2
2017	UKIP	594,068	1.0	0	0
2019	Brexit Party	644,257	2.0	0	0
2024	Reform UK	4,117,610	14.3	5	0.8

European parliament elections UK

	Party	Votes	Vote %	Seats	Seat %
1999	UKIP	696,057	6.3	2	2.4
2004	UKIP	2,660,768	16.2	12	16.0
2009	UKIP	2,498,226	16.5	13	18.1
2014	UKIP	4,352,051	27.5	24	32.3
2019	Brexit Party	5,248,533	31.6	29	39.7

Note: Figures are UK-wide.
Source: House of Commons Library (https://commonslibrary.parliament.uk/research-briefings/).

UKIP and successor parties have found it difficult to establish themselves in the House of Commons. UKIP never got more than one seat in a general election (in 2015, plus two by-election victories in 2014).

The performance of UKIP and successor parties in devolved institutions has been patchy. UKIP won two seats in elections to the London Assembly in 2004 and 2016, while Reform UK got one in 2024. In the Welsh Assembly, UKIP won seven seats in 2016, but neither it nor Reform UK got any seats in 2021. Scotland has been a difficult hunting ground. UKIP did get one Scottish seat in the 2014 EU election, but neither UKIP nor Brexit/Reform UK have so far been represented in the Scottish Parliament. On local councils, UKIP had some success, with over 400 councillors in 2016. In late 2024, Reform UK had forty-three councillors.

3. General Election 2024: polls, candidates and campaigns

A year before the general election, opinion polls suggested the Greens and Reform UK were oscillating around 5 and 6% in voting intentions, and both were well behind the Liberal Democrats. Some polls put the Greens slightly ahead of Reform UK. The Greens' poll standing remained stable during the campaign (Fig. 6.1). Reform UK, meanwhile, saw their support climb steadily from the end of 2023, overtaking the Liberal Democrats in early 2024. A dip in May was followed by a surge in early June when Nigel Farage took over the party leadership and decided to stand in the constituency of Clacton (held by UKIP 2014–7). From then support for the party grew quickly, the average reaching 17% by the end of June. During the same period, support for the Conservatives and Labour declined. Multilevel regression and post-stratification poll (MRP) polls suggested an average seat projection of two (ranging between zero and four) for the Greens; and an average of three (ranging between zero and seven) for Reform UK (Bunting 2025).

In 2017 and 2019, the Greens attempted cooperation with other progressive parties, standing down some candidates. In 2024, they had a dual strategy, giving all electors the opportunity to vote Green coupled with a targeting of resources in a small number of constituencies deemed winnable. The GPEW fielded 574 candidates, covering all but one constituency in England and Wales; the Scottish Greens put forward forty-three candidates across Scotland's fifty-seven constituencies. More than four in ten (44%) of Green candidates were female, compared to 16% for Reform UK (Cracknell and Baker 2024: 39).

The Brexit party presented 275 candidates in 2019, desisting in constituencies where its votes could threaten the Conservatives, whose main campaign pledge was to 'Get Brexit Done'. The Reform UK approach in 2024 was different, Richard Tice declaring his intention to 'obliterate' the Conservatives. The party put forward candidates in 609, or 96%, of the 632 constituencies in Great Britain, including all seats in Scotland. This was fewer than the 624 candidates fielded by UKIP in 2015.

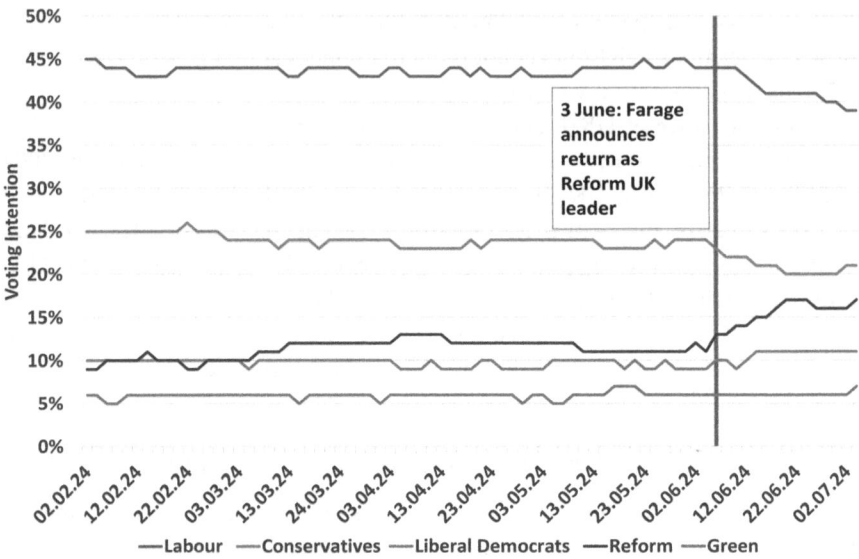

Figure 6.1. Voting intentions in six months before general election
Source: Poll of polls BBC News (https://www.bbc.co.uk/news/articles/cyxx9vxwjk9o).

The candidate selection process appeared rushed, with inadequate vetting in at least some cases. There were several reports about Reform UK candidates who had problematical backgrounds or had made inappropriate comments. Two of the party's candidates stood down in protest against what they saw as irresponsible conduct by others in the party. Five days before the election, the party disowned three of its candidates for allegedly racist or offensive comments.

High-profile Reform UK candidates included Lee Anderson, a former Labour councillor and Conservative MP. In early 2024 he refused to apologise for saying that Islamists had 'got control' of London and its Mayor Sadiq Khan. He was suspended from the Conservative whip, and the following month defected to Reform UK, becoming the party's first MP. Another relatively well-known name was Richard Tice, who had been forced to hand over the leadership to Nigel Farage a month before the election. A former Conservative and Leave campaigner, and part owner of the party as a limited company, Tice had a key role in the campaign, although he played second fiddle to Farage. The most important candidate was of course Farage, arguably one of the best-known British politicians within as well as outside the UK. He gave the party's campaign momentum, as shown in the poll ratings.

Donations to Reform UK increased dramatically after Farage declared his candidacy and return as leader. According to media reports the party raised £1.5

million in less than two weeks after Farage's announcement, and there was a surge in supporter registrations (Quinn and Dodd 2024). The Greens, meanwhile, received few large donations, instead relying on crowd funding and small individual donations. The total sum of donations to the Greens during the campaign was tiny compared to that of Reform UK (Electoral Commission 2024). Membership of the Greens increased in the run-up to the election, but not dramatically.

The campaigns run by the two parties emphasised contrasting themes. The Green campaign, on the ground and digitally, focussed on the theme of 'Real Hope, Real Change', promoting a progressive, left-wing agenda. The Greens' co-leaders, Carla Denyer and Adrian Ramsay, were the main figureheads, certainly in the national campaign. Denyer took part on behalf of the Greens in the BBC and ITV seven-party election debates, on 7th June and 13th June respectively. The Greens were critical of the two main parties' 'timid' approach on climate policy, as well as their position on the conflict in Gaza. They aligned with the SNP and Plaid Cymru on other issues, stressing the benefits of immigration, and advocating investment in public services and greater equality.

This positioning was in stark contrast to Nigel Farage who fronted for Reform UK in both debates. He talked of a 'population crisis', the necessity of border control, the benefits of a low-tax economy and expressed scepticism about the climate agenda. The Conservative party was also restrictive on immigration, but was outflanked by Reform UK, who accused the Conservatives as well as Labour of inability and unwillingness to deliver reduced immigration. In the BBC debate, Farage employed a populist rhetoric about 'uncomfortable truths', urging voters to 'join the revolt'. The debates demonstrated that the Greens and Reform UK are, to a significant degree, ideological polar opposites.

4. General Election results

The 2024 General Election made history in several ways. One of them was the disproportionality between votes and seats. The main beneficiary was the Labour party, winning an overwhelming majority of seats despite receiving only one-third of the popular vote. The reverse of Labour overrepresentation was the underrepresentation of outsider challenger parties. The Greens attracted over 1.9 million GB votes, 6.9%, and won four seats, representing 0.6% of all 632 seats in England, Scotland and Wales. The underrepresentation of Reform UK was even more striking, with 4.1 million votes, 14.7% of GB votes, and five seats (0.8%). This illustrates that the House of Commons is something of a closed shop for challenger parties (Thompson 2020). Nevertheless, the 2024 election was a great success for both the Greens and Reform UK, each winning more seats and votes in a general election than ever before.

The Greens more than doubled their vote, adding a million votes to their 2019 tally. Even more satisfying for the party, their four MPs were elected in exactly those constituencies identified as key target seats. This involved long-term planning and concentration of campaign resources in areas where the party had a record of local council success, and energetic local campaigns, as well as variation in local messaging, with more emphasis on the natural environment, community and rural issues in the seats where they were challenging the Conservatives. In addition to holding the seat of Brighton Pavilion (with a new candidate) the party took one seat from Labour and two from the Conservatives (Table 6.3). In the seats they gained from the Conservatives, Green support jumped from single figures to over 40%, while the Conservative vote was halved. In both seats 16% of the votes went to Reform UK, which split the right of centre vote and aided the Greens. The Green co-leaders became MPs, as did former co-leader Siân Berry and Ellie Chowns who was previously a Green MEP and councillor. Turnout in these seats was well above the national average.

Reform UK employed a much less targeted strategy, their aim appearing to be to spread support widely and to hurt the other parties, particularly the Conservatives. A lot of attention was focused on Farage's chosen constituency of Clacton, but this was probably more a consequence of his status as a media celebrity than a

Table 6.3. Seats won by the Greens and Reform UK at the 2024 General Election

Party	Constituency	Winning candidate	Vote share (%)	Majority	Result	2nd place
Green	Brighton Pavilion	Siân Berry	55.0	14,290	Green hold	Labour
	Bristol Central	Carla Denyer	56.0	10,407	Gain from Labour	Labour
	North Herefordshire	Ellie Chowns	43.2	5,894	Gain from Con	Conservative
	Waveney Valley	Adrian Ramsay	41.7	5,594	Gain from Con	Conservative
Reform UK	Ashfield	Lee Anderson	42.8	5,508	Gain from Con	Labour
	Boston and Skegness	Richard Tice	38.4	2,010	Gain from Con	Conservative
	Clacton	Nigel Farage	46.2	8,405	Gain from Con	Conservative
	Great Yarmouth	Rupert Lowe	35.3	1,426	Gain from Con	Labour
	South Basildon and East Thurrock	James McMurdock	30.8	98	Gain from Con	Labour

Source: Cracknell and Baker (2024: 71).

pre-planned allocation of resources. If there was a strategy, it seemed to be that the attention paid to Farage would stretch far beyond Clacton, and so it proved. The five seats won was a case of serious underrepresentation, but the 4.1 million votes indicated a potential to hurt the main parties. The Reform UK seats were all gains from the Conservatives, but in three cases Labour finished second. As noted by Pippa Norris (2024), the all-out strategy by Reform UK split right-wing support by taking Conservative votes. It is notable that all successful Reform UK candidates were men, compared to one of the Greens'.

The number of a party's lost deposits is an indicator of the extent of support and whether it is concentrated. In 2024, Green candidates lost over 40% of election deposits (at a cost of £130,000), while Reform UK lost only 5% (£16,000). This reflects a widespread, relatively high level of support for Reform UK—indeed, they received half a million more votes than the Liberal Democrats—and underlines the disproportionality of the result.

A closer look at the regional distribution of the parties' votes (Fig. 6.2) reveals that Greens registered 7.3% of the vote in England, compared with 4.7% in Wales, 3.8% in Scotland and 1.1% in Northern Ireland. The party's regional performance suggests broadly even support across England, with seats won in the South East, South West, West Midlands and East of England. A standout feature of Fig. 6.2 is how well the party performed in the London area, attracting one in ten voters, but without bearing fruit in terms of seats. The geographical character of Green

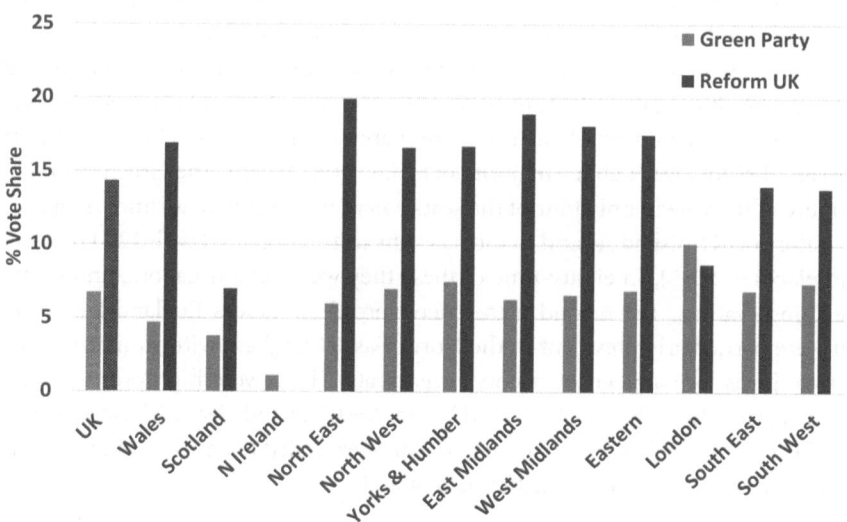

Figure 6.2. Greens and Reform UK in the countries and regions of the UK (% vote)
Source: Cracknell and Baker (2024), p.18-21.

support now appears rather varied, maintaining strength in big cities, many with large numbers of students and young professionals, but making inroads in formerly Conservative, small-town and countryside areas.

Support for Reform UK varied between 8.7% (London) and 19.9 % (North East). London, however, was an outlier. Elsewhere in England the lowest share of the vote was 13.8% in the South West, and the party was well supported in the Home Counties surrounding the capital. Another area of relative weakness was Scotland, where Reform UK received 7% of the vote, compared with over 15% in England and 17% in Wales. Even in Scotland, however, the result was an improvement on previous general election performances, which may suggest future potential. The party recorded 14.6% of the vote in Aberdeenshire North and Moray East, enabling the SNP to depose the Scottish Conservative leader at the time. The overall distribution of Reform UK support could be said to reflect the all-out campaign strategy, with support quite evenly spread across most of England and Wales, which is a key explanation for why the party's nearly 15% of the vote only brought five seats. The geographical profile of those seats could somewhat crudely be summarized as what Heath et al. (2024) call "'left behind' places", including three east coast seaside resorts and a Nottinghamshire former mining seat.

An interesting feature of the election was the distribution of second places. In 2019, the Greens finished second in one seat; in 2024, this figure rose to forty, and in all but one of these they were second to Labour. The party's vote share increased across Britain, but especially in England. The seats where the Greens finished second reflect this pattern. Nearly half—eighteen—were in London. Others were spread across England, one was in Wales but none in Scotland. This might suggest that the Greens are in a good position to challenge for Labour seats next time, although Labour majorities in these seats were sizeable. The closest second place positions for the Greens were Huddersfield in Yorkshire (Labour majority of 4,533 = 11.3% point gap) and Bristol East (Labour majority of 6,606 = 14.3% gap). The Greens won 25% or more of the vote in only four of the seats where they finished as runners-up.

Reform UK finished second in ninety-eight seats (compared with 120 UKIP second places in 2015). In eighty-nine of these they were behind Labour, and in nine the Conservatives. The second places were spread out across England and Wales, but were particularly prevalent in the North East of England with runner-up spots in two-thirds, or eighteen of twenty-seven seats. There were high proportions of second places also in Wales (41%), and North West England (38%). These races were not always close. In fifty-eight cases the distance exceeded twenty percentage points. There were no second place finishes in Scotland.

5. The social and issue profile of Green and Reform UK voters

Previous work has developed a detailed picture of green and radical right voters in the UK and elsewhere (van Haute 2016; Arzheimer 2017). This leads us to expect that the

Table 6.4. Socio-demographic profile of voters (%)

	Con	Lab	Lib Dem	Green	Reform UK	All voters
Age 18-35	7.8	27.6	26.6	**40.6**	14.5	21.7
Age 36-55	27.6	40.9	37.6	**38.8**	36.0	36.3
Age over 55	64.6	31.5	35.9	**20.6**	49.5	42.1
Men	47.3	49.2	45.7	**43.8**	57.7	49.0
Women	52.7	50.8	54.3	**56.2**	42.3	51.0
University qualification	41.8	54.6	56.1	**58.2**	32.5	44.3
Gross annual household income £50,000 or above	25.4	30.3	31.7	**26.1**	21.2	26.7
Not religious	37.9	61.6	60.2	**69.1**	51.6	54.1
Upper middle class	17.6	19.2	21.5	**17.0**	13.4	17.7
Middle/lower middle class	68.5	64.9	63.7	**64.4**	64.5	65.5
Routine occupations	13.9	15.9	14.7	**18.7**	22.1	16.7
Private sector employment	63.7	51.5	53.7	**50.7**	66.3	56.3
Public sector employment	30.4	41.0	36.3	**34.3**	27.6	35.6
Third/voluntary sector employment	5.9	7.5	9.9	**15.0**	6.1	8.1

Source: British Election Study, wave 29, fielded 5–19 July 2024. For documentation, see BES 2024.

two parties are fishing for votes in dissimilar sociodemographic pools. By and large this is supported by our analysis of British Election Study data, reported in Table 6.4. The composition of Green voters contains few surprises. The party is clearly overrepresented in the youngest (18–35) age group. The party's electorate is disproportionately female, and it has the highest proportion of university graduates of all parties. The proportion with a household annual income of over £50,000 is 26%, below those of both Labour and the Liberal Democrats, which reflects the comparatively young age profile. Green voters appear the least religious, they are dominated by middle to lower class occupations and are the most likely to be third sector employees.

The profile of Reform UK voters is almost a mirror image. The age breakdown resembles that of the Conservatives, with older voters overrepresented. In other aspects, Reform UK stands out from all other parties by being disproportionately male, having the lowest proportion of university graduates, the lowest proportion earning £50,000 a year or more and the highest proportion of routine occupations and privately employed. These characteristics closely resemble erstwhile UKIP voters, suggesting that Reform is not broadening its vote base but may be building a stable, loyal following (Heath et al., 2024).

As for previous voting behaviour, the BES data (not reported in table) indicate that 77% of Reform UK voters had voted Conservative, and 8% for the Brexit party, in 2019. Amongst Greens, previous voting patterns were more diverse—52% voted Labour last time, 19% Green, 12% Conservative and 9% Liberal Democrat.

In Table 6.5, we report issue saliency among party voters. This is based on an open-ended question in the British Election Study, where respondents are asked to indicate one issue they consider the most important facing the country. Answers were coded into fifty categories, and then merged into the twelve categories reported in the table (BES 2024). The most frequently cited issues by Green voters were the economy and the environment, the latter including climate and sustainability. Green voters are the most likely of all to identify inequality as the most important issue.

For Reform UK voters, the dominant issue was immigration, mentioned by 58%. Immigration was a concern also among Conservative voters, but the percentage of thirty-two was much lower than that of Reform UK. The second-most cited issue among Reform UK voters was the economy, on 19%. This is a diverse category, covering a wide range of subcategories. For most parties, including Reform UK and the Greens, the main concern within this category was cost of living, followed by inflation and the economy in general (not reported in table). Former Reform UK profile issues, such as Europe and terrorism, appeared to have limited saliency among the party's voters in 2024.

Table 6.5. Most important issue facing the country among party voters (%)

	Con	**Lab**	**Lib Dem**	**Green**	**Reform UK**	**All voters**
Europe	0.4	1.8	2.5	**1.1**	**0.1**	1.3
Immigration & asylum	32.3	5.0	5.5	**3.6**	**58.4**	20.1
Economy	33.2	49.2	43.7	**34.3**	**18.9**	38.3
Health	10.6	18.6	18.3	**12.7**	**5.5**	13.7
Terrorism	0.2	0.1	0.2	**0.1**	**0.3**	0.2
Inequality	1.3	7.3	6.0	**9.9**	**1.8**	5.0
Environment	2.3	7.7	10.6	**24.5**	**0.9**	6.9
Austerity/spending	1.3	2.4	2.5	**3.0**	**0.8**	1.9
Negativity	9.2	2.3	4.0	**3.1**	**6.5**	5.2
Other lib-auth	7.5	4.2	4.8	**5.7**	**5.3**	5.6
Other left-right	0.1	0.3	0.2	**1.3**	**0.4**	0.3
Other	1.6	1.1	1.5	**0.7**	**1.1**	1.4
Total	100.0	100.0	100.0	**100.0**	**100.0**	100.0
N	5175	7361	2684	**1569**	**3328**	21832

Source: British Election Study, wave 29. For documentation, see BES 2024.
Notes: Other lib-auth = other issues on which voters primarily divide on a libertarian/authoritarian axis. Other left-right = other issues on which voters primarily divide on a left-right axis.

The social and attitudinal profile of Green and Reform UK voters align closely with what we know from comparative research. Green voters are younger, more highly educated, liberal and left-leaning. Reform UK voters tend to be older, more male, without higher education qualifications and with immigration as the most prioritised issue. The latter aspect is particularly marked in the context of the 2024 General Election, given that Brexit has occurred. Although the party tries to present a comprehensive policy package, its voters appear primarily motivated by immigration (see also Heath et al., 2024).

6. Independents

The total number of candidates in this election was unprecedented. The Greens and Reform UK were two of five Britain-wide parties to present over 600 candidates. In addition, however, there exists a large universe of other parties and independents. Nearly 100 organisations were registered as parties to stand in the election. A total of 518 candidates came from parties other than Labour, Conservative, Liberal Democrat, SNP, Plaid Cymru, Reform UK or Green; of these, 459 were independent candidates, more than double the number in 2019 (Cracknell and Baker 2024: 10). Even more significantly, six independents became MPs, the highest number in post-1945 elections (Table 6.6).

Jeremy Corbyn won Islington North easily. Having served as a Labour MP there for forty years, he was suspended in 2020 and stood as an independent after being refused readmission. In Northern Ireland, Alex Easton won North Down as an independent, having left the Democratic Unionist Party (DUP) in 2021. The other four independent MPs were elected as part of a movement against the Labour party's position on the conflict between Israel and Hamas in Gaza. They won in seats with a high concentration of Muslim voters. A high-profile loss for Labour was Jonathan Ashworth in Leicester South. Other Labour MPs, such as Wes Streeting who would become Health Secretary, defeated independent challengers by narrow margins. The loosening of ties between Muslim voters and Labour was a prominent story to emerge from this election, although this process had begun earlier. As in 2019, Labour won most seats with large Muslim populations, but there was a noticeable decline in support for the party in these communities.

George Galloway, a long-term pro-Palestinian campaigner, can be regarded as part of this Israel-critical network. Previously an MP for the Labour and, later, Respect parties, his Workers Party of Britain stood more than 150 candidates in the election. It received 210,252 votes, 0.73% overall, but got more than 20% in some ethnically diverse constituencies (for example, 29.3% in Birmingham Yardley which has a large Muslim population). The party was runner-up in three seats, including Rochdale which Galloway had won in a by-election in February 2024, but lost to Labour in the general election.

Table 6.6. Seats won by independents in the 2024 General Election

Constituency	Winning candidate	Vote share (%)	Majority	Result	2nd place
Birmingham Perry Barr	Ayoub Khan	35.5	507	Gain from Labour	Labour
Blackburn	Adnan Hussain	27.0	132	Gain from Labour	Labour
Dewsbury and Batley	Iqbal Mohamed	41.1	6,934	Gain from Labour	Labour
Islington North	Jeremy Corbyn	49.2	7,247	Gain from Labour	Labour
Leicester South	Shockat Adam	35.2	979	Gain from Labour	Labour
North Down	Alex Easton	48.3	7,305	Gain from Alliance	Alliance

Source: Cracknell and Baker (2024: 84).

7. Conclusion: can the small parties build on this success?

A story which emerges from this election is that the underrepresentation of smaller parties was maintained. British general elections are essentially rigged against these parties. Nevertheless, the Greens and Reform UK—two very different parties—experienced simultaneous success. Four seats for the Greens and five for Reform UK represented a breakthrough. In the context of declining support for the major parties, and in the face of issues which mainstream politicians seem unable or unwilling to grapple with, the Greens and Reform UK are likely to remain significant. The parliamentary impact of these increases should not be overstated, as small parties face considerable parliamentary obstacles (Thompson 2020). However, the 2024 breakthrough for the Greens and Reform UK enhances the possibilities for both parties to make their voice heard in debates and in the work of the parliament. Previous research has shown that parliamentary presence can help a small party to grow (Dinas et al., 2015).

A question that remains is whether the parties are well-placed organisationally to be able to build on this success. In the case of the Greens, they have a healthy membership of close to 60,000, and an organisational structure which has been professionalised and involves a UK-wide network of local parties. The party has media-savvy leadership and clear issues driving support, especially amongst the young. However, the Greens find it difficult to compete with the larger parties financially and, as green parties elsewhere know only too well, electors can be fickle. Success is often followed by a downturn.

As for Reform UK, there are more question-marks about organisational durability. The structure of the party changed when a new constitution was adopted at the party conference in September 2024. A more conventional form of membership and more internal democracy was introduced. The party leader will be directly elected by the annual conference, and motions of no confidence against the leader are possible. There will be a party board with eight voting members, although only three are directly elected by the conference (Reform UK 2024b). These changes appear to involve democratisation. Nigel Farage also announced that he would give up his shares in the party. The party remains a limited company but is attempting to broaden its organisational presence. Towards the end of 2024 it claimed to have branches in around 300 constituencies, and a membership of 100,000, more than the Greens or SNP (Pidd and Ktena 2024). The party has some key strengths, notably a popular leader and a large amount of money received in donations. To maintain these advantages, and to build-up more permanent organisational strength across the country, may prove difficult. Nigel Farage is idolised by his party's followers, but his leadership is more focused on punditry and performance politics than mundane party work. The challenge for Reform UK is to create a more robust party organisation, with an active and united membership.

A final reflection is that the performance of these parties highlights a paradox in British politics. Despite having left the EU, and an election campaign focused on a post-Brexit future, the British party system moved closer to a European model, where green and radical right parties are permanent fixtures. There are countries without a strong green party, but in these countries the green agenda is upheld by other parties, usually the radical left. Radical right parties exist in almost every EU and EEA country. Even though the British Greens and Reform UK are still punished by the electoral system, their recent performance suggests that they may have a more successful future. Following the election, Vernon Bogdanor (2024) noted that the electoral system continues to make the UK an outlier; but, he asked, 'for how long?'.

References

Arzheimer, K. (2017) 'Electoral Sociology – Who Votes for the Extreme Right and Why – and When?' in: C. Mudde (ed.) *The Populist Radical Right: A Reader*, pp. 277–90. Abingdon and NY: Routledge.

Bennie, L., Mitchell, J. and Johns, R. (2024) *Surges in Party Membership: The SNP and Scottish Greens After the Independence Referendum*. London: Routledge.

BES (2024) *British Election Study 2014-2024*. Combined Waves 1-29 Internet Panel Codebook, https://www.britishelectionstudy.com/data-object/wave-29-of-the-2014-2024-british-election-study-internet-panel/, accessed 5 Aug. 2025.

Bogdanor, V. (2024) 'Whisper it, but the election shows that Britain is fast turning French', *The Telegraph*, 7 July 2024, https://www.telegraph.co.uk/news/2024/07/07/election-shows-that-britain-is-fast-turning-french/, accessed 5 Aug. 2025.

Bunting, H. (2025) 'The Results: How Britain Voted in 2024', in: A. Clark, L. Thompson and S. Wilks-Heeg (eds.) *Britain Votes: The 2024 General Election*. Oxford: Oxford University Press.

Copus, C. et al. (2009) 'Minor Party and Independent Politics beyond the Mainstream: Fluctuating Fortunes but a Permanent Presence', *Parliamentary Affairs*, 62: 4–18.

Cracknell, R. and Baker, C. (2024) *General Election 2024 Results*, House of Commons Library, 18 July 2024, Briefing Paper Number 10009, https://commonslibrary.parliament.uk/research-briefings/cbp-10009/, accessed 5 Aug. 2025.

Dennison, J. (2020) 'How Niche Parties React to Losing Their Niche: The Cases of the Brexit Party, the Green Party and the Change UK', *Parliamentary Affairs*, 73: 125–41.

Dewsnip, K. (2024) "How to Constitute a Political Party", Blog post, The Constitutional Society, 22 October 2024, https://consoc.org.uk/how-to-constitute-a-political-party/, accessed 5 Aug. 2025.

Dinas, E., Riera, P. and Roussias, N. (2015) 'Staying in the First League: Parliamentary Representation and the Electoral Success of Small Parties', *Political Science Research and Methods*, 3: 187–204.

Electoral Commission (2024) 'Political parties accept £55.5m in donations in second quarter of 2024', https://www.electoralcommission.org.uk/media-centre/political-parties-accept-ps555m-donations-second-quarter-2024, accessed 5 Aug. 2025.

Green Party (2024) 'Real Hope, Real Change: Manifesto for a Fairer, Greener Country', General Election Manifesto, https://greenparty.org.uk/about/our-manifesto/2024-manifesto-downloads/, accessed 5 Aug. 2025.

Heath, O. et al. (2024) 'The 2024 General Election and the Rise of Reform UK', *The Political Quarterly*, 96: 91–101.

Kuenssberg, L. (2024) 'Unfathomable errors and "cinnamon bun" strategy: Political end-of-term report cards', *BBC News* online, 24 July: https://www.bbc.co.uk/news/articles/cpwd65nwq5yo, accessed 5 Aug. 2025.

Mudde, C. (2019) *The Far Right Today*. Cambridge: Polity Press.

Müller-Rommel, F. and Poguntke, T. (2002) (eds.) *Green Parties in National Governments*. London: Frank Cass.

Norris, P. (2024) 'How Nigel Farage opened the door to No. 10 for Keir Starmer' in: D. Jackson et al. (eds) *UK General Election Analysis 2024: Media, Voters and the Campaign*. Bournemouth: Centre for Comparative Politics and Media Research (Bournemouth University): 12-3, https://eprints.bournemouth.ac.uk/40269/1/UKElectionAnalysis2024_Jackson-et_al_v1-COMPRESSED.pdf, accessed 5 Aug. 2025.

Pedersen, M. N. (1982) 'Towards a New Typology of Party Lifespan and Minority Parties', *Scandinavian Political Studies*, 5: 1–16.

Pidd, H. and Ktena, N. (2024) 'Growing up with Nigel Farage: Inside Reform UK's push for the next election', *The Guardian*, 22 November, https://www.theguardian.com/politics/2024/nov/22/growing-up-with-nigel-farage-inside-reform-uks-push-for-the-next-election, accessed 5 Aug. 2025.

Quinn, B. and Dodd, V. (2024) 'Reform UK raises £1.5m after Nigel Farage's return as leader', *The Guardian*, 12 June, https://www.theguardian.com/politics/article/2024/jun/12/reform-uk-raises-donations-nigel-farage-return, accessed 5 Aug. 2025.

Reform UK (2024a) 'Our Contract With You', General Election Manifesto, https://assets.nationbuilder.com/reformuk/pages/253/attachments/original/1718625371/Reform_UK_Our_Contract_with_You.pdf?1718625371, accessed 5 Aug. 2025.

Reform UK (2024b) Party constitution, https://web.archive.org/web/20241002055707/https://assets.nationbuilder.com/reformuk/pages/2206/attachments/original/1726655475/Reform_UK_Constitution.pdf, accessed 5 Aug. 2025.

Thompson, L. (2020) *The End of the Small Party? Change UK and the challenges of parliamentary politics*. Manchester: Manchester University Press.

van Haute, E. (2016) (ed.) *Green Parties in Europe*. Abingdon/NY: Routledge.

Widfeldt, A. and Brandenburg, H. (2018) 'What Kind of Party Is the UK Independence Party? The Future of the Extreme Right in Britain or Just Another Tory Party?', *Political Studies*, 66: 577–600.

Shifting sands: Sources of voter volatility in the 2024 UK General Election in Scotland

Ailsa Henderson* and James Mitchell

Politics & International Relations, University of Edinburgh, 15a George Square, Edinburgh, EH8 9LD, UK

*Correspondence: ailsa.henderson@ed.ac.uk

In one sense, the 2024 UK General Election in Scotland provided a significant departure from what we have come to expect from elections in the aftermath of the 2014 independence referendum, returning thirty-seven Labour MPs on just over a third of the vote. The declining support for the SNP, down fifteen percentage points but losing thirty-nine seats while support for independence remained at 45%, suggested that the Scottish electorate had decoupled constitutional and partisan preferences, which marked a radical change from the 2021 devolved election. An analysis of voter decisions reveals, however, that high levels of tactical voting, late deciding from voters, low turnout, and a desire to remove the Conservatives from office were driving change, more than newly positive evaluations of the Scottish Labour party. This was a volatile election, in Scotland as in England, with voters arranging themselves into a series of extreme two-party contests, seeking to punish two sets of governing incumbents: the Conservatives in London and the SNP in Edinburgh. The 2024 election, therefore, provides yet another example of how Scottish electors navigate their multi-level political worlds.

The 2015 UK General Election in Scotland was conducted in the shadow of the Scottish independence referendum, and to a certain extent, this has been true of each election since 2014. As Labour, Conservatives, and Liberal Democrats scrambled for the larger unionist vote, the SNP scooped up the independence vote securing fifty-six of Scotland's fifty-nine seats. Even a sizeable swing from the SNP to the Conservatives in 2017 delivered thirty-five seats to the SNP, a figure on which they improved in 2019 with 80% of the seats on 45% of the votes. But in

© The Author(s) 2025. Published by Oxford University Press on behalf of the Hansard Society. All rights reserved. For commercial re-use, please contact reprints@oup.com for reprints and translation rights for reprints. All other permissions can be obtained through our RightsLink service via the Permissions link on the article page on our site—for further information please contact journals.permissions@oup.com.

the years preceding the 2024 UK General Election it was unclear whether we had witnessed a critical juncture in Scottish electoral politics. Was the SNP making an enduring valence argument (Green and Jennings 2017), convincing enough Scots that it was best capable of delivering on the range of devolved, and possibly many retained, competences? And as the salience of constitutional issues waned, how did enduring features of Scottish voting, including negative partisanship towards the Conservative party, influence voter preferences? We explore these possibilities in an analysis of the 2024 UK General Election in Scotland.

1. Background

The 2024 UK General Election in Scotland occurred within the wider context of increasing support for Labour in England making the prospect of a change of government more likely. Two things are, therefore, critical to understanding the most recent UK General Election in Scotland: first, that changed *English* preferences altered the decision-making calculus of *Scottish* voters and second, this served to accelerate a departure of support from the SNP, which had begun shortly after the 2021 devolved election.

It is now routine to note that the 2014 independence referendum changed electoral behaviour in Scotland (see inter alia Henderson et al., 2022). This included an increased symmetry between constitutional and partisan preferences. At the time of the 2011 devolved election, 52% of the Scottish electorate cast a vote for a party that shared their constitutional preferences (i.e. independence supporters backing the SNP, those opposed to independence backing, for example, the Conservatives). Ten years later, constitutional consistency in vote choice was in excess of 90% (McMillan and Henderson 2021). Post-indyref voting also saw an increased symmetry between Westminster and Holyrood preferences. In 2011, 55% of voters cast a ballot for the same party at both the Scottish and preceding UK election. By 2021 this had risen to 71%. This reflected a tendency after the independence referendum to see Westminster elections in Scotland as second-order electoral contests with the constitutional question assuming first-order importance, useful for sending representation to stand up for Scotland but not necessarily to elect one of the two parties likely to form the eventual UK government.

Just as the 2014 independence referendum influenced subsequent electoral behaviour, so too did the 2016 Brexit referendum. This is visible with respect to both electoral and constitutional preferences. The presence of two constitutional referendums in 2014 and 2016 created four constitutional tribes composed of different combinations of constitutional preferences: Yes Remain; Yes Leave; No Remain; and No Leave (Mitchell and Henderson 2019). The post-2016 period therefore saw two forms of political sorting. First, the respective tribes swung behind the parties best perceived to be issue owners on the pro-change side. In this process, voter support left the Liberal Democrats and Labour for the Yes-supporting SNP and Leave-supporting Conservatives. However, independence exerted an asymmetrical pull on voters. Yes Leavers, forced to choose between a party that supported their independence preferences or their Brexit preference, broke to the SNP. The result was a hollowing out of the political centre, away from parties advocating the status quo in both referendums. The same process specifically hollowed out the No Remain tribe, which had been the largest cluster of voters in 2016. Instead, by 2021, the modal Scottish voter was a Yes-supporting Remainer. The result of all of this was that voters showed greater consistency across their electoral and constitutional preferences, but also across the two constitutional issues as well, sorting themselves out of cross-pressured groups (Henderson et al., 2022). Many of these features reached a peak in 2021 (Johns 2021; McMillan and Henderson 2021; McMillan and Johns 2021) but thereafter had started to wane by the time the 2024 UK General Election was called.

Viewed through a longer lens, Scottish voting had two enduring features, a centre of gravity that was to the left of English electoral preferences, and a strong negative partisanship for the Conservative party in particular (Brown et al., 1999; Denver, Carman, and Johns 2012). Negative partisanship (Rose and Mishler 1998; McGregor, Caruana, and Stephenson 2015; Abramowitz and Webster 2018) ensured a level of anti-Conservative tactical voting among the Scottish electorate. In recent elections that had endured but to a smaller degree, with 6% of the Scottish electorate claiming in 2019 that they had cast a tactical vote against the Conservative party. After the independence referendum, just as voters moved to the constitutional "issue owners"—prioritizing support for the party most obviously associated with a constitutional preference—the resulting polarization also introduced a greater level of anti-SNP tactical voting (rising from only 9% in 2019). This served to introduce a more symmetrical form of negative partisanship in Scottish voting behaviour.

Three other features warrant careful attention. First, to say that Scottish Labour struggled in both UK (in Scotland) and devolved elections is to underestimate the scale of electoral loss. From 2014 to 2016, it lost approximately half its electoral support at each devolved, UK and European contest and by the 2019 UK General Election was still struggling in Scotland (Henderson and Mitchell 2018; Henderson et al. 2020; Henderson, Awan-Scully, and Tonge 2021). Continuing a pattern from previous devolved elections (Carman, Johns, and Mitchell 2014), competence evaluations placed the party well behind the SNP on a range of issues and this was true of those questions that forced respondents to choose a single competent party (which party is best at handling this area) as well as questions that asked respondents to evaluate the competence of each party in turn across a range of areas. On competence, the SNP was rated by respondents as ahead on each policy area, but particularly so on 'Standing up for Scotland' (Henderson et al., 2022).

Second, much of any UK 'national' election campaign focuses on devolved matters (extra spending on education, the hiring of more teachers), policy areas that are devolved in Scotland and are therefore the responsibility of the Scottish Parliament, though funding decisions at Westminster do have knock-on consequences for the allocation of Treasury grant to the Scottish Government. At each UK election since devolution, however, Scottish parties have, by calculated intent or ignorance, campaigned on devolved policy issues specific to Scotland that cannot be decided at the level of a UK election. No party has been immune to this. There has been a low thrum of 'cross-level campaigning', with policy issues and performance evaluations for areas of jurisdiction outwith the responsibility of the Parliament being elected. This includes attacks on the SNP government's handling of areas such as education or health.

Last, the period between the 2021 devolved election and the 2024 election witnessed a slow ebbing away of support for the SNP, a party previously seemingly immune from paying the costs of governing. This was visible in patterns of vote intention, with declining support, particularly in any future UK contest, but visible also in decreased levels of support for the SNP-led Scottish Government, particularly so among SNP supporters. The three-year period can best be summed up as one where SNP supporters fell out of love with the Scottish Government, if not necessarily with independence. While some of this can be attributed to the resignation of the previously popular First Minister Nicola Sturgeon, her less-popular and short-lived replacement Humza Yousaf (Mitchell 2023), and the return of John Swinney as party leader, the decrease in support was visible before this, and has three other origins. First is a standard 'costs of governing' argument, that the SNP's policy troubles, much like any party in government for a long time, had finally caught them up. Falling education standards, as tracked in international evaluations, would explain why on competence evaluations it was on education that parties caught the SNP faster than with other policy areas. Second, decreased support for the SNP accelerated after the Supreme Court ruled that the Scottish Parliament had no legal competence to hold an independence referendum, making the route to a second referendum uncertain. The issue of another independence referendum declined in importance even amongst its supporters, evident in the proportion of voters who do not want another referendum any time soon (Difford 2024).[1] A third further decline occurred around the introduction of the Gender Recognition Reform bill in Scotland. This last might explain why the gender gap in support for both the SNP and independence, which post-2014 showed greater support among women, saw a reversal, with lower levels of support among women by 2024.

In short, as the UK General Election campaign began, the Scottish electorate existed in a world that was partly post-indyref creation, partly old normal. This

---

[1] One in six want a referendum within the next year.

was a multi-level political world, with a shifting sense of first- and second-order electoral levels, where Scottish voters were influenced by English preferences making the possibility of a change of government in London appear more likely, but also where the boundaries of legislative competence were deliberately blurred by parties. It was also a world of post-referendum political sorting into constitutionally coherent tribes but with the enduring presence of negative partisanship, trained as ever on the Conservative party but increasingly so on the SNP, where patterns of competence and evaluations of leaders provided a lens through which to anticipate vote choice.

2. Results

This election (results for which are summarised in Table 7.1) saw new electoral boundaries throughout the UK. In Scotland, this reduced the number of constituencies from fifty-nine to fifty-seven. This was far less volatile than had been experienced in Wales, for example, which was reduced from forty to thirty-two seats. The new boundaries reflected a greater attention to electoral parity and the need for constituencies to lie within 5% of the UK electoral quota of 73,393. Scotland also houses two of the UK's five protected constituencies: Orkney and Shetland, and Na h-Eileanan an Iar (the Western Isles). These changed boundaries made it difficult to track changes in performance, since the previous election results used for comparison were modelled rather than actual. Those modelled results at times changed the 'notional' results of the 2019 electoral contests from what had actually occurred in those constituencies (suggesting that the Liberal Democrats would have lost North-East Fife, as well as Caithness, Sutherland and Easter Ross, for example).

Turnout was low, falling below 60% (59.2) which represented a more than eight-point drop on the last election and the lowest since 2001 (58.2), which itself had been a marked drop from the previous election. This was only marginally lower than the turnout for the whole of the UK. The turnout literature might well have led us to expect low figures (e.g. Blais 2006). Close contests drive turnout, and this was predicted to deliver a clear winner. In addition, the election was called for the first week of the Scottish school holidays in all but two local authorities (Aberdeen City, Aberdeenshire). The Scottish Election Study asked respondents whether they were likely to be away from their usual homes on election day, holidaying in a different part of the UK or internationally. Just under 12% said they were not at home on election day. This perhaps explains the rise in postal ballot requests, from 732,718, representing 18.1% of the Scottish electorate in 2019 to 26% in 2024 according to respondents in the Scottish Election Study. Across Scotland, turnout varied from a low of 47% in Glasgow North-East to a high of 72% in Mid Dunbartonshire. Seats won by Labour had a statistically significant lower level of

Table 7.1. UK General Election 2024 results in Scotland

	Labour	SNP	Con	LibDem	Reform UK	Green	Alba
% votes	35.3 (+ 16.7)	30.0 (−15.0)	12.7 (−12.4)	9.7 (+ 0.2)	7.0 (+ 6.5)	3.8 (+ 2.8)	0.5 (+ 0.5)
Seats[a]	37 (+ 36)	9 (−39)	5 (−1)	6 (+ 2)	0	0	0
% seats	64.9 (63.2)	15.8 (−65.6)	8.8 (−1.4)	10.5 (+ 3.7)	0	0	0
Candidates	57	57	57	57	57	44	19
Deposits lost	0	0	16 (28%)	30 (53%)	10 (18%)	32 (73%)	19 (100%)
Strongest constituency	Edinburgh South 53.3	Angus & Perthshire Glens 40.4	Berwickshire, Roxburgh & Selkirk 40.5	Orkney & Shetland 55.1	Aberdeenshire N & Moray E 14.6	Glasgow South 13.1	Cowdenbeath & Kirkcaldy 2.8
Weakest constituency	Orkney & Shetland 7.2	Edinburgh South 16.5	Orkney & Shetland 2.8	Coatbridge and Bellshill AND Glasgow NE 1.7	Edinburgh N & Leith 3.7	Dumfries and Galloway 0.5[b]	Mid Dunbartonshire 0.9
Biggest change	East Renfrewshire + 31.1	Na H'Eileanan an Iar −24.0	Central Ayrshire −19.9	Inverness, Skye and West Rosshire +22.7	na	Glasgow South +10.5	na
Smallest change[c]	Caithness, Sutherland and Easter Ross 2.1	Perth and Kinross −7.5	Glasgow North −4.9	Berwickshire, Roxburgh & Selkirk −0.1	na	North Ayrshire and Arran + 0.8	na
Westminster leader's seat	Ian Murray, Edinburgh S (as above)	Stephen Flynn Aberdeen S 32.8 (−11.9)	Douglass Ross Aberdeenshire N and Moray E 32.8 (−17.3)[d]	Christine Jardine Edinburgh W 50.8 (+ 10.9)	na	na	Alex Salmond—didn't run

Notes: In 2024, Labour and Liberal Democrats did not have Westminster leaders as such but Ian Murray was Scottish Labour's only MP and Labour's Shadow Secretary of State for Scotland. The equivalent post in the Liberal Democrats was held by Christine Jardine, Edinburgh West.
[a] Boundary changes resulted in a reduction in Scottish seats at this election from fifty-nine to fifty-seven.
[b] Although the Scottish Greens didn't stand candidates in thirteen Scottish constituencies.
[c] This is based on notional results, assuming the 2024 boundaries had operated in 2019.
[d] Calculated from 50.1 for David Duguid in Banff and Buchan in 2019.

turnout, a function perhaps of the typical relationship between socio-economic profile and turnout rather than a lack of enthusiasm for voting Labour. The same constituencies that had lower turnout in 2019 re-appeared at the lower end of engagement in 2024.

First Past the Post (FPTP) distorts electoral preferences. In Scotland, Scottish Labour emerged in 2024 as the largest party for the first time since the 2010 UK General Election, achieving 35% vote share compared to 42% fourteen years previously. This also marked a 16.7-point jump for Labour on the previous election. A fifteen-point drop in support for the SNP took them from forty-eight seats in 2019 back to single digits, on nine. The effects of FPTP mean that Labour won almost two-thirds of Scottish seats on the back of just over one-third of the vote, while the SNP earned around 15% of seats, having earned twice that proportion of votes. Ironically for such long-term advocates for PR, the Liberal Democrats have a near equal proportion of votes and seats (around 10% in each case) while the Conservatives were slightly disadvantaged, earning less than 10% of seats on around 13% of the vote.

Looking at the constituency contests, there are obvious signs of trouble for both the Conservatives and SNP in that their best constituency showing was the weakest among the constituency contests (around 40% support each, compared to over 50% support for the Liberal Democrats and Labour). As for the Scottish party leaders, the defeat of the Conservatives' Douglas Ross in Aberdeenshire North and Moray East could well be interpreted as bruising, losing seventeen points to earn 32.8% of the vote, but further south, SNP Westminster leader Stephen Flynn earned an identical percentage of the vote in Aberdeen South and held his seat. The difference was less their individual popularity and more the performance of Reform UK, only 6.9% in Aberdeen South (in a crowded field with eight candidates) but more than double that in Ross's constituency (where only five candidates stood). The Reform UK performance in Ross's seat, the highest in Scotland, could be attributed to the circumstances in which he came to be the candidate, replacing a popular sitting Conservative MP, or it could be that with the redrawing of the boundaries, Reform UK had more favourable terrain in a new constituency that, had it existed in 2016, would have been the only one in Scotland to have voted Leave.

Party support is best understood in comparison with earlier elections. Across the 2017 and 2019 elections in Scotland, the Scottish Conservatives were on less than 10% of the vote in only three constituencies out of a possible 118 contests over the two elections (i.e. 59 × 2). By 2024, almost two-thirds of Scottish constituencies (63%) had a Conservative candidate on less than 10% of the vote. If it was a remarkably poor election for the Conservatives in England there are various measures to suggest that the bottom had fallen out of Conservative support in Scotland. Part of this feeds into a wider trend of voter volatility (Fieldhouse et al., 2019).

We can measure the volatility of Scottish seats using the Pedersen Index, which takes the absolute change in party vote share since 2019 and divides by two. To calculate this, we have relied on the changes across the SNP, Labour, and Conservative parties, since this leaves the index less vulnerable to larger swings in smaller parties. The score for Scotland as a whole was 22.1 in this election, compared to less than half that (10.0) in 2019. We have mapped the distribution across constituencies in Fig. 7.1.[2] Average volatility ranges from 11.9 in Orkney and Shetland to 35.3 in Alloa and Grangemouth. Eighteen constituencies have volatility scores greater than 25, which would place them at the high end of voter volatility.

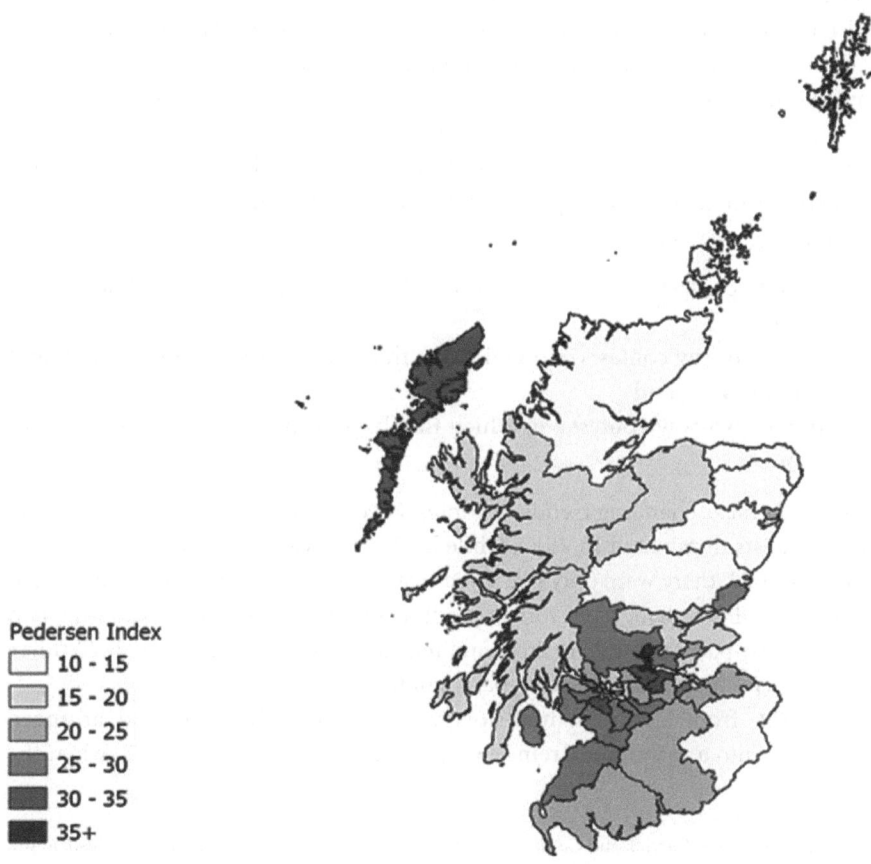

Figure 7.1. Pedersen Volatility Index 2024 Scotland

---

[2]We must urge caution here. Given the new boundary changes, our volatility measures are calculated against modelled data that estimated the proportion of votes for each party building up from local election results. Because Scottish local elections employ the single transferable vote and Westminster elections use first past the post, and also because of the high number of independent candidates in certain parts of Scottish local elections, we should be cautious with the model estimates.

These are predominantly in the central belt with the exception of Na h-Eileanan an Iar.

The volatility in constituency results hints at trends in tactical voting. The 2.8% earned by the Conservatives in Orkney and Shetland could be attributed to electors disliking the UK party of government, or it could be because almost the entire unionist vote swung behind Liberal Democrat incumbent Alistair Carmichael. Labour, after all, only earned 7.2% in the same constituency. The same could be said of North East Fife, which also had single-digit showings for both the Conservatives and Labour, with similarly depleted figures for the Conservatives and Liberal Democrats in Edinburgh South. Indeed, in twenty-nine constituencies, the SNP appeared to be facing a single unionist candidate, with voters largely leaving other No-supporting parties to single-digit support in favour of the eventual victor (which in thirty-seven instances, was Labour).

It was, therefore, not just that party fortunes differed, but the nature of party competition in Scotland changed in 2024. To illustrate this, we can classify contests into three categories:

- three-way contests—in which even the third party earned more than 20% of the vote;
- 'classic' two-way contests—in which the third party earned between 10% and 20% of the vote; and
- 'extreme' two-way contests, in which the third party earned less than 10% of the vote.

Fig. 7.2 tracks changing trends in contests over the past three elections. Three-party contests dominated in 2017, while by 2019 classic two-way contests dominated. By 2024, there were only five three-way contests[3] and two-way contests had dropped by almost half, from forty constituencies to twenty-two. From only two 'extreme' two-party contests in 2017 and ten such contests by 2019, in 2024 thirty constituencies, were 'extreme' two-party contests.[4]

By 2024, from a vibrant multi-party world, Scottish voters had arranged themselves into a series of extreme two-party contests. Unlike in 2019, when the

---

[3] Aberdeen South; Ayr, Carrick and Cumnock; Dumfries and Galloway; Dumfriesshire, Clydesdale and Tweeddale; and Mid Dunbartonshire

[4] Airdrie and Shotts, Alloa and Grangemouth, Bathgate and Linlithgow, Coatbridge and Bellshill, Cowdenbeath and Kirkcaldy, Cumbernauld and Kirkintilloch, Dunfermline and Dollar, Edinburgh East and Musselburgh, Edinburgh North and Leith, Edinburgh South, Falkirk, Glasgow East, Glasgow North, Glasgow South, Glasgow South West, Glasgow West, Glenrothes and Mid Fife, Inverclyde and Renfrewshire West, Kilmarnock and Loudon, Livingston, Midlothian, Motherwell, Wishaw and Carluke, Na h-Eileanan an Iar, North East Fife, Orkney and Shetland, Paisley and Renfrewshire North, Paisley and Renfrewshire South, Rutherglen, and West Dunbartonshire. In one further constituency (Dundee Central), the same pattern was not enough to take the seat from the SNP.

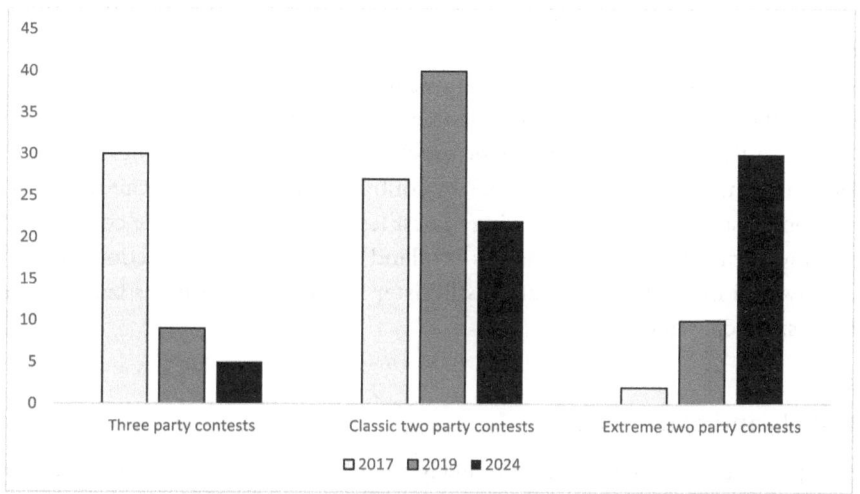

Figure 7.2. Types of constituency contest 2017–24

Conservatives had been able to capitalize on around half of these instances, winning areas like Dumfries and Galloway, Dumfriesshire, Clydesdale and Tweeddale, or Banff and Buchan, and unlike in 2017 when they won *both* the extreme two-way contests, by 2024 there was not a single constituency in Scotland in which unionist voters depleted their support for Labour and the Liberal Democrats below 10% in favour of the Conservative party. The Conservatives won familiar areas (Dumfries and Galloway; Dumfriesshire, Clydesdale and Tweeddale; Berwickshire, Roxburgh and Selkirk) but in three-way contests. This served as a structural disadvantage to Conservatives, who appeared in 2024 to be unable to capitalize on unionist vote lending.

These patterns also raise questions about the sustainability of Labour's electoral fortunes in Scotland. In an election perceived as 'all hands to the pump' to unseat an unpopular Conservative government in London, voters could be expected to move around the unionist parties. The Conservatives themselves had benefited from this in 2017 but by 2024 their capacity to continue to do so proved so short-lived it should sound a note of caution to Scottish Labour. Party support built on tactical voting is not an enduring recipe for success.

Another measure of party performance is party deposits, the £500 a political party pays per candidate. Those deposits are returned so long as the candidate earns 5% of the vote in that constituency. The four main parties each fielded fifty-seven candidates. Neither Labour nor the SNP lost any deposits. The Conservatives lost sixteen of their deposits in Scotland, a figure notable because it represents more than half of all the deposits they lost in Great Britain as a whole. The Liberal Democrats lost twice as many (thirty), which represents around

13% of all deposits lost by their candidates. Equally interesting are the patterns for the smaller parties. Greens stood forty-four candidates and held on to only one deposit outside the city constituencies in Edinburgh and Glasgow, in Orkney and Shetland. Reform UK fielded fifty-seven candidates but lost only ten, faring poorest in the very same constituencies where Greens performed best. Alba, the Alex Salmond-led split from the SNP, by contrast, fielded nineteen candidates and each one lost their deposit, securing at best less than 3% in a single constituency and fewer than 12,000 voters across Scotland as a whole. Two elections in—one at Holyrood in 2021 and one at Westminster in 2024—and Alba is barely worth discussing separately.

3. Polls and expectations

Polls provide an early indication of likely events but for pollsters this was a challenging contest as it took place against the backdrop of two data-relevant events. The first of these were the aforementioned boundary changes, and thus the reliance on modelled data to track change. This election also saw a greater use of MRP—multi-level regression post-stratification—models, which from large samples create profiles of likely party supporters according to their demographics and socio-economic characteristics, then use constituency demographic and socio-economic data to look for the presence of typical Labour supporters, SNP supporters, and so on. Since the Scottish census was delayed by more than a year after the England and Wales census, the constituency-level data for the new Scottish constituencies was more limited than that available in England, which in turn made it difficult to build constituency-level predictions. The result was a high degree of volatility across MRP predictions, with only ten of fifty-seven constituencies called the same way in each of the eight MRP polls. Not a single seat was predicted consistently across all MRP models to be won by the Liberal Democrats, SNP, or Conservatives.[5] Most difficult to call were Motherwell, Wishaw and Carluke, and Stirling and Strathallan, which different MRPs predicted were either safe Labour or safe SNP seats. In the end, both seats swung to Labour, comfortably so in the former case, but by only a two-point margin in Stirling.

4. Campaign themes

In the 2024 campaign, Scottish parties attempted, as usual, to highlight their differences, emphasizing their constitutional views as well as their policy preferences. While Scottish Labour campaigned on a general UK message of change

---

[5]See https://electiondatavault.co.uk/charts/model-comparisons/ for a comparison of different MRP predictions.

they also had specific policy pledges, including a commitment to locate a new publicly-owned GB Energy company in Scotland. The Conservatives committed to asylum flights to Rwanda, increased defence spending and national service for youth but clearly suffered as the constitutional question declined in significance. The SNP committed to independence talks if it won a majority of seats, a ceasefire in Gaza, opposition to anticipated public sector cuts and support for a just transition fund for the oil and gas sector, much of which is based in the North East of Scotland. That said, the campaign was overshadowed both by the SNP's internal troubles and its record in office, with opponents criticizing its devolved record on education targets, health waiting lists, reduced resources across a range of public services, and council tax funding, providing continued evidence of 'cross-level campaigning'.

Before she left office, former First Minister Nicola Sturgeon had suggested the SNP should treat the next UK general election as if it offered a proxy referendum on constitutional preferences, having tried throughout her leadership to keep the prospect of another independence referendum alive. In 2022, Sturgeon had set out a 'route map' to a referendum (Sturgeon 2022). She also asked Scotland's senior law officer to refer a proposed Holyrood Referendum Bill to the Supreme Court for guidance on whether it was within reserved powers. In November 2023, the Supreme Court decided that the Scottish Parliament could not legislate for an independence referendum. Sturgeon had prepared for such a judgment in her 'route map' to a referendum: in its event, the next general election would be a 'de facto referendum' in which the SNP would fight on the single question of whether Scotland should be independent.[6] The prospect of the SNP winning over 50% of the vote seemed improbable on the basis of the polls. It would have required the SNP to exceed its 2015 election result at a time when the polls had last shown SNP support over 40% in May 2023. It also assumed any new UK Government would accept such an interpretation of Scottish election results.

In March 2023, when Nicola Sturgeon announced her resignation she stated 'I free the SNP to choose the path it believes to be the right one' in pursuit of independence, an apparent concession that the de facto referendum would be abandoned in light of internal criticism. The ensuing SNP leadership contest was bitter between Sturgeon's preference Humza Yousaf and Kate Forbes (Mitchell 2023). Party officials were forced to admit that they had been dishonest about SNP membership figures, forcing the resignation of Peter Murrell, SNP chief executive and Sturgeon's husband. The party's hopes that the surge in membership after

---

[6]There had been some confusion as Deputy First Minister John Swinney suggested that having a majority of votes from Scottish *seats* would constitute a mandate to start independence negotiations before he corrected himself and stated that a majority of *votes* would be required.

the independence referendum (Johns and Mitchell 2016; Bennie, Mitchell, and Johns 2021) would provide financial security and a considerable body of activists in the event of another referendum proved forlorn.[7] This cast a cloud over the SNP and made it difficult to raise money for campaigns. Yousaf resigned as leader just over a year after becoming First Minister and was replaced by John Swinney, who returned without a contest. It is difficult to estimate the extent to which these problems impacted the SNP's ability to campaign effectively at the 2024 General Election but it is equally difficult to conclude other than that they damaged both activist morale and appeals for funding in the long campaign leading to the 2024 General Election.

The initial objective for Scottish Labour had been to replace the Conservatives as the main challenger to the SNP. Labour was at a disadvantage so long as the positional issues of independence and Brexit, perceived as binary choices, were dominant. Greater focus on valence issues such as cost of living and the delivery of public services would open opportunities first to challenge the Conservatives as Scotland's second party and then to challenge the SNP. Labour gained a consistent lead over the Conservatives in Scottish polls from February 2022—two months after UK Labour pulled ahead of the UK Conservatives—and by September 2022 Scottish Labour had pulled significantly ahead of the Conservatives. Labour only started to show a marginal and occasional lead over the SNP from October 2023, more than seven months after Yousaf became First Minister, and immediately after the Rutherglen and Hamilton by-election in which the Labour candidate won the seat left vacant by the recall of SNP MP Margaret Ferrier. Modern Studies teacher Michael Shanks won with 59% of the vote, representing a twenty-four-point jump in Labour fortunes.

5. Explaining the vote

The Scottish Election Study provides helpful evidence to understand when, how, and why voters reached their decisions on election day in 2024. Seven things are worth highlighting. First, we must question the impact of high-profile campaign events on vote choice. In this election, as in previous elections, very few reported that the election debates influenced their vote. Indeed, only nine people in the entire dataset of over 2,000 respondents reported that the election debates changed their mind on how to vote. Second, voters continued to decide very late in the campaign how they would vote, with more than a third of voters deciding

---

[7]Police enquiries into the SNP's finances had been launched in 2021 but had received little media coverage, other than in sections of social media, until the police arrested Murrell shortly after Yousaf was elected leader. He was later re-arrested and charged with embezzlement. Sturgeon and the SNP Treasurer were also arrested.

either in the last few days (25%) or at the polling station itself (11%) how they would vote. This represents an increase of about five percentage points on late deciding in 2019.

Third, this was an election about removing the Conservatives from office more than it was about sending constitutional messages (as seen in Fig. 7.3). Over 40% of the Scottish electorate as a whole expressed a wish to remove the Conservatives from office and there were more respondents who wished to maximize the number of pro-union MPs than to maximize the number of independence MPs. In an election that under one formulation was supposed to send a constitutional message from Scottish voters to the prospective government in London, the message was not very loud, nor was it the one the SNP would have hoped to send.

It should not be assumed from this that constitutional preferences are no longer relevant to vote choice or indeed that they do not provide a useful means for understanding why voters back different parties. Support for independence remains well above its pre-2014 level, at 43% of participants in the SES. It is perhaps more helpful if we locate independence within a range of different constitutional options. Asked whether the Scottish Parliament should be abolished, there should be no change, it should have more powers, or whether Scotland should be independent either within or outside the EU, then the most popular option is independence in the EU (30%) followed by no change (28%), the abolition of the Parliament (16%), more powers for the Parliament (15%) then independence outside of Europe (4%). As Fig. 7.4 makes clear, the plurality response for the SNP and Green voters is independence, while the most popular option for Conservative,

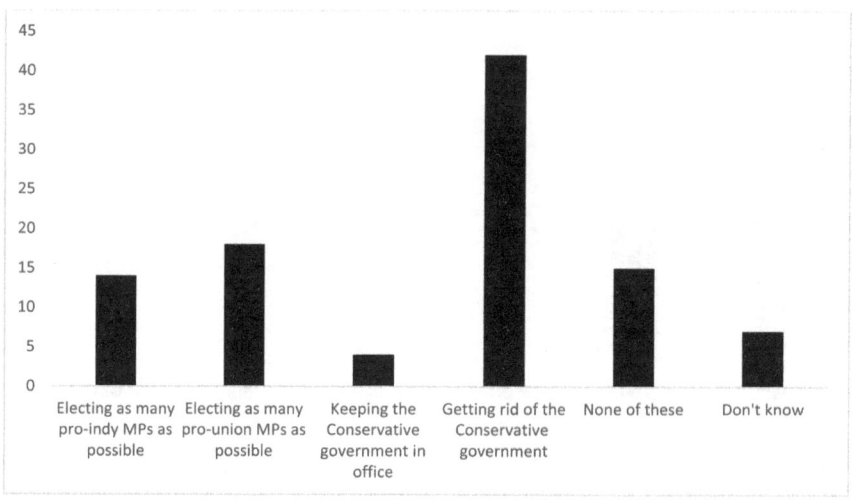

Figure 7.3. What voters wanted from the 2024 UK General Election
Source: Scottish Election Study pre-election wave 2024.

Labour, and LibDem voters is 'no change'. The most popular option for Reform UK voters is to abolish the Scottish Parliament, and while a higher proportion of Conservative voters believe this (45%) it is only because of the strength of support among Conservatives for the status quo that this is not the most popular option. With Reform UK, it is the plurality option in part because there is also a cluster of Reform UK support for independence outside Europe (6%). Indeed, that view is as popular within Reform UK as it is within the SNP.

Fourth, by examining vote switching (patterns of which are detailed in Table 7.2) we can understand the sources of Labour support in 2024. The party managed to retain a higher proportion of its vote than in previous elections, and more than any other party. Retention rates of three in four previous voters would not have been considered high in previous years, when both the Conservatives and SNP managed to retain more than four in five previous voters, but both of these parties failed to hold on to their previous voters compared to earlier elections, with the Conservatives holding on to only four in ten previous supporters. Both proportionately, and in terms of absolute numbers, more Conservative supporters moved to Labour in 2024 than SNP voters moved to Labour.

Fifth, competence evaluations show that the SNP has lost considerable ground. In earlier devolved elections, as in 2019, the SNP was perceived by voters to be more trusted to handle policy areas than any other party. By 2021, Labour was neck and neck with the SNP on education but the SNP retained a lead on all policy areas and particularly on standing up for Scotland. By 2024, Labour was perceived to be more competent in its handling of the economy, on immigration and

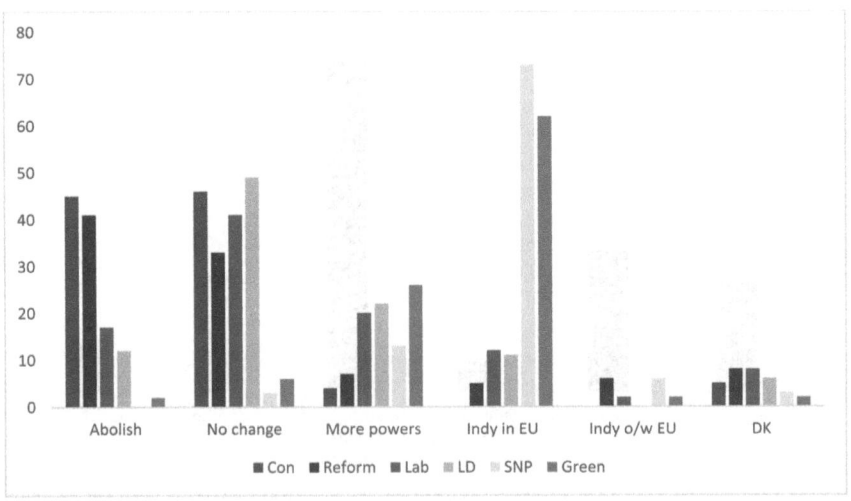

Figure 7.4. Constitutional preferences by party vote, 2024
Source: SES post-election wave 2024.

Table 7.2. Vote switching in 2024

	Vote in 2019			
Vote in 2024	Con	Lab	LD	SNP
Con	41	1	8	1
Lab	33	77	33	19
LD	6	6	51	5
SNP	2	6	3	65
Green	0	3	1	4
Reform UK	16	4	2	3

Source: SES 2024.

education. On standing up for Scotland, the SNP retained its lead over other parties, with 53% perceiving the SNP stands up for Scotland 'well'. By contrast, 39% believed the same of Labour, with less than half that figure (16%) saying the same of the Conservatives.

Sixth, to help understand why voters might have opted to back different parties in 2024 the SES asked about political attitudes as well as support for a range of policy areas. Respondents were asked where they placed themselves on a 0–10 scale of left to right, and then were asked to assess the location of political parties on the same scale. This helps us to assess whether Scottish voters see any party as close to them, and where the parties are perceived to be relative to the average Scottish voter. Here we see that both SNP and Labour supporters placed their own *parties* at 3.7 on a scale of 0–10. The average left-right score for SNP *supporters* was 3.2, and for Labour it was 4.3, so both made errors in their estimation but Labour supporters believed their party was to the left of where it was and SNP supporters placed it slightly to the right of where it was. Conservative voters believed that both groups were significantly more left-wing, placing the SNP at 1.9 on a scale of 0–10, and Labour at 2.6. Conservative supporters believed that their party was at 7.3, very much on the right-wing end of the scale, while the average score for supporters was 6.5. SNP and Labour supporters both placed the Conservatives to the right of where they are, at 7.8 according to Labour supporters, and at 8.9 according to SNP supporters. Looking across these results, party supporters have a habit of exaggerating the left-right placement of parties, perceiving Scottish politics to be more polarized than it is. Table 7.3 compares the perceived and actual left-right differences between parties. Positive numbers mean voters think that rival parties are to the right. Negative numbers mean voters think that rival parties are to the left. Conservative voters, for example, believe Labour is 4.7 points to the left of their own party, but in fact, there is only a 2.2 gap between the two groups of supporters.

Table 7.3. Perceived and actual difference between party supporters

	Perceived distance to SNP	Actual distance to SNP	Perceived distance to Labour	Actual distance to Labour	Perceived distance to Cons	Actual distance to Cons
View of SNP voters	–	–	+1.5	+1.1	+5.2	+4.3
View of Lab voters	0	−1.1	–	–	+4.1	+3.3
View of Con voters	−5.4	−3.3	−4.7	−2.2	–	–

Source: SES 2024.

The SES policy questions (in Table 7.4) include those promoted by different parties in the election, including national service for young people (Conservatives), charging VAT on private school fees (Labour), and an immediate ceasefire in Gaza (SNP). These policies allow us to identify the most popular options, with the electorate, and their relative popularity among groups of party voters, both of which help us to understand the nature of Scottish party space. What we see is that Green voters are consistently at one end of the spectrum of policy views in Scotland and that Reform UK or Conservative supporters are typically at the other end, but that Labour, Liberal Democrats, and SNP supporters vary both in their ordering and in how close they are to each other. SNP supporters are often closer to Labour and the Liberal Democrats—for example, on oil and gas jobs, pensions, and freezing council tax—than to supporters of their former coalition partners, the Greens.

Despite losing a considerable number of seats, not all SNP policies were unpopular. Asked about the freezing of council tax, a policy former FM Humza Yousaf announced to the surprise of many, almost two-thirds of the electorate and a majority in all parties clearly supported it. As a sign of the troubles the party faced over gender recognition reform, however, only 10% supported the participation of transgender women in women's sports. This makes it the least popular policy by some margin, less popular than two Conservative policies, withdrawal from the European Convention on Human Rights and national service for young people. The figures also provide hints about why it was so easy for 2019 SNP voters to swing to Labour in this election. The high-profile Labour policy of VAT on private school feels, criticized by many journalists (many of whom themselves were privately educated), was a remarkably popular policy across Labour, the SNP, and Greens.

Seventh, we discussed earlier the introduction of extreme two-party contests, all of which suggest a degree of tactical voting in 2024. In fact, one-third said they

Table 7.4. Support for policy options by party vote, 2024, %

	Scotland	Reform UK	Cons	Lab	LibDems	SNP	Greens
Do more to protect pensions	85	92	94	86	83	88	67
Immediate ceasefire in Gaza	69	35	47	70	73	85	95
VAT on private school fees	68	43	36	74	57	85	91
Freezing council tax	64	80	62	59	54	67	52
Asylum seekers remain in UK while claims processed	49	9	18	45	53	73	83
Supporting oil and gas jobs over environmental targets	48	83	77	50	42	39	4
National service for young people	31	51	65	29	38	18	11
Withdraw from ECHR	23	76	60	20	19	7	0
Transgender women in women's sport	10	3	1	6	8	14	35

Source: SES 2024. Results are % of party supporters agreeing with each policy area.

voted for a party based on its policies and one-fifth said they always vote that way, but 22% said it was a tactical vote, and almost half of these voters backed Labour in this election. Who were people trying to stop? Almost three-quarters of the tactical voting (74%) in Scotland was to stop the SNP, 22% was to stop the Conservatives, with the remainder trying to stop other parties. Another measure of voter volatility is whether people considered voting for another party. Around 40% of Conservative and Liberal Democrat voters and around 30% of Labour and SNP voters reported that they considered backing another party before settling on their vote choice. All of this suggests that, however, dramatic the results in 2024, we should not assume that a similar pattern will be repeated in the 2026 devolved elections. A combination of vote switching, tactical voting, and late deciding presents something of a shifting sand on which parties can build support.

6. Conclusion

By some indicators, the 2024 election appears to suggest that Scottish politics is returning to its pre-2014 roots. Scottish Labour is once more the largest party although without the dominance it previously experienced in UK elections in Scotland. But assuming that it will remain as such may be premature, if not wrong. Support for independence remains stable and even if it has lost some salience amongst voters, there remains a much larger base that could be capitalized upon at some future election. A return to, or at least greater relevance of, valence issues might have undermined the SNP as voters failed to distinguish between devolved and retained matters. But a return to valence and the decreased salience of constitutional issues would not necessarily mean the end of an electoral threat from the SNP. The SNP had, after all, won Holyrood elections in 2007 (Johns et al., 2010) and even more so in 2011 (Carman, Johns, and Mitchell 2014) campaigning on government competence rather than the constitution. Given the volatility in the electorate, captured by the timing of vote decisions, levels of switching, tactical voting, and certainty over vote choice, the 2024 UK General Election in Scotland could well be viewed as an event to be considered in isolation rather than an enduring realignment.

Funding

This study was supported by the Economic and Social Research Council (ESRC) through the Scottish Election Study [grant number ES/V01000X/1].

References

Abramowitz, A. I., and Webster, S. W. (2018) 'Negative Partisanship: Why Americans Dislike Parties but Behave Like Rabid Partisans', *Political Psychology*, 39: 119–35.

Bennie, L., Mitchell, J., and Johns, R. (2021) 'Parties, Movements and the 2014 Scottish Independence Referendum: Explaining the Post-referendum Party Membership Surges', *Party Politics*, 27: 1184–97.

Blais, A. (2006). 'What affects voter turnout?', *Annual Review of Political Science*, 9: 111–25.

Brown, A. et al. (1999) *The Scottish Electorate: The 1997 General Elections and Beyond*. Basingstoke: Macmillan.

Carman, C., Johns, R., and Mitchell, J. (2014) *More Scottish than British: The 2011 Scottish Parliament Election*. Basingstoke: Palgrave Macmillan

Denver, D., Carman, C., and Johns, R. (2012) *Elections and Voters in Britain*, 3rd edn. Basingstoke: Palgrave.

Difford, D. (2024) 'Scottish Independence 10 Years On', *YouGov*, https://yougov.co.uk/politics/articles/50536-scottish-independence-10-years-on, accessed 05 Aug. 2025.

Fieldhouse, E. et al. (2019) *Electoral Shocks: The Volatile Voter in a Turbulent World*. Oxford: Oxford University Press.

Green, J., and Jennings, W. (2017) *The Politics of Competence: Parties, Public Opinion and Voters*. Cambridge: Cambridge University Press.

Henderson, A., Awan-Scully, R., and Tonge, J. (2021) 'The Devolved Nations' in: R. Ford, T. Bale, W. Jennings, and P. Surridge (eds) *The British General Election of 2019*. Basingstoke: Palgrave Macmillan.

Henderson, A. et al. (2020) 'Scottish Labour as a Case Study in Party Failure: Evidence from the 2019 UK General Election in Scotland', *Scottish Affairs*, 29: 127–40.

Henderson, A. et al. (2022) *The Referendum that Changed a Nation: Scottish Voting Behaviour 2014 to 2019*. Basingstoke: Palgrave.

Henderson, A., and Mitchell, J. (2018) 'Referendums as Critical Junctures? Scottish Voting in British Elections', *Parliamentary Affairs*, 71: 109–24.

Johns, R. (2021) 'As You Were: The Scottish Parliament Election of 2021', *The Political Quarterly*, 92: 493–9.

Johns, R., and Mitchell, J. (2016) *Takeover: Explaining the Extraordinary Rise of the SNP*. Hull: Biteback.

Johns, R. et al. (2010) *Voting for a Scottish Government: The Scottish Parliament Election of 2007*. Manchester: Manchester University Press.

McGregor, R. M., Caruana, N. J., and Stephenson, L. B. (2015) 'Negative Partisanship in a Multi-party System: The Case of Canada', *Journal of Elections, Public Opinion and Parties*, 25: 300–16.

McMillan, F., and Henderson, A. (2021) 'Scotland's Future? The 2021 Holyrood Election', *Political Insight*, 12: 37–9.

McMillan, F., and Johns, R. (2021) 'Nats Whae Hae: The SNP's Enduring Success', *Progressive Review*, 28: 153–63.

Mitchell, J. (2023) 'From Team Nicola to Team Humza: The SNP Leadership Contest in Perspective', *Scottish Affairs*, 32: 263–89.

Mitchell, J., and Henderson, A. (2019) 'Tribes and Turbulence: The 2019 UK General Election in Scotland', *Parliamentary Affairs*, 73: 142–56.

Rose, R., and Mishler, W. (1998) 'Negative and Positive Party Identification in Post-communist Countries', *Electoral Studies*, 17: 217–34.

Sturgeon, N. (2022) 'Independence Referendum: First Minister's Statement—28 June 2022', https://www.gov.scot/publications/ministerial-statement-independence-referendum/, accessed 5 Aug. 2025.

The 2024 UK General Election in Wales

Jac M. Larner*, and Richard Wyn Jones

Wales Governance Centre, School of Law and Politics, Cardiff University, Museum Avenue, Cardiff, Wales, CF10 3AX, UK

*Correspondence: larnerJM@cardiff.ac.uk

1. Introduction

That Labour emerged victorious from the 2024 UK General Election in Wales must count among the least surprising political outcomes imaginable. It has, after all, been the largest party in terms of both votes and seats after *every* general election in Wales since 1922; a record of one-party domination at the sub-state level that is without parallel in the democratic world. Given that, overall, the 2024 General Election delivered the worst result in the long history of the incumbent Conservatives—and, concomitantly, one of Labour's best ever—anything other than a decisive victory for Labour in Wales was surely unthinkable. In the event, Labour duly won 84% of Welsh seats in the House of Commons (twenty-seven out of a total of thirty-two) with the Conservatives losing all of their Welsh MPs (see Table 8.1). The latter's calamitous result was thrown into even starker relief by the fact that the party had secured their best ever general election result in Wales in 2019 and that their result in the 2021 election for the devolved Welsh Parliament or Senedd represented another high-water mark: for the Conservatives this was a truly precipitous fall from grace.

Yet Labour's remarkable haul of Welsh seats serves to mask clear signs that Labour's hegemonic position in Wales may at last be under threat. In contrast to both England and Scotland, in Wales Labour saw their vote share fall. Indeed, at 37.5%, its vote share in 2024 was the fourth lowest in the party's storied history of electoral success west of Offa's Dyke, and the lowest ever achieved by an incoming Labour administration. It is also the case that in every seat in which there was a credible non-Labour alternative to the Conservatives, it was that alternative that

© The Author(s) 2025. Published by Oxford University Press on behalf of the Hansard Society. All rights reserved. For commercial re-use, please contact reprints@oup.com for reprints and translation rights for reprints. All other permissions can be obtained through our RightsLink service via the Permissions link on the article page on our site—for further information please contact journals.permissions@oup.com.

Table 8.1. UK General Election result in Wales, 2024 (change from 2019)

	Seats	Seat Share (%)	Vote Share (%)
Labour	27 (+ 9)	84.4	37.5 (-3.9)
Plaid Cymru	4 (+ 2)	12.5	14.8 (+ 4.9)
Lib Dem	1 (+ 1)	3.1	6.5 (+ 0.5)
Conservative	0 (-12)	0	18.2 (-17.9)
Reform UK	0 (-)	0	16.9 (+ 11.5)

Note: Notional results for 2019 compiled by Professors Colin Rallings and Michael Thrasher on behalf of BBC News, ITV News, Sky News, and the Press Association.

triumphed—this was true even in the case of Caerfyrddin, a constituency into which Labour poured considerable resources and which hosted an eve-of-poll visit by Sir Keir Starmer.

Two things served to render the 2024 General Election in Wales distinctive. The first was a reduction of 20% in the number of Welsh constituencies since the previous election, reducing Welsh representation in the House of Commons to the lowest number since 1865. This meant that with the sole exception of the island constituency of Ynys Môn, every constituency in the country was fought on new boundaries. Second, unlike Scotland or England, in Wales Labour found itself defending the record of an increasingly unpopular devolved Welsh Government; this at a moment of particular controversy in the immediate aftermath of the installation of Vaughan Gething as First Minister following a divisive leadership election. After nearly a quarter of a century in which Labour had appeared to be able to defy political gravity and in which the 'Welsh Labour' brand had proven an electoral asset even in the context of Westminster elections, the party was finally paying the cost of governing. The beneficiaries of Labour's travails and Tory collapse were, as we shall see, Plaid Cymru and Reform UK respectively.

In the following, we discuss the 2024 General Election in Wales in three steps. First, we elaborate on the context in which the election took place, focusing in particular on Welsh Labour's internal difficulties. Second, we analyse the results of that election through the prism of the various political parties themselves. Finally, we consider the prospects for the next Senedd election scheduled for May 2026. This election will not only take place against a backdrop of public dissatisfaction with the performance of the incumbent devolved administration. It will also feature a new closed-list PR voting system that is set to be substantially more proportional than the voting system previously used for devolved elections. As a result, Labour's dominant position in Wales currently appears more fragile than at any point in the preceding century. Yet paradoxically, the party's very success in terms of expanding its Westminster parliamentary representation in 2024 may

2. Context and campaign

Labour's historical dominance in Welsh electoral politics (see Table 8.2) has traditionally shaped how both media outlets and academic research discuss campaigns in Wales, with a focus on the party's relative strength or weakness. In 2024, this narrative became even more pronounced due to several factors: Wales's reduction in parliamentary representation, polling data suggesting few competitive constituencies, and an internal crisis within Welsh Labour. For most of the past twenty-five years, Labour in Wales has benefited from the existence of a distinctive 'Welsh Labour' brand identity embraced and deliberately promoted by a series of popular leaders. Primarily associated with the devolved level, this brand has been associated with an inchoate yet powerful sense that it—Welsh Labour—embodies particular 'Welsh values' that are distinguishable not only from those dominant in other parts of the state but even in other parts of the Labour Party (Moon 2013; Davies 2024).

The party's hand has been further strengthened by a long-standing tendency across large swathes of the Welsh electorate to blame the UK level of government for any perceived deficiencies in the delivery of public services in Wales. There are doubtless several explanations for the latter state of affairs including,

Table 8.2. Westminster election results in Wales, 1979–2024, vote share (seats)

Election	Con	Lab	Lib Dem*	Plaid Cymru	Others
1979	32.2 (11)	47.0 (21)	10.6 (1)	8.1 (2)	2.2 (1)
1983	31.0 (14)	37.5 (20)	23.2 (2)	7.8 (2)	0.4 (0)
1987	29.5 (8)	45.1 (24)	17.9 (3)	7.3 (3)	0.2 (0)
1992	28.6 (6)	49.5 (27)	12.4 (1)	8.8 (4)	0.7 (0)
1997	19.6 (0)	54.7 (34)	12.4 (2)	9.9 (4)	3.4 (0)
2001	21.0 (0)	48.6 (34)	13.8 (2)	14.3 (4)	2.3 (0)
2005	21.4 (3)	42.7 (29)	18.4 (4)	12.6 (3)	4.9 (1)
2010	26.1 (8)	36.2 (26)	20.1 (3)	11.3 (3)	6.2 (0)
2015	27.2 (11)	36.9 (25)	6.5 (1)	12.1 (3)	17.3 (0)
2017	33.6 (8)	48.9 (28)	4.5 (0)	10.4 (4)	2.5 (0)
2019	36.1 (14)	40.9 (22)	6.0 (0)	9.9 (4)	7.1 (0)
2024	18.2 (0)	37.5 (27)	6.5 (1)	14.8 (4)	23.0 (0)

*Formerly Liberal (1979) and Liberal-SDP Alliance (1983 and 1987).

inter alia: the widely held view that Wales is unfairly treated in terms of the allocation of public finance (Henderson and Wyn Jones 2023); a degree of ignorance among the electorate as to which level of government is responsible for what policy area (Larner et al., 2022); relatedly, the fact that the powers of the devolved legislature, in particular, were very limited for at least the first decade of devolution; and deliberate blame-shifting by a Welsh government eager to point out that the austerity policies pursued by successive UK governments have had a disproportionately negative impact in economically disadvantaged Wales (Ifan and Siôn 2019). Whatever the cause, the end result is that the electorate has tended to view the Welsh level of government in essentially benevolent terms.

In retrospect, it is clear that the Covid-19 pandemic represented the zenith of this 'Welsh Labour' approach. The pandemic catapulted then-newly installed First Minister Mark Drakeford to fame and made him, for a period at least, the most popular political figure in the UK (Surridge and Larner 2021). Drakeford's calm, cautious and characteristically communitarian approach to crisis management was widely contrasted with that of UK Prime Minister Boris Johnson. This was a comparison that, in Wales at least, was regarded as rebounding almost wholly in the First Minister's favour. It also appeared to redeem the claim that Welsh values are indeed different. In 2021, Drakeford's popularity and the perception that the Welsh Government had performed creditably at a testing time was enough to power Labour to a convincing victory in a devolved election almost wholly overshadowed by the pandemic (Larner et al., 2022).[1]

Yet in the post-pandemic period, the incumbent government's popularity, as well as the popularity of its leading figure, waned in a rather dramatic fashion. This appears to have been an almost universal experience for incumbents in both state and sub-state governments across western democracies (Burn-Murdoch 2024). In the Welsh iteration of this wider phenomenon, Labour's standing seems to have been damaged, first, by the way in which its heightened profile as guardian of the health service during the pandemic transmogrified into a sense that it was responsible for the deficiencies of that same service once the pandemic period had been negotiated. In addition, the government's decision to introduce an upper-speed limit of 20mph in most built-up areas elicited a fierce popular and populist backlash (Redfield and Wilton 2023). This hostility appears to have remained undimmed even as evidence mounts that the policy is having its intended effect of reducing road traffic casualties (BBC News 2024c).

Indeed, the 2024 election arrived at a point when satisfaction with both the UK and Welsh governments had hit all-time lows (at least as far as survey research allows us to measure). Fig. 8.1 plots the percentage of respondents who thought

---

[1] A remarkable recovery from 2019 opinion polls which suggested Labour was on course to finish third in the next Senedd election.

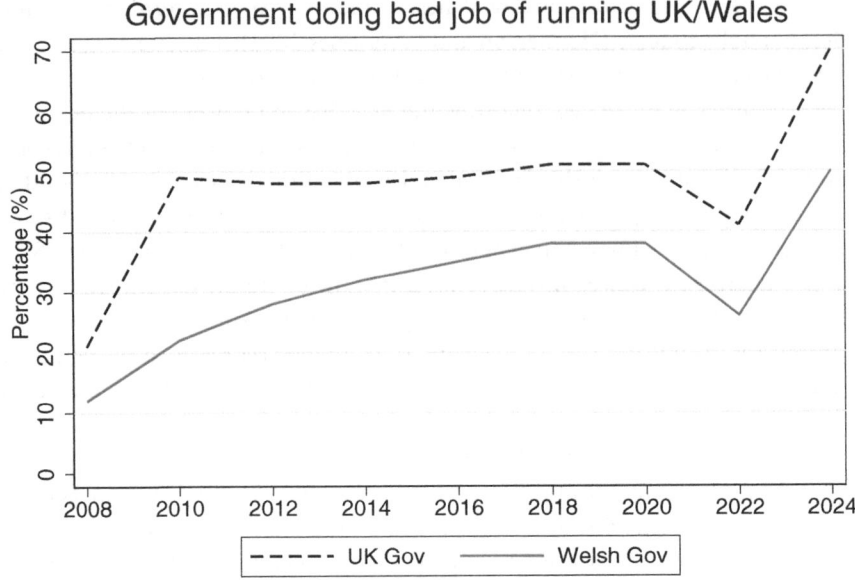

Figure 8.1. Satisfaction with government over time
Source: Welsh Election Studies 2007–24.

that the UK/Welsh Government was doing a bad job of running the UK/Wales over the previous decade and a half. While we see an initial divergence between the two governments around 2010—the moment when the Conservatives were first elected at Westminster—the two trend lines have moved in parallel, with discontent reaching over 70% in the UK Government and over 50% for the Welsh Government. While views of the UK Government were obviously considerably worse than those of the Welsh Government, 2024 nevertheless was the first time that a majority of voters in Wales thought the Welsh Government were doing a bad job of running Wales. The question for Labour in Wales, therefore, was whether they would pay the price of governing in Wales for so long, or whether the relative positive ratings of the Welsh Government would save them.

Even more damaging for the party's standing was the controversy surrounding the internal party election to find a successor for Mark Drakeford who, in December 2023, had announced his intention to step down from the role of First Minster. The result (in March 2024) was a victory by the narrowest of margins for Vaughan Gething—a candidate who had been heavily backed by the party establishment and who had massively outspent his only rival for the post thanks to a (in Welsh terms) large donation from a company controlled by a businessman previously convicted of environmental crimes (Wyn Jones 2024). It was to prove a pyrrhic victory both for Gething and his party. Not only was the new First Minister deeply unpopular with the wider public, but the limited polling that takes place in Wales suggested that Labour itself was losing support at the devolved level, in particular. While Gething would eventually be forced to step down, this was not to occur until just *after* the general election (on 16th July).

Data from the Welsh Election Study supports the idea that the First Minister was at best neutral and, at worse, a detriment to the party in the July election. Using 0–10 likeability scales, Gething fell far below the three most popular leaders in Wales—Rhun ap Iorwerth, Ed Davey and Keir Starmer—and was on par with Welsh Conservative leader Andrew RT Davies and Nigel Farage (the lowest ever mean score for a Welsh First Minister in a Welsh Election Study). This popularity also had real-world cut through in the electorate. In an open-ended unprompted question about the most important issue facing Wales, the fifth most common write-in was mention of Vaughan Gething (Larner 2024b). Matters were likely made worse by a series of high-profile Labour politicians publicly dismissing the scandal, either as a 'political stunt' or as a 'gimmick' (LBC 2024; S4C 2024). In Wales, at least, Labour's general election campaign was very much overshadowed by Vaughan Gething and the travails of the Labour administration in Cardiff.

Perhaps of even greater long-term significance than all of this was the clear shift in Labour's messaging in Wales that occurred in the first half of 2024. As it became increasingly apparent that the party was set for victory at the UK general election this shift in messaging was personified, above all, by Vaughan Gething, who was very much the choice of Welsh Labour (Westminster) MPs for the First Minister. As has already been noted, for the past quarter of a century the Labour Party in Wales has embraced a distinctive 'Welsh Labour' branding emphasising its distinctiveness not least vis-à-vis the wider British party. In 2003, then First Minister Rhodri Morgan pointed to the 'clear red water' that separated the Welsh party from Tony Blair's UK government, positioning Welsh Labour as the guardian of both 'classic Labour' values and Welshness against New Labour's market-oriented reforms. In more recent years, as Labour languished on the opposition benches in the House of Commons, Welsh Labour has emphasized its willingness to 'fight Wales's corner' against successive UK governments accused of short-changing Wales (Henderson and Wyn Jones 2023).

All the evidence suggests that this approach has paid rich dividends for Welsh Labour in multiple electoral contests over more than two decades (Davies 2024). Despite this, the party would seem to have shifted with remarkable alacrity to embrace a new framing encapsulated in the carefully calibrated campaign message 'Two Labour governments, working together for Wales's and Britain's future'. With Labour returned to power at the UK level, the differentiation that was the essence of the 'Welsh Labour' brand—Welsh Labour as the inheritor and advocate of authentically Labour and distinctively Welsh values—and arguably a buffer that shielded them from an increasingly unpopular Labour Westminster government, has been replaced by a claim that there exists a fundamental harmony of both values and interest between the UK and Welsh levels of government and between the British and Welsh leadership of the Labour party (Welsh Labour 2024).

The Conservative betting scandal emerged as one of the campaign's most significant moments, achieving substantial media cut-through beyond Labour's internal difficulties. The controversy centered on Craig Williams, the Conservative MP for Montgomeryshire—the party's safest Welsh seat—who had placed a £100 bet on the election date just three days before it was officially announced (BBC News 2024a). Williams won the bet, raising immediate questions about potential access to privileged information. The scandal dominated electoral coverage for several days, with both the Prime Minister and Cabinet members facing repeated questions about whether Williams had received inside information about the election timing. As the story developed, multiple Conservative politicians became implicated in similar betting activities, leading to a significant expansion of the investigation's scope. In response to mounting pressure, the Conservative Party announced the withdrawal of financial support from Williams's campaign. They further declared that should he win re-election, he would not receive the Conservative whip in Parliament. The scandal's reach extended into Welsh devolved politics, though this aspect received comparatively less attention in the UK national press. Russell George, the Member of the Senedd for Montgomeryshire, also came under investigation by the Gambling Commission for similar election betting activities, adding a distinctly Welsh dimension to what had become a national controversy (Guardian 2024).

Elsewhere, Plaid Cymru was focused on maintaining their representation of four MPs from the reduced Welsh crop, including winning back the Conservative held Ynys Môn and winning the three-way marginal Caerfyrddin. The Liberal Democrats, once a force to be reckoned with in Welsh electoral politics, were focused on the single largely rural seat of Brecon, Radnor, and Cwm Tawe—another Conservative 'safe' seat that had a strong Liberal history and a boundary change that moved the seat decidedly away from the Conservatives in demographic terms.

3. The result

The election took place on a turnout of just 56%—a decline of 10.6 points compared to 2019 and the largest decline by a considerable margin of any of the UK's four constituent countries. In a pattern repeated elsewhere across the UK, turnout was particularly low in uncompetitive constituencies. The result saw an emphatic Labour victory, with the party winning twenty-seven of Wales's thirty-two seats on a vote share more than double that of any other party. Plaid Cymru won four seats on a record high vote share of 14.8%, and the Liberal Democrats won the final seat in a largely tactical contest. However, the Conservative Party's elimination from Welsh parliamentary representation in 2024 was perhaps the most striking feature of the result in Wales. Indeed, if you needed to identify a single story of the election in Wales, you would have to tell of the complete collapse of Conservative support, rather than any surge in support for a challenger. The election left Wales without any Conservative MPs for the third time in the post-war period. What marks this as distinct from the previous two times—1997 and 2001—is that it did not occur following a decade-long trend of Conservative decline. Instead, the party descended from its 2019–21 apex, when it secured both its best Westminster performance (14 seats) and strongest Senedd showing (sixteen seats), representing an unprecedented acceleration of electoral decay.

Most concerning for the Conservatives will be *where* the party lost most votes and *among whom*. The party's greatest losses occurred precisely in those areas where it had made its most dramatic gains in 2019. Rather than representing a genuine realignment of Welsh politics, the 2017–21 Conservative surge increasingly appears as an aberrant interlude—a temporary suspension of Wales's traditional anti-Conservative disposition (Wyn Jones, Scully, and Trystan 2002), rather than its permanent transformation. Even where the party had majorities large enough to withstand the national-level losses, local factors appear to have played a decisive factor. The safest Conservative seat in Wales—Montgomeryshire and Glyndŵr—saw their vote share drop 36 percentage points, double the Welsh average. The incumbent was the aforementioned Craig Williams whose supposed transgressions allowed the Labour Party to be the apparent beneficiaries of significant levels of tactical voting to win in one of the very few areas of Wales it had never represented before. The Conservatives also saw the near total collapse of support among younger voters in Wales. While the party has always enjoyed far more substantial support among older voters, data from the Welsh Election Study paints a particularly stark picture for the party; just 5% of under-30s and 7% of those aged 30 to 50 voted for them, with less than 10% of all under-65s voting for the party (Larner 2024b).

Labour's capture of twenty-seven seats out of thirty-two appears, at first glance, to represent a triumph of electoral strategy and political dominance and suggests the previously discussed internal problems did little to dampen enthusiasm among voters. The raw numbers suggest a remarkable recovery from 2019's relatively 'weak' showing of twenty-two seats from forty. The party comfortably won constituency contests across the entirety of South Wales including areas that have demographically moved to be less favourable for the party such as Monmouthshire and the Vale of Glamorgan. More importantly for the party however was that it managed to reclaim ground lost to the Conservatives in the heavy Leave-voting areas in the North East of Wales and expanded into areas where it had never won representation before. Yet this apparent triumph masks a more complex—and potentially troubling—reality about the state of Labour's political hegemony in Wales. Labour's four percentage point decline from its already disappointing 2019 performance places its 2024 vote share among the party's four worst results in Welsh electoral history, and represents the lowest vote share ever in Wales for an incoming Labour government. And while the party was successful in every two-way Labour-Conservative contest, the party failed to win in any of the three seats where it faced a credible challenger (Caerfyrddin, Ynys Môn, and Brecon, Radnor, and Cwm Tawe).

The party's strategic response to this contradiction has been to frame it as a triumph of tactical resource allocation—a deliberate choice to concentrate efforts in marginal constituencies while accepting reduced majorities in safer seats. This explanation aligns with contemporary campaign theory about the efficient distribution of finite resources under first-past-the-post electoral systems (e.g. Sudulich and Trumm 2019). However, such tactical rationalization fails to address the broader pattern of declining Labour support across Wales, a pattern that manifests across multiple electoral arenas. Perhaps most concerning for Welsh Labour strategists is the emerging gap between Westminster and Senedd voting intentions. Recent polling data reveals a growing disparity between support for UK Labour and its Welsh counterpart, with Westminster voting intentions consistently outperforming Senedd constituency preferences (Larner 2024a). The implications of this paradox extend beyond mere political arithmetic. Labour's longstanding dominance of Welsh politics has been predicated on its ability to lean on its Welsh identity and represent Welsh interests while acting as a bulwark against the 'nationalism' of Plaid Cymru (Moon 2013). The combination of declining vote share and diverging levels of support between different electoral arenas suggests that in the absence of a challenger facing electoral collapse, the party's foundations are not as strong as they have been in the past, with the party increasingly dependent on the vagaries of first-past-the-post mathematics rather than genuine popular enthusiasm.

Plaid Cymru was one of the few parties in Wales to have an unambiguously 'good' election, winning its highest-ever share of the vote at a Westminster election (14.8%) and equalling its record of four MPs. Two of the party's seats—Dwyfor Meirionydd and Ceredigion Preseli—are now the safest constituencies in Wales with majorities of over 14,000 votes, representing a remarkable consolidation of Plaid's position in Y Fro Cymraeg (Welsh-speaking Wales). This is particularly striking in Ceredigion which, as recently as 2015, was considered a marginal contest between Plaid and the Liberal Democrats. Equally significant was Plaid's success in securing victories in both Caerfyrddin[2] and Ynys Môn—constituencies characterized by genuine three-way competitions between Plaid, Labour, and the

---

[2]Caerfyrddin was also the seat of Government's chief whip and former Secretary of State for Wales, Simon Hart.

Conservatives and heavily targeted by Labour campaigning in particular with Keir Starmer visiting Whitland in Caerfyrddin on the final day of the campaign.

However, the 2024 results also highlight Plaid Cymru's persistent geographic and cultural limitations. Outside Y Fro Cymraeg, the party's electoral presence remains minimal, managing only distant second-place finishes in five constituencies. The downside of successfully investing the party's resources and campaign focus in Caerfyrddin and Ynys Môn came at the cost of ceding second-place positions across much of the South Wales valleys to Reform UK. While this might seem a reasonable strategic choice for a Westminster election in which expectations are usually low for the party, it could have longer-term implications for Plaid's ambitions to establish itself as the primary challenger to Labour across wider swathes of Wales. This pattern reinforces long-standing questions about Plaid's ability to transcend its traditional linguistic and cultural boundaries to build a truly national presence (Balsom, Madgwick and van Mechelen 1983). Yet the focus for Plaid Cymru will inevitably turn now to the devolved election of 2026. Labour's declining support in Senedd voting intentions, combined with the implementation of a new electoral system and systematic multilevel voting, may create openings for Plaid to expand its influence beyond its traditional geographic and linguistic heartlands.

3.1 Other parties

The Liberal Democrats were the only other party to win representation in Wales, in the large rural constituency of Brecon, Radnor, and Cwm Tawe, an area that the party has historically been very strong in. However, the combination of general Liberal decline across Wales and the addition of the post-industrial northern Tawe valley into the seat meant that the seat's demographics had shifted away from the party. Liberal Democrat incumbency is now largely reliant on tactical voting.

The emergence of Reform UK as the primary challenger to Labour across the South Wales valleys represents one of the more significant stories of the election in Wales. Their decision to launch their manifesto in Merthyr Tydfil (BBC News 2024b)—a symbolic heartland of Welsh Labour tradition and working-class politics—signalled a motivation to force the region's potential for political realignment. These areas have historically exhibited a deep-seated antipathy toward the Conservative party brand and the persistence of what might be termed 'anti-Tory affect'—emotionally charged memories of deindustrialization and Thatcherite policies—that has rendered these communities relatively immune to recent Conservative electoral advances across the rest of Wales (Wyn Jones, Scully, and Trystan 2002; Larner et al., 2022). Yet these same areas also voted heavily to Leave the European Union, with Reform UK targeting their campaign messages to these voters. The party's targeting of these areas was validated by the result: the party finished second in thirteen Welsh constituencies, including in eight of ten valleys seats. Reform UK's relative success in these areas suggests they may have identified a route to mobilizing socially conservative sentiment while circumventing the toxic associations of the Conservative brand. This represents a potentially significant shift in the valleys' political dynamics – building on the previous success of UKIP in 2015 and 2016 (Bradbury 2015; Scully and Larner 2017) where previous right-wing challenges—whether from UKIP or the Conservatives—have struggled to overcome the region's ingrained political memory.

Yet data from the Welsh Election Study suggests that Reform UK was largely unsuccessful at persuading former Labour voters to vote for them. Instead, the party was the clear and obvious beneficiary of the Conservative decline: approximately 35% of 2019 Conservative voters voted for Reform UK, compared with 39% for the Conservatives. Those who switched tended to be much younger and economically left-wing compared with remaining Conservative voters. The other distinctive feature of these switchers is the relative dissatisfaction with how the UK Government has handled Brexit, as illustrated in Fig. 8.2. The source of Reform UK's support raises several intriguing questions about the future of political competition in these areas. First, there is the question of whether their second-place finishes represent a ceiling or a foundation for future growth. The

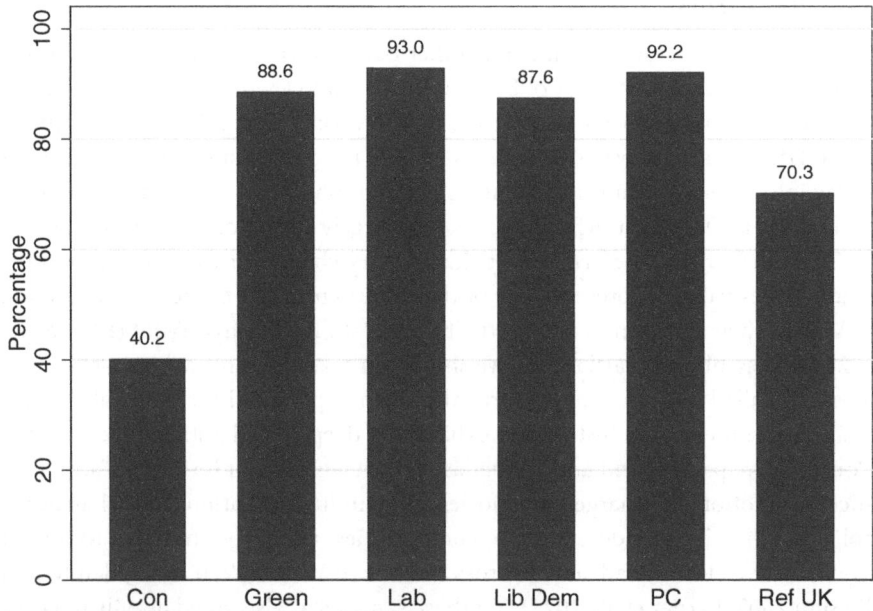

Figure 8.2. Proportion of respondents who thought the UK Government has done a bad job of Brexit, by 2024 vote

spatial dimension of Reform UK's support—concentrated in areas where turnout has historically been low—suggests potential for electoral expansion if the party can successfully mobilize disengaged voters. Yet this same pattern might also indicate the limitations of their appeal: strong enough to attract protest votes in low-turnout elections but perhaps insufficient to challenge Labour's structural advantages when participation increases.

4. Conclusion

A century after Labour's ascendance in Welsh politics, the 2024 General Election offered a paradoxical reinforcement of the party's dominance: an expanded parliamentary presence masking an increasingly fragile electoral foundation. While Labour's 1922 breakthrough established its hegemony in Welsh politics, its 2024 performance suggests both the resilience and potential vulnerability of that century-old supremacy. This pattern echoes similar warning signs observed in 2015 (see Bradbury 2015), though these were temporarily obscured by Labour's exceptional surge in the 2017 election. The backdrop to this electoral landscape is particularly striking. The 2019-24 Parliament witnessed the most severe stagnation in Welsh average incomes since records began in 1971, surpassing even the profound economic disruption of 1979-83 when Wales lost approximately 100,000 manufacturing and mining jobs (Ifan et al., 2022). This economic context, combined with the most extensive constituency boundary changes in recent history—reducing Welsh parliamentary representation to its lowest level since 1865—has created unprecedented pressures on traditional voting patterns.

Looking ahead, several factors suggest continued evolution in Welsh electoral behaviour. The implementation of an expanded Senedd and reformed electoral system in 2026 will likely accelerate the trend toward multilevel voting (Henderson et al., 2022: 182-7). The growing divergence between Westminster and Senedd voting preferences, particularly evident in Labour's drastically reduced advantage in devolved contexts, indicates an electorate increasingly willing to calibrate its political choices according to governance level. Meanwhile, the Conservative base's partial migration toward explicitly devosceptic positions in Senedd elections points to deepening ideological fissures in Welsh conservatism. These developments suggest that Welsh politics may be approaching an inflection point. While Labour's century-long dominance of Welsh Westminster politics appears secure for now, the party's ability to maintain its historical supremacy across all levels of governance faces unprecedented challenges.

Acknowledgements

This work was supported by the Economic and Social Research Council (grant number ES/V009559/1).

References

Balsom, D., Madgwick, P. J., and van Mechelen, D. (1983) 'The Red And The Green: Patterns Of Partisan Choice in Wales', *British Journal of Political Science*, 13, 299–325.

BBC News (2024a, 13 June) 'Tory Candidate Tells BBC Election Bet Was "Huge Error of Judgement"', https://www.bbc.co.uk/news/articles/cneevz8278eo, accessed 2 Nov. 2024.

BBC News (2024b, 17 June) 'Farage: Wales Shows What a Labour Government Will Do', https://www.bbc.co.uk/news/articles/c0vvy8y0ze1o, accessed 5 Nov. 2024.

BBC News (2024c, 1 August) 'Serious Road Casualties Drop in Wales since 20mph', https://www.bbc.co.uk/news/articles/cydvr2rnm4ro, accessed 1 Dec. 2024.

Bradbury, J. (2015) 'Wales: Still a Labour Stronghold but Under Threat?', in: A. Geddes and J. Tonge (eds) *Britain Votes 2015*. Oxford: Oxford University Press, pp. 101-16.

Burn-Murdoch, J. (2024, 7 November) 'Democrats Join 2024's Graveyard of Incumbents', *Financial Times*, https://www.ft.com/content/e8ac09ea-c300-4249-af7d-109003afb893, accessed 1 Dec. 2024.

Davies, N. (2024) 'The Language of Priorities: Aneurin Bevan, Welsh Labour and the Politics of the Past', *The British Journal of Politics and International Relations*, 26: 62-78.

Guardian (2024, 25 June) 'Election Betting: Fifth Tory Investigated in Growing Scandal', https://www.theguardian.com/politics/article/2024/jun/25/election-betting-fifth-tory-investigated-in-growing-scandal, accessed 1 Dec. 2024.

Henderson, A. et al. (2022) *The Referendum that Changed a Nation: Scottish Voting Behaviour 2014–2019*, London: Springer Nature.

Henderson, A. and Wyn Jones, R. (2023) 'The Ambivalent Union: Findings from the State of the Union Survey', *Institute for Public Policy Research*, https://ippr-org.files.svdcdn.com/production/Downloads/the-ambivalent-union-sept23.pdf, accessed 1 Nov. 2024.

Ifan, G. and Siôn, C. (2019) 'Cut to the Bone? An Analysis of Local Government Finances in Wales, 2009-10 to 2017-18 and the Outlook to 2023-34', *Wales Fiscal Analysis*, https://www.cardiff.ac.uk/__data/assets/pdf_file/0010/1448920/local_government_finance_report_Feb19_final.pdf, accessed 1 Dec. 2024.

Ifan, G. et al. (2022) 'Welsh Budget Outlook 2022', *Wales Fiscal Analysis*, https://www.cardiff.ac.uk/__data/assets/pdf_file/0007/2688199/wbo_2022_full_report_final.pdf, accessed 1 Dec. 2024.

Larner, J. (2024a, 25 July) 'Welsh Labour and the Travails of Single-Party Dominance', *UK in a Changing Europe*, https://ukandeu.ac.uk/welsh-labour-and-the-travails-of-single-party-dominance/, accessed 3 Nov. 2024.

Larner, J. (2024b, 7 November) 'The 2024 UK General Election and Wales - Etholiad Cyffredinol y DU 2024 a Chymru', *Wales Governance Centre*, https://www.youtube.com/watch?v=7CMXfpiWfso, accessed 2 Dec. 2024.

Larner, J. et al. (2022) 'Incumbency and Identity: The 2021 Senedd Election', *Parliamentary Affairs*, 76: 857–78.

LBC (2024, 9 June) Interview between Lewis Goodall and Emily Thornberry, https://x.com/LBC/status/1799767840561439014?lang=en, accessed 1 Dec. 2024.

Moon, D. S. (2013) 'Rhetoric and Policy Learning: On Rhodri Morgan's "Clear Red Water" and "Made in Wales" health policies', *Public Policy and Administration*, 28: 306-23.

Redfield and Wilton (2023, 18 October) 'Majority of Welsh Voters Now Oppose New 20mph Speed Limit', https://redfieldandwiltonstrategies.com/majority-of-welsh-voters-now-oppose-new-20mph-speed-limit/, accessed 1 Dec. 2024.

S4C (2024, 17 June) 'Newyddion Interview between Catrin Haf and Jo Stevens', https://x.com/NewyddionS4C/status/1802786241852707250, accessed 1 Dec. 2024.

Scully, R. and Larner, J. (2017) 'A Successful Defence: the 2016 National Assembly for Wales Election', *Parliamentary Affairs*, 70: 507–29.

Sudulich, L. and Trumm, S. (2019) 'A Comparative Study of the Effects of Electoral Institutions on Campaigns', *British Journal of Political Science*, 49: 381–99.

Surridge, P. and Larner, J. (2021) 'Elections 2021: What Happens in Cardif Stays in Cardiff?', *Political Studies Association Blog*, https://www.psa.ac.uk/psa/news/elections-2021-what-happens-cardiff-stays-cardiff, accessed 1 Dec. 2024.

Welsh Labour (2024) *Change: Welsh Labour Manifesto 2024*, https://labour.org.uk/wp-content/uploads/2024/06/Change-Welsh-Labour-Manifesto-2024-large-print.pdf, accessed 1 Dec. 2024.

Wyn Jones, R. (2024, 6 June) 'Vaughan Gething's Leadership Crisis is a Disaster – for Wales, for Labour and maybe even for devolution', *The Guardian*, https://www.theguardian.com/commentisfree/article/2024/jun/06/vaughan-gething-labour-wales-devolution, accessed 1 Nov. 2024.

Wyn Jones, R., Scully, R. and Trystan, D. (2002) 'Why do the conservatives always do (even) worse in Wales?' *British Elections & Parties Review*, 12: 229–45.

Northern Ireland: Sinn Féin completes a hat-trick

Jonathan Tonge* and Stuart Wilks-Heeg

Department of Politics, School of Histories, Languages and Cultures, University of Liverpool, Liverpool, L69 7WZ, UK

*Correspondence: j.tonge@liverpool.ac.uk

Northern Ireland's election saw Sinn Féin complete a hat-trick few would have envisaged at the start of the century. The party became the region's largest at Westminster, to add to its status as the biggest seat-holder in both the devolved power-sharing Northern Ireland Assembly and in local government, lead positions attained in 2022 and 2023, respectively. Sinn Féin continued, however, to refuse to take its seven seats in the House of Commons, declining to swear an oath of allegiance to a British monarch. Two re-elected Social Democratic and Labour Party (SDLP) MPs, Colum Eastwood and Claire Hanna, continued as the only Irish nationalist representatives within the Westminster parliament.

Sinn Féin became Northern Ireland's largest Westminster contingent merely by retaining all their seats at the 2024 election, as unionist representation fragmented and the Democratic Unionist Party (DUP) endured reverses. At the previous two general elections, the DUP had been the only unionist party elected. Now, remarkably, three unionist parties plus an Independent Unionist were elected across the eight constituencies which sent a unionist representative to Westminster. 543 English seats managed to send just five parties and a sprinkling of independents to the Commons. Such are the divisions within unionism, however, that it came close in party diversity with 535 fewer constituencies. The DUP had a poor election, the only Northern Ireland party to endure a net seat loss, three in total. The party was joined in representing unionism in the Commons by the Ulster Unionist Party (UUP) and, unexpectedly, the Traditional Unionist Voice (TUV) along with a former DUP member turned Independent Unionist, Alex Easton. Beyond the unionist and nationalist ideological blocs, the Alliance Party lost its North Down seat to Easton but gained Lagan Valley from the DUP.

This contribution analyses the contests and outcomes. It begins by assessing the continuing salience of the traditional voting faultline. Northern Ireland remains a polity where party choices are shaped by religious community background more than any other in Europe. Continuing Protestant-British-Unionist versus Catholic-Irish-Nationalist inter-communal rivalry was nonetheless accompanied by significant intra-bloc division within unionism over the degree of European Union (EU) influence upon the region's post-Brexit trading arrangements. This controversy collapsed Northern Ireland's power-sharing Assembly and Executive for two years from Spring 2022 and influenced unionist party choice at the election. Such fracture contributed to the DUP's losses to rival unionists. We analyse the continuing dominance of Sinn Féin within nationalism, evident for more than two decades, before assessing why electoral unionism is so disparate. Finally, the final section considers whether the solitary sizeable party located beyond unionism and nationalism, Alliance, has plateaued following its recent surge in support.

1. The results

Table 9.1 shows the overall results, in terms of votes, percentage shares and seats. Table 9.2 displays party fortunes in each constituency and Table 9.3 shows the constituency placings of each party that won a seat. At 57%, turnout was, as usual, below the UK average. Postal voting in Northern Ireland requires a reason and a

Table 9.1. The Northern Ireland General Election result 2024

	Seats contested and change from 2019	Votes	% Vote	% Change from 2019	Seats won	Seat change from 2019	Seats with increase in vote share from 2019	Seats with decrease in vote share from 2019
SF	14 (−1)	210,891	27.0	+4.2	7	NC	11	3
DUP	16 (−1)	172,058	22.1	−8.5	5	−3	3	13
Alliance	18 (NC)	117,191	15.0	−1.8	1	NC	6	12
SDLP	18 (+3)	86,861	11.1	−3.8	2	NC	1	14
UUP	17 (+1)	94,779	12.2	+0.5	1	+1	7	9
TUV	14 (+14)	48,685	6.3	DNS	1	+1	NA	NA
Others	39 (+18)	48,751	6.3	+3.1	1	+1		

Turnout: 57% (-4.5%).
Notes: NC = No change. NA = Not applicable. DNS = Did not stand.

Table 9.2. Northern Ireland constituency results, Westminster Election 2024

Constituency	Result	Winning Majority	DUP	UUP	Alliance	Sinn Féin	SDLP	TUV	Others	Turnout	Turnout change
Belfast East	DUP HOLD	2,676	46.6 (−1.3)	4.3 (−1.5)	40.3 (−1.8)	DNS (DNS)	1.4 (DNS)	4.5 (DNS)	2.9	64.3	−5.8
Belfast North	SF HOLD	5,612	29.8 (−10.5)	DNS (DNS)	10.6 (+0.8)	43.7 (−4.4)	3.5 (DNS)	7.1 (DNS)	5.3	54.4	−12.5
Belfast South & Mid Down	SDLP HOLD	12,506	15.8 (−9.6)	6.1 (+2.5)	20.3 (+4.9)	DNS (DNS)	49.1 (−4.2)	5.1 (DNS)	3.6	67.9	−9.6
Belfast West	SF HOLD	15,961	10.8 (−7.4)	1.2 (+0.3)	2.7 (−4.4)	52.9 (+4.4)	10.9 (+3.5)	5.1 (DNS)	16.4	53.0	−6.9
East Antrim	DUP HOLD	1,306	28.9 (−13.0)	23.9 (+7.3)	25.6 (−0.4)	7.5 (−0.3)	2.2 (−1.4)	10.4 (DNS)	1.5	54.0	−3.5
East Londonderry	DUP HOLD	179	27.9 (−12.1)	8.3 (−0.8)	9.0 (−5.5)	27.4 (+12.0)	12.7 (−3.7)	10.6 (DNS)	4.1	55.0	−1.8
Fermanagh & S Tyrone	SF HOLD	4,571	DNS (DNS)	39.7 (−1.9)	4.7 (−0.7)	48.6 (+6.1)	4.7 (−2.5)	DNS	2.3	65.6	−4.5
Foyle	SDLP HOLD	4,166	10.2 (+1.5)	3.7 (+1.7)	3.3 (+0.6)	29.9 (+8.7)	40.8 (−17.4)	DNS	12.1	52.0	−11.2
Lagan Valley	ALLIANCE GAIN FROM DUP	2,959	31.9 (−11.5)	22.7 (+4.2)	37.9 (+10.8)	DNS	2.1 (−2.0)	4.5 (DNS)	0.9	60.0	−0.2
Mid Ulster	SF HOLD	14,923	20.2 (−3.6)	5.0 (−2.5)	4.4 (−3.2)	53.0 (+7.3)	8.2 (−5.7)	6.6 (DNS)	2.6	61.4	−1.9

Table 9.2. Northern Ireland constituency results, Westminster Election 2024

Constituency	Result	Winning Majority	DUP	UUP	Alliance	Sinn Féin	SDLP	TUV	Others	Turnout	Turnout change
Newry & Armagh	SF HOLD	9,287	12.8 (−7.4)	6.9 (−0.8)	5.9 (−2.5)	48.5 (+7.5)	14.8 (−4.6)	8.9 (DNS)	2.2	59.1	−3.7
North Antrim	TUV GAIN FROM DUP	450	27.2 (−23.6)	9.5 (−7.4)	10.9 (−3.4)	18.7 (+7.4)	4.0 (−1.9)	28.3 (DNS)	1.4	55.0	−2.0
North Down	IND. GAIN FROM ALLIANCE	7,305	DNS	15.6 (+3.7)	31.4 (−13.5)	DNS	1.5 (DNS)	DNS	51.5 IND U = 48.3 (+9.6)	59.0	−1.6
South Antrim	UUP GAIN FROM DUP	7,512	20.5 (−15.7)	38.0 (+8.9)	10.7 (−7.7)	18.7 (+7.3)	3.7 (−1.3)	6.3 (DNS)	2.1	56.0	−3.9
South Down	SF HOLD	9,280	16.2 (+0.9)	3.1 (−3.5)	7.0 (−6.9)	43.6 (+11.2)	23.0 (−6.2)	4.2 (DNS)	2.9	59.0	−3.4
Strangford	DUP HOLD	5,131	40.0 (−0.5)	10.1 (+0.9)	26.8 (+0.6)	7.2 (−0.4)	4.6 (−5.4)	8.1 (DNS)	3.2	52.2	−4.6
Upper Bann	DUP HOLD	7,406	45.7 (+4.9)	7.7 (−4.8)	13.3 (+0.6)	30.1 (+5.4)	3.2 (−6.2)	DNS	0.0	58.0	−2.0
West Tyrone	SF HOLD	15,917	15.5 (−6.2)	6.1 (−0.5)	5.2 (−4.4)	52.0 (+11.9)	13.3 (−5.2)	5.8 (DNS)	2.1	59.0	−3.9

Notes: 2019 election figures in brackets. DNS denotes 'did not stand'.

countersigned application and, at 22,924, formed only 3% of votes cast, way below the percentage in Great Britain.

2. Still sectarian head-counting?

Given the depth and seeming permanence of its divide, the fluidity of Northern Ireland's constituency outcomes may surprise. Only two of its eighteen seats, the Sinn Féin strongholds of Mid Ulster and West Belfast, have not changed hands this century. Nonetheless, the balance of religious community background usually shapes whether a constituency returns a unionist or nationalist candidate. Tables 9.4 and 9.5 indicate the solidity of this linkage. Table 9.4 shows where parties drew their support from in 2024 in terms of the self-declared religious affiliation of voters. As can be seen, no Catholics admitted voting for unionist parties and very few Protestants voted for nationalist ones. Table 9.5 shows the Protestant, Catholic and no-religion percentages of electors in each constituency and provides the percentage votes for unionists, nationalists and 'neithers'.

Table 9.3. Party constituency placings

	1st place	2nd place	3rd place
Sinn Féin	7	3	2
DUP	5	6	4
SDLP	2	2	4
Alliance	1	5	3
UUP	1	1	4
TUV	1	0	1

Note: Seat-winning parties only.

Table 9.4. Party votes by self-declared religious affiliation of voters, 2024 Northern Ireland Westminster Election (%)

	Catholic	Protestant	No religion	Other religion	Total
Sinn Féin	96.9	1.4	1.7	0.0	100
DUP	0.0	92.5	7.1	0.4	100
SDLP	83.9	5.2	10.3	0.6	100
UUP	0.0	94.4	5.6	0.0	100
Alliance	22.0	52.2	25.3	0.5	100
TUV	0.0	92.1	7.9	0.0	100

Source: Tonge et al. (2024b); Northern Ireland General Election survey 2024.

Table 9.5. Constituency outcomes by religion and vote shares by pro-Northern Ireland (NI) in the UK versus pro-United Ireland (UI) candidates, Northern Ireland election 2024

Constituency	Protestant % of the constituency	Roman Catholic % of the constituency	% Unionist vote	% Nationalist vote	No religion % of the constituency	% Non-Unionist and non-Nationalist vote	Constitutional position of winning candidate
Belfast East	52.7	13.0	55.4	1.4	32.0	43.2	Pro-UK
Belfast North	31.2	44.2	36.9	49.5	19.0	13.6	Pro-UI
Belfast South & Mid Down	29.9	38.0	27.0	49.1	27.4	23.9	Pro-UI
Belfast West	17.2	70.7	17.1	78.8	10.6	4.1	Pro-UI
East Antrim	55.9	17.8	63.3	9.7	25.2	27.0	Pro-UK
East Londonderry	43.7	40.4	47.3	42.6	15.2	10.1	Pro-UK
Fermanagh & S Tyrone	31.4	58.5	39.7	54.4	9.2	5.9	Pro-UI
Foyle	17.0	72.5	13.9	82.4	9.4	3.7	Pro-UI
Lagan Valley	53.8	21.6	59.1	2.1	23.2	38.8	No Position
Mid Ulster	27.8	64.1	31.8	63.8	7.6	4.4	Pro-UI
Newry & Armagh	23.9	65.9	28.9	65.2	9.4	5.9	Pro-UI
North Antrim	55.3	27.8	65.3	23.8	16.2	10.9	Pro-UK
North Down	54.6	10.7	63.9	1.5	33.4	34.6	Pro-UK
South Antrim	47.1	30.0	64.8	23.2	21.8	12.0	Pro-UK
South Down	23.4	65.4	23.6	68.4	10.6	8.0	Pro-UI

Table 9.5. Constituency outcomes by religion and vote shares by pro-Northern Ireland (NI) in the UK versus pro-United Ireland (UI) candidates, Northern Ireland election 2024

Constituency	Protestant % of the constituency	% Unionist vote	Roman Catholic % of the constituency	% Nationalist vote	No religion % of the constituency	% Non-Unionist and non-Nationalist vote	Constitutional position of winning candidate
Strangford	52.8	58.6	21.2	11.8	25.0	29.6	Pro-UK
Upper Bann	40.5	53.4	41.6	33.3	16.5	13.3	Pro-UK
West Tyrone	26.0	27.6	67.0	67.2	6.5	5.2	Pro-UI

Notes: People Before Profit is classed as an 'Other' party in the Northern Ireland Assembly but favour a United Ireland, so its vote is added to the UI tally. The Greens, Alliance and all bar two independents are classed as constitutional neutrals. Religious figures exclude the small percentages for other religions.
Source for religious compositions: Northern Ireland Census 2021; Religion, UK Data Service CKAN.

Table 9.5 shows that in only two constituencies, South Antrim and Upper Bann, did the unionist vote vary by more than ten percentage points from the proportion of Protestants resident in the seat (North Antrim was not far behind). In these cases, strong intra-unionist competition boosted the combined unionist vote. There were only three constituencies where the nationalist vote varied by more than ten percentage points from the proportion of Catholics. Relatively low support for a nationalist candidate in Lagan Valley and Belfast East is explained by nationalist willingness to back an Alliance Party constitutional neutral to try to oust a unionist, whilst a particularly high vote for the nationalist SDLP in South Belfast and Mid Down is explained by the popularity of its candidate.

Every constituency containing more Catholics than Protestants returned a pro-United Ireland MP except for Upper Bann, where the religious split is almost equal. Lagan Valley, a mainly Protestant constituency, returned a constitutionally neutral Alliance MP amid exceptional local circumstances relating to the former MP, explained below. Unionists may take some comfort from Table 9.4 in indicating that support for unionist candidates is not dependent exclusively upon Protestant identifiers. In fifteen constituencies the percentage vote for pro-Union candidates exceeded the percentage of Protestants in the seat but the excess was very modest.

The scatterplot in Fig. 9.1 shows the continuing strength of the relationships between Catholic religious affiliation and support for nationalist parties. Fig. 9.2

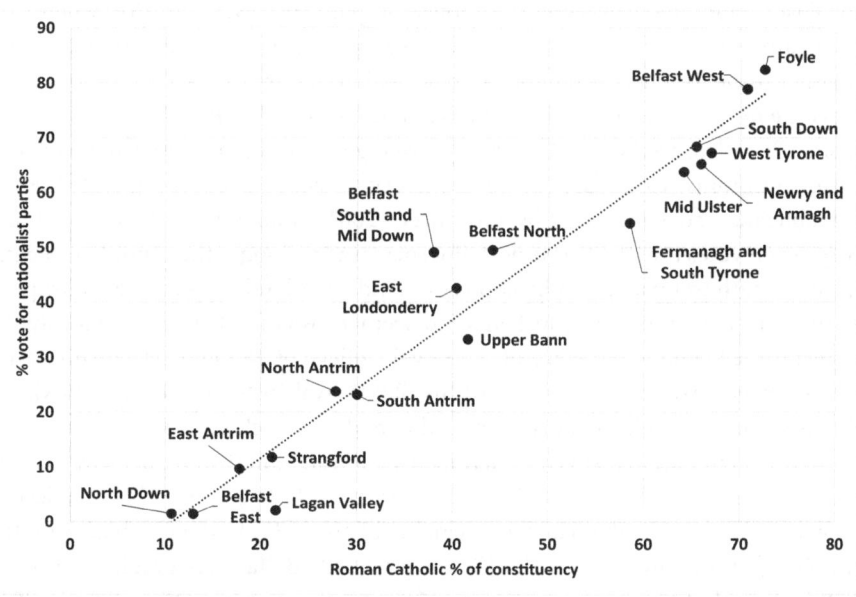

Figure 9.1. Roman Catholic population (%) by constituency and vote share for nationalist parties (%), Northern Ireland 2024 General Election (r = 0.98)

demonstrates a very similar relationship between Protestant affiliation and support for unionist parties. More than two-and-a-half decades after the Good Friday Agreement, progress towards electoral rapprochement, in terms of voting for a party on the other side of the sectarian divide, is very slow. Thawing is evidenced mainly via an increased willingness to vote for a non-bloc party, Alliance, not the casting of ballots beyond the divide for the rival bloc's parties.

3. A treble, abstention, and the timing of a border poll: the contest within nationalism

In advancing to become Northern Ireland's largest Westminster party, Sinn Féin was the only party to significantly improve its vote share, up by more than four percentage points. The party's Assembly and local government gains in the two preceding years had followed a poor performance at the 2019 General Election. At that contest, a drop in vote share of seven percentage points and the loss of Foyle to the SDLP was masked only partly by the gain of North Belfast from the DUP, with Sinn Féin blamed for collapsing the devolved power-sharing Assembly two years earlier.

In 2024, Sinn Féin comfortably held all their seats and came within 179 votes of a shock victory over the DUP in East Londonderry. There, Sinn Féin turned what had been the DUP's second safest seat into a marginal, Gregory Campbell retaining East Londonderry by a mere 179 votes compared with 9,607 in 2019 when Sinn Féin came third behind the SDLP. Remarkably, Sinn Féin made Fermanagh and South Tyrone look a safe republican seat, with a majority of 4,571. Although the constituency had been held by Sinn Féin's Michelle Gildernew since 2001, apart from a 2015 loss to the UUP, the party's average winning majority when faced by a single unionist candidate (all elections except 2005) had been just 272 votes. Republicans had triumphed by fifty-three (2001), four (2010), 875 (2017) and fifty-seven votes (2019). This time, Gildernew was no longer the candidate, having headed south to unsuccessfully contest Ireland's Midlands-North-West European Parliament constituency. Sinn Féin's replacement was Pat Cullen, previously the high-profile General Secretary of the Royal College of Nursing. Meanwhile, Sinn Féin's Chris Hazzard easily defeated his SDLP rival in South Down, enjoying a five-fold increase in his majority from what had been a close contest in 2019.

In the main nationalist versus nationalist contest, Sinn Féin reduced the SDLP's Colum Eastwood's majority in Foyle by more than 12,000 votes. This was despite Eastwood appearing the 'runaway winner' of the BBC leaders' debate and 'triumphing' in the previous week's UTV equivalent (Belfast Telegraph 2024a). An SDLP stronghold since its creation in 1983, Foyle was lost to Sinn Féin in 2017 amid an SDLP Westminster wipeout. The seat was recaptured by Eastwood in 2019 with a remarkable 17,000 majority, Eastwood polling a higher vote than even

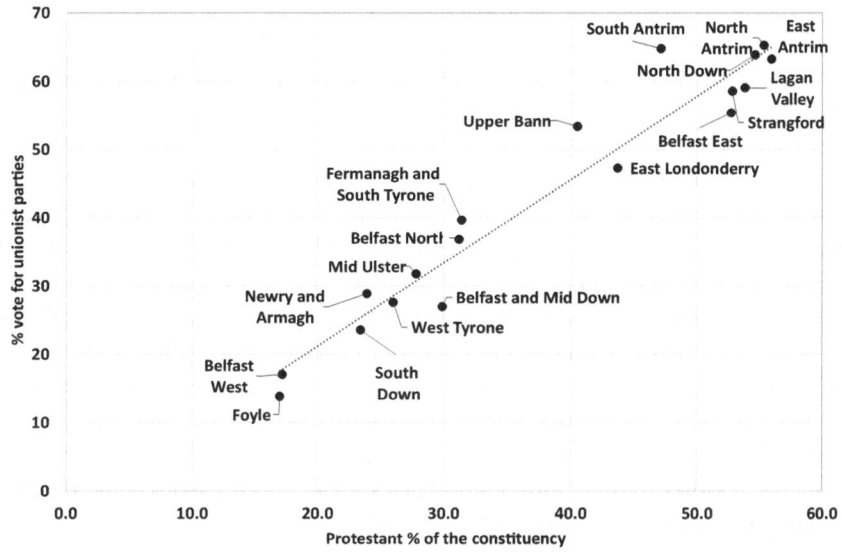

Figure 9.2. Protestant population (%) by constituency and vote share for unionist parties (%), Northern Ireland 2024 General Election (r = 0.97)

John Hume, SDLP leader from 1979 to 2001 and the closest thing to a local saint, ever managed. The reduction in Eastwood's majority may have contributed to his decision to step down as SDLP leader after the 2024 election, to concentrate on defending the seat next time. Eastwood was replaced as leader by the SDLP's other MP, Claire Hanna.

Hanna's re-election in South Belfast and Mid Down with a five-figure majority was assisted by Sinn Féin's absence, for the second successive election. Hanna also enjoys considerable personal popularity, part of the reason Sinn Féin stood aside, asking supporters to back 'progressive candidates' (Irish News 2024). The 'Hanna factor', contributing to her ascent to the party leadership, is evident when comparing her Westminster triumph with the SDLP's poor fourth on vote share in South Belfast at the previous year's local elections.

At ten pages, Sinn Féin's election manifesto was decidedly flimsy (Sinn Féin 2024). Yet the party's performance was much stronger than that south of the border in European and local elections during the previous month. Then, the party had been afflicted by immigration issues, with a tougher line demanded from sections of its working-class base. In the North, Sinn Féin has no such problems and the erosion of SDLP support, temporarily reversed in 2019, was resumed. Sinn Féin's domination of nationalist politics owes much to how the party has changed from its conflict incarnation. Its leader in Northern Ireland, Michelle O'Neill, insists she is 'First Minister for all'. That has involved appearances at the late Queen's funeral and the King's coronation, attendance at a Northern Ireland football match and even occasional use of the term 'Northern Ireland', steps unthinkable for the previous republican generation.

A traditional republican position, abstention from Westminster, divides Sinn Féin and the SDLP. Throughout the campaign, the SDLP talked up the value of sending representatives to sit in the Commons. The SDLP also emphasised the value of its status as a 'sister party' of the Labour Party given the seeming certainty of a change of government. The SDLP's overall vote share, however, fell for the sixth time in seven Westminster elections this century, to its lowest level since the party first contested a general election in February 1974. Sinn Féin leads the SDLP in all age categories under-65, as those politically socialised in an era of SDLP dominance enter senior years. The 'sister party' claim is contested by those wanting Labour to field candidates in Northern Ireland, who argue no such status exists in either party's constitution (Black 2024). Both parties were, however, founding members of the Party of European Socialists.

There are few policy differences between the SDLP and Sinn Féin. The latter holds the obvious structural advantage of being an all-Ireland party. Believing in a United Ireland but only standing in one corner and unable to secure a permanent arrangement with a party south of the border does not assist the SDLP. The party has insufficient Stormont seats for a place in the Northern Ireland Executive, although fronting the official Opposition may do no harm.

Both nationalist parties desire a border poll, a constitutional referendum on whether Northern Ireland remains in the UK or forms part of United Ireland, but differ on optimum timing. Sinn Féin argues a date should be set for such a contest, preferably within a decade; the SDLP is more circumspect on the calendar. The Secretary of State for Northern Ireland decides when a contest takes place and is obliged to call one only when it appears there is a majority in favour of constitutional change. Hilary Benn, as current postholder, will not be rushing. Immediately post-election, Prime Minister Keir Starmer did affirm that, in the unlikely event of a poll being called during his premiership, the UK government would be an honest broker, whereas in opposition he indicated he would campaign for the Union, but a contest was not envisaged (Irish Times 2024). Legal efforts to create the criteria on which the Secretary of State must make a judgement on whether to call a border poll have floundered.

Did the election bring a border poll any nearer? Sinn Féin's largest party status is juxtaposed with less favourable indicators for Irish unity. Averaging across post-Brexit opinion polls, support for Northern Ireland remaining in the UK averages 49% – hardly a resounding endorsement – but backing for a United Ireland only reaches 35%. Assessment of recent elections offers something for both camps. Support for pro-United Ireland candidates at the 2023 local elections totalled almost 44%, exceeding backing for candidates preferring the constitutional status quo by almost four points (O'Leary and Pow 2023). In the 2022 Assembly elections the two blocs were almost tied, with votes for unionists exceeding those for nationalists by a mere 0.6 of a percentage point. The 2024 General Election offered slightly greater reassurance for unionism in that it saw a reversion to the norm of unionist votes exceeding those cast for nationalists. However, the gap of 2.7 percentage points was the lowest ever recorded for a Westminster contest and it is worth remembering that Sinn Féin stood in the fewest seats of the main five parties. Fig. 9.3 shows the bloc percentage votes at general elections since the 1998 Good Friday Agreement. As can be seen, the unionist bloc vote has subsided, down nine percentage points this century but nationalism has not advanced its vote share. The percentage of votes cast for pro-United Ireland candidates was lower in 2024 than in 2001. The bloc that has grown has been that of 'others', those neither unionist nor nationalist.

4. Another Brexit election: fragmentation within unionism

Within unionism, another Brexit election took place. The acceptability or unacceptability of the terms of Northern Ireland's departure from the EU was the faultline within unionist politics. The issue had raged for years. The 2017-19

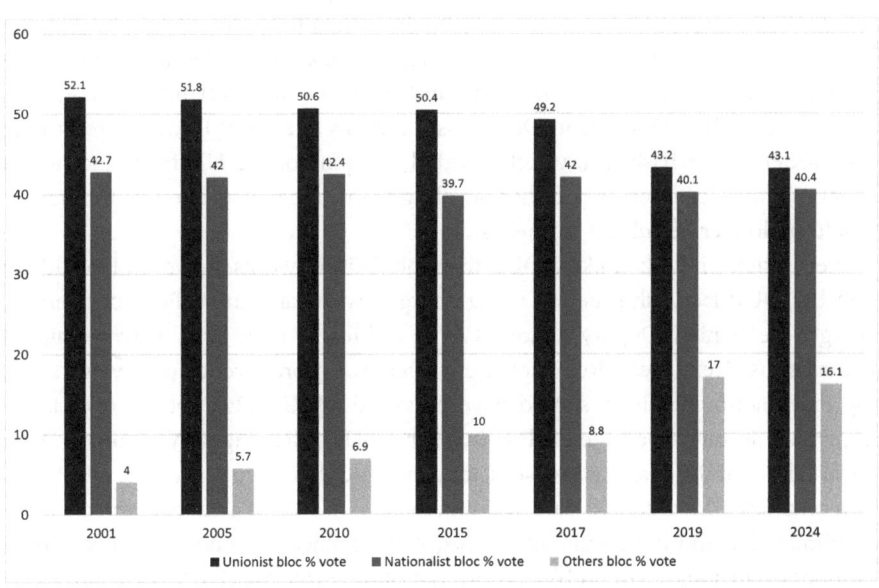

Figure 9.3. Unionist, Nationalist and 'Others' bloc votes, Northern Ireland general elections 2001-24

Conservative government eventually cut adrift the DUP when Boris Johnson replaced Theresa May as Prime Minister in July 2019 and immediately cut a deal with the Taoiseach, Leo Varadkar, and the EU to accept a bespoke alignment of Northern Ireland to EU trading rules. These stipulations included a border at Northern Irish ports (the 'Irish Sea border'), with goods deemed at risk of entering the EU subject to customs checks and EU regulations. Such terms were the opposite of what Johnson had promised the DUP's 2018 conference, months before he became Prime Minister when he asserted that no British Conservative government should sign up to such an arrangement dividing one part of the UK from another.

It was immediately apparent that Johnson's deal with the EU, the Ireland/Northern Ireland Protocol, placed restrictions upon trade between Great Britain and Northern Ireland unacceptable to many with the DUP. With some (not all) Northern Ireland businesses also unhappy, the Conservative government strove to remove or mitigate the bureaucratic excesses of what had been agreed. Pressure to do so increased markedly when the DUP collapsed power-sharing in 2022. The DUP set itself seven tests against which progress would be measured, including the removal of the 'Irish Sea border'.

In response, the government and the EU agreed the Windsor Framework of February 2023 (HM Government 2023) which diminished, but did not eliminate, checks on goods and offered the possibility of a 'Stormont brake' on new EU laws. Insufficiently impressed, the DUP's boycott of the political institutions continued into the following year. The decision to finally return to Stormont was announced by the DUP leader Jeffrey Donaldson early in 2024, as he claimed the government's Safeguarding the Union Command Paper (HM Government 2024) as a great victory. The 'Donaldson Deal' was hailed by the DUP leader as removing the border in the Irish Sea, which divided one part of the UK from another in economic and legal terms. Goods travelling from one part of the UK to another would no longer be subject to checks.

Very briefly, it looked like a DUP triumph. Within weeks, however, Donaldson quit the DUP leadership before being charged with rape and other sex offences, charges he denies. Deputy Leader Gavin Robinson took over. Having lauded Donaldson's Brexit deal, Robinson now offered a more circumspect view, arguing that 'cautious realism' should have prevailed (BBC 2024) not the overclaiming which accompanied the deal. Four of the DUP's then eight Westminster MPs always thought the deal was oversold and never hid their scepticism. The DUP election manifesto downgraded 'Safeguarding the Union' from a great bargain to a mere 'roadmap' that 'did not secure all our negotiating objectives and did not remedy a number of the long-term problems born out of the Protocol' (DUP 2024: 14).

Amid this disquiet, the three unionist parties entered the election with distinct positions. The DUP argued that it had improved Northern Ireland's post-Brexit trading arrangements but conceded, after initial triumphalism, that not all it wanted had been achieved. The TUV claimed the DUP had sold out and surrendered leverage by returning to Stormont having gained very little. Jim Allister's party argued the DUP had attempted to deceive unionist voters but that the strategy had unravelled. Uncompromising, it implacably opposes any EU law operating in Northern Ireland and demands 'No Sea Border'. The TUV leader was dismissed as a 'dead-end unionist' by the DUP's Paul Givan in the Stormont chamber on the day the Assembly was revived. Now, the TUV smelt blood over the overselling of (non-)revised trading arrangements and stood against the DUP in all constituencies except where there was any perceived risk of a Sinn Féin victory. Whilst unhappy over the EU's continuing rule-setting, the UUP insisted it had never been appropriate to collapse power-sharing as a result and urged maximum use of the political institutions to influence trade rules.

The DUP had been the largest Northern Ireland party at Westminster since its 2005 eclipse of the UUP but entered the election with a difficult political argument—effectively, 'what we told you about the deal we negotiated was not entirely true'—and several awkward constituency defences. A three-way TUV-UUP-DUP split in the unionist vote created problems for the DUP. The TUV announced an election pact with Reform UK in March 2024. The latter's then leader, Richard Tice, addressed Allister's party conference and demanded full Brexit for Northern Ireland. The memorandum became one of misunderstanding when Tice's replacement, one Nigel Farage, promptly endorsed DUP candidates Sammy Wilson and Ian Paisley, even though the latter was standing against the TUV leader, Jim Allister, in North Antrim!

The denouement of the fragmentation of unionism was a trio of DUP seat losses. Defeat in Lagan Valley could be ascribed to the circumstances of Jeffrey Donaldson's departure. Donaldson had held the seat since 1997, initially for the UUP, then the DUP since 2005. His majority was slashed from 19,000 to 6,500 in the 2019 electoral surge of the Alliance Party, which again fielded Sorcha Eastwood in 2024, against the DUP's Jonathan Buckley, both Assembly members. The expectation was a DUP hold, given the demographics (fourth-most Protestant) and history (unionist-held since creation in 1983) of the constituency. Yet Eastwood won by almost 3,000 votes, her majority exceeding that of the 2,186 votes which the TUV may have taken mainly from the DUP. The UUP's improved performance, its deputy leader, Robbie Butler, putting on 2,560 votes, may also have contributed to the DUP's demise, as unionist voters looked for alternatives.

South Antrim offered the only real DUP versus UUP contest, the latter's Robin Swann coming out on top. Health Minister in the power-sharing Executive and high-profile given he had been the postholder during the Covid-19 lockdown, Swann ousted the DUP's Paul Girvan. This DUP defeat was the least surprising. Even as the DUP eclipsed the UUP electorally in the post-Good Friday Agreement years, South Antrim remained marginal. The UUP recaptured the seat in 2001 after a by-election defeat to the DUP and again in 2015. Only 2,689 votes separated the two parties in the DUP's favour in 2019. What did surprise, however, was the size of the UUP's majority, Swann triumphing by a comfortable 7,512 votes, the largest victory the constituency had seen since 1997. This restoration of UUP fortunes did not necessarily constitute a major rebirth, however. The party leader, Doug Beattie, quit soon after the election citing differences with party officers. His departure saw the return of Mike Nesbitt as leader, the fifth change of UUP leader in seven years.

The biggest shock of the entire election came in the DUP's loss of North Antrim to the TUV, Jim Allister defeating Ian Paisley Jr. The last time a Paisley was not winning the seat, constituents were watching on black-and-white television sets. Ian Paisley Snr. became North Antrim's MP upon first contesting the constituency in 1970, standing as leader of the Protestant Unionist Party, before it became the DUP in 1971, a party he led until 2008. His son, Paisley Jnr., replaced him as North Antrim's MP at the 2010 election and seemed secure. Paisley Jnr. was the only MP to have survived a parliamentary recall petition. Such a petition is triggered if an MP is suspended by the House of Commons for ten working days or more. Paisley's thirty-day exclusion in 2018 for failing to declare holidays paid for by the Sri Lankan government, for whom he lobbied, led to a recall petition requiring 10% of his constituents to sign to necessitate a by-election. Only 9.4% did so (Tonge 2019). Paisley declared that '90.6% said: "we are keeping you, big fella, we like you"' (BBC 2018). Paisley's 2024 election vote fell by more than twenty percentage points, Allister triumphing with 28.3% of the vote, the lowest winning percentage of any UK constituency.

The good news for the DUP came in East Belfast. Gavin Robinson made the regular general election head-to-head with the Alliance Party leader Naomi Long 4-0 in his favour. Robinson had only 1,819 votes spare in 2019 and the reappearance of the TUV, whose last foray into this parliamentary seat contributed to Long's 2010 victory over the then DUP leader Peter Robinson, made an Alliance victory appear very possible. Unlike in 2019 however, the Greens and SDLP stood this time and polled a combined 1,696 votes, many of which might otherwise have gone to Alliance, almost offsetting the 1,918 TUV votes which may have peeled from the DUP. Robinson retained most of his 2019 vote share and may have taken some from the UUP, to increase his majority by more than 800 votes.

Robinson's victory was crucial for the DUP. Although he would head back into Westminster in reduced circumstances for the DUP given the party's poor overall performance, it meant a difficult leadership contest or embarrassing co-option of the leader into the Assembly was swerved (the DUP leader must be drawn from among its Westminster or Assembly elected representatives). Robinson's triumph reflected his enduring local popularity and perhaps some unionist recognition of both the tightness and importance of the contest. The DUP had outpolled Alliance by a mere 141 first preference votes at the 2022 Assembly election but extended that slender lead. The party has now held East Belfast, unionism's only remaining parliamentary seat in the capital, for forty of the last forty-five years.

5. Beyond Unionism and Nationalism: Alliance stable but no longer surging

The election was also a difficult test for the party that straddles Northern Ireland's divide, Alliance. The party has made considerable strides in recent years. The 'Alliance surge' saw the party average 16% of the vote across three different types of election, general, local and European, in 2019, double its average share since its foundation in 1970. Alliance also more than doubled its Assembly representation to seventeen seats in 2022 and made further gains in local elections in 2023. Those contests were perfect storms benefitting Alliance. The context of considerable hostility to Brexit, anger over collapsed devolved political institutions and a willingness of voters to transfer to the centre but not across the divide, saw the party soar. Alliance has a large reservoir of potential voters. Since 2006, those saying they are 'neither unionist nor nationalist', Alliance's position, has been the largest category of elector; 38% of electors declared themselves as such in 2023, compared to 30% self-identifying as a unionist and 28% as nationalist (Northern Ireland Life and Times survey 2023).

Alliance's election pitch was to change the rules of the game. Institutional reform is a key plank of its platform, removing the unionist versus nationalist divide by scrapping such designations in the Assembly, introducing weighted majority voting to replace sectarian counting and abolishing communal designation. Alliance also demanded the retitling of the First and deputy First Ministers as Joint First Ministers to accurately reflect their co-equal powers (Alliance Party 2024). The party called for an end to the system whereby if either the First or deputy First Minister from the rival blocs quits the Executive, Northern Ireland's government falls. Most recently, this happened when Sinn Féin's Martin McGuinness quit in 2017 and again when the DUP's Paul Givan walked out in 2022. The devolved power-sharing Executive was collapsed for 70% of the period from January 2017 to February 2024 and missing in action for nearly 40% of the post-Good Friday Agreement era up to its restoration shortly before the 2024 election. This has contributed to the worst crisis in the NHS anywhere in the UK, with one in four adults on a waiting list, the absence of a coherent programme for the government and chronic dependence upon the UK Treasury. The Assembly has also struggled to deal with contentious issues due to communal vetoes. Westminster legalised same-sex marriage and abortion and introduced Irish language provisions between the 2019 and 2024 elections despite each supposedly being a devolved matter.

Alliance retained a Westminster presence for the second consecutive election for the first time ever, via Sorcha Eastwood's impressive gain in Lagan Valley. A seemingly overwhelmingly unionist constituency, where Alliance was polling at a mere 11% only two elections previously, was now captured by a non-unionist party. Nonetheless, this remarkable triumph for Alliance was set against an overall slight fall in vote share across Northern Ireland, accompanied by the party leader's failure to gain East Belfast and offset by the loss of the North Down constituency gained in 2019. In East Belfast, Naomi Long was not helped by controversies over the timing of her selection as a candidate, claiming no decision had been made even though it emerged she had already been selected. Alliance argued the selection was conditional and had to be revisited after the Executive and Assembly were restored (Belfast Telegraph 2024b). There was also the suspicion that Long preferred to remain as Justice Minister in the Executive, even though she was temporarily embroiled in difficulties in that role during the election campaign, over a court decision striking down the law banning the identification of sex offenders. Long initially wished to appeal the verdict but retreated.

In North Down, Deputy Leader Stephen Farry strived to become the first Alliance MP to retain their parliamentary berth but was ousted by Independent Unionist Alex Easton. Alliance rose without trace to claim the seat in 2019; previously the party's vote share in the constituency had been in single percentage figures, so this was a tough defence. Despite quitting the DUP three years earlier, Easton was backed by his former party (and the TUV). Moreover, following his success, Easton co-opted the DUP's Stephen Martin into the Assembly as his replacement. Clearly, an 'independent' brand was perceived as more electorally favourable than a DUP label. To survive, Farry needed a more even split in the unionist vote but the UUP candidate, Colonel Tim Collins, was involved in a series of gaffes. One such episode involved his complaint of how it was cheaper to service his Rolls-Royce back home in England than a Ford Fiesta in Northern Ireland. That raised eyebrows even in the region's most affluent constituency. Collins conceded early on election night, claiming North Down's voters were 'not interested in international affairs – they're interested in potholes and hedges' (News Letter 2024).

Alliance's electoral problem remained that its big reservoir of potential voters is difficult to fish. Those saying they are 'neither unionist nor nationalist' are far less likely to vote, whereas most unionists and nationalists do. More than 80% of votes in the region's elections are cast for unionist or nationalist parties. Alliance has other problems, notably its inability to expand its vote and membership westward beyond the Greater Belfast area (Tonge et al., 2024a). Alliance profited electorally from the absence of the devolved executive when voters punished the perceived culprits for the collapses. The party demanded institutional changes to secure the institutions but ironically may attract the most sympathy when they are downed.

6. Conclusion

The main features of the election were the ascent of Sinn Féin to become Northern Ireland's largest party in all three types of elections—a notable hat-trick—and the fragmentation of unionism over post-Brexit trading arrangements. Sinn Féin's triumph is remarkable. When the Good Friday Agreement was reached, few would have envisaged the republican party becoming the most important force in Northern Irish politics.

That said, another Sinn Féin electoral triumph does not a United Ireland make. The party needs to match its success in attracting nationalists to winning support for Irish unity from those who are neither unionist nor nationalist. Given that the overall pro-United Ireland vote appears static and still trails that in favour of the Union in opinion polls, the constitutional agnostics and 'don't knows' in Northern Ireland's centre ground need to break overwhelmingly for Irish unity. More Alliance Party members now favour unity than Union (Tonge et al. 2024a) but with lots of undecideds. It would need their voters to think likewise to increase the prospect of a referendum being called and for it to yield constitutional change but most Alliance voters (68%) at the 2024 election offered a preference for the Union (Tonge et al. 2024b). Demographic change favours those backing a United Ireland as Catholics now outnumber Protestants – but Protestants are more united in backing the Union than are Catholics in wanting a United Ireland. Constitutional unionism is performing better than party political unionism, with much division evident within the latter.

Divisions over whether to accept continuing EU shaping of post-Brexit trading arrangements dominated the contest within unionism. Concerns over how the DUP had handled such issues contributed to the party sustaining losses. Although still unionism's largest force, the DUP's Westminster contingent is now half the size of its 2017-9 heyday. It appeared doubtful that the variety of voices of unionism now present in the Commons would achieve further modifications on Brexit trade issues. Another withdrawal from the power-sharing assembly appeared unlikely nonetheless, any supposed leverage seemingly spent. Abstention would be confined to Sinn Féin's absence from Westminster. In the centre ground, Alliance nonetheless made the argument that, with their rules unchanged, Northern Ireland's political institutions remained vulnerable. If the main unionist or nationalist party withdraws, everything collapses.

Yet institutional reform appears a low priority for a new UK government content that power-sharing has been restored. The Labour government's main priority for Northern Ireland is improving Anglo-Irish relations, difficult since Brexit and strained further by the outgoing Conservative government's Legacy Act which created immunity from prosecution in some circumstances for actions committed during the Troubles. One of Labour's few specific pledges for Northern Ireland in its election manifesto was to repeal and replace that Act. That pledge, unusually, united all the region's MPs elected in 2024.

Funding

Professor Tonge acknowledges with thanks the support from the Economic and Social Research Council, grant reference ES/Z503058/1, 'The 2024 Northern Ireland General Election study'.

References

Alliance Party (2024) *Leading Change for Everyone*. Westminster Election Manifesto. Newtownabbey: Alliance Party.

BBC (2018) 'Ian Paisley: DUP MP "stunned" and "humbled" at keeping seat', https://www.bbc.co.uk/news/uk-northern-ireland-45574495, accessed 25 Jul. 2024.

BBC (2024) 'DUP Leader Accepts Party Oversold Stormont Deal', https://www.bbc.co.uk/news/articles/cp33kgypdp3o, accessed 27 Jul. 2024.

Belfast Telegraph (2024a) 'Colum Eastwood Runaway Winner of BBC NI Leaders' Debate, Snap Poll Finds', https://www.belfasttelegraph.co.uk/news/politics/colum-eastwood-runaway-winner-of-bbc-ni-leaders-debate-snap-poll-finds/a1319042245.html, accessed 28 Jul. 2024.

Belfast Telegraph (2024b) 'Alliance minister adds 'context' to confusion over Naomi Long east Belfast selection meeting', https://www.belfasttelegraph.co.uk/news/northern-ireland/alliance-minister-adds-context-to-confusion-over-naomi-long-east-belfast-selection-meeting/a803784071.html, accessed 28 Jul. 2024.

Black, B. (2024) 'NI like the rest of the UK, wants change but we cannot vote for it', *Letter to Belfast Telegraph*.

DUP (2024) *Speaking Up for Northern Ireland*. Westminster Election Manifesto. Belfast: DUP.

HM Government (2023) *The Windsor Framework*. London: HMSO, CP806.

HM Government (2024) *Safeguarding the Union*. London: HMSO, CP1021.

Irish News (2024) 'Sinn Féin "Wants to Return as Many Progressive MPs as Possible From N Ireland"', https://www.irishnews.com/news/northern-ireland/sinn-fein-wants-to-return-as-many-progressive-mps-as-possible-from-n-ireland-QU36OYNLUFHU5IEVDWT6UGRKRE/, accessed 27 Jul. 2024.

Irish Times (2024) 'UK Will Act as "Honest Broker" on Question of Border Poll, Says Starmer', https://www.irishtimes.com/politics/2024/07/08/keir-starmer-in-belfast-for-meetings-with-northern-ireland-political-leaders/, accessed 28 Jul. 2024.

News Letter (2024) 'Alex Easton "Confident" about North Down as Tim Collins Concedes Accusing Voters of Being More Interested in Potholes', https://www.newsletter.co.uk/news/politics/alex-easton-confident-about-north-down-as-tim-collins-concedes-accusing-voters-of-being-more-interested-in-potholes-4691646, accessed 27 Jul. 2024.

Northern Ireland Census (2021) 'Religion', UK Data Service CKAN, https://statistics.ukdataservice.ac.uk/dataset/northern-ireland-census-2021-ms-b19-religion/resource/cca5cfe2-9a53-40f5-8972-780e7a8ed9ca/view/262ef9be-5e3d-4e10-b870-9ba519f5a306, accessed 28 Jul. 2024.

Northern Ireland Life and Times survey (2023) 'Political Attitudes', https://www.ark.ac.uk/nilt/2023/Political_Attitudes/UNINATID.html, accessed 25 Jul. 2024.

O'Leary, B. and Pow, J. (2023) *'The Turning Point? The Northern Ireland Local Government Elections of 18 May 2023'*, Dublin: Royal Irish Academy, https://www.ria.ie/blog/the-turning-point-the-northern-ireland-local-government-elections-of-18-may-2023/, accessed 26 Jul. 2024.

Sinn Féin (2024) *Strong Leadership; Positive Change. Westminster Election Manifesto.* Belfast: Sinn Féin.

Tonge, J. (2019) 'Petitions, Polling Stations and Paisley: the First Outworking of the Recall of MPs Act 2015', *Political Quarterly*, 90: 143–7.

Tonge, J. et al. (2024a) *The Alliance Party of Northern Ireland: Beyond Unionism and Nationalism*. Oxford: Oxford University Press.

Tonge, J. et al. (2024b) *The Northern Ireland General Election survey 2024*. Liverpool: ESRC.

Party finance: Labour exploits its advantage

Justin Fisher*

Department of Social & Political Sciences, Brunel University of London, Uxbridge, UB8 3PH, UK

*Correspondence: Justin.fisher@brunel.ac.uk

The 2024 General Election took place in the context of important legislative change related to party finance, together with Labour's growing popularity ultimately being reflected in significant growth in its income as the election approached. The combination of increased campaign spending limits and Labour's relative success in fundraising in the months leading up to the election meant that Labour was better able to exploit its ability to raise income and spend accordingly in the election campaign. By way of contrast, both the Conservatives and Liberal Democrats were financially far worse off than they had been in 2019.

1. The Elections Act 2022

As with a number of electoral cycles since 1997, the 2019–24 Parliament included some key legislative changes of importance relating to party finance. The first was the Elections Act, which received Royal Assent in 2022. The act was wide-ranging and included a number of provisions that related to party finance.

1.1 Digital imprints

Digital campaigning has been increasing in importance over several elections though it is also true that its pre-eminence as a campaign technique has frequently been overstated (Fisher 2020: 205). Printed campaign material for candidates has required an imprint—information stating who is responsible for the material—since the 1883 Corrupt and Illegal Practices Act, and for national party campaign materials since the Political Parties, Elections and Referendums Act

2000 (hereafter PPERA) when national parties were first regulated (though this requirement did not come into force until 2007). Imprints serve two purposes: they generate transparency with respect to the origin of the material and also create the means to audit the cost in order to enforce expenditure limits. However, unlike printed election material, digital campaign content previously required no such imprint. This was purely a function of the fact that digital campaigning was fairly minimal beyond websites, emails and text messages when PPERA was drafted. The Electoral Commission called for digital imprints as early as 2003. However, a significant growth in spending on this mode of campaigning did not really occur until the 2015 election (Johnston 2023: 15). Legislation finally sought to catch up with the digital world with the introduction of digital imprints via the Elections Act. This new requirement put digital communications on a par with the imprint regulations on printed communications, leading to greater transparency in terms of party and candidate (and non-party campaigner) spending.

1.2 Third parties

The Elections Act tightened regulations on 'third parties' to prevent political parties also registering as third parties. Third parties (or non-party campaigners) are organisations that campaign in elections but do not themselves put up candidates. On the one hand, this tightening of the regulations was a logical step to close an unexpected loophole and also prevent spending limits from being artificially inflated through the combination of third-party and political party spending. However, it was arguably a disproportionate response. This problem was by no means widespread. Since 2014, there had been only one instance of an organisation registering as both a political party and a non-party campaigner (at the 2019 General Election). Furthermore, in that single case, the organisation only reported spending against the political party limit.

1.3 Overseas voters

Keeping foreign money out of domestic politics is a recognised issue in most democracies. Prior to PPERA, there were no restrictions on where donations to any political party could come from. PPERA introduced legislation such that citizens were permitted to make political donations only if they were registered to vote in the UK. It also stipulated that British citizens resident overseas for up to fifteen years were eligible to register to vote so long as they had been registered to vote before they left the UK (unless they were too young to register when they left). This meant that overseas electors could quite legitimately make political donations to British parties using money from outside the UK for up to fifteen years, so long as they had renewed their registration at the time of making a donation.

That risk of foreign money (or at least money emanating from outside the UK) legally entering domestic politics has therefore existed for some time. However, the risk was mitigated somewhat by the numbers actually registering to vote. Before 2015, that figure never exceeded 35,000 (Johnston and Uberoi 2023: 24). However, at the 2015 General Election, it increased to 106,000, rising to 285,000 at the 2017 General Election and 233,000 (of an estimated 1.4 million eligible citizens) registered in time for the snap 2019 General Election (Johnston and Uberoi 2023: 24–7). The scale of registration since 2015 arguably presented significant risks for money from overseas entering domestic politics (albeit entirely legally).

This potential problem was amplified by provisions in the Elections Act. The Act removed the fifteen-year limitation and there was no longer a requirement for citizens to have been registered to vote at the time of leaving the UK. In addition, registration will ultimately be required only every three years as opposed to the annual registration requirements that were previously in place. The *potential* impact is significant. Government estimates put the number of eligible British citizens resident overseas as being 3.2–3.4 million and that, by 2029, the number registering would be around 302,000 (Johnston and Uberoi 2023: 28).

However, were registrations to be at the level of the 2017 General Election (just over 20% of eligible overseas voters), this would be around 692,000 (based on an eligible population of 3.4 million). Regardless of which figure is more accurate, that would still represent a significant potential issue with respect to overseas money entering domestic politics. This would be entirely legal but arguably raises problematic issues with respect to the sources of party income, with the potential to lead to significant sums of money feeding into British domestic politics from abroad (Fisher 2023).

At present, we have no idea of the extent of any potential problem. The Electoral Commission does not collect (and is not required to collect) any data on donations made by citizens based abroad. Political parties are similarly not required to declare such data. So, the issue may be negligible, but equally, it may potentially be a very significant one if substantial donations are made by voters who do not live in the country. In that respect, were practice to change and the published register of donors to indicate whether the citizen is a resident overseas, this would be more in line with PPERA's principles of transparency.

1.4 The Electoral Commission

MPs have selectively expressed concerns about the Electoral Commission ever since it was established by PPERA, despite the Commission always having been overseen by a Speaker's Committee. However, new concerns emerged following the 2015 General Election, when a number of candidates' spending returns were investigated. Most cases were dropped, but one MP, his agent and a Conservative Party official did end up in court, with the official prosecuted (Fisher 2018: 174–6; Fisher 2020: 191–2). The Act sought greater parliamentary accountability for the Commission, by the introduction of a Strategy and Policy Statement, to be approved by Parliament. This was intended to provide the Commission with guidance on how to discharge its functions.

Such proposals were challenging, not least because political oversight already existed, together with the argument that for the Commission to function effectively and independently, it should—as far as is possible—be free from interference from those whom it sought to regulate. One particular criticism was that far from requiring additional oversight, the Commission already delivered excellent work in ensuring high levels of satisfaction in the integrity of the electoral process amongst those who are most knowledgeable and closely involved. A survey of electoral agents at the 2019 General Election, for example, showed high levels of satisfaction with the work of the Commission (Fisher and Kumar 2020). Overall, many critics argued that the proposal represented both disproportionate and unnecessary measures. These arguably threatened the independence and therefore the effectiveness of the Electoral Commission, and there was little evidence to support the need for further parliamentary accountability.

Unbowed, the responsible department (Levelling Up, Housing and Communities, LUHC) issued a draft statement in August 2022. As part of the consultation, the statement was reviewed by the LUHC Select Committee (Levelling Up, Housing and Communities Committee 2022). Its verdict was damning, stating that the government had not provided independent evidence to justify bringing forward the draft statement and that no such statement should be made at this time. Moreover, even if the government decided to proceed, the draft statement would need to be fundamentally rewritten. In light of the significant criticism, the draft statement was withdrawn in June 2023. However, the government remained of the view that a Policy and Strategy Statement was necessary (Department for Levelling Up, Housing and Communities 2023a), and though it emphasised that it had no desire to direct the Commission, a revised Policy and Strategy Statement was published in February 2024 (Department for Levelling Up, Housing and Communities 2024).

2. Revised spending and reporting limits

Perhaps ironically, the most significant party finance change in advance of the 2024 election was made (quite legitimately) by secondary rather than primary legislation—the uplift in elections spending limits and thresholds for the declaration of donations.

In December 2020, the then Minister of State for the Constitution and Devolution, Chloe Smith, signalled that the government would be seeking to increase party and candidate spending limits in line with inflation (Hansard 2020). However, it was not until July 2023 that Michael Gove, the Secretary of State responsible for overseeing party finance regulation, announced the change, with donation declaration thresholds also being increased on the same basis (Hansard 2023).

Party (rather than candidate) spending limits were introduced by PPERA. Setting the period of regulation as 365 days before a general election, the act devised a formula for parties based on the number of constituencies in which a party fielded a candidate. The overall party spending limit was set at the number of seats contested multiplied by £30,000. Thus, at the 2019 General Election, if a party fielded candidates in the 631 constituencies in Great Britain (assuming they did not contest the seat of the Speaker), the national party spending limit would be £18,930,000. However, the sum per constituency (£30,000) set by PPERA had never been adjusted for inflation. As a result, the national party limit in 2023 was approximately 45% lower in real terms using the Consumer Prices Index (CPI) than when it was introduced. Using the more comprehensive Retail Prices Index, the figure was closer to 50%.

The intention to increase the limit was a sensible one. Most obviously, the value of the spending limits introduced by PPERA bore little relation to the real value in 2023. But more specifically, there were three potential issues. First, the previous failure to adjust this figure for inflation challenged the ability of parties to campaign effectively. As the Secretary of State observed, the cost of printing, postage and communication—which is vital for parties and candidates to engage with voters—had risen, while the spending limit had not. Second, with these and other costs rising while the spending limit was static, there were growing potential difficulties in terms of party compliance with the rules. Parties had rarely pushed up close against the existing limit (though the Conservatives came very close in 2017) but left unchecked, this would have been likely to cause difficulty. It was in no one's interest for there to be regulation with which parties struggle to comply.

Third, the previous failure to adjust party spending limits for inflation presented a challenge to a principle laid out by PPERA—namely that parties and candidates should be the principal actors in elections. Third-party (sometimes known as non-party) campaigning had always existed and was regulated by PPERA. But, there was growing evidence that third parties were becoming increasingly cognisant of the possibilities of extensive campaign activity. Electoral Commission data showed that in 2019, there was a record number of registered non-party campaigners (sixty-one), together with a record level of expenditure—over £6m—compared with less than £2m (at 2019 prices)[1] in 2015. These levels of third-party activity had the potential to threaten the primacy of parties in electoral contests—particularly if the distribution of third-party activity was asymmetric and overwhelmingly negative towards one party.

There were however some concerns about the move. First, other parties suggested that this was a partisan change designed to benefit the Conservative Party, which had a previously stronger record of fundraising. In 2019, for example, the Conservatives raised over £19 million in the campaign period alone (Fisher 2020) and were also very successful in 2017 (Fisher 2018). Second, it would be very likely to widen the spending gap between the two largest parties and their competitors. While returns to the Electoral Commission showed that the Liberal Democrats actually outspent Labour in 2019, having received a donation of some £8 million just prior to the campaign (Fisher 2020), the typical pattern has been that the Liberal Democrats have spent between 24% and 37% of the Conservatives' campaign expenditure. Given the Liberal Democrats' lack of a natural pool of large donors, the gap between higher- and lower-spending parties would be likely to widen quite significantly.

The spending changes, nevertheless, were introduced by a statutory instrument in November 2023 (SI 1235, 2023). The previous limit informing the national party spending limit was raised from £30,000 per constituency contested to £54,010, in line with inflation as measured by the CPI. This meant that the limit for a party contesting 631 constituencies would now be £34,080,310. Candidate spending limits in the 'short' campaign (from dissolution) were also increased. The base sum went up from £8,700 to £11,390 with the pence per elector increasing from 9p to 12p in county (rural) seats, and from 6p to 8p in borough (urban) ones. This meant that the average candidate expenditure limit was roughly £18,855. 'Long' campaign base expenditure (not applicable in this election) was raised from £30,700 to £40,220. Finally, declaration thresholds for donations at the national level were raised from £7,500 to £11,180 beginning in Quarter 1 of 2024 (and at the local level, from £1,500 to £2,230).

3. Trends in party income and expenditure

The normal pattern of party income is that it cycles with general elections—rising sharply in the year before an election and falling away again in the year after. This happened for all three parties, unlike the period after the 2015 election when Labour's post-election finances were buoyed significantly by the two leadership elections of 2015 and 2016 (Fisher 2018). Party funding was not, however, immune to the effects of the pandemic. The parties' accounts in 2020 showed that Covid-19

---

[1] All real terms calculations are made using the Retail Prices Index unless stated.

had taken its toll. All three reported significant drops in income, in part because of cancelled conferences. The year after a general election typically leads to a sharp drop in income. Yet Conservative central income in 2020 was at its lowest in real terms since 2003.

That said, parties were affected to different degrees. While Conservative income declined after the 2019 election, the party still had a very good financial year in 2023, securing £59.3m in income, boosted by the receipt of a £10m legacy to the Conservative Party Foundation (Conservative Party 2024: 3). Labour too enjoyed a significant leap in income in 2023 (to £58.6 million), generating over £6m more in donations in absolute terms than in 2022. Labour engaged in significant spending in preparation for the 2024 election, increasing its full-time national and regional staff by 42% and increasing its running costs by £10.5m in absolute terms (Labour Party 2024: 15–6). This meant that after a surplus of £2.7m in 2022, the party recorded a deficit of £0.85m in 2023. By way of contrast, the Liberal Democrats' post-2019 income was notably low. Even after the pandemic-hit year of 2020, Liberal Democrat income in both 2021 and 2022 was, in real terms, lower than any year since the mid-1990s. In 2023, however, there was an uplift with income increasing by over £2m, which included an increase of over £1m in donations (Liberal Democrats 2024: 10). In historical terms, however, income in 2023 was still lower in real terms than any years since 2002 (bar 2020, 2021, and 2022, which were lower still).

At the time of writing (October 2024), full accounts are only available up to the end of 2023. However, a review of annual central party income since 1989 (when the Liberal Democrats first filed accounts) shows a series of phases with respect to the Conservatives and Labour (see Fig. 10.1). First, the phase of 'normal service', where the Conservatives were clearly the wealthier of the two main parties—a longer standing position that predates these graphs (Fisher 2010). Second, there is the 'Blair revolution', where Labour became not only the party of government but also the wealthiest party by some margin. Third, the resumption of 'normal service', from soon after the 2005 election, with the Conservatives again generating the most income. Finally, since 2011, Labour has generally enjoyed higher levels of annual income than the Conservatives, though the difference between them and the Conservatives was not as marked as during the 'Blair revolution'.

Two years do, however, provide an exception to this post-2010 rule. First, in the election year of 2019, the Conservatives generated significantly more income than Labour (£68m compared with £57.3m). Second, in 2023, the Conservatives generated marginally more than Labour (£59.3m compared with £58.6m).

These patterns are clearly illustrated in Fig. 10.2, which calculates Labour annual income as a percentage of that of the Conservatives. Where the line rises above 100 on the graph, Labour is generating more income, and *vice versa*. For the Liberal Democrats, however, there is only one real phase throughout this

Party finance 189

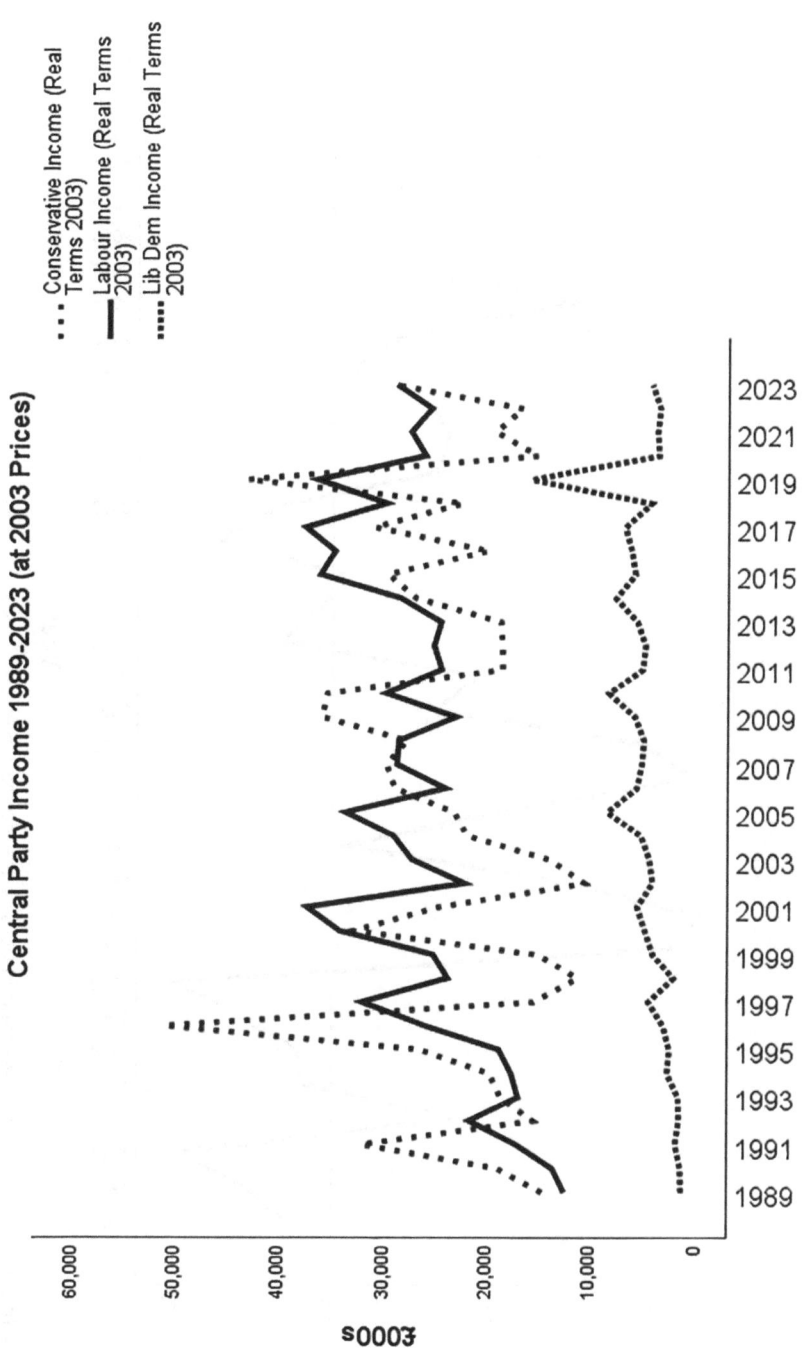

Figure 10.1. Central party income 1989–2023

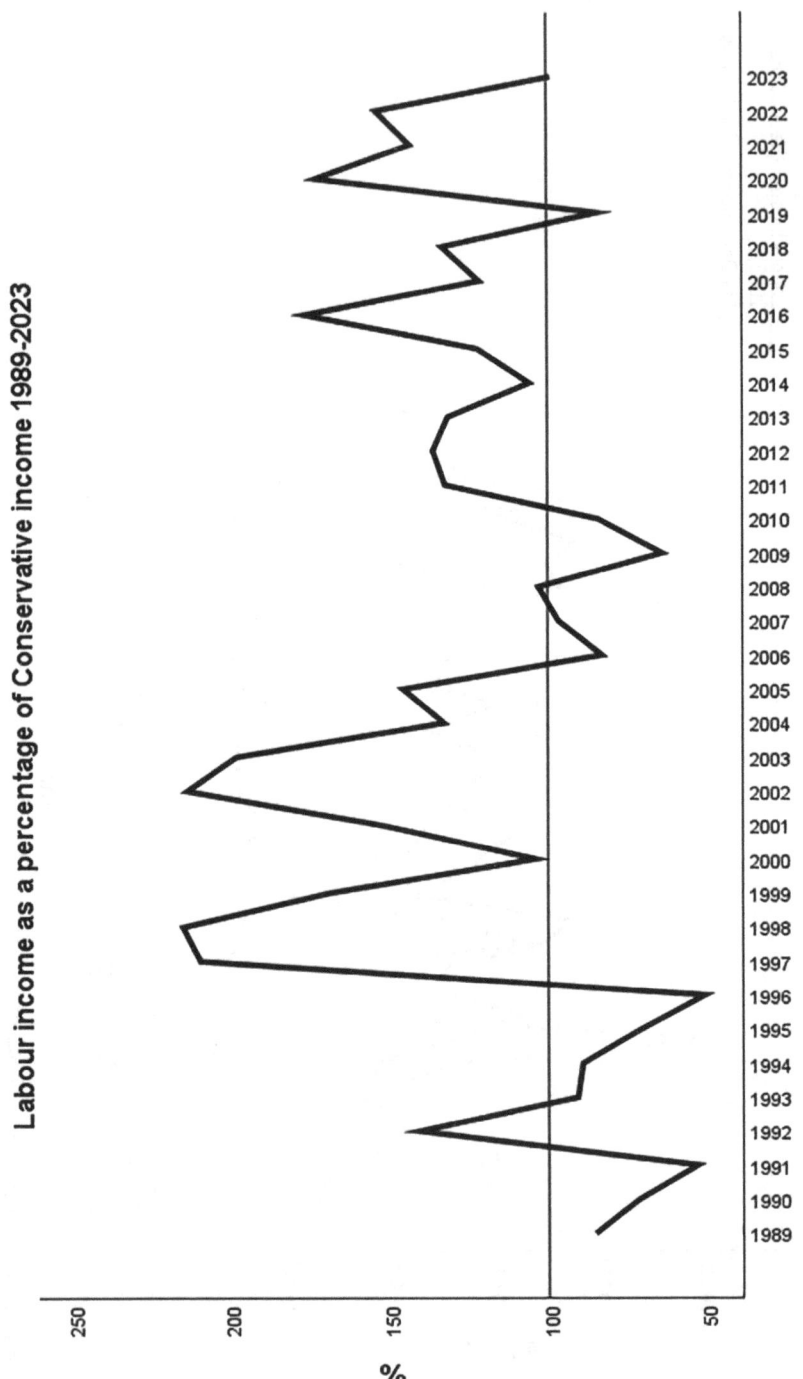

Figure 10.2. Labour income as a percentage of Conservative income 1989–2023

period—that of relative poverty compared with the Conservatives and Labour. As Fig. 10.1 shows, Liberal Democrat annual income only came close to that of either of the main two parties in the depths of the Conservative malaise in the late 1990s and early 2000s. The Liberal Democrats did enjoy a considerable spike in income in 2019, though that was largely a function of a single donation of £8m from Lord (David) Sainsbury of Turville (Fisher 2020: 198).

In terms of annual expenditure (Fig. 10.3), as we might expect, similar patterns are evident. Not surprisingly, those parties that generate more income on an annual basis, generally spend more, and the periods of Conservative or Labour annual financial advantage are mirrored, as is the gap in expenditure levels between the Liberal Democrats and the main two parties. Again, however, 2019 and 2023 proved to be slight exceptions to this rule. Labour actually spent more than the Conservatives in 2019 as a whole (£57.2m compared with £54.6m), and in 2023, despite the party's fundraising success, the Conservatives spent considerably less (£41m) than it generated (£59.3m), leaving it in a promising financial and organisational position ahead of election year, having also expanded its staff body by 37% since January 2022 (Conservative Party 2024: 3).

What has been an important change, however, is the parties' financial prudence since the late 2000s. Fig. 10.4 shows annual central expenditure as a percentage of annual central income. Where the lines on the graph fall above 100, parties are spending more than they generate each year, and *vice versa*. In the period up until 2007–8, parties regularly spent more in any year than they generated income—considerably so in some years. This was for many reasons, not least that the income required for parties' annual operating costs was not well served by a cycle of income that reflected the timing of the general election. With parties fighting elections in every year and seeking to maintain their organisations, the flow of income was not matching their regular financial needs. Since 2007–8, however, the parties have clearly exercised significant levels of financial restraint. The Conservative and Labour parties have only rarely spent more in one year than they have generated since then. The picture for the Liberal Democrats has been slightly less positive. The party has continued to struggle to generate more than it needs to spend on an annual basis, though the overspends have generally been rather lower than in the pre-2007 period. However, this pattern was interrupted by the Covid-19 pandemic. In 2020, all three parties' expenditure exceeded their income—in the case of the Conservatives and Liberal Democrats by some margin (over 20%). Since 2021, however, the parties have moved back towards a position where their income and expenditure were more balanced.

Overall, however, it shows that parties have become much more financially responsible. Indeed, in many ways, it would not be an exaggeration to think of them as models of efficiency—undertaking a great deal of activity with relatively little money. Of course, the loss of a major fundraising opportunity (party

192 J. Fisher

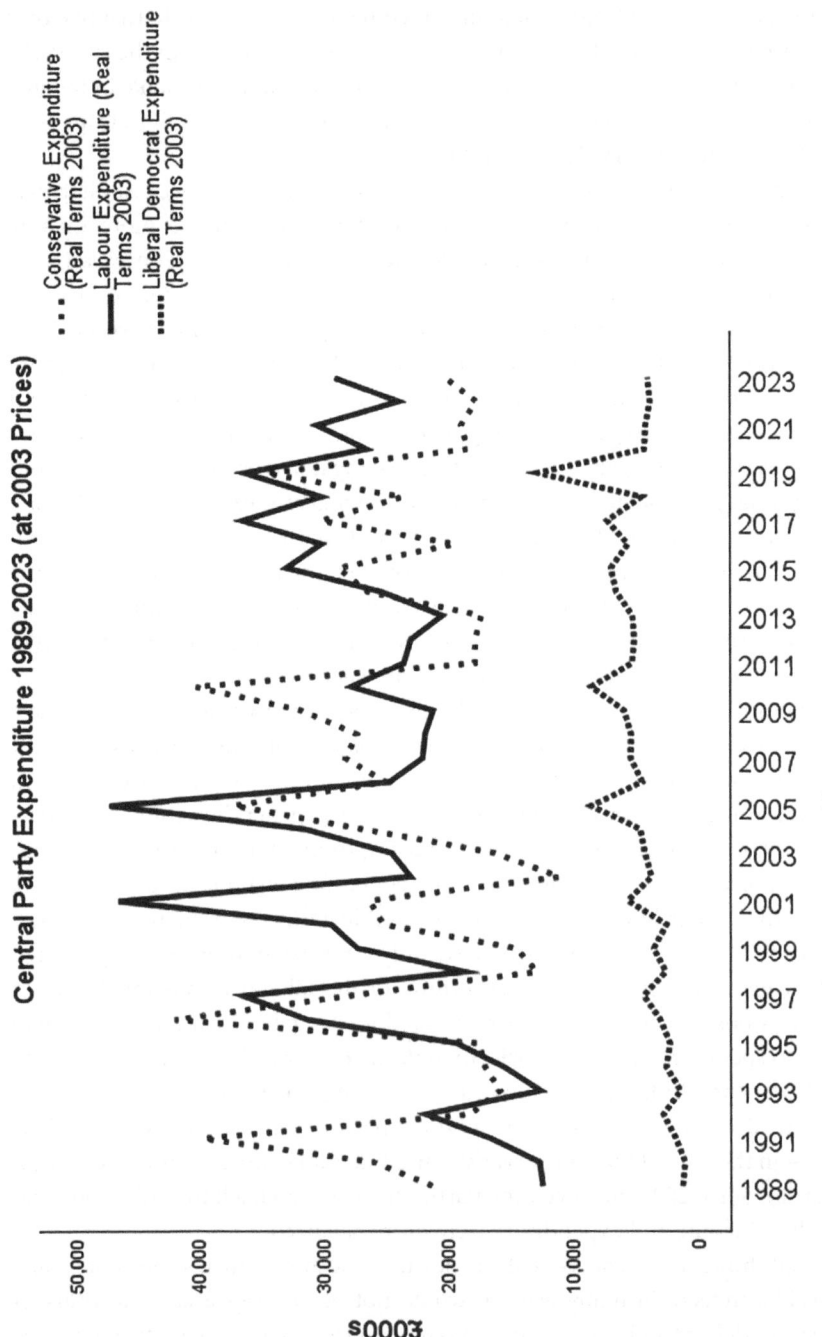

Figure 10.3. Central party expenditure 1989–2023

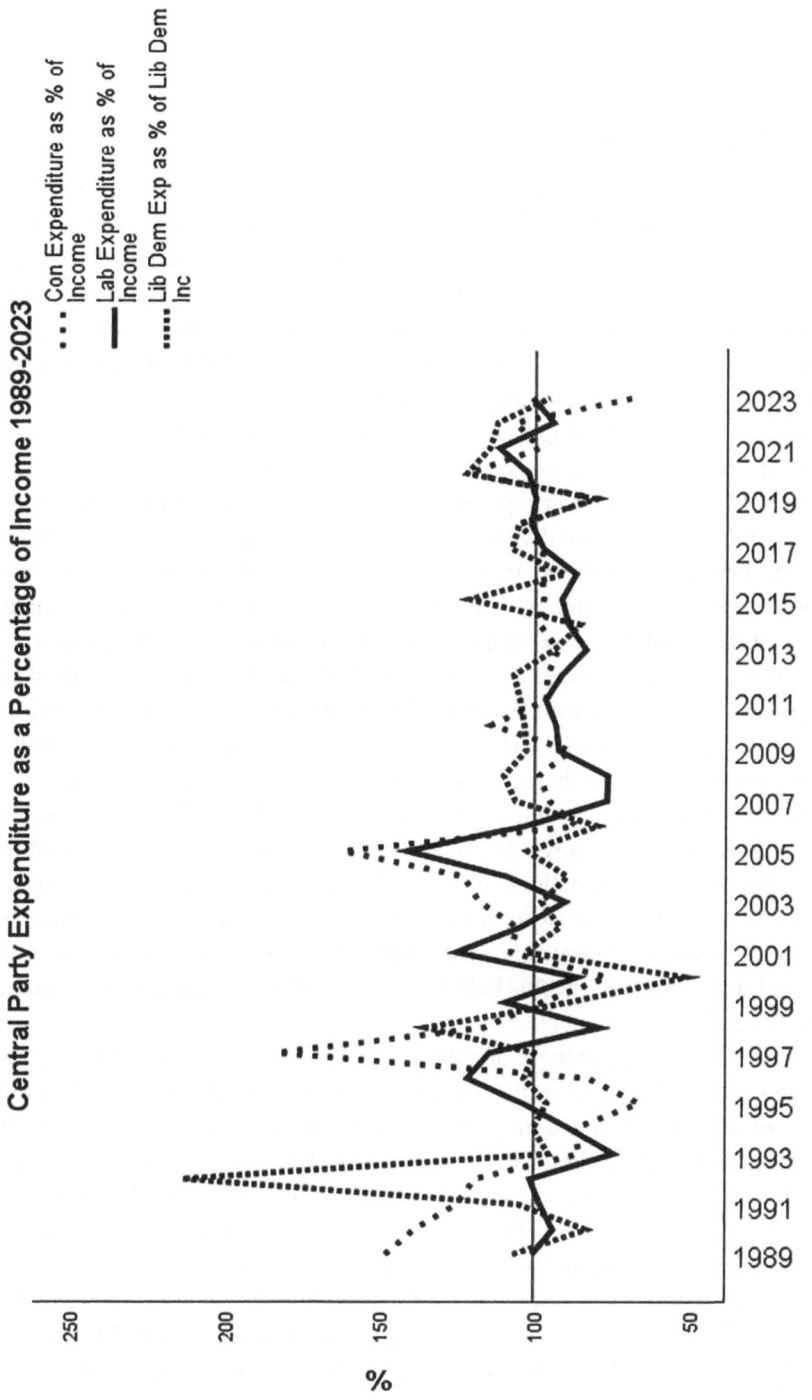

Figure 10.4. Central party expenditure as a percentage of income 1989–2023

conferences) as a result of the pandemic illustrates that party finance can be highly susceptible to shocks.

4. Donations 2010–24

Figs. 10.1– 10.4 provide excellent context to the finances of the 2024 election, but of course, only go up to the end of 2023. So—to gain a fuller picture of central party income, we examine declared cash donations in each quarter from Quarter 3 in 2010 (the first quarter after the 2010 election) to Quarter 2 in 2024, which ended four days before the 2024 election. A description of some terminology is important. Declared donations were (until January 2024) all donations of £7,500 or more made to the national party (rather than to a constituency one). £7,500 was the threshold for reporting donations to the Electoral Commission, until the uplift to £11,180 was implemented in January 2024. Donations are published by the Electoral Commission every quarter (and weekly from dissolution until polling day). Cash donations are distinct from non-cash donations, which are more commonly known as payments-in-kind. So—these data do not provide a complete picture of party income (as any donations below the declaration threshold are not captured), but they do reveal clear patterns in terms of sizable donations.

Fig. 10.5 shows the number of declared cash donations. It reveals a number of things. First, in the first three elections in this period (2015, 2017, and 2019), the Conservatives experienced a significant boost in income in the run-up to the elections, particularly sharply in the 'snap' elections of 2017 and 2019. In 2024 however, it was Labour that was able to attract the most (220), albeit only marginally more than the Conservatives (210). Indeed, the advantage that Labour had in terms of the number of donations in the final quarter of the parliamentary term was more a function of the steep fall in the number of Conservative donations relative to the comparable quarter in 2019 (Q4). The number of Labour donations in the final quarter before the 2024 election increased only marginally compared with that of 2019.

Fig. 10.6 illustrates how these donations translated into income. Not surprisingly, the peaks and troughs in income from declared cash donations reflect the numbers of donations (indeed they correlate at 0.85), but what was very different in this election was the Labour advantage. In Quarter 2 2024, Labour generated some £22.5m in declared donations (the figure in the graph being lower as it is adjusted for prices over time). By way of contrast, the Conservatives attracted £12.7m in the same period (compared with some £33.6m in the comparable quarter in 2019). The £12.7m included a donation of £5m made by The Phoenix Partnership (Leeds) Ltd, a company owned by Frank Hester. In March 2024, it was reported that in 2019 Hester had made highly offensive comments about Diane Abbott MP saying that she made him 'want to hate all black women' and that she

Party finance 195

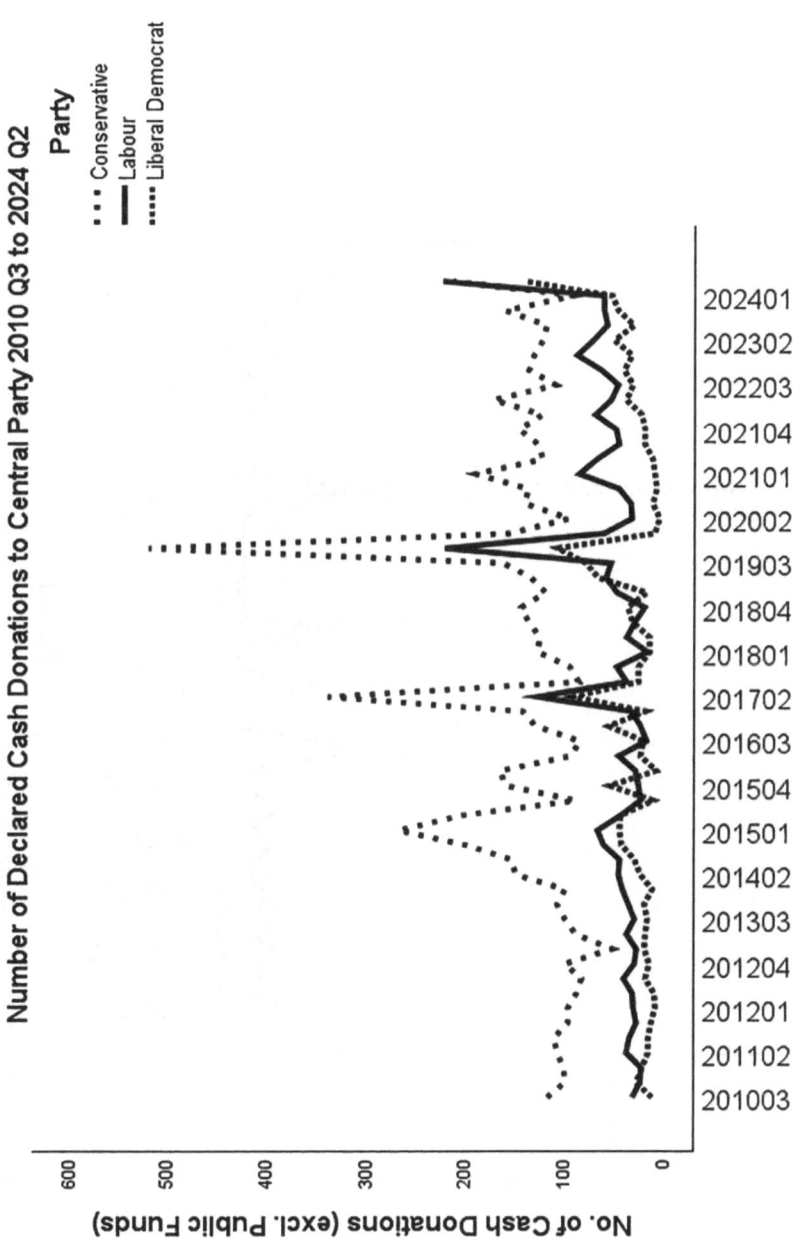

Figure 10.5. Number of declared cash donations 2010 Q3 to 2024 Q2

196 J. Fisher

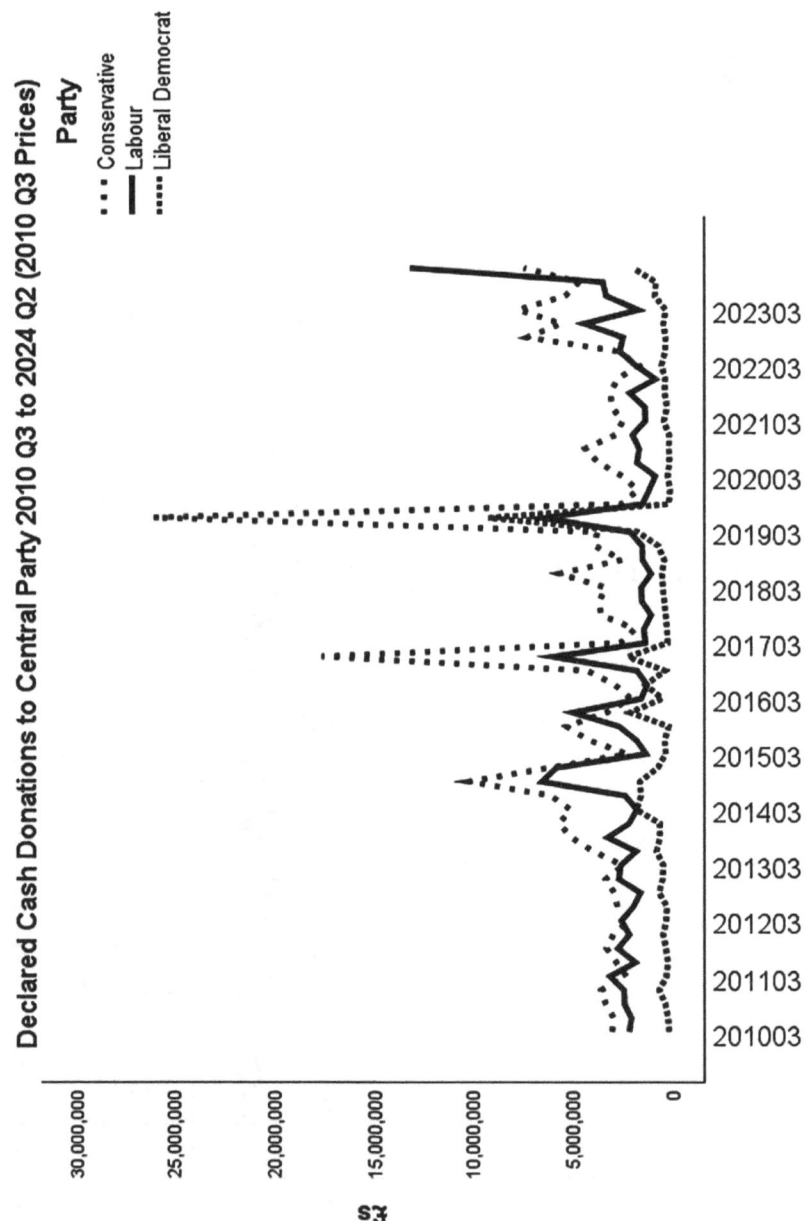

Figure 10.6. Declared cash donations 2020 Q3 to 2024 Q2

'should be shot' (BBC News 2024a). Mr Hester had previously donated £5 million to the Conservatives himself, and over £5 million through his company. Following a significant outcry, he admitted that the remarks had been 'rude', but said that they 'had nothing to do with her gender nor colour of skin' (BBC News 2024b). The Conservatives, while condemning the remarks, did not return the donations. Further donations of over £5m were accepted in the first quarter of 2024 (which were revealed after the story broke) together with the £5m accepted just before the election was called.

The Liberal Democrats attracted £3.2m; much less than the £11.8m the party attracted in the fourth quarter of 2019, albeit with £8 million coming from one single donation (Fisher 2020: 198). Combined, the volume of declared donations received by the Conservatives and the Liberal Democrats represented only 70% of the amount received by Labour.

Labour, then, had a significant financial advantage over their political opponents in the final quarter before the election date. In elections at the beginning of the century, this might not have mattered so much with respect to the campaign as the lead time for many campaigning techniques such as direct mail and billboards meant that the more significant income for a party's campaign needed to be generated some months before polling day. That remains the case for campaigning techniques such as direct mail which endure. But the growth of digital campaigning is very significant in this respect as the lead time is considerably shorter, and therefore 'late money'—money that comes in during the campaign—can still be spent with the potential, at least, to be effective. The Labour financial advantage in declared donations must be seen in that context, particularly when the overall spending limit had been increased so substantially. In effect, the increase in spending limits by the Conservative government, which were criticized as a ploy to benefit the Conservative campaign, was likely to be of greater benefit to Labour, who were able to raise so much more in the build-up to the election.

5. Campaign donations

PPERA requires donations to be reported weekly during the period between dissolution and polling day. When the legislation was first introduced, what appeared like a well-intentioned provision in terms of transparency was of limited use because of the lead time associated with major campaign initiatives. However, as we have seen, the growth of digital campaigning, with significantly shorter lead times, means that this level of transparency is now much more informative.

Table 10.1 details all declared donations (cash and non-cash) and the category of cash donor over the period. What is striking first is the reversal of fortunes of the Conservatives relative to 2019. In that election period, the party received just under £19.4m (equivalent to approximately £25.8m in real terms in 2024[2]).

Table 10.1. Source of election period declared cash donations and levels of declared non-cash donations

	Conservative		Labour		Lib Dems	
	£s	No.	£s	No.	£s	No.
Individual	922,111	31	6,011,800	30	1,071,147	27
Company	496,000	10	574,752	3	584,982	12
Trade union	0	0	2,413,426	12	0	0
Unincorporated associations	373,500	9	0	0	0	0
Total cash donations	1,791,612	50	8,999,978	45	1,656,129	39
Total non-cash donations	78,780	4	537,080	3	0	0
Total all donations	1,870,392	54	9,537,058	48	1,656,129	39

Source: The Electoral Commission.

In this election, the Conservatives were able to raise just £1,870,392 in declarable donations during the campaign period—only marginally more than the Liberal Democrats, who raised £1,656,129. For the Liberal Democrats, this was an almost identical figure in real terms to the amount raised in the 2019 campaign. Labour, by way of contrast, raised over £9.5m—more than five times more than the Conservatives. Not surprisingly this also easily exceeded the amount raised by Labour in 2019, which amounted to £7.2m at 2024 prices.

There was a similar reversal for the Conservatives in terms of the number of donations. In 2019, there were 272 declarable cash donations. In 2024, there were just fifty, thirty-one of which were made by individuals and only ten by companies. In 2019, the cash donation numbers from individuals and companies were 193 and seventy-six, respectively. The Liberal Democrats received an almost identical number of declarable campaign donations as in 2019—thirty-nine in 2024 compared with thirty-eight in 2019. As in 2019, the bulk came from individuals. Interestingly, however, the party was able to attract twelve donations from companies in 2024—twice the number that was generated in 2019 (and approaching twice the value in real terms).

Labour, too, received an identical number of declarable cash or non-cash campaign donations as in 2019—forty-eight. What changed, however, was the balance in the sources of those donations. In 2019, Labour received twenty-eight cash donations from trade unions totalling £5,039,754 (c. £6.7m at 2024 prices). In 2024, there were twelve such donations totalling £2,413,426. By way of contrast, there were thirteen declarable cash donations from individuals in 2019 amounting to £159,442 (£212,058 at 2024 prices). In 2024, there were thirty cash donations

---

[2]All real terms calculations are made using the Retail Prices Index comparing Q4 2019 with Q2 2024.

from individuals amounting to £6,011,800. This included £2,500,000 from Lord (David) Sainsbury of Turville. Furthermore, in 2019, 95% of Labour's campaign cash donations came from trade unions. In 2024, it was 27%. By way of contrast, 3% of Labour's declarable cash donations came from individuals in 2019. In 2024, it was 67%—the highest proportion donated by individuals to Labour ever recorded since these data were first made public in 2001. Labour also benefitted from a non-cash donation of £500,000, made by Anthony Gormley.

One area where there was more similarity was with respect to cash donations for Labour from companies. Labour received just three declarable cash donations in 2024, compared with four in 2019. The value of these donations was, however, higher in 2024—£574,752 compared with £120,000 (£159,600 in real terms) in 2019. However, while Labour performed no better in attracting company donations during the campaign than the Corbyn-led party, it was also the case that companies made far fewer campaign donations to parties overall. Companies were not rushing to support Labour financially, but also considerably fewer supported the Conservatives financially in 2024. If the threat of a Corbyn-led Labour government had likely stimulated higher numbers of corporate donations to the Conservatives in 2017 and 2019 (Fisher 2020), a potential Starmer-led Labour government in 2024 had no such effect.

Table 10.2 details when the cash and non-cash donations were received by parties. Labour outperformed the Conservatives and Liberal Democrats in all weeks, except Week 4 (Week 6 consisted of only one day—polling day on 4th July). Indeed, so strong was Labour's campaign fundraising, that it raised more in Week 2 than the combined totals raised by the Conservatives and Liberal Democrats over the whole campaign period. And, even in its weakest week, Labour still raised over £450,000, eclipsed only by the Liberal Democrats, who raised just over £500,000.

6. Election period expenditure

6.1 Conservatives

The Conservatives' campaign was much more strongly weighted in favour of digital than print in 2024. In the two years leading up to the election, there was a concerted effort using mainly print media (leaflets and direct mail) to promote

Table 10.2. Timing of weekly declared cash and non-cash donations

£s	Week 1	Week 2	Week 3	Week 4	Week 5	Week 6	Total
Conservative	574,919	292,500	375,000	378,945	249,028	0	1,870,392
Labour	926,908	4,383,400	3,309,918	451,232	465,600	0	9,537,058
Lib Dems	454,999	335,000	193,945	515,982	137,500	18,703	1,656,129

Source: The Electoral Commission.
Notes: Excludes public funds. Week 6 is 4th July only.

local communications from MPs and candidates in seats the party was trying to hold (accounting for around 60% of campaigning costs). However, in the last six months, attention shifted to digital. While the party had used digital extensively in the past, the emphasis in 2024 was not driven principally by a strategic shift in campaign approach. Rather, it was driven by cash limitations. As Fig. 10.6 and Table 10.1 illustrate, income from donations fell after the Autumn of 2023 and those in the campaign itself were comparatively modest, and from February 2024 onwards, raising income for the election became a significant challenge. As a consequence, while print expenditure during the short campaign would normally have been around £3.5m (comparable with the digital spend), in 2024, the party was able to spend only around £1m on print after the election was called.

In light of the party's relative lack of income, the principal spend after February 2024 was on digital mainly because that mode offered more coverage with the available cash. Of course, there was still expenditure on print, particularly with direct mail when the election was called. But, at both the national and local levels, the message was clear to focus on digital campaigning. Not only were postal costs rising significantly but the cost per acquisition via digital was much lower.

In terms of platforms, the Meta apps (Facebook and Instagram) were favoured. Indeed, Facebook became the dominant platform, with some expenditure (but much less) on YouTube and Google ads—Facebook was regarded as being better at reaching key voters. In addition, there was a significant growth in organic content on X/Twitter, but in terms of paid activity, Facebook dominated, both at national and constituency levels. The party also invested strongly in supporting local campaign teams in target seats with their digital content.

The party's financial position also affected the level of polling undertaken to some extent. A series of constituency-level polls in target seats were undertaken from the Spring of 2023 and into the early part of 2024. But campaign polls were less frequent than in previous elections. The party had some MRP (multi-level regression and poststratification) partners, and while fewer pieces of research were conducted, the emphasis was on more internal scenario modelling and forecasting using different MRP criteria. Publicly available MRPs were used to validate and sense-check the party's own estimates.

6.2 Labour

As with the 2019 election, Labour's 2024 campaign again demonstrated the increasing importance of digital campaigning while continuing to use print on a significant scale. Digital expenditure matched or possibly slightly exceeded that spent on print, with Labour making extensive use of both the Meta platforms (Facebook and Instagram) and especially YouTube. Like other parties, the links between Facebook and Instagram were attractive in terms of reach. But there were practical issues too. Political advertising was no longer permissible on X/Twitter nor on the other prominent platform, TikTok. Instead, content on platforms such as X and TikTok was organic rather than paid for. However, the micro-targeting that was previously seen as being critical for digital campaigning was not possible. The match rates with individuals were too poor, and so targeted advertising on Meta platforms and YouTube was by postcode sector rather than individuals, though even then, the targeting could generally not be achieved at full postcode level. Nonetheless, the ability to deploy new digital expenditure during the campaign proved to be very useful.

While digital campaigning continued to grow, it was integral to all the other modes, including print and traditional campaigning locally. To that end (and unlike the 2019 campaign) the various campaigning modes were joined up to help identify key target voters. A key group here were so-called 'hero voters'—voters who supported the Conservatives in 2019 but were now open to voting Labour. Such voters were more likely to be economically insecure, were middle-aged with families, were working-age non-graduates, and who had voted Leave in the EU referendum.

A key difference from 2019 (and previous elections) was the amount of polling that Labour conducted. The party ran a large internal MRP exercise. This was a rolling MRP with new data added daily. These combined data were bought in regularly from a range of polling companies with Labour's own data. Critically, it was Labour who weighted the polling data. This approach marked a key change from the tradition of a single company acting as the party's pollster. The rolling MRP played a number of roles. Critically, it formed a key part of the seat targeting process. Labour had used MRP polling before (Fisher 2020), but the key difference in 2024 was the buy-in at all levels of the party as a means of driving the distribution of resources that derives from targeting. While the receipt of daily data created some challenges (interpreting small shifts, for example), the party credited this innovation with helping them identify new emerging potential target seats that were winnable. In those cases, the party was able to quickly deploy additional digital resources to support the campaigns.

6.3 Liberal Democrats

A significant difference for the Liberal Democrats compared with 2019 was the party's relative poverty. While in 2019, a generous pre-campaign donation meant that the party could effectively decide on campaign priorities in advance, in 2024 much of the activity involved hypothecating campaign donations. The three main national spending priorities were print, digital and the leader's programme. More was spent on print, in part because of the inherently higher costs associated with that mode. Critically, however, compared with 2019 there was no acceleration to digital. This was in part because of the continuing effectiveness of print, and in part because of doubts of the utility of some digital campaigning. For example, the party's view was that if anything, print could be becoming increasingly effective. Voters were receiving less mail in general, so printed communications from the party were seen by recipients as being more of a novelty and therefore more likely to be effective. Coupled with that, an internal party review had shown a strong relationship between expenditure on print and votes won, while the relationship with digital was less clear. Print therefore continued to be seen as a vital part of the campaign. There was also some continuing scepticism about the reach of digital campaigning. Party officials highlighted that the impact of digital adverts was subject to 'a lot of scrolling' or watching with the sound muted. Not only that, in the aftermath of a by-election, an internal party study showed that recall rates for digital contacts were much lower than for other campaign modes. For the Liberal Democrats, there was a hierarchy of voter recall of campaign contacts: in-person conversations, print, and then digital. Notwithstanding, digital was regarded as the best mode for interaction, with the mode being more likely to generate responses or participation in activities such as surveys or petitions. Like other parties, Facebook and Instagram were the dominant paid-for platforms, with organic activity occurring elsewhere.

The leader's programme garnered good media coverage, but less was spent on it than in 2019 due to the party's financial position. The leader did visit target seats (with the party having to again be mindful of the cost attribution of leaflets—national or constituency level—see Fisher 2020). But critically, the programme was designed around media centres in key electoral areas for the party, to boost media coverage.

Unlike 2019, the Liberal Democrats did not conduct their own MRP poll. This was in part because the party had significantly less money than in 2019, but mostly because of the large number of MRP polls that were published during the campaign. These provided a very useful source of free data, and the party took the view that there was little point in commissioning their own. This approach came with some downsides, however. There was significant variation in the many published MRP polls, and while the large number of polls was generally helpful, the variation could make the management of expectations difficult if a particular poll showed some seats doing much better than the party believed was the case. Like other parties, the YouGov MRP matched the party's own data and estimations most closely.

7. Conclusions

Three things dominated party finance in the 2024 election. The first was the varying financial positions of the parties. Reflecting its relative popularity, Labour was able to raise considerable sums (though rather less than the Conservatives managed in 2019). By way of contrast, the Conservatives and Liberal Democrats found themselves in relative poverty, meaning both that they had less money than Labour and that they had to curtail some activities in their respective campaigns.

The second was the significant legislative change—in particular the uplift in campaign expenditure limits meaning that parties could spend far more than previously. Critics had suggested that the increase in spending limits had been motivated by partisan concerns, given the Conservatives' financial advantage in previous elections. Such criticism may have been unjustified, given that the uplifts were well overdue, but regardless, the increase in spending limits only benefitted one party—Labour. The financial circumstances in which the Conservatives found themselves, coupled with Labour's relative wealth meant that if the uplift was motivated by partisan concerns, it backfired.

The third was the continued growth in importance of digital campaigning, with Labour, in particular, exploiting it to a significant degree. But, it would be wrong to characterise this continuing shift to digital as being wholly strategic. The Conservatives' focus on digital was motivated to a significant extent by its financial position. All parties continued to use print on a significant scale, but its growing cost meant that digital frequently offered greater reach relative to expense. It's also important to note that parties' assessments of the effectiveness of digital campaigning varied. The Liberal Democrats were more sceptical of digital and were even of the view that print could be re-asserting its effectiveness. Overall, digital continued to grow in importance in terms of campaign expenditure. But print is far from obsolete.

References

BBC News (2024a) 'Diane Abbott calls Tory donor's comments frightening', https://www.bbc.co.uk/news/uk-politics-68542624, accessed 26 Sep. 2024.

BBC News (2024b) 'Frank Hester: Tory donor accused of racist Diane Abbott remarks', https://www.bbc.co.uk/news/uk-politics-68539981, accessed 26 Sep. 2024.

Conservative Party (2024) *Annual Report and Financial Statements for the Year Ended 31 December 2023*.

Department for Levelling Up, Housing and Communities (2022) Draft Electoral Commission Strategy and Policy Statement, https://www.gov.uk/government/publications/draft-electoral-commission-strategy-and-policy-statement, accessed 15 Aug. 2024.

Department for Levelling Up, Housing and Communities (2023) Government response to the consultation on the draft Strategy and Policy Statement for the Electoral Commission, https://assets.publishing.service.gov.uk/media/648c44155f7bb7000c7fac-0c/2023-06-08-Government_response_to_consultation_on_the_SPS.pdf, accessed 23 Sep. 2024.

Department for Levelling Up, Housing and Communities (2024) Electoral *Commission strategy and policy statement*, Electoral Commission strategy and policy statement - GOV.UK, accessed 15 Aug. 2024.

Fisher, J. (2010) 'Party Finance—Normal Service Resumed?', *Parliamentary Affairs*, 63: 778–801.

Fisher, J. (2018) 'Party Finance', *Parliamentary Affairs*, 71: 171–88.

Fisher, J. (2020) 'Party Finance in 2019—Advantage Conservative Party', *Parliamentary Affairs*, 73: 189–207.

Fisher, J. (2023) 'The regulation of political finance. Choppier waters ahead?' Institute for Government / Bennett Institute for Public Policy Review of the UK Constitution, https://www.instituteforgovernment.org.uk/publication/regulation-political-finance, accessed 15 Oct. 2024.

Fisher, J., and Kumar, J. (2020) *Attitudes of Electoral Agents on the Administration of the 2019 General Election*. Report produced for the Electoral Commission.

Hansard (2020, 3 December) 'Election Spending Limits Uprating', https://hansard.parliament.uk/commons/2020-12-03/debates/20120378000008/ElectionSpendingLimitsUprating, accessed 16 Aug. 2024.

Hansard (2023, 20 July) 'Written Statement made by Michael Gove, Secretary of State for Levelling Up, Housing and Communities and Minister for Intergovernmental Relations', Statement UIN HCWS985, https://questions-statements.parliament.uk/written-statements/detail/2023-07-20/hcws985, accessed 16 Aug. 2024.

Johnston, N. (2023) *Imprints on Election and Campaign Material*, CBP 02174, House of Commons Library.

Johnston, N., and Uberoi, E. (2023) *Overseas Voters*, CBP 5923, House of Common Library.

Labour Party (2024) *Financial Statements for the Year Ended 31 December 2023*.

Levelling Up, Housing and Communities Selection Committee. (2022) *Draft Strategy and Policy Statement for the Electoral Commission HC 672*.

Liberal Democrats (2024) *Annual Report for the Year Ended 31 December 2023*.

SI 1235 (2023) The Representation of the People (Variation of Election Expenses, Expenditure Limits and Donation etc. Thresholds) Order 2023.

The first TikTok election? Social media, generative AI, and data-driven campaigning in the 2024 UK General Election

Filip Biały[1,2,*] **and Rachel Gibson**[1]

[1]*Politics, University of Manchester, Oxford Rd, Manchester, M13 9PL, UK*
[2]*Collegium Polonicum, Adam Mickiewicz University Poznań, Kościuszki 1, 69-100 Słubice, Poland*

Correspondence: filip.bialy@amu.edu.pl

1. Introduction

The development of new communication technologies over the past century is intrinsically linked with the development of new modes or phases of campaigning (Norris 2000; Schmitt-Beck and Farrell 2003). Recent and rapid expansion in the amount and granularity of voter data available along with the opportunities for more precise and personalized message delivery through social media platforms has led to campaigns being labelled as 'data-driven' (Dommett et al., 2024). As well as prompting deeper shifts in campaign organization, strategy, and resources, the emergence of new technologies can lead parties to engage in more experimental and innovative communication techniques, particularly in the lead-up to a national election. The snap UK General Election in 2024 was no exception in this regard. As parties continued to invest heavily in microtargeting—a technique that lies at the heart of the new data-intensive mode of campaigning—media speculation was rife over whether we were about to see "the first TikTok election" (Tapper and Smith-Galer 2024; Titcomb 2024). Or, whether the new wave of generative artificial intelligence (AI) would flood the internet with believable 'deep fake' content and throw the outcome of the vote into question (Judson 2023). Surrounding this process of evolution and innovation in digital campaign practices, we also witnessed the introduction of a new regulatory regime, the explicit mission of which was to require greater transparency and accountability from those promoting online political material.

In this contribution, we examine these deeper and more surface-level developments in the UK digital campaign of 2024. First, we look at the evolution in the use of data-driven methods, particularly targeted advertising on social media. Despite ongoing debate over its effectiveness, political parties invested record-breaking amounts of money in their paid advertising campaigns on social media platforms such as Meta and Google. We then investigate whether the more sensationalist claims that we witnessed 'the TikTok election' were justified. The 2024 election campaign arguably offered the first opportunity for parties to reach out to the younger demographic of TikTok users. However, the specificities of the platform were a challenge in getting their message across. In a third step, we examine the role played by generative AI, both in terms of its actual use by practitioners and the fears it prompted for wider electoral integrity. Here we draw on findings from a recent and original campaign survey that measured public perceptions of the prevalence and impact of AI-generated political content during the election. Finally, we assess the impact of the new requirements for digital imprints on political content during the campaign. How 'fit for purpose' was the new regulatory regime particularly in the context of the new wave of generative AI tools? We conclude by reflecting on what our findings suggest about the future of digital campaigning in the UK. Will we see the incremental intensification of trends toward more data-driven campaigning (DDC), or did the experience of 2024 point toward a more disruptive and unpredictable future for online elections?

2. A data-driven election?

The literature on political campaigning has long recognized the relationship between emerging communication technologies and the approaches that parties use to reach existing and new audiences (Norris 2000; Schmitt-Beck and Farrell 2003; Owen 2018). The early 'premodern' era of campaigning, which relied mostly on localized 'low tech' personal interactions and print communication, was superseded by a more nationalized form of 'modern' campaigning that revolved around the centralized mass media of radio and particularly television. The advent of cable TV and the internet, and the increasing fragmentation this produced in the media landscape in the 1990s, helped usher in a third 'postmodern' phase of campaigning in which political communication was professionalized and placed in the hands of specialized operatives and strategists (Blumler and Kavanagh 1999). The claim that we have entered a new fourth, data-driven era is one that has gained traction in recent years (Blumler 2016; Semetko and Tworzecki 2017). While still emergent, a core feature is that political parties employ a more scientific approach to their communication activities, combining data from diverse sources in order to inform decision-making in relation to advertising and canvassing, as well as intra-party organization (Roemmele and Gibson 2020).

Much of the empirical research on DDC has focused on the case of the USA (Baldwin-Philippi 2017), although more comparative approaches have been expanding (Kefford et al., 2023; Vliegenthart et al., 2024). In particular, it has been established that the uniform 'one size fits all' approach to understanding DDC is too narrow and misses the role of cultural, organizational, and regulatory contexts in shaping the value given to, and applications of, data and data-driven tools by parties (Barclay, Dommett, and Russmann 2024). A recent 'working' definition arrived at through a systematic literature review reflects this need for nuance in describing it as:

> DDC relies on accessing and analyzing voter and/or campaign data to generate insights into the campaign's target audience(s) and/or to optimize campaign interventions. Data is used to inform decision-making in either a formative and/or evaluative capacity, and is employed to engage in campaigning efforts around either voter communication, resource generation and/or internal organization. (Dommett, Barclay, and Gibson 2024: 2)

A key component of the DDC definitions presented to date is the practice of microtargeting—the harnessing of increasingly fine-grained voter data to tailor messages toward ever narrower segments of the electorate. Judging by the scale of spending on this type of voter communication in the UK 2024 General Election, it appears that DDC had reached something of a peak. From the date Rishi Sunak announced the election to polling day, parties, individual candidates, and non-party campaigners spent £11.2 million on online advertising, eight and half million pounds of which went to Meta and £2.7m to Google platforms, resulting in the airing of two billion ads (Who Targets Me 2024b). In comparison, the total expenditure by all parties in 2019 on advertising on social media and other online platforms stood at £7.6 million (Dommett et al., 2024). The increase can be explained in part by the lifting of external restraints on election spending. Since paid television and radio advertising in the UK remained prohibited, digital advertising became an obvious outlet for the excess funds. However, the size of the increase in spending, by around a third of the 2019 total, signals that the parties were viewing the virtual campaign as a serious battleground for voters' attention.

The spending differential across parties in 2024 was something of a talking point, particularly between the two main parties. According to the Who Targets Me data (Who Targets Me 2024b), the Labour Party alone accounted for more than half of the total expenditure, with £6.1 million funnelled into its digital advertising campaign, possibly exceeding the amount spent on print media, as Justin Fisher argues in this volume. This was almost three times more than the Conservative Party, which spent a paltry £2.1 million by comparison. In terms of the differential across platforms, advertising on Meta—which includes Facebook and Instagram—was favoured over Google and its subsidiary video channel YouTube by a ratio 3:1 (Who Targets Me 2024b). The two major political parties, however, again differed in the way they chose to target voters online. The Labour Party made extensive use of geotargeting, focusing particularly on reaching middle-aged voters in those constituencies where a small to moderate swing would yield seats. By contrast, the Conservatives were more likely to exploit platforms' audience matching facility, which meant reaching users similar to those that previously engaged with their content (Ewing 2024). These approaches aligned with the broader campaign strategies of each party, in that Labour were widely seen as seeking to reach beyond their core electorate and those already committed to supporting them (young voters), to tap into the large seam of voters that were highly disaffected with the ruling Conservative Party. Conversely, the Conservatives were primarily concerned with maintaining the support of their base of older voters, and retaining the 'red wall' seats they had captured with tight margins in the 2019 election (Hern et al., 2024).

Spending on paid online advertising by the three smaller parties, the Liberal Democrats, Greens, and Reform UK, albeit much lower overall, was arguably even better targeted in terms of the 'return on investment'. The Liberal Democrats' campaign, which saw the party win a record number of seats, focused mostly on constituencies in the South and South West of England (Savage 2024). With total spending on digital advertising by the party and its candidates being just over £450,000, the Liberal Democrats' online campaign proved to be the most efficient and effective. Looked at in terms of their spending on Meta platforms, they paid around £3,700 per seat won, which was considerably lower than the two main parties (Who Targets Me [@WhoTargetsMe] 2024). The Green Party, despite putting up candidates in all constituencies, pursued a similar strategy and invested most of its £285,000 spent on battlegrounds in Wales and South West England. Notably both the Liberal Democrats and Greens were in the end outspent by Reform UK and Nigel Farage, whose Meta page was responsible for the vast majority of the £680,000 spent by the party on digital adverts (Who Targets Me 2024a).

In terms of digital campaign messages, while Labour ran ads heavily critical of the Conservative government, they also leveraged their challenger status to focus on their credentials as the party of change in both their paid and organic communication. The Conservative Party by contrast adopted an almost entirely negative tone. *Who Targets Me* research identified just seven policy Facebook ads compared with several thousand attack ads from the party in the lead-up to election day (Who Targets Me 2024b). The Liberal Democrats heavily relied on the individual popularity of Ed Davey whose picture was featured on ads promoting candidates in particular constituencies. The party also used paid advertising to recruit new members and election-day volunteers. Reform UK's adverts frequently publicized longer conference speeches of the party officials, but many of them were focused on anti-immigration policies, while attacking both the Labour and the Conservatives. In contrast, the Green Party adverts were mostly policy-oriented (with a focus on NHS, climate action, and education), with some presenting the party as the one able to win seats that the Labour Party could not win (Facebook Ad Library 2024).

Results from a specially commissioned YouGov survey by the DiCED project, funded by the European Research Council, indicated that digital forms of contact reached a smaller portion of voters than the more traditional ones. While 54% of respondents received party communication by mail or leaflet delivered to their house, only a little over 10% received information by email, 7% while searching or browsing the Internet, and almost 7% through their social media[1]. It would suggest that the future increase in investment in DDC, and in particular in microtargeted advertising, is an open question, considering that the current social media landscape is increasingly less conducive to the use of such methods. In the aftermath of the Facebook–Cambridge Analytica scandal, the platforms have imposed greater restrictions on the targeting options of advertisers. The regulators in Europe introduced limitations for targeting (Council of the EU 2024) and new transparency requirements, including digital imprints in the UK that we examine below. Furthermore, the effectiveness of microtargeting has been debated. While some studies have suggested it is useful as a means to reach one's base and known supporters (Lavigne 2021) whether it can find new or undecided voters is questioned. Recent evidence has shown that targeting messages with an ever greater set of characteristics did not yield significant persuasive gains (Tappin et al., 2023).

3. Was it 'the TikTok election'?

Within this broader cycle of political campaign change and questions of where the UK is located in relation to a new fourth era, there were a number of other more practical and tactical innovations that emerged that overlaid these deeper historical trends. While the digital campaign playbook over the past few election cycles has been dominated primarily by Facebook and Twitter (now X), younger audiences

---

[1] The online survey for the Digital Campaigning and Electoral Democracy (DiCED) project was conducted by YouGov on 6-24 June and 11-24 July 2024 on a nationally representative sample (N) of 5142. In calculating the results, a subset of 4193 respondents completed a specialist module of question regarding the online campaign and weights provided by YouGov were applied to optimise the representativeness of responses to all UK adults. More information about the project: https://sites.manchester.ac.uk/diced/

have now migrated away from these older platforms. One of the most popular new online spaces by the time of the election was TikTok, a social media app launched in 2017 by Chinese company ByteDance with a clear skew to younger voters (Schapals 2024). In 2024 the platform was used by more than 23% of all UK adults and by more than 53% in the 18-24 age group (YouGov 2024). For candidates, and particularly party leaders struggling to introduce themselves to the new crop of Gen Z voters, TikTok offered potentially high rewards but also carried high risks.

The platform itself faced controversy over data privacy, with concerns about user information being shared with the Chinese government (Levine 2023). By 2024, over thirty countries, including the UK, had banned the app or restricted its use on government devices (Gordon 2024a). Despite this, the company denied any wrongdoing and emphasized its commitment to helping users and governments safeguard elections through transparency initiatives.

Despite TikTok's challenges, its popularity among younger audiences made it appealing to most parties. The Greens and Reform UK adopted the platform early, with others joining as the election day loomed closer. Since TikTok did not allow paid political ads, parties had to create content suited to its algorithms rather than simply buying impressions. As late adopters, they had to build their follower base from scratch, so even their most popular content lagged behind established creators and influencers. By 4th July Labour had 223,000 followers and the Conservatives 74,000—dwarfed by leading UK accounts like Gordon Ramsey, who had 40.5 million followers (Social Blade 2024). The meme and parody-filled nature of the medium, however, offered rewards to those willing to adopt a more irreverent and 'populist' style. The content produced by Reform UK leader Nigel Farage gained some notable traction, with his campaign travel diary offering an effective combination of conversational authenticity and entertaining spontaneity. A widely watched and shared post involved him singing along to an Eminem song, while policy-oriented posts focused on an anti-immigration message (Jorgensen 2024). Similarly, the madcap antics of Liberal Democrat leader Ed Davey to highlight sewage problems in Britain's rivers gained him a sizeable audience.

Although the smaller parties may have punched above their weight in terms of providing memorable content creation, the Labour Party was arguably the biggest winner in extracting votes from TikTok. Even before they opened an account a survey of users showed they were 31% more likely to vote for the Labour than people of the same age and background who did not use the app (Waterson 2024). Certainly, once on the platform, Labour proved much more active than the Conservatives, with a total of 175 posts by election day, compared with only 48 by the Conservatives. In terms of content, Labour's profile was a mixture of issue-based videos and parodies attacking Conservative manifesto pledges, particularly from the youth angle. One of the highest performing videos, which gained over five million views, ridiculed Rishi Sunak's plan to reintroduce National Service for young people by juxtaposing it with the theme tune from "Surprise, Surprise", a TV dating show hosted by pop star Cilla Black.

Despite the healthy media attention that the new platform generated, claims that the UK saw its first TikTok election in retrospect appear to be inflated, if not "massively overblown" (Wheeler 2024). While posts on all parties' social media feeds were down in 2024 overall (Fletcher 2024), TikTok still ranked significantly below Facebook, X, and Instagram in terms of the frequency of party posts, and activity subsided rapidly after 4th July. Furthermore, as the legacy media pointed out, the mainstream news channels were still pivotal in setting the agenda (The Economist 2024). The sudden spike and fall of interest in TikTok, combined with the more general decline of effort spent on organic versus paid content by parties, suggests that for this electoral cycle, at least, most parties saw social media platforms as 'standard' advertising tools rather than channels for organic communication. Whether that might change in the future if other platforms move to impose bans on paid political content is an interesting question. Also, it may be the case that parties begin to see their potential for building ongoing relationships with segments of the electorate, much in the style of the current crop of popular online microinfluencers.

4. Was it the generative AI election?

In previous electoral cycles, parties' use of AI was limited and focused more on internal tasks such as modelling and predicting voter turnout. The new wave of generative AI tools, particularly the large language models or LLMs such as ChatGPT released in November 2022, changed the communications landscape rapidly. Campaigns and their supporters now had the ability to easily create and distribute sophisticated campaign memes and messages at scale. Similarly to TikTok, however, as much as the tools inspired enthusiasm, they also provoked concern and even fear about their consequences for democratic systems' integrity.

Much of the concern centred on the capacity of AI to spread disinformation. The ease with which it was now possible to manipulate and doctor images, and create entirely false content in the form of deepfake videos or cloned audio of politicians, was seen to pose a major risk to the integrity and trustworthiness of the electoral process and democracy more generally (Pawelec 2022). The fears were not without foundation. In Autumn 2023, an AI-generated audio clip that purportedly contained a secret recording of London Mayor Sadiq Khan supporting pro-Palestinian marches went viral (Spring 2024). Just before the Labour Party conference of that year, video footage of leader Keir Starmer allegedly swearing at his staff was posted on X. While in both instances the footage was later debunked and dismissed, these events highlighted the vulnerability of the upcoming UK election and many others occurring worldwide in 2024, to malicious attempts to disrupt and influence the results (Ambrose 2024). Moves by some of the major AI companies to install new 'guardrails' around the technology to prevent any misuse in elections further served to emphasize the reality of the threat it now posed. OpenAI for example prohibited the use of ChatGPT to develop applications that could be used for political campaigning and lobbying such as 'candidate' chatbots that could interact with, and provide information to voters (OpenAI 2024).

From a campaigner's perspective, however, generative AI offers clear benefits, enabling cheap, rapid creation of personalized content based on individual data. This could allow campaigns to craft tailored video ads and press releases, tested and refined using AI tools. In response, the Demos think-tank published an open letter urging UK political parties to 'safeguard election integrity in the era of AI'. It called on parties to avoid using AI to produce or amplify misleading content; to label AI-generated materials, and to provide transparent AI usage guidelines to campaign staff (Demos 2024). The UK Government issued online security guidance for candidates, focusing primarily on risks from high-quality 'fake content' (UK Government 2024).

Again, rather like TikTok, the role played by AI in the election proved ultimately to be quite limited. For the parties, this was perhaps not too surprising given the negative publicity that was likely to flow from the discovery of any deliberate misuse. Also, their need to maintain control of the message made dabbling with the software potentially dangerous. Current versions of widely used LLMs suffered from so-called 'hallucinations'—a malfunction that led them to produce plausible but at times wildly factually incorrect text in response to user prompts. Furthermore, and perhaps most importantly, it was not yet clear whether the technology actually returned any votes. Although recent studies have suggested that voters consider AI-generated content to be persuasive, it is argued that it still requires effective microtargeting to exert any real influence on their attitudes (Dobber et al., 2021; Goldstein et al., 2024).

The evidence regarding malicious use of AI also suggests that activity levels were lower than feared. A post-election report, based on evidence cited in news articles and public reports between 22nd May and 30th August, revealed that during the course of the campaign a total of sixteen cases of AI-generated disinformation or deepfakes that went viral were identified (Stockwell 2024). This included a doctored video of Shadow Health Minister Wes Streeting, published on X, and deepfaked pornographic pictures of high-profile UK politicians. Anti-immigrant appeals also featured an AI-generated picture of Keir Starmer surrounded by women in hijabs posted on X in a bid to show how Labour had deserted its white working-class voter base. Otherwise, initial media reports that Reform UK was generating AI candidates in order to fulfil their mission of competing in every constituency were later exposed as themselves 'fake' news stories (Pike and Kemp 2024). By way of counter-balance, the report sought to highlight a number of potentially beneficial uses of AI such as its capacity to fact check and rapidly debunk false claims and news content. It also provided a new way to connect voters more directly with candidates through synthetic personas. One example of this that generated national headlines was an independent candidate from Brighton who generated an avatar, 'AI Steve', to exchange and communicate with voters on his policy ideas (Davis 2024).

The low profile of AI in the election is highlighted by YouGov survey data from the DiCED project. Of 4,193 respondents, only 13% believed they had seen AI-generated content. Among them, 37% reported seeing AI-generated images, about 25% mentioned news articles or social media posts, and 20% thought they had seen AI-produced videos. Most respondents (71%) ignored the content, while 15% consumed it without further action. Only 5% fact-checked the content, 5% reported it, and 1.5% shared it. Reactions were mostly neutral or negative, with 25% unbothered, 20% irritated, and 18% concerned (YouGov 2024). Overall, therefore, this preliminary evidence suggests the impact of the AI-generated content on the electorate was likely to be minimal. That said, there are important questions as to how well average users of social media platforms are able to detect AI-generated content and whether exposure levels might in fact be significantly higher than recorded through self-reported surveys (Hameleers, Van Der Meer, and Dobber 2024; Nas and De Kleijn 2024). Certainly, the small number of individuals that actually undertook countermeasures to check the content or report it to the platforms is an indication that regulatory intervention in this sphere may be necessary in the future (Jungherr, Rauchfleisch, and Wuttke 2024).

5. Was it the digital imprint election?

Calls for greater oversight and accountability of digital political advertising have increased in recent elections with some describing the existing system as akin to an 'unregulated Wild West' (Dommett, and Power 2020: 5). In the aftermath of the 2019 General Election, the government conducted a consultation exercise, which produced a series of recommendations designed to enhance the transparency of online political advertising, and empower the Electoral Commission to monitor and sanction transgressions (Dommett and Power 2020). At the core of the proposals were requirements for placing digital imprints on online campaign content to clearly identify its source. Political parties and candidates had to indicate responsibility for all content—texts, images, videos, music, and speech, whether paid or unpaid. The imprint needed to include the promoter's name and address and the person on whose behalf the content was published.

The Elections Act of 2022 formalized these new provisions. Although the new rules did impose stronger obligations on parties to disclose their authorship of online election content there were some significant 'gaps' or areas of uncertainty regarding their application. Content produced by social media influencers who were paid by a party for example did not have to carry an imprint. Exemption was also made for unpaid material that appeared on a website or app run as a journalistic source. Also, the understanding of what constituted campaign material was defined in somewhat general and subjective terms as material that could be 'reasonably regarded as intended to promote a candidate or party, persuade a voter to vote for a particular candidate or party, or vote in a particular way in a referendum' (Tumbridge 2024).

Findings from a recent study examining the implementation of the new imprints regime in 2024 reflect these ambiguities, with the general conclusion drawn that its application was not 'consistent or necessarily informative' (Dommett, Luke, and Gordon 2024: 17). Notably, compliance differed significantly across the four main digital platforms (Facebook, Instagram, X, and TikTok) and across political entities. Overall, a significant majority (68.9%) of the campaign materials analysed were found to be compliant, with Facebook adverts topping the charts (85.5%) followed by X (72.8%). Content on TikTok and Instagram was less so (59.9% and 57.1% compliant, respectively). National parties were the most compliant, with 93.3% of assessed posts containing the required information, while smaller parties, individual candidates, and non-party campaigns adhered at lower rates, although typically still the majority of their content carried an imprint. Diving below the presence or absence of the required information, visibility also proved to be a factor. Only half of the imprints provided were embedded directly in the campaign content (50.2%) and just under a third (29.2%) of imprints were immediately visible, with less than one-fifth (17.6%) of materials on the X platform displaying them visibly.

Given the sizeable upswing in party spending on social media advertising, it does not appear that the new transparency rules reduced investment in this new mode of voter communication. That said, it is also evident that the new rules on transparency of digital campaigning were selectively adhered to in 2024. One might expect future elections to see a strengthening and tightening in their application. Whether this curbs parties' enthusiasm remains to be seen. Of course, increasing the requirements for transparency in the source of messages cannot guarantee their accuracy and trustworthiness, which is arguably the bigger problem that governments and voters will face in future elections, particularly in the era of generative AI (Gordon 2024b). Whether current restrictions will extend to policing content and the promotion of misinformation poses both significant normative questions and technical challenges. Arguably, the speed of change in the technological landscape makes the remit and scope of the Electoral Commission in this area particularly challenging. Policymakers might, with good reason, want to see how the new tools play out before imposing new laws on their use.

6. Conclusions

Based on this brief overview of the 2024 digital election one might argue that it was in many ways a continuity or 'no change' election. Data-driven methods in the form of targeted online advertising were a 'staple' in all of the parties' campaign toolboxes and saw a significant financial uplift. Overlaying this continuity there were some instances of innovation and unanticipated creativity, particularly among the smaller parties on TikTok. However, the snap nature of the election did not leave much time and space for advance experimentation, leading parties to fall back more on previously tested channels.

The general consensus that the hopes and fears for generative AI and TikTok went largely unrealized is in keeping with the prior cycles of techno-hype that have greeted each election since 1997 when the World Wide Web first entered the race. However, whether this failure of the technological 'dog to bark' will place a pause on legislative intervention is questionable. The lack of consistent application of the current controls on digital imprints revealed in post-election analysis suggests that the current rules will be insufficient to capture and deal with any new wave of AI-powered mis- and disinformation campaigns in the future. Even if fully and consistently implemented, the rules on digital imprints only extend to ensuring the transparency of the source of the material, not the veracity of its content. Although the direct impact of generative AI has to date been marginal, continuing extensive media coverage of its manipulation and misuse and the very real barriers that automated methods of detection are now facing will very likely build a narrative supportive of increasing regulation. Purveyors of this narrative, however, would do well to be mindful of its consequences for voters' already shaky trust in their institutions.

Funding

This research received funding from the European Research Council (ERC) under the European Union's Horizon 2020 research and innovation programme (Digital Campaigning and Electoral Democracy (DiCED), Grant agreement no. 833177).

References

Ambrose, T. (2024) 'UK's Enemies Could Use AI Deepfakes to Try to Rig Election, Says James Cleverly', *The Guardian*, https://www.theguardian.com/uk-news/2024/feb/25/uks-enemies-could-use-ai-deepfakes-to-try-to-rig-election-says-james-cleverly, accessed 1 Oct. 2024.

Baldwin-Philippi, J. (2017) 'The Myths of Data-Driven Campaigning', *Political Communication*, 34: 627–33.

Barclay, A., Dommett, K., and Russmann, U. (2024) 'Data Driven-Campaign Infrastructures in Europe: Evidence from Austria and the UK', *Journal of Political Marketing* 1–20.

Blumler, J. G. (2016) 'The Fourth Age of Political Communication', *Politiques de Communication*, 6: 19–30.

Blumler, J. G. and Kavanagh, D. (1999) 'The Third Age of Political Communication: Influences and Features', *Political Communication*, 16: 209–30.

Council of the EU (2024) 'EU Introduces New Rules on Transparency and Targeting of Political Advertising', https://www.consilium.europa.eu/en/press/press-releases/2024/03/11/eu-introduces-new-rules-on-transparency-and-targeting-of-political-advertising/, accessed 21 Oct. 2024.

Davis B. (2024) 'Meet AI Steve: The Bot-Driven Politician Using Artificial Intelligence on the Campaign Trail', *The Independent*, https://www.independent.co.uk/news/uk/politics/election-politics-uk-ai-steve-brighton-b2559777.html, accessed 15 Nov. 2024.

Demos (2024) 'Open Letter Calling for UK Political Parties to Safeguard Election Integrity in Era of AI, Demos', https://demos.co.uk/research/open-letter-to-uk-political-parties-to-safeguard-the-next-general-election-from-generative-ai/, accessed 12 Oct. 2024.

Dobber, T., et al. (2021) 'Do (Microtargeted) Deepfakes Have Real Effects on Political Attitudes?', *The International Journal of Press/Politics*, 26: 69–91.

Dommett, K., Barclay, A., and Gibson, R. (2024) 'Just What is Data-Driven Campaigning? A Systematic Review', *Information, Communication & Society*, 27: 1–22.

Dommett, K., Luke, S., and Gordon, H. (2024) 'Making Elections More Transparent? Lessons from the Implementation of Digital Imprints at the 2024 UK General Election', https://doi.org/10.31219/osf.io/unb26, accessed 12 Oct. 2024.

Dommett, K., and Power, S. (2020) *Democracy in the Dark Digital Campaigning in the 2019 General Election and Beyond*. London: Electoral Reform Society.

Dommett, K., et al. (2024) 'Understanding the Modern Election Campaign: Analysing Campaign Eras through Financial Transparency Disclosures at the 2019 UK General Election', *Government and Opposition*, 60: 141–67.

Ewing, T. (2024) 'Anatomy of an Election, The 2024 Labour landslide Part 1: Digital Marketing Strategy', https://medium.com/station10/anatomy-of-an-election-the-2024-labour-landslide-part-1-digital-marketing-strategy-f53c79dd6e3d, accessed 7 Oct. 2024.

Facebook Ad Library (2024) *Facebook Ad Library*, https://www.facebook.com/ads/library/, accessed 15 Oct. 2024.

Fletcher, R. (2024) 'Which Social Networks Did Political Parties Use Most in 2024?', *UK Election Analysis*, https://www.electionanalysis.uk/uk-election-analysis-2024/section-6-the-digital-campaign/which-social-networks-did-political-parties-use-most-in-2024/, accessed 12 Oct. 2024.

Goldstein, J. A., et al. (2024) 'How Persuasive is AI-Generated Propaganda?", *PNAS Nexus*, 3: 1–7.

Gordon, A. (2024a) 'Here Are All the Countries With TikTok Bans and Restrictions', *TIME*, https://time.com/6971009/tiktok-banned-restrictions-worldwide-countries-united-states-law/, accessed 12 Oct. 2024.

Gordon, T. (2024b) 'The Dawn of the AI Election', *Prospect*, https://www.prospectmagazine.co.uk/politics/64396/the-dawn-of-the-ai-election, accessed 11 Oct. 2024.

Hameleers, M., Van Der Meer, T. G. L. A., and Dobber, T. (2024) 'They Would Never Say Anything Like This! Reasons To Doubt Political Deepfakes', *European Journal of Communication*, 39: 56–70.

Hern, A., et al. (2024) 'Tories Pursuing "ostrich strategy" on Facebook Campaign Ads', *The Guardian*, https://www.theguardian.com/politics/article/2024/jun/03/tories-pursuing-ostrich-strategy-on-facebook-campaign-ads, accessed 30 Sept. 2024.

Jorgensen, K.-W. (2024) 'Farage on TikTok: The Perfect Populist Platform', *UK Election Analysis*, https://www.electionanalysis.uk/uk-election-analysis-2024/section-6-the-digital-campaign/farage-on-tiktok-the-perfect-populist-platform/, accessed 13 Oct. 2024.

Judson, E. (2023) '2024 will be a Litmus Test for AI's Effect on Elections – and Voters' Faith in Them', *The Guardian*, https://www.theguardian.com/commentisfree/2023/jul/07/2024-litmus-test-ai-elections-voters-trust, accessed 1 Oct. 2024.

Jungherr, A., Rauchfleisch, A., and Wuttke, A. (2024) 'Deceptive Uses of Artificial Intelligence in Elections Strengthen Support for AI Ban', http://arxiv.org/abs/2408.12613, accessed 8 Oct. 2024.

Kefford, G., et al. (2023) 'Data-Driven Campaigning and Democratic Disruption: Evidence from Six Advanced Democracies', *Party Politics*, 29: 448–62.

Lavigne, M. (2021) 'Strengthening Ties: The Influence of Microtargeting on Partisan Attitudes and The Vote', *Party Politics*, 27: 965–76.

Levine, A.S. (2023) Exclusive: TikTok Confirms Some U.S. User Data Is Stored In China, *Forbes*, https://www.forbes.com/sites/alexandralevine/2023/06/21/tiktok-confirms-data-china-bytedance-security-cfius/, accessed 12 Oct. 2024.

Nas, E., and De Kleijn, R. (2024) 'Conspiracy Thinking and Social Media Use are Associated with Ability to Detect Deepfakes', *Telematics and Informatics*, 87: 102093.

Norris, P. (2000) *A Virtuous Circle: Political Communications in Postindustrial Societies*. Cambridge: Cambridge University Press.

OpenAI (2024) 'How OpenAI is Approaching 2024 Worldwide Elections', https://openai.com/index/how-openai-is-approaching-2024-worldwide-elections/, accessed 11 Oct. 2024.

Owen, D. (2018) 'New Media and Political Campaigns' In: K. Kenski and K. Hall Jamieson (eds) *The Oxford Handbook of Political Communication*, pp. 823–36. Oxford: Oxford University Press.

Pawelec, M. (2022) 'Deepfakes and Democracy (Theory): How Synthetic Audio-Visual Media for Disinformation and Hate Speech Threaten Core Democratic Functions', *Digital Society*, 1: 1–37.

Pike, J., and Kemp, P. (2024) 'Reform UK Fake Candidate Conspiracy Theories Debunked', https://www.bbc.com/news/articles/ckvgl9kzwzjo, accessed 12 Oct. 2024.

Roemmele, A., and Gibson, R. (2020) 'Scientific and Subversive: The Two Faces of the Fourth Era of Political Campaigning', *New Media & Society*, 22: 595–610.

Savage, M. (2024) 'Lib Dems Step up Frantic Tactical Voting Effort to Oust Conservatives in Blue Wall', *The Observer*, https://www.theguardian.com/politics/article/2024/jun/30/lib-dems-step-up-frantic-tactical-voting-effort-to-oust-conservatives-in-blue-wall, accessed 14 Oct. 2024.

Schapals, A. (2024) 'Winning Voters' Hearts and Minds… Through reels and Memes?! How #GE24 Unfolded on TikTok', https://www.electionanalysis.uk/uk-election-analysis-2024/section-6-the-digital-campaign/winning-voters-hearts-and-minds-through-reels-and-memes-how-ge24-unfolded-on-tiktok/, accessed 12 Oct. 2024.

Schmitt-Beck, R. and Farrell, D. M. (2003) 'Do Political Campaigns Matter? Yes, But it Depends' In: D. M. Farrell, and R. Schmitt-Beck (eds), *Do Political Campaigns Matter?*, pp. 183–93. London and New York: Routledge.

Semetko, H. A., and Tworzecki, H. (2017) 'Campaign Strategies, Media, and Voters'. In: J. Fisher et al. (eds) *The Routledge Handbook of Elections, Voting Behavior and Public Opinion*, pp. 293–304. Abingdon: Routledge.

Social Blade (2024) 'YouTube, Twitch, Twitter, & Instagram Statistics', https://socialblade.com/, accessed 13 Oct. 2024.

Spring, M. (2024) 'Sadiq Khan Says Fake AI Audio of Him Nearly Led to Serious Disorder', https://www.bbc.com/news/uk-68146053, accessed 12 Oct. 2024.

Stockwell, S. (2024) 'AI-Enabled Influence Operations: Threat Analysis of the 2024 UK and European Elections', Centre for Emerging Technology and Security.

Tapper, J. and Smith-Galer, S. (2024) '"The First TikTok Election": Are Sunak and Starmer's Digital Campaigns Winning Over Voters?', *The Observer*, https://www.theguardian.com/politics/article/2024/jun/01/parties-starmer-sunak-digital-campaigns-social-media-tiktok, accessed 1 Oct. 2024.

Tappin, B. M., et al. (2023) 'Quantifying the Potential Persuasive Returns to Political Microtargeting', *Proceedings of the National Academy of Sciences*, 120: 1–10.

Titcomb, J. (2024) 'Inside the First TikTok Election', *The Telegraph*, https://www.telegraph.co.uk/business/2024/05/27/inside-first-tiktok-election/, accessed 1 Oct. 2024.

The Economist (2024) 'Why This Isn't Britain's TikTok Election', *The Economist*, https://www.economist.com/britain/2024/06/15/why-this-isnt-britains-tiktok-election, accessed 13 Oct. 2024.

Tumbridge J. (2024) 'Digital Imprints and The Spread of Misinformation in Elections', https://www.lexology.com/library/detail.aspx?g=dca8984b-69a7-4c37-9317-4eb2670536fd, accessed 15 Nov. 2024.

UK Government (2024) 'Online Disinformation and AI Threat Guidance for Electoral Candidates and Officials', https://www.gov.uk/government/publications/security-guidance-for-may-2021-elections/online-disinformation-and-ai-threat-guidance-for-electoral-candidates-and-officials, accessed 12 Oct. 2024.

Vliegenthart, R. et al. (2024) 'Citizens' Acceptance of Data-Driven Political Campaigning: A 25-Country Cross-National Vignette Study', *Social Science Computer Review*, 42: 1101–9.

Waterson, J. (2024) '"Almost Everyone Supports Labour": Why 2024 isn't the TikTok Election', *The Guardian*, https://www.theguardian.com/technology/article/2024/jun/08/almost-everyone-supports-labour-why-2024-isnt-the-tiktok-election, accessed 12 Oct. 2024.

Wheeler, B. (2024) 'Is This Really the TikTok General Election', *BBC*, https://www.bbc.com/news/articles/cjerdlw4jeqo, accessed 13 Oct. 2024.

Who Targets Me (2024a) 'Standing For Attention: Minor Parties in the Spotlight', https://fulldisclosure.whotargets.me/p/standing-for-attention-minor-parties, accessed 14 Oct. 2024.

Who Targets Me (2024b) 'Two Billion Ads', https://fulldisclosure.whotargets.me/p/two-billion-ads, accessed 7 Oct. 2024.

Who Targets Me [@WhoTargetsMe] (2024) 'Reform bought £108,400 worth of Meta ads for every seat won. The Greens spent £60k for each of theirs. The Liberal Democrats just £3,700, https://x.com/WhoTargetsMe/status/1809544871050420479, accessed 14 Oct. 2024.

YouGov (2024) 'UK 2024 General Election Survey for Digital Campaigning and Electoral Democracy Project'.

There may be trouble ahead: Women's representation, voters, and issues in the 2024 election campaign

Emily Harmer* and Rosalynd Southern

Department of Communication and Media, University of Liverpool, 19 Abercromby Square, Liverpool, L69 7ZG, UK.

*Correspondence: E.Harmer@liverpool.ac.uk

1. Introduction

Just when many commentators had settled on the idea of an Autumn campaign, Rishi Sunak surprised many by calling a July vote, much to the distress of several members of his own party (Crerar 2024). Sunak's prime ministerial term had been fraught from the start; after gaining the leadership because of the fallout from Liz Truss' disastrous mini budget, he had struggled to take charge of a party that had run out of ideas after being in power for so long. The government had been dogged by their repeated failure to fulfil their own controversial policy pledges to prevent refugees arriving in small boats, the cost-of-living crisis which was pushing more people into poverty, and the proliferation of sewage in Britain's waterways to name but a few political pressures. Consequently, speculation about when he would call an election had been rife for months. Here we analyse the significance (or lack of it) placed on women during the 2024 General Election by first discussing how they featured in the campaign. We then go on to discuss the parties' attempts to appeal to women voters through an analysis of their manifesto offerings. Next, we analyse the extent to which the representation of women in the House of Commons was altered as a result of the election, and finally we assess how women voted.

1.1 The campaign

In the previous two general elections, several of the larger parties were led by women, but many of these leaders had moved aside before the 2024 election.

Sinn Fein retained its female leader in Northern Ireland Michelle O'Neill, who by this time had become First Minister, and The Green Party continued its balanced co-leadership structure with Carla Denyer sharing the leadership. Aside from formal leadership, there were plenty of fairly visible women. Labour and the Liberal Democrats both had female deputy leaders, Angela Rayner and Daisy Cooper respectively, who featured heavily in the series of televised debates. Televised debates have become a fixture of UK election campaigns, after being introduced for the first time in 2010. Such debates can sometimes have gendered dynamics which can disadvantage women participants (Harmer et al., 2017). However, early analysis into the reception of the 2024 iteration suggests that the subsequent news coverage of them was not explicitly gendered (Shaw 2024).

Despite their inclusion in these high-profile events, media coverage of the campaign in general tended to be much more male-dominated. In their real-time study of legacy press and broadcast coverage of the campaign, Loughborough University's content analysis showed that women politicians were marginal in the campaign. For example, only 19.2% of politicians cited in news coverage were women, and moreover in the final week of the campaign women accounted for just six of the top twenty most visible individuals, five of whom were Labour candidates, and just one Conservative (Deacon et al., 2024). This marginalization is not untypical during election campaigns, and in fact continues a trend over the past century (Harmer 2021).

However, the election did result in some interesting milestones for women. Firstly, 264 women were elected accounting for an historic 40.6% of MPs in the House of Commons for the first time. This was a significant increase from the previous record of 34.2% in 2019 (Murray 2024). Labour's victory resulted in the first female Chancellor of the Exchequer in the form of Rachel Reeves. The election also saw two former female Prime Ministers leave the Commons. Theresa May had already announced her retirement from her role as MP in March (Baker and Seddon 2024), while Liz Truss lost her 23,000 majority in her South West Norfolk constituency to Labour's Terry Jermy who won by just 630 votes (Seddon 2024a).

The circumstances of the election led to problems with the selection of constituency candidates across the board. In the months running up to the campaign, many Conservative MPs had announced their intention to stand down at the next election, meaning that there were a significant number of constituencies with no selected candidate when the election was announced. This led to a large volume of last-minute selections which largely seem to have benefited male candidates (Murray 2024).

While the Conservatives were in a perilous position from the start, Labour was not immune from selection problems either, but these were largely self-inflicted. One of the biggest stories at the start of the campaign focused on Diane Abbott and whether she would be allowed to stand as a Labour MP. Some months previously, Abbott had the Labour whip removed after she wrote a letter to *the Observer* which suggested that Jewish, Irish, and Travellers were not subject to racism 'all their lives' (Crew and Catt 2023). She withdrew the comments but an investigation on restoring the whip had been ongoing. Just before parliament was dissolved Abbott had the whip restored, but shortly after an anonymous briefing in the press stated that she would be blocked from standing for re-election as a Labour MP (Seddon 2024b). This caused uproar among many, particularly among the Black community, as Abbott was the first Black woman MP and was, according to another Labour candidate Miatta Fahnbulleh an 'iconic figure' (Church 2024). The incident also led to the UK's most prominent Black newspaper, *The Voice*, questioning whether Labour was the natural home for Black voters (Sudan 2024). Following pressure, Abbott was allowed to run as a Labour candidate (later becoming the first black Mother of the House), but it somewhat marred the start of the campaign for Labour.

A second similar story also broke around this time. The Labour candidate for Chingford and Woodford Green at the last two general elections, Faiza Shaheen, was also barred from standing, reportedly over problematic Twitter/X 'likes'. This led to a tearful appearance by Shaheen on Newsnight (BBC News 2024a). Here she recounted what she felt were shaky grounds for her suspension, stating that she had been night feeding her small son at the time and may have liked the offending tweet by accident, meaning to like a post containing a Jon Stewart sketch rather than a quote tweet of the sketch containing antisemitic tropes. The two stories together were interpreted by some as Labour being hostile to women of colour (Aziz 2024), potentially overshadowing Labour's attempts to seem competent and progressive. Shaheen later ran as an independent, with her deselection leading to a split vote on election day and Iain Duncan Smith retaining the seat he had been projected to lose (Leach and de Hoog 2024). This was a rare disappointment on a night of triumphs for Labour.

Selection problems also beset other parties. Reform UK came under fire for selecting a number of candidates who had previously made misogynistic (as well as racist) comments in their public remarks or on their social media accounts. For example, their candidate for Orkney and Shetland posted on social media calling Nicola Sturgeon a 'bitch' and suggesting she should be shot (BBC News 2024b). Moreover, at least two candidates selected by Reform UK defected to the Conservatives during the campaign over claims that they had failed to tackle sexism and racism in the party (Quinn and Stacey 2024). Such incidents cast a shadow over the tone of campaign, compounded by the fact that several women candidates, including Jess Phillips and Shabana Mahmood, reported experiencing harassment and intimidation on the campaign trail (Lawson 2024). This underscores a recent trend in politicians experiencing abusive and harassing behaviour in British politics, both online and in person which threatens women's participation in the public sphere (see Collignon and Rüdig 2021; Southern and Harmer 2021).

2. Parties appeal to women voters: the manifestos

While parties attempt to appeal to voters through a variety of means, the clearest way of analysing their efforts to target and represent women is by paying attention to the formal pledges made by parties in their manifestos (Campbell and Childs 2015). Of course, women will be affected by all the policies that parties propose, but here we analyse the manifesto policies which explicitly or implicitly invoke women or gender because this shows the way women's needs are perceived by parties (Harmer and Southern 2020). In this section, we present a summary of nine political party manifestos of parties that achieved House of Commons representation: the Labour Party, the Conservatives, Liberal Democrats, the Scottish National Party (SNP), Reform UK, Sinn Fein, the Democratic Unionist Party (DUP), The Green Party and Plaid Cymru. Importantly, many policy areas affecting women are devolved to the respective national governments of Northern Ireland, Scotland, and Wales, therefore the manifesto commitments of parties who only contest seats in the devolved nations (the SNP, Plaid Cymru, Sinn Fein, the DUP) are aimed at a much smaller set of electors than the other parties discussed here. As a result, some of the smaller parties' manifestos were much briefer than the larger parties. Nevertheless, including gendered proposals in their manifestos for the general election signals a set of priorities as far as women are concerned. While there are more parties who gained seats in the House of Commons, including the six independent MPs, we have tried to reflect the policy issues aimed at voters across the UK without being exhaustive.

Just as in the previous elections, there is consensus around the kinds of policy areas where women are most visibly invoked, although the parties often offer different solutions to common problems. The following discussion will attempt to contextualize the policy positions of each party, since although there is a consensus on the range of issues associated with women, the approaches of each party can be very different. The policies that are included in the manifestos mainly fall into seven main areas: violence against women and girls, legal/judicial rights and protections, employment, social security, education, health, and political representation. Some parties do explicitly refer to women in other policy areas, for example Plaid Cymru mention prioritizing women's safety on public transport, but by far the most explicit appeals to women appear under the headings mentioned above. These will now be addressed in turn.

2.1 Violence against women

The issue which took up the most space in the majority of manifestos was violence against women. All parties (except for Reform UK, who did not mention it at all beyond a vague allusion to stopping grooming gangs) offered related policies. Plaid Cymru and Labour made pledges on stalking protections. Domestic violence was emphasized by most parties, with various pledges such as the instigation of a Domestic Violence Register to better keep track of repeat offenders (Plaid Cymru), tougher prison sentences for perpetrators (Conservatives), and the installation of trained experts in police control rooms to provide help and assistance (Labour). These measures all emphasize the criminal justice angle of intimate partner violence rather than seeking a more holistic approach. The Greens pledged to implement a UK-wide strategy to tackle domestic violence and Sinn Fein supported an 'ending violence against women and girls strategy', although neither proposal laid out any specific detail.

In relation to sexual violence, the Conservatives pledged a new investigatory model for investigating rape and to allow prerecorded cross-examination of victims in Crown courts, while Labour emphasized their plans for specialist rape teams and units for all police forces, as well as to fast-track such cases in the courts. Crucially, only three parties explicitly mentioned any specific funding for services aimed at tackling violence against women. The Greens offered a pledge to fund local authorities to meet local needs for domestic violence and rape crisis services while the Liberal Democrats promised to expand the number of refuges and rape crisis centres and to ensure sustainable fundings for these services. Similarly, the DUP pledged to address funding gaps in support for survivors of domestic abuse but did not specify what that support would entail.

Several parties sought to address the growing issue of digital threats to women and girls through legislation. Labour, Conservatives, and Plaid Cymru also mentioned new measures to tackle nonconsensual image sharing or sexually explicit deepfakes, while the DUP pledged to improve the response to online abuse without giving details. Labour promised to amend the Online Safety Bill while the Liberal Democrats pushed for measures to require social media companies to publish the actions they were taking to protect women and girls online. Both the Greens and Liberal Democrats also pledged to make misogyny a hate crime. The Liberal Democrats were the only party to mention implementing the Istanbul Convention which makes addressing and monitoring violence against women in all its forms an obligation of the state (Council of Europe 2011). Across the board, the issue of violence against women tended to be framed as a police or criminal justice matter, suggesting parties are more focused on punishment than prevention. Crucially, despite the subject taking up a lot of space, there was very little specific detail about funding or improving services for women from any of the parties.

2.1.1 Legal/judicial rights and protections The parties also sought to appeal to women by strengthening a range of legal rights and protections, although this was an area where parties showed more divergence than in other policy areas. Three parties (Reform UK, Conservatives, and Liberal Democrats) pledged to address perceived shortcomings in the child maintenance system, with the Liberal Democrats and Conservatives emphasizing their goals to support those who have experienced domestic violence. When it comes to reproductive rights, only three parties used the manifesto to reaffirm their position on abortion rights and services. The Liberal Democrats and SNP pledged to uphold women's rights to safe and high-quality healthcare, including terminations. The DUP reasserted its antichoice position, opposing the provision of abortion services in Northern Ireland. There were also some pledges from parties that sought to increase rights for cohabiting couples (Liberal Democrats and Labour).

Most parties had sections where they addressed LGBTQ + rights as well, although there were clear ideological differences between the parties. Plaid Cymru, Liberal Democrats, and Labour all pledge to ban conversion therapy practices that relate to gender and sexuality. The Conservatives included some vague text that discussed how difficult it was to legislate and that they wanted more time to address it, which constitutes a watering down of their previous commitments under Theresa May (Cowburn 2018). There was more variation over the issue of gender recognition. Plaid Cymru, Liberal Democrats, and the Greens pledged support for a de-medicalised, self-identification approach. Labour, on the other hand, opted for a vaguer commitment to 'modernize, simplify, and reform' gender recognition laws but also reiterated their support to retain the need for medical diagnosis and restated the idea that there should be single-sex exemptions in line with the Equality Act 2010. This pledge represents a key change from the 2019 manifesto (see Harmer and Southern 2020). Strikingly, the SNP did not reiterate its commitment to introducing self-identification for trans people, despite attempts under its former leader to reform this issue through the Scottish Parliament which placed it in conflict with the previous Conservative government in Westminster.

The Conservatives also promised to guarantee single-sex services, but they went much further by choosing to heavily emphasize an attachment to biological sex as a means of categorizing people and also choosing to position trans people's rights in opposition to those of cis women and girls. Similarly, Reform UK also pledged support for single-sex spaces, specifying toilet facilities and changing areas. It is perhaps instructive that this was the only mention of women's rights in Reform UK's entire manifesto. The hardening of rhetoric about gender politics shows a clearly regressive move away from progressive policies for women and LGBTQ + people in general. Luxton (2024) argues that this represents a clear strategy of some of the mainstream parties accommodating more conservative positions on gender in the race for votes, which has the potential to harm LGBTQ + rights in the longer term. Another concerning trend for women in this area was the Conservative and Reform UK pledges to reduce diversity, equality, and inclusion measures in some sectors. Reform UK particularly targeted the police, using the far-right rhetoric about 'two-tier' policing to accuse them of being too concerned about infringing on the rights of minorities. Considering the very public failures of various police forces to take sexual offences and domestic violence seriously, it seems that such policy pledges conflict with delivering better policing.

2.1.2 Social security Social security was another issue that foregrounded women. Issues falling into this category included: childcare provision, child benefit, and pensions inequality. All parties, apart from Reform UK discussed their childcare proposals. Most of the parties pledged to expand free childcare provision, although some parties were more ambitious (and provided more detail) than others. For example, the Greens pledged 35 hours for children aged nine months and above, while both Labour and the SNP merely pledged to "expand childcare". Child benefit was more sparsely included. The Conservatives pledged to change its distribution while the SNP was the only party to explicitly pledge to remove the two-child cap on child benefit, in contrast to the 2019 General Election where Labour also promised to address this specific inequality. Pension inequality was addressed by five of the parties. The Liberal Democrats, Plaid Cymru, and SNP all pledged to provide compensation for the WASPI women who were disadvantaged by changes to the state pension age without adequate notice. The Conservatives and DUP gave more vague assurances about addressing pensions inequality.

2.1.3 Health Some of the parties chose to make explicit references to women in their sections on public health and the NHS specifically. Once again, much of this referred specifically to trans issues, with a variety of different positions adopted. Plaid Cymru pledged to improve the service provided by gender clinics and to ensure timely care for those affected. The Conservatives pledged to expand the ban on puberty blockers and referred to gender-affirming care as 'ideologically driven' while ignoring the role of ideological consideration in their own position. Similarly, the Conservatives also stressed their opposition to inclusive language within maternity services which once again shows their increasingly socially conservative approach to gender and is perhaps a strange thing to include in a party manifesto. Labour adopted a position in the middle on gender identity care, where the manifesto pledged to ensure that those presenting to medical services about their gender identity will receive high-quality care, without specifying what that might look like. Some parties also made specific pledges about maternity services. The Conservatives and Liberal Democrats both detailed some proposed improvements to neonatal services and also mental health support for those experiencing pregnancy. The Liberal Democrats and Labour explicitly pledged to improve the experiences and address the maternal mortality gap for black women. The Conservatives also mentioned improving menopause support.

2.1.4 Education Five of the parties refer to education in their manifesto, although, much like some of the policy areas discussed already, there is a clear focus from the right-wing parties on sex and gender within schools. Reform UK pledged to ban what they refer to as 'transgender ideology' in schools so that pupils cannot openly question their gender or ask to be referred to by different pronouns. Similarly, the Conservatives pledged to disallow any teaching that relates to gender identity which, in addition to being hostile to trans pupils, also seems to lack sufficient definition. They also emphasized the rights of parents to know about their child's identity over the potential safety of the child. The Greens, Liberal Democrats, and Labour simply pledged to provide high-quality sex and relationships education in schools, with the Greens specifying that this will be LGBTQ + inclusive, and Labour emphasizing the need to teach consent and address misogyny.

2.1.5 Criminal justice Women were also explicitly referred to in relation to the criminal justice system, as both offenders and victims of crime. Plaid Cymru emphasized the need to ensure women prisoners could be held nearer home to ensure that their families were not disrupted, as well as pledging to provide more centres to address women's offending in Wales. The Liberal Democrats emphasized the need for specialists in police stations and emergency operator centres to deal with gender-based violence, as well as pledging to speed up referrals to the Crown Prosecution Service for domestic abuse. Other parties chose to emphasize the need for better training for police around such issues. For example, the Labour Party pledged to implement minimum professional standards for police officers. The Liberal Democrats and Greens also suggested the police need to address historic problems with racism, homophobia, and misogyny amongst their number to repair their relationship to the public. Hate crime legislation was another area that addressed gender explicitly, for example, Plaid Cymru and Labour both pledged to ensure the police took LGBTQ + hate crime offences seriously, with Labour pledging to make it an aggravated offence.

2.1.6 Employment Only five of the parties sought to offer specific policies that might improve women's experiences in the workplace. These proposals tend to be focused on three key areas: pay inequality, flexible working, and parental leave. Labour, the Liberal Democrats, and Greens both pledged to require reporting on gender pay gaps, and crucially to extend this reporting to include other characteristics such as disability and ethnicity. Labour and the Greens also pledged to ensure that employers act on any pay gaps that are identified, although neither provided any detail on what that action would look like or whether noncompliance would be punished. The Liberal Democrats and Greens also agreed on the need to extend flexible working to benefit women and other carers. The Liberal Democrats and SNP both pledged to make changes to parental leave. The SNP promised to increase maternity leave to one year and to increase the shared parental leave entitlement from fifty-two weeks to sixty-four (including twelve-week paternity leave). The Liberal Democrats in contrast pledged to introduce one extra month of paternity leave and to make parental leave a day-one right, as well as extending rights to adoptive parents and those who are self-employed. Labour simply pledged to review the parental leave system within the first year of being elected. Similarly, Plaid also only included a brief mention of reforming parental leave. Labour was however, the only party to mention plans to address discrimination in the workplace, such as pregnancy and menopause discrimination, as well as what they call 'dual' discrimination, which presumably encompassed other social inequalities such as discrimination based on ethnicity, sexuality, and disability. The right-wing parties (Reform UK, Conservatives, and DUP) on the other had nothing to say on these issues which affect women's everyday lives.

2.1.7 Politics Perhaps the area which was most drastically reduced in focus when compared to previous elections, were measures to improve or maintain women's political representation. Only three of the nine parties discussed the issue, in contrast to the 2019 campaign when it featured in the manifestos of five out of the six parties studied (see Harmer and Southern 2020). The Greens pledged to advocate for ways to make politics more accessible to underrepresented groups by introducing job sharing for MPs and a permanent fund to help meet election costs for candidates, while Plaid Cymru reaffirmed their commitment to gender quotas in the Senedd. The Liberal Democrats, on the other hand, pledged to bring into force Section 106 of the Equality Act 2010 which would require political parties to publish candidate diversity data, as well as promising legislation to empower constituents to recall MPs who commit sexual harassment. The silence on this issue from other parties perhaps reflects the progress which has been made in women's Westminster representation over the past three decades, however, it is particularly striking to see the Labour Party who led on this issue for such as long time, fail to even mention it. This brings us to a closer look at the candidates and MPs (see Table 12.1).

3. Candidates and MPs

Assessing the gender split of candidates, overall, Labour's share of candidates who were not men fell compared to their 2019 figures. In 2019 over half (53%) of the

Table 12.1. Candidate gender by party, 2019 and 2024

	2019 (Women or NB)	% Women	2024 (Women or NB)	% Women
Con	635 (194)	31	635 (216)	34
Lab	631**(335~)	53	629 (295~)	47
Lib Dem	611**(186~)	30	630** (177~)	28
UKIP (2019)	44 (8)	18	-	
Reform (2024)	-		609 (96)	16
Green	497^ (203~)	41	585*** (261~~)	45
SNP	59 (20)	34	57 (22)	39
PC	36 (9)	25	32** (10)	31
Sinn Fein	15 (4)	27	14 (5)	36
SDLP	15 (8)	53	18 (7)	39
DUP	17 (2)	12	16 (3)	19
WEP	3 (3)	100	4 (4)	100
Total		38		39

** Including one non-binary candidate ^ Including four non-binary candidates ~ Including one trans woman ~~ Including two trans women *** Including 3 non-binary candidates.
Sources: Uberoi, Baker, and Cracknell (2020): 41; Cracknell, Baker, and Pollock (2024); Hansford (2024).

party's candidates were women whereas this time just under half were (47%). Despite being fairly close to parity, this is still a reduction in the number of women being selected, and a report by the Labour Women's Network suggested that even fewer women (44%) were selected for winnable seats (Jones 2024). It also suggests that the removal of formal rules around selections does default to women missing out. Labour was advised that all women shortlists were not legal for the 2024 election as their 2019 class of MPs was more female than male (Jones 2024). The figures below suggest this may have contributed to a fall in women candidates for them.

Other parties increased their share of women candidates compared to the 2019 election, with the Conservatives increasing the percentage of women candidates from 31% in 2019 to 34% in 2024, although this still means they were far from parity. The Green Party also increased their share from 41% to 45% - coming very close to an equal split of men and women candidates. Conversely, the Liberal Democrats had slipped very slightly back, from 30% in 2019 to 28% in 2024. The party with the lowest percentage of women candidates was, perhaps not surprisingly, Reform UK, with just 16% of their candidates being women. At the other end of the scale, and again not surprisingly, the Women's Equality Party had an all-women line-up of candidates, just as they did in 2019.

Assessing who was actually elected to parliament by gender reveals some potentially concerning patterns (see Table 12.2). This was billed by Labour as they

Table 12.2. Woman MPs by party after the 2024 General Election

	N	%	Woman representatives in 2019 (%)
Conservatives	29	24	87 (24)
Labour	190	46	104 (51)
Lib Dems	32	44	7 (64)
SNP	1	11	16 (33)
Green	3	75	1 (100)
Other	8	17	5 (22)
All	263	40	220

Source: Allen (2024).

entered government as the 'most diverse' parliament in history in terms of both gender and race (Morton 2024). On the raw figures, this is correct. 260 women MPs is the highest number of women MPs there has ever been in parliament. However, when looking at some of the percentages, women MPs as a percentage of their party's parliamentary group have slipped back. Labour's landslide was responsible for the record-breaking number here, by dint of their huge majority and their almost-equal candidate selection. However, they have fewer women MPs, as a percentage than they had in 2019. If they had kept the 51% of women MPs they achieved in 2019, the Parliament would have been even more diverse. This suggests, as stated above that parties need to strengthen their informal rules around selections, as the removal of formal rules (here all-women shortlists) does appear to have impacted women's descriptive representation negatively. The Liberal Democrats had a good result in this election, achieving their highest number of MPs in over a decade. However, in terms of gender representation, they too slipped back on their 2019 percentage going from 64% to 44% women MPs. The SNP did particularly poorly in this regard too, although for different reasons as they lost so many seats on the night. Here, they retained just one woman MP, making up 11% of their representation in parliament, compared to 33% at the 2019 election. These figures underline the need for parties to keep pressure up internally and in the work they do around recruitment and selections, or there is an ever-present danger of progress made on equal representation slipping away.

4. The voters

In terms of how the voters behaved, there were very small gender differences in votes for the two main parties (see Fig. 12.1). There was a very slight lead among women voters for the Conservative Party (24% of women compared to 22.4% of

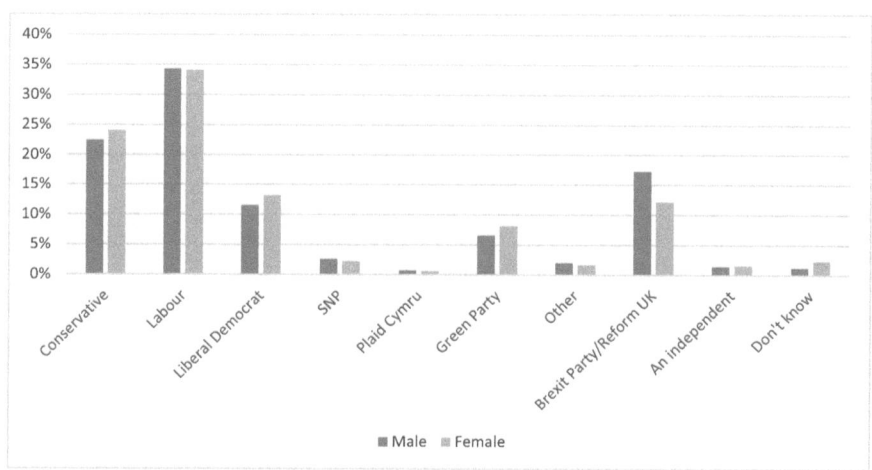

Figure 12.1. The General Election recalled vote by gender
Source: BES wave 2024 twenty-nine (5th July 2024 and 19th July 2024) *N* = 24,796), weighted.

men) and Labour trailed among women very slightly (34.1% compared to 34.3%), although Labour's vote was essentially an even gender split. This contrasts with the previous election where Labour held a lead among women voters, (34% of women voted for Labour in 2019 compared to just 31% of men) and where the Conservatives were two percentage points behind with women. This is an interesting development as Labour often courts women's votes, focussing on family-friendly policy and other equalities issues. Here, this advantage among women voters has all but disappeared. The largest gender difference was in votes for Reform UK, with 17.3% of men voting for them compared to 12.1% of women.

Finally, assessing votes, by gender and age for the two largest parties, there seemed to be few large gender differences in voting patterns within age groups (Fig. 12.2). Again, this contrasts, and here rather starkly, with the last election. As discussed in our contribution to this series about the 2019 election (Harmer and Southern 2020), there were large gender differences in voting patterns within age groups in 2019. Young women (18-25) were far more likely to vote Labour than young men with 58% of young women voting Labour compared to almost 43% of men. Similarly for the 26-35 age group in 2019, 43% of women voted for Labour compared to 38% of men their age. While there is still a small advantage for Labour among the youngest age group here (with 42% voting Labour compared to 40% of young men) the huge lead they had among young women at the last election has all but disappeared. This may suggest that some of the policies that were offered by Labour at the last election but since abandoned (e.g. free university tuition or nationalized broadband) may have been particularly appealing to young women.

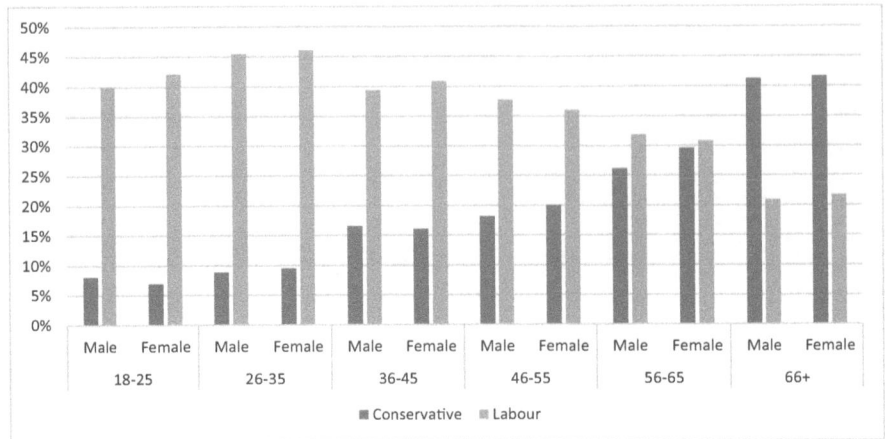

Figure 12.2. The 2024 General Election recalled vote for the Conservative and Labour parties by gender and age
Source: BES wave twenty-nine (5th July 2024 and 19th July 2024) *N* = 24,796), weighted.

Although not shown in this chart, some of this difference has now opened up within the Green Party vote with 18–25 year old women voting Green at over 5 percentage points higher than their male counterparts (18.8% compared to 13.2%). There were also large gender age differences in the Reform UK vote, with 13% of 18–25 year old men voting for Reform UK compared to 5% of 18–25 year old women.

Despite the very similar vote for the main parties, these latter two results suggest that the gender vote among young people may be becoming more polarized, which is a phenomenon occurring in many other countries too (Burns-Murdoch 2024). It will be interesting to see how this develops over the course of the 2024 Parliament and whether it will cause issues for women and parties alike.

5. Conclusion

The 2024 campaign seemed generally unremarkable as far as women were concerned. There were some highlights such as women MPs breaching the 40% threshold of parliamentary seats and the appointment of the UK's first female Chancellor of the Exchequer. However, the economic landscape that Labour inherited means that it remains to be seen whether these milestones will translate into tangible gains for women citizens. While the election may have been unexceptional in some ways, there were also some concerning developments including the tone of the campaign for some women candidates who received harassment on the campaign trail, and the indisputable move rightwards on policies around gender identity by the main parties, if left to fester, could prove extremely regressive and harmful. If it were to continue, the gender gap in voting among younger electors could also signal trouble ahead for women.

References

Allen, G. (2024) 2024 General Election: How many women were elected? *House of Commons Library Insight Briefing*. https://commonslibrary.parliament.uk/2024-general-election-how-many-women-were-elected/, accessed 22 Aug. 2024.

Aziz, S. (2024, 3 June) 'White male MPs make mistakes and are mostly forgiven. Not so women of colour like Faiza Shaheen', *The Guardian*, https://www.theguardian.com/commentisfree/article/2024/jun/03/faiza-shaheen-deselection-labour-party, accessed 23 Sept. 2024.

Baker, G. and Seddon, P. (2024, 8 March), Theresa May: Conservative ex-PM to stand down at next election', *BBC News*, https://www.bbc.co.uk/news/uk-politics-68509239, accessed 22 Aug. 2024.

BBC News (2024a, 30 May) 'Labour candidate shocked after being blocked from standing as candidate', *BBC News*, https://www.bbc.co.uk/news/av/uk-politics-69075181, accessed 18 Sept. 2024.

BBC News (2024b, 2 July) 'Reform admits 'mistakes' after candidate's Sturgeon post', *BBC News*, https://www.bbc.co.uk/news/articles/c51y4gm467zo, accessed 24 Aug. 2024.

Burns-Murdoch, J. (2024, 26 January) 'A new global gender divide is emerging', *Financial Times*, https://www.ft.com/content/29fd9b5c-2f35-41bf-9d4c-994db4e12998, accessed 26 Sept. 2024.

Campbell, R. and Childs, S. (2015) 'All Aboard the Pink Battle Bus? Women Voters, Issues, Candidates and Party Leaders', *Parliamentary Affairs*, 68, 206–23.

Church, S. (2024, 31 May) 'Black Londoners "Really Hurt" By Diane Abbott Row', *Politics Home*, https://www.politicshome.com/news/article/black-community-hurt-diane-abbott-treatment-says-labour-candidate, accessed 18 Sept. 2024.

Collignon, S. and Rüdig, W. (2021) 'Increasing the cost of female representation? The gendered effects of harassment, abuse and intimidation towards Parliamentary candidates in the UK', *Journal of Elections, Public Opinion and Parties*, 31: 429–49.

Council of Europe (2011) 'Council of Europe Convention on preventing and combating violence against women and domestic violence', https://www.coe.int/en/web/istanbul-convention/about-the-convention, accessed 26 Nov. 2024.

Cowburn, A. (2018, 3 July) 'Theresa May vows to eradicate 'abhorrent' gay conversion therapy as part of LGBT+ equality plan', *The Independent*, https://www.independent.co.uk/news/uk/politics/gay-conversion-therapy-uk-theresa-may-lgbt-equality-plan-a8427406.html, accessed 26 Sept. 2024.

Cracknell, R., Baker, C., and Pollock, L. (2024, 24 September) 'General Election 2024: Results and Analysis', *House of Commons Library Briefing*, https://commonslibrary.parliament.uk/research-briefings/cbp-10009/, accessed 22 Aug. 2024.

Crerar, P. (2024, 24 May) 'Tory MPs mull over their fate after Rishi Sunak's election call', *The Guardian*, https://www.theguardian.com/politics/article/2024/may/24/tory-mps-mull-over-their-fate-after-rishi-sunaks-election-call, accessed 26 Nov. 2024.

Crew, J. and Catt, H. (2023) 'Diane Abbott suspended as Labour MP after racism letter'. BBC News, 23 April 2023. https://www.bbc.co.uk/news/uk-politics-65365978, accessed 18 Sept. 2024.

Deacon, D. et al. (2024, 5 July) Report 5: 30 May–3 July 2024, https://www.lboro.ac.uk/news-events/general-election/report-5-2024/, accessed 5 Aug. 2024.

Hansford, A. (2024, 5 July) 'These inspiring trans and non-binary candidates stood for election – here's how they fared', *Pink News*, https://www.thepinknews.com/2024/07/05/general-election-trans-non-binary-candidates/, accessed 22 Aug. 2024.

Harmer, E. (2021) *Women, Media and Elections: Representation and Marginalisation in British Politics*. Bristol: Bristol University Press.

Harmer, E., Savigny, H. and Ward, O. (2017) "Are You Tough Enough?' Performing Gender in the UK Leadership Debates 2015', *Media, Culture and Society*, 39: 960–75.

Harmer, E. and Southern, R. (2020) 'Girly Swots and The Most Diverse Parliament Ever: Women's Representation, Voters and Issues in the 2019 Election Campaign', *Parliamentary Affairs*, 73: 243–58.

Jones, M (2024, 8 March) 'Without all-women shortlists, can Labour maintain gender balance among its MPs?', *Politics Home*, https://www.politicshome.com/thehouse/article/without-allwomen-shortlists-labour-maintain-gender-balance-among-mps, accessed 23 Sept. 2024.

Lawson, E. (2024, 5 July) 'Female MPs call harassment an assault on democracy', *BBC News*, https://www.bbc.co.uk/news/articles/c4ng3j1pnpqo, accessed 24 Sept. 2024.

Leach, A. and de Hoog, N. (2024, 3 July) 'Which seats are the Tories set to lose if the polls are right?', *The Guardian*, https://www.theguardian.com/politics/ng-interactive/2024/jul/03/general-election-uk-opinion-polls-seats-tories-lose, accessed 26 Nov. 2024.

Luxton, L. (2024) "Take the Next Right: Mainstream Parties' Positions on Gender and LGBTQ+ Equality Issues'. In: D. Jackson et al. (eds) *UK Election Analysis: Media, Voters and the Campaign*. Bournemouth: Centre for Comparative Politics and Media Research, https://www.electionanalysis.uk/uk-election-analysis-2024/section-5-policy-and-strategy/take-the-next-right-mainstream-parties-positions-on-gender-and-lgbtq-equality-issues/, accessed 5 Aug. 2025.

Morton, B. (2024, 9 July) 'Starmer proud of 'most diverse' Parliament ever', *BBC News*, https://www.bbc.co.uk/news/articles/cv2gn0jj541o, accessed 23 Sept. 2024.

Murray, R. (2024, 5 July) 'What Labour's election means for women: the good and the bad', *The Conversation*, https://theconversation.com/what-labours-election-means-for-women-the-good-and-the-bad-234117, accessed 18 Sept. 2024.

Quinn, B. and Stacey, K. (2024, 2 July) 'Second Reform candidate quits, accusing party of 'racism and misogyny'', *The Guardian*, https://www.theguardian.com/politics/article/2024/jul/02/second-reform-candidate-quits-over-racism-and-misogyny, accessed 24 Sept. 2024.

Seddon, S. (2024a, 5 July) 'The big winners and losers on election night', *BBC News*, https://www.bbc.co.uk/news/articles/c4ng3vz5gdno, accessed 22 Aug. 2024.

Seddon, P. (2024b, 2 June) 'Abbott says she intends to run and win for Labour', *BBC News*, https://www.bbc.co.uk/news/articles/cd11zp9kxw4o, accessed 18th Sept. 2024.

Shaw, S. (2024) '"Well that was Dignified, wasn't it?": Floor Apportionment and Interaction in the Televised Debates'. In: D. Jackson et al. (eds) *UK Election Analysis: Media, Voters and the Campaign*. Bournemouth: Centre for Comparative Politics and Media Research, https://www.electionanalysis.uk/uk-election-analysis-2024/section-8-personality-politics-and-popular-culture/well-that-was-dignified-wasnt-it-floor-apportionment-and-interaction-in-the-televised-debates/, accessed 5 Aug. 2025.

Southern, R. and Harmer, E. (2021) 'Twitter, Incivility and "Everyday" Gendered Othering: An Analysis of Tweets Sent to UK Members of Parliament', *Social Science Computer Review*, 39: 259–75.

Sudan, R. (2024, 24 June) 'Is it time for black voters to abandon Labour?', *The Voice*, https://www.voice-online.co.uk/news/uk-news/2024/06/24/is-it-time-for-black-voters-to-abandon-labour/, accessed 23 Sept. 2024.

Uberoi, E., Baker, C., and Cracknell, R. (2020) 'General Election 2019: Results and Analysis', House of Commons Library, https://commonslibrary.parliament.uk/research-briefings/cbp-8749/, accessed 22 Aug. 2024.

Ethnic minority voters and the 2024 General Election

Nicole S. Martin*

Department of Politics, University of Manchester, Oxford Road, Manchester, M13 9PL, UK

*Correspondence: nicole.martin@manchester.ac.uk

Ethnic minorities are a bigger part of the electorate than ever; 14% of registered voters in England and Wales in 2024,[1] compared to 8% in 2010 (Heath et al., 2013). This contribution argues that competition for ethnic minority votes in 2024 was high, cementing the growing electoral fragmentation of this broad and heterogeneous group. It might be tempting to believe that the first British Indian Prime Minister caused a mass shift of Indian voters to the Conservatives or that the conflict in Israel-Palestine created a unique circumstance pushing British Muslim voters away from the Labour Party. This would be mistaken. Already in 1972, a Rochdale by-election showed that Muslim voters could be prompted to support a different party on the back of a foreign policy disagreement with the Labour Party (in this case the India–Pakistan war) and a Liberal candidate who campaigned more astutely (Anwar 1973). Meanwhile, polling data suggests that a plurality of Indian Hindu voters already supported the Conservatives in 2019,[2] and greater support for the Conservatives among Indian voters has been noted for decades (Saggar and Heath 1999). The 2024 election completes a process of growing competition for ethnic minority votes and corresponding voter volatility. What is new is the extent of these shifts compared to prior elections and the greater electoral power of different ethnic minority groups as compared to fourteen years ago. However, strong evidence

---

[1] Author's estimate, methodology explained below.
[2] 47% Conservative compared to 41% Labour. *Understanding Society* data.

suggests that Labour still remain the most popular party by some way among almost all ethnic minority groups.

This contribution proceeds as follows. First, I look at pre-election fears that voter identification would make it harder for ethnic minorities to vote, finding that gaps in electoral registration are likely to be much more important. Next, I consider the different parties. I show that Labour did markedly better than the Conservatives in more ethnically diverse seats. However, this masks the fact that Labour lost sizeable numbers of votes in these most diverse constituencies, where turnout declined more than average, and now face a broader range of opposing parties. I question the evidence that Black voters were less likely to vote for Labour in 2024 than before, instead pointing to lower turnout as more likely. Next, I present new data on the independent and small party candidates that challenged Labour in constituencies with many Muslim voters. All twenty-eight seats where at least 25% of residents are Muslim had an explicitly pro-Palestinian independent candidate, who received on average 24.6% of the vote. Finally, I consider whether evidence of higher support for the Conservative Party among Indian ethnicity voters reflects a longer-term realignment or a Sunak-specific phenomenon.

This contribution relies on ecological analysis of election results published by the House of Commons Library (Cracknell, Baker, and Pollock 2024) combined with information from the most recent Censuses of England and Wales, and Scotland. As constituency boundaries changed between 2019 and 2024, I use the notional results provided by Colin Rallings and Michael Thrasher (Rallings and Thrasher, 2024: 202). Any reference to 2019 results should be interpreted as referring to these notional results unless indicated otherwise. I also use 2021 Census Microdata from England and Wales to estimate voter eligibility among different ethnic groups and adjust these figures for electoral registration rates. Other sources of data (e.g. polling companies) are referenced directly.

1. Holding the balance of power?

Ethnic minority voters are a larger part of Britain's electorate than ever and hold the numerical balance of power in a significant number of constituencies. In 1996, Operation Black Vote argued that ethnic minorities could overturn the election in more than 100 seats by comparing incumbent MPs majorities to the number of Black and Asian residents in their constituency. This was clearly inaccurate (the total number of residents includes children, for instance, and the figure assumes that all members of ethnic minority groups could be persuaded to vote against an incumbent). However, if we repeat the exercise today, we find that there were 361 seats where the number of ethnic minority residents[3] was greater than the 2019

---

[3] People of Black, Asian or Mixed ethnic backgrounds, to be comparable with OBV.

(notional) margin of victory, and 470 seats where it was greater than the 2024 (actual) margin of victory.

A more realistic view is presented in Table 13.1, which shows the numbers of seats where ethnic minorities are at least 30% of residents (158 in total) and their location in the UK. London accounts for almost half (46.8%) of all seats where ethnic minority residents are more than 30%. These numbers should not surprise us, since the 2021 Census showed that 9.3% of the population of England and Wales belonged to an Asian ethnic group, 4.0% to a Black ethnic group, and 5.0% to a mixed or other ethnic minority group.[4]

But not everyone participates in elections. In 2024, the introduction of mandatory photo voter ID was expected to pose more of a barrier to voting for ethnic minorities (House of Lords Select Committee on the Constitution 2023). Did this threat materialize? Electoral Commission statistics report the numbers of voters who came to a polling station to vote but were turned away

Table 13.1. Ethnic diversity in constituencies in different regions

Region	Average % ethnic minority[5]	Ethnic minorities >= 30%	N seats
East Midlands	19.1	9	47
East of England	20.6	12	61
London	62.1	72	75
North East	8.9	1	27
North West	18.1	15	73
Scotland	9.7	0	57
South East	11.9	16	91
South West	8.0	3	58
Wales	9.1	1	32
West Midlands	26.3	18	57
Yorkshire and the Humber	18.3	11	54
Total	22.5	158	632

Source: Derived from Census for England and Wales 2021, Table TS021, and Scotland Census 2022, Table UV201.

---

[4]Even in Scotland—historically less ethnically diverse—4.0% of the population in the 2022 Census identified as Asian, Caribbean, African, Black, Mixed or Other.
[5]100–the percentage whose ethnicity is White British.

for lack of a valid photo ID (Electoral Commission 2024). In most seats, the proportion of voters turned away was very small—the average was 0.2% or 1 in 500 would-be voters.[6] However, seats with the highest numbers of voters turned away include many of the most ethnically diverse seats. If we rank seats from low to high in terms of how many people were turned away from voting in the top 10% an average 61% of residents were White British, compared to an average of 79% in the bottom 10%. Looking at the top five seats, where an average of 1% of would-be voters were turned away for want of a valid photo ID,[7] only one seat (Birkenhead, 90% White British) does not have a large ethnic minority population.[8] There are other common factors, including higher levels of deprivation. In two seats with large ethnic minority populations, the number of voters initially turned away was larger than the winning candidate's majority.[9]

Further research is undoubtedly needed to ascertain how voter ID may shape electoral power. However, the small numbers of voters turned away on average suggest that electoral registration remains a bigger factor reducing ethnic minority political participation than voter ID.[10] Ethnic gaps in electoral registration have long been noted and were likely evident in 2024 as well; in December 2022, the Electoral Commission found that completeness of electoral registers—that is, whether someone who is entitled to vote is actually on the electoral register—remains highest among people from a White ethnic background at 87%, and lower for all other groups (Electoral Commission 2023). I use these figures to estimate the number of registered voters from each ethnic group in England and Wales. Registered voters matter in particular because their numbers are used to draw electoral boundaries, and so if ethnic gaps persist in registration, MPs for more diverse areas are likely to have more eligible voters in their constituency, a

---

[6] This is much smaller than the 6.7% of ethnic minority voters and 2.5% of White British voters who reported being turned away from a polling station in a poll by More In Common (More In Common 2024). If this poll's results are extrapolated, it would suggest that 406,000 people tried to vote but were unable to for lack of a valid ID and did not return later in the day, whereas Electoral Commission data records only 16,000 cases.
[7] A majority of these voters (69%) returned with a valid ID and were allowed to vote.
[8] The other four seats were Oldham East and Saddleworth (69% White British), Birmingham Perry Barr (16% White British), Bradford West (24% White British), and Bradford East (41% White British).
[9] Blackburn: majority 132, voters initially turned away 204, although only 62 did not return. Hendon: majority 15, voters initially turned away 118, of which 34 did not return.
[10] Turnout was also lower in seats with more ethnic minority voters; average turnout in the 25% most diverse constituencies in Great Britain was 56.1%, compared to 61.0% in the others. However, there are many other factors at play here (e.g. age, deprivation, seat marginality), and this difference is dwarfed by the change in overall turnout from 2019 to 2024 (average −7.7 points).

form of voter dilution. I first estimate from 2021 Census Microdata (England and Wales) the number of eligible voters in each ethnic group. For three of the largest ethnic minority groups—Indian, Pakistani, Bangladeshi—voter eligibility is 99%, the same as for those of White British ethnicity.[11] Voter eligibility is marginally lower for Black groups; 96% for Black Caribbean and 82% for Black African—but still the overwhelming majority of people in these ethnic groups are eligible to vote. However, estimates in Table 13.2 that account for voter registration show that while people in White ethnic groups are 84.8% of adults eligible to vote in England and Wales, they are 86.3% of registered voters. For minorities, the gap is proportionally much more significant; Asian/British Asian people are 8.6% of people eligible to vote, but 8.0% of those registered—a decrease of 7%. And Black/British Black adults are 3.6% of those eligible to vote, but 3.0% of those actually registered, a decrease of 20%.

2. Labour losing support?

Despite suffering its worst result since 1935 (Goes 2020), Labour remained the party supported by a majority of ethnic minority voters in 2019, as in previous elections (UK in a Changing Europe 2024). But as the 2024 results came in, it was clear by the early hours of 5th July that Labour's night of electoral triumph was tempered by a downwards shift in fortunes in the country's most diverse seats. This was preceded before the election by low net satisfaction with Starmer among ethnic minorities. In the second half of 2023, this was already in negative territory at −21 points, and more tellingly, there was no gap between minorities and white British respondents; a stark contrast to evaluations of his predecessors Corbyn and Miliband, who—even at their most unpopular (−17 for Corbyn and −1 for

Table 13.2. Voter eligibility and registration by ethnicity

Ethnic group	% of eligible voters	Completeness (%) (December 2022)	% of registered electors	Estimated number of registered electors
White	84.8	87	86.3	36,945,830
Asian	8.6	80	8.0	3,424,874
Black	3.6	72	3.0	1,284,328
Mixed	1.8	72	1.5	642,163
Other	1.5	71	1.2	513,731

[11] Both UK and Commonwealth citizenship qualifies someone to vote in UK general elections, which has been responsible for the historically high levels of voter eligibility among immigrants in the UK.

Miliband)—were much more popular among minorities than white Britons (Ipsos 2024).

The challenges for Labour with minority groups were foreshadowed in the pre-election period as candidate selections were finalized. In late May, a row erupted as veteran MP Diane Abbott—the first Black woman to be elected to the House of Commons in 1987—said she had been banned from standing for re-election. Abbott was eventually allowed to stand and later returned as the MP for Hackney and Stoke Newington, but her treatment proved controversial, with prominent figures like the co-founder of Operation Black Vote David Weaver suggesting it symbolized the 'disrespect' that Black voters felt (Bakare 2024), and MP for Streatham Bell Ribiero-Addy saying that it was 'clouding' how Black voters felt about Labour (Holloway 2023). Similarly, a left-wing Muslim candidate Faiza Shaheen was deselected over social media posts. Shaheen resigned from Labour, saying it had 'a palpable problem with black and brown people' (Thomas 2024), and stood as an independent instead in the same seat, Chingford and Woodford Green, held by former Conservative leader and cabinet minister Iain Duncan Smith. Duncan Smith comfortably retained his seat with 17,281 votes; fewer than the combined total from Labour runner-up Shama Tatler (12,524) and third-placed Shaheen (12,445).

Shaheen and Abbott were both prominent on Labour's left wing, which might have something to do with their (attempted) deselections (BBC News 2024a). But another reading of their cases epitomizes the party's perceived difficulties with Black and Muslim voters in 2024. Starmer was introduced before his 2021 conference speech by Baroness Lawrence, who thanked him for helping (as a barrister) to prosecute the murder of her son Stephen Lawrence. Yet in 2024, Lawrence was reported to have said to a private group of ethnic minority parliamentarians that she was 'appointed as the race adviser but I haven't been listened to' (Huskisson 2024), whilst an anonymous Black Labour MP told *The Voice* newspaper that they did not expect race equality to be a priority for a future Labour government (Sudan 2024). The report by barrister Martin Forde suggested there was a 'perception of a hierarchy of racism', where anti-black racism was perceived to be taken less seriously than antisemitism by the party, and that the party was an 'unwelcoming place for people of colour' (White 2022).

Meanwhile, multiple waves of Labour councillors resigned from the party over its stance on the conflict in Israel-Palestine, citing not only the party's position on a ceasefire, but framing this in terms of Islamophobia. A former councillor in Oxford said 'the hierarchy of racism is 100% clear' and that 7th October (the day of the terrorist attack by Hamas in Israel) 'was the straw that broke the camel's back' (Piñeda 2024). The leader of Burnley Council, on resigning his Labour Party membership, warned that 'I just don't think the message is getting through in terms of how our communities…are feeling about this' (Sky News 2023a). Fifty-six Labour

MPs voted for an SNP motion in favour of a ceasefire in November 2023, and eight shadow ministers gave up their positions over the issue (Sky News 2023b). Notably, almost all represented constituencies with large Muslim populations, including Jess Phillips (Birmingham Yardley), Afzal Khan (Manchester Gorton), and Naz Shah (Bradford West).

So what evidence is there that Labour lost votes among ethnic minorities in 2024, even whilst they gained votes and seats overall? Labour's decline should not be overstated. If we look at the top 25% of seats with the fewest White British residents, Labour won (notionally) 70% (110) of these seats in 2019, but in 2024, this increased to 82%, and polling suggests that Labour won among Black and Asian voters overall (Focaldata 2024; YouGov 2024). However, this comparatively rosy picture for Labour is undermined when we look at their actual vote share in the most diverse seats, which in many of these seats was lower than the 2019 notional result. Table 13.3 shows the average change in vote share in seats with different characteristics; Labour's vote share declined in all different types of seats with more ethnic minorities. For instance, in the top 25% most ethnically diverse seats, Labour's vote share decreased by 7.6 points, compared to an average increase of 1.9 points.

Alongside falling vote shares, the other change in 2024 is that Labour's challengers in the most diverse seats are different opponents. In 2019, the Conservatives came second in 105 (66%) of the top 25% most diverse seats, and Labour were second in thirty-six (23%). By 2024, however, the Conservatives were a much smaller proportion of runners-up (seventy or 44%), and though Labour won a majority of these most diverse seats, their nearest opponents were almost as likely to be from the Greens (20%), other parties including independents (11%), or even Reform UK (11%). If we go even further to examine the eighty-one seats where White British residents are fewer than 50%, we can see the changing structure of party competition more clearly; in 2019, Labour won sixty-eight (84%) of these seats, and the Conservatives won the remainder. In 2024, however, Labour won seventy-one (88%) of these seats, but the others were split between the Conservatives (four seats), independents (five seats), and the Liberal Democrats. This shows the fragmentation of political competition in seats with the most ethnic minority voters.

What evidence is there then that Labour lost voters from ethnic minorities in 2024—either to other parties, or through lower voter turnout? I answer this question in two parts, looking firstly at Black voters, and secondly at the Muslim voters.

3. Black voters and turnout

It is not obviously true that Labour did worse than expected among Black voters. Of the twenty-eight seats where at least 15% of residents are Black, Labour won twenty-seven,

Table 13.3. Average change in vote share in constituencies according to ethnic diversity

Change 2019–24	All seats	Top 25% diversity	Black >=15%	Indian >=15%	Pakistani >=15%	Bangladeshi >=15%	Muslim >=15%	Hindu >=15%
Turnout	**–7.7**	–9.3	–10.7	–9.5	–10.6	–12.6	–9.9	–7.4
Conservatives	–20.6	–14.3	–9.0	–11.5	–15.2	–8.8	–12.7	–5.1
Labour	+1.9	–7.6	–11.3	–16.0	–23.1	–26.0	–16.9	–10.9
Liberal Democrats	+0.4	–1.8	–2.2	–1.6	+0.5	–2.0	–0.9	–1.4
Green	+4.2	+7.0	+10.5	+4.4	+5.8	+9.3	+6.8	+3.7
Reform UK	**+12.6**	+8.3	+5.1	+6.9	+9.2	+4.4	+7.6	+5.0
All others	+2.6	+8.3	+6.9	+17.7	+22.8	+23.1	+16.1	+8.7
N	632	158	28	20	20	5	64	5

compared to 28 in 2019. We see a similar pattern in polling data: YouGov before the election concluded that 72% of Black Britons were intending to vote for Labour (YouGov 2024), compared to 11% for the Conservatives.[12]

However, there is some evidence consistent with lower enthusiasm for the Starmer-era Labour Party. Turnout dropped everywhere (7.7 points overall), but by more in seats with the most Black residents; by 10.7 points on average in seats where at least 15% of residents were Black. And whilst Labour retained its MPs in constituencies with the most Black residents, their vote share in these seats fell, from 63.7% in 2019 to 52.4% in 2024—an average drop of 11.3 points, whilst the Green Party's vote share in the same seats increased by 10.5 points. However, it need not be the case that it was Black voters moving to the Greens for this pattern to be true; it could also be that other people in seats with more Black residents were more likely to vote for the Greens in 2024 than before, and polling data suggests lower on average support for the Greens among Black Britons (Focaldata 2024; YouGov 2024). Diane Abbott was re-elected in Hackney North and Stoke Newington with a large majority, but a reduced vote share by 10.3 points, but this drop is almost nothing compared to the more Starmerite David Lammy in Tottenham, whose vote share decreased by 20.3 points.

It is hard to infer much about differences in vote choice between different Black groups from ecological data.[13] It is notable, however, that despite sustained efforts to recruit more ethnic minority politicians (Sobolewska 2013), the Conservatives have only elected one MP from a Black Caribbean background, Darren Henry (MP for Broxtowe from 2019 to 2024), compared to a much larger number of prominent politicians from Black African families. Other evidence suggests that there might be more of an opening for the Conservatives among Black African Britons, with more positive evaluations of the party (UK in a Changing Europe 2024), and a lower lead to Labour over the Conservatives among Londoners of African descent (Africans by sixty-four to twenty-one points; people from the Caribbean by eighty-three to five points) (Hussain 2023).

4. Muslim voters and the Labour Party

If the evidence that Black voters deserted Labour for other parties is scant, the opposite is true for Muslim voters. Table 13.3 shows that Labour's vote share fell by an astonishing 23.1 points in areas where at least 15% of the population were of Pakistani ethnicity, and 26.0 in seats with at least 15% Bangladeshi residents.

---

[12]Focaldata polling suggests the same; 59% Labour support compared to 21% Conservative (Focaldata 2024).
[13]There are no constituencies where at least 15% of residents were of Black Caribbean heritage, and only six where Black African residents were at least 15%.

Turnout also decreased by more than average; −10.6 points in areas with the most Pakistani residents, −12.6 in seats with the most Bangladeshi residents, compared to a drop of 7.7 overall. The beneficiaries of these falls were the Greens, and independents and minor parties like the Workers Party for Britain.

I investigate these parties further in the next section. However, it is important not to overstate the extent of this shift, which was a meaningful challenge to Labour's electoral dominance—but not a wholesale desertion of the party. Pro-Palestine independents won four seats in areas with large Muslim populations; but most seats in these areas were retained by Labour. Post-election polling suggests that around 12% of British Muslims voted for the Greens, and 15% for other party candidates (Focaldata 2024), which accounts for the twenty-eight-point drop in Labour support among this group—but the remainder of British Muslims did not support the Conservatives[14] or Reform UK instead. Independents and the Green Party offered more pro-Palestinian options, but this was not an issue that motivated all—or even a majority—of Muslim voters to switch parties in 2024.

5. Pro-Palestine candidates

The potential for pro-Palestine candidates in July 2024 was visible in the Rochdale by-election, where George Galloway greeted his win saying 'this is for Gaza' (BBC News 2024b), and the May local elections, which saw candidates from the Workers Party of Britain or local independents succeeding in cities with significant Muslim populations. But it has longer precedents in the success of the Liberal Democrats in mobilizing Muslim voters against the Iraq war (Curtice, Fisher, and Steed 2005), Galloway's previous successes with the Respect Party (Peace 2013), and other local parties like the Birmingham People's Justice Party that integrated local concerns with international politics. What is unusual about 2024 is the scale of their success, returning four MPs to Parliament.[15] Indeed, in some seats, better co-ordination between independent pro-Palestine candidates could have could have resulted in more losses for Labour. Labour MP Tahir Ali in Birmingham Hall Green and Moseley received 12,798 votes, but in both second and third place were two independents, who received 7,142 and 6,159 votes respectively. Naz Shah, Labour MP for Bradford West, was re-elected with 11,724 votes; the runner-up independent candidate received 11,017, but there were two further independents, receiving 3,547 and 334 votes.

---

[14]Indeed, disapproval of Rishi Sunak's handling of the Gaza response was higher at 88% of British Pakistani or Bangladeshi voters, compared to 78% who disapproved of Starmer's (YouGov 2024).
[15]Not including Jeremy Corbyn, who has joined these four MPs in a new parliamentary grouping, Independent Alliance.

Other races were extremely close; in Ilford North, the future Health Secretary Wes Streeting (15,647 votes) was almost unseated by independent Leanne Mohamad (15,119 votes). The electoral majority of Labour MP for Bethnal Green and Stepney, Rushanara Ali, was reduced from 31,655 votes in 2019 (notional) to 1,689 in 2024; however, in addition to the second-placed independent challenger (14,207 votes), there were another three pro-Palestine candidates who together totalled 911 votes. What had been an extremely safe seat is now very marginal. And it is noteworthy too that discontent with Labour was mostly not funnelled through existing political parties which on the face of the policy issue would be compatible such as the Greens.

To understand the extent of these candidates, this contribution looks at the 117 seats where candidates not standing for one of the main parties[16] gained at least 5% of the vote. Pro-Palestine candidates (independents or minor parties) were identified using local media, candidate websites, and social media. These candidates account for a large proportion of the increase in support for independents and minor parties in 2024; a pro-Palestine candidate stood in 77% of seats where independents won at least 5% of the vote, and in 44% of them, there was more than one such candidate. These seats are especially likely to have more Muslim residents; the average proportion of Muslims living where a pro-Palestine candidate stood (and independents won at least 5% of the vote) is 21.4%, compared to 2.9% in all other seats. The majority (79%) of pro-Palestine candidates studied here were themselves Muslim, but this was not universally the case; 6% were from another ethnic minority background, and 14% were White British.

These candidates clearly hurt Labour more than other parties, as we would expect for parties seeking to attract Muslim voters, an estimated 83% of whom voted for Labour in 2019.[17] Pro-Palestine candidates stood most often in seats that Labour won (notionally) in 2019; 81% were in 2019 Labour seats, but only 18% in Conservative.[18] And these differences are yet more stark when we look at vote share; the average vote share of pro-Palestine candidates in seats notionally held by the Conservatives in 2019 was 0.4%, compared to 5% in Labour seats, and there were only two Conservative seats where a pro-Palestine candidate received at least 15% of the vote[19], compared to twenty-three for Labour. Where information is

---

[16]Conservatives, Labour, Liberal Democrats, Scottish National Party, Green/Scottish Greens, or Reform UK
[17]*Understanding Society* data.
[18]One stood in SNP seat Dundee Central
[19]One was Chingford and Woodford Green, where Faiza Shaheen stood, and the second was Walsall and Bloxwich, which although notionally a Conservative 2019 win, was being defended Labour incumbent Valerie Vaz.

available about the prior party affiliation of these candidates, it was much more likely to be Labour (24%), compared to only three candidates (0.2%) who were previously Conservatives, but the majority did not have an obvious previous affiliation. Most were true independents (59%), in the sense that they were not registered under a political party, but 39% were candidates for the Workers Party of Britain, led by George Galloway. This made the WPB the party which stood the highest number of candidates (152) without gaining a single seat.

Some were clearly standing as single-issue candidates; however, what is also apparent is how other candidates combined Palestine with other issues. A common theme was degradation and neglect in the local area, often accusing both Conservatives (neglect at the national level) and a local Labour MP who did not work enough. Noor Begum, standing as independent candidate for Ilford South, declared her reasons for running; 'Tired of Empty Promises: For too long, mainstream parties have made promises they fail to keep. I'm running to break this cycle of disappointment' (Begum 2024). In Birmingham Edgbaston, Ammar Waraich's campaign website lists 'Peace, Dignity and Justice for Palestine' as the last of his promises, behind saving the NHS, rebuilding and investing in the community, reducing economic hardship, and saving the planet (Waraich 2024). Running in Slough, Azhar Chohan seamlessly combined the local and international, calling on 'the government to reassess its role in the ongoing genocide in Gaza, [and] build more affordable housing' (Clark 2024). Aside from the large number of Muslim candidates, and the references to Palestine and sometimes Kashmir, the appeals of these candidates sound very similar to other populist candidates mobilizing voters who feel their areas are 'left behind'. However, some candidates have clear disagreements with the Labour Party on policy issues that predate October 2023. Shakeel Afsar stood as an independent in Birmingham Hall Green and Moseley, but first became prominent as a leader during protests outside a primary school against a pro-LGBT programme known as No Outsiders, and confronted Batley and Spen MP Kim Leadbeater during her election campaign on (alongside other issues) LGBT issues in education (Haynes 2024).

What does the relative success of independents and the Workers Party of Britain mean for the future relationship between Muslim voters and Labour? Previous breaks have been repaired; for instance, under Corbyn's leadership, 83% of British Muslims voted for Labour in 2019.[20] However, the much higher numbers of independent candidates, the potential for some 'easy wins' in future through better co-ordination of candidates, and the strong geographical concentration of Muslim voters suggests some potential pre-conditions for the formation of a new party (or parties). The example of Tower Hamlets here is instructive, where many Bengali

---

[20]*Understanding Society* data. For Labour the figures are as follows; Indian—53%; Pakistani—86%; Bangladeshi—85%, Black Caribbean—78%; Black African—85%.

voters no longer support Labour, who no longer control the council. Regardless, the greater competition for Muslim voters means that the majorities of a number of urban Labour MPs are much slimmer. Electoral arithmetic alone suggests that the party will pay attention.

6. The Conservatives and Indian voters

Talking about strong support for Labour among ethnic minorities might seem an anachronism; after all, it was the Conservatives who went into the election led by Sunak, the first ethnic minority Prime Minister since Disraeli. Conservative governments appointed more diverse cabinets than ever and bore joint responsibility for making ethnic minority parliamentarians the "new normal" (Sobolewska 2013). However, the party by and large remained unsupported by ethnic minority voters in previous elections; in 2019, 36% of Indian heritage Britons voted for the Conservatives, the highest proportion compared to 12% of Bangladeshi, 9% of Pakistani, or 10% of either Black Caribbean of Black African heritage voters.[21] Some analysts highlight that far from being seen as substantive representatives of the interests of racialized minorities in politics, prominent minority Conservative politicians engage in "post-racial gatekeeping" and legitimize xenophobia in the party (Saini, Bankole, and Begum 2023). The 2024 Conservative campaign emphasized toughness on immigration, raising its issue salience through "Stop the Boats". And as the party responsible for the Windrush scandal, where British citizens were denied jobs, healthcare, and even deported due to a lack of documentation, and also the compensation scheme with a 'litany of flaws' (Waitzman 2024), the Conservative Party's prospects in 2024 for changing the minds of voters who see them as ill at ease with Britain's multiculturalism was slim. There was also a strong valence case against the Conservative Party, compounded by the fact that some of the catastrophes of the 2019–24 period, such as illness and financial hardship stemming from the Covid-19 pandemic hit some ethnic minority groups particularly hard. So, whilst Labour faced challenges to their electoral dominance among Pakistani and Bangladeshi voters from pro-Palestine independents and may have damaged their reputation among Black voters by their treatment of Abbott, on the whole the Conservatives would not have been expected to gain many new ethnic minority voters in 2024.

There were two important exceptions, however. The first is difficult to test with existing data, but ethnic minority voters who feel that race ought not to be the most important factor in their vote choice or who believe their ethnicity is not a significant hurdle (Martin and Sobolewska 2023) may have felt more comfortable voting for Rishi Sunak's post-racial message than previous Conservative leaders.

---

[21] *Understanding Society* data.

Asked by Eastern Eye about being the first UK Prime Minister of South Asian descent, Sunak characterized it as 'not a big deal, and I think that that is a good thing…because people think that it's just something which is British' (Solanki and Choudhury 2024). This echoes the first attempts by the Conservatives to attract minority voters in 1983, showing pictures of Black and Asian men with a tagline 'Labour Says He's Black - Tories Say He's British' (Peace and Meer 2020).

The other exception is more well-evidenced; British Indian voters retained higher support for the Conservatives in 2024 than other minority groups. Already in 2019, a plurality of Hindu voters supported the Conservatives (as noted above). Greater support for the Conservatives among middle-class British Indians has been noted since at least 1997 (Saggar and Heath 1999), with more recent analyses invoking both economic and ideological explanations (Saini 2024). This also means that Sunak's election as party leader in October 2022 cannot be solely responsible, although it might be expected that his leadership could cement this stronger support for the Conservatives (or more even split between Labour and Conservatives) among Indian voters.

There are some indications that this is true. For instance, although the Conservative vote share dropped on average 20.6 points, in the twenty seats where at least 15% of the residents were of Indian ethnicity, this was reduced to a drop of 11.5 points, and in the five seats where at least 15% of the residents are Hindu, even less at 5.1. Areas with high ethnic diversity also had lower than average drops, but because of a very low floor; however, the five seats with the most Hindu voters had just as high levels of support for the Conservatives as the rest of the country in 2019, suggesting that there was indeed room for it to have fallen in 2024. Polling of Londoners showed that 47% of Indians in the capital were satisfied with Sunak's premiership, compared to 26% of all Londoners (Hussain 2023). Leicester East was the only seat gained by Conservatives, and whilst this is a special case as not one but two former Labour MPs for the seat were standing as independents against the selected Labour candidate, it is also true that in Harrow East (−1.3), Harrow West (−5.6), or Brent West (−1.3), the Conservative vote share did not suffer large falls.

There is some suggestion also that Labour's perceived pro-Pakistan position on Kashmir might also have undermined Labour support among Indian voters. Before the 2019 election, the BJP (India's ruling Hindu-nationalist party) had urged Indians not to support Labour after a conference motion passed in favour of a self-determination referendum (Canton 2019). Since then, Labour MPs have been prominent campaigners on human rights in Kashmir; Debbie Abrahams, Labour chair of the All Party Parliamentary Group on Kashmir, was refused entry to the region in 2020, and Labour MP Tahir Ali called for the Indian high commissioner to be prevented from entering Parliament (House of Commons Debate 2021a). On the other side, Conservative MP for Harrow East, Bob Blackman, also raises issues related to Kashmir in Parliament, defending India in the debate

(House of Commons Debate 2021b). Polling data suggests that this issue does matter somewhat; 42% of Indian Londoners said it would affect how they voted—only marginally fewer than the 46% of Pakistani Londoners who felt the same (Hussain 2023). But given Starmer's less clear position on the issue than Corbyn's, it is debateable if this issue can explain any further change from 2019.

7. Conclusion

In 2024, Labour achieved a parliamentary victory but no great increase in their share of the vote. In this contribution I have argued that ethnic minority voters contributed substantially to this lower vote share; either through lower turnout, or through voting for other parties. Scholars have argued that support for Labour is deeply socialized (Martin and Mellon 2020) and has important historical policy roots (Heath et al., 2013; Sobolewska and Ford 2020). In 2024, however, we see more clearly than ever that the rules of the game have changed; ethnic minority loyalty to Labour is no longer a habit that is so universally engrained. This does not mean that ethnicity is unimportant to vote choice; it means that meaningful political competition and realistic alternative vote choices to Labour have arrived.

Funding

This work benefitted from funding from the John Rylands Research Institute and Library Pilot Grant Scheme (University of Manchester); From protests to party? How do parties representing minorities emerge in England?

References

Anwar, M. (1973) 'Pakistani Participation in the 1972 Rochdale by-Election', *Journal of Ethnic and Migration Studies*, 2: 418–23.

Bakare, L. (2024) '"Such Disrespect": Diane Abbott Row Looms Over Race for Hackney North Seat', *The Guardian*, https://www.theguardian.com/politics/article/2024/jun/17/such-disrespect-diane-abbott-row-looms-over-race-for-hackney-north-seat, accessed 9 Dec. 2024.

BBC News (2024a) 'Keir Starmer Denies Purge of Left-Wing Candidates', *BBC News*, https://www.bbc.com/news/articles/c800pzlz9k8o, accessed 9 Dec. 2024.

BBC News (2024b) 'Rochdale By-Election: Landslide Win for George Galloway', *BBC News*, https://www.bbc.com/news/uk-politics-68443430, accessed 9 Dec. 2024.

Begum, N. (2024) 'Noor 4 Ilford South', https://www.noor4ilfordsouth.com/, accessed 9 Dec. 2024.

Canton, N. (2019) 'Labour Passes Controversial Kashmir Motion, India's UK Mission Cancels Annual Dinner', *The Times of India*, https://timesofindia.indiatimes.com/world/uk/labour-passes-controversial-kashmir-motion-indias-uk-mission-cancels-annual-dinner/articleshow/71300614.cms, accessed 9 Dec. 2024.

Clark, N. (2024) 'Slough General Election Candidate Names "Genocide in Gaza" in Campaign', *Slough Observer*, https://www.sloughobserver.co.uk/news/24341977.slough-general-election-candidate-names-genocide-gaza-campaign/, accessed 9 Dec. 2024.

Cracknell, R., Baker, C., and Pollock, L. (2024) 'General Election 2024 Results', https://commonslibrary.parliament.uk/research-briefings/cbp-10009/, accessed 5 Dec. 2024.

Curtice, J., Fisher, S. D., and Steed, M. (2005) 'Appendix 2: The Results Analysed – The General Election of 2005', in *The General Election of 2005*. Basingstoke: Palgrave Macmillan.

Electoral Commission (2023) '2023 Report: Electoral Registers in the UK', https://www.electoralcommission.org.uk/research-reports-and-data/electoral-registration-research/accuracy-and-completeness-electoral-registers/2023-report-electoral-registers-uk, accessed 05 Aug. 2025.

Electoral Commission (2024) 'Voter ID at the 2024 UK General Election', https://www.electoralcommission.org.uk/research-reports-and-data/our-reports-and-data-past-elections-and-referendums/voter-id-2024-uk-general-election, accessed 5 Dec. 2024.

Focaldata (2024) 'How Britain Voted', https://www.focaldata.com/blog/how-britain-voted-2024, accessed 9 Dec. 2024.

Goes, E. (2020) 'Labour's 2019 Campaign: A Defeat of Epic Proportions', *Parliamentary Affairs*, 73(Supplement_1): 84–102.

Haynes, J. (2024) 'Shakeel Afsar Wants to be the Next MP for Hall Green and Moseley and Some People Aren't Happy', *Birmingham Mail*, https://www.birminghammail.co.uk/news/midlands-news/shakeel-afsar-wants-next-mp-29359581, accessed 9 Dec. 2024.

Heath, A. et al. (2013) *The Political Integration of Ethnic Minorities in Britain*. Oxford: Oxford University Press.

Holloway, L. (2023) 'Diane Abbott Saga "Clouding" How Black Voters See Labour – MP', *Voice Online*, https://www.voice-online.co.uk/news/uk-news/2023/10/08/diane-abbott-saga-clouding-how-black-voters-see-labour-mp/, accessed 9 Dec. 2024.

House of Commons Debate (2021a) 'vol. 701 col. 500 (vol. 701 col. 500 vol)', https://hansard.parliament.uk/Commons/2021-09-23/debates/BB35EDC2-CCB6-4E7D-941B-6E0929F2DC6D/HumanRightsKashmir, accessed 9 Dec. 2024.

House of Commons Debate (2021b) 'vol. 701, col. 510 (vol. 701, col. 510 vol)', https://hansard.parliament.uk/Commons/2021-09-23/debates/BB35EDC2-CCB6-4E7D-941B-6E0929F2DC6D/HumanRightsKashmir, accessed 9 Dec. 2024.

House of Lords Select Committee on the Constitution (2023) 'Findings of the House of Lords Constitution Committee's Inquiry into the Introduction of Voter ID', https://committees.parliament.uk/publications/42629/documents/211942/default/

Huskisson, S. (2024) 'Doreen Lawrence Says Keir Starmer Not Listening Despite Asking for Race Advice', *The Mirror*, https://www.mirror.co.uk/news/politics/doreen-lawrence-says-keir-starmer-32406405, accessed 9 Dec. 2024.

Hussain, F. (2023) *The Diversity of Ethnic Minority Londoners*. Mile End Institute, London: Queen Mary University of London, https://www.qmul.ac.uk/mei/media/mei/tgc-media/filesx2fpublications/The-Diversity-of-Ethnic-Minority-Londoners.pdf, accessed 24 Mar. 2025.

Ipsos (2024) 'Ipsos Analysis Shows Falling Satisfaction with Rishi Sunak and Keir Starmer Amongst Ethnic Minorities in Britain', https://www.ipsos.com/en-uk/ipsos-analysis-shows-falling-satisfaction-rishi-sunak-and-keir-starmer-amongst-ethnic-minorities, accessed 9 Dec. 2024.

Martin, N., and Mellon, J. (2020) 'The Puzzle of High Political Partisanship Among Ethnic Minority Young People in Great Britain', *Journal of Ethnic and Migration Studies*, 46: 936–56.

Martin, N. S., and Sobolewska, M. (2023) 'The End of the Ethnic Bloc Vote? Ethnic Minority Leavers After the Brexit Referendum', *Political Science & Politics*, 56: 566–71.

More In Common (2024) 'July 2024 Polling Tables, More in Common Polling on Voter ID', https://www.moreincommon.org.uk/media/qjzpzvb4/voter-id-july-2024.xlsx, accessed 5 Dec. 2024.

Peace, T. (2013) 'All I'm Asking, Is For a Little Respect: Assessing the Performance of Britain's Most Successful Radical Left Party', *Parliamentary Affairs*, 66: 405–24.

Peace, T. and Meer, N. (2020) 'Ethnic Diversity', in: M. Garnett and H. Pillmoor (eds) *The Routledge Handbook of British Politics and Society*, 1st edn, pp. 188–98. Abingdon, Oxon; New York, NY: Routledge, Series: Routledge International Handbooks.

Piñeda, N.L. (2024) '"My Conscience Would Not Allow Me to Carry On": Local Councillors on Why they Left Labour', *Hyphen Online*, https://hyphenonline.com/2024/04/19/my-conscience-would-not-allow-me-to-carry-on-local-councillors-on-why-they-left-labour/, accessed 9 Dec. 2024.

Rallings, C. and Thrasher, M. (2024) 'Estimates of the 2019 General Election Result in New Constituencies', https://electionresults.parliament.uk/general-elections/5/political-parties/3/elections/won, accessed 5 Dec. 2024.

Saggar, S. and Heath, A. (1999) 'Race: Towards a Multicultural Electorate?', in: G. Evans and P. Norris (eds) *Critical Elections: British Parties and Voters in Long-Term Perspective*, pp. 102–23. London: Sage.

Saini, R. (2024) *Politics, Identity and Belonging Across the British South Asian Middle Classes: Between Privilege and Prejudice*. Cham: Springer Nature Switzerland (Palgrave Politics of Identity and Citizenship Series).

Saini, R., Bankole, M., and Begum, N. (2023) 'The 2022 Conservative Leadership Campaign and Post-Racial Gatekeeping', *Race & Class*, 65: 55–74.

Sky News (2023a) '11 Councillors Quit Labour Over Stance on Ceasefire in Gaza – After Calling for Sir Keir Starmer to Resign', *Sky News*, https://news.sky.com/story/leader-of-burnley-council-and-11-councillors-resign-from-labour-party-over-starmers-gaza-ceasefire-stance-13001632, accessed 9 Dec. 2024.

Sky News (2023b) 'Who Are the Rebel Labour MPs That Resigned Over the Vote for a Gaza Ceasefire?', https://news.sky.com/story/who-are-the-rebel-labour-mps-that-resigned-over-the-vote-for-a-gaza-ceasefire-13009351, accessed 9 Dec. 2024.

Sobolewska, M. (2013) 'Party Strategies and the Descriptive Representation of Ethnic Minorities: The 2010 British General Election', *West European Politics*, 36: 615–33.

Sobolewska, M., and Ford, R. (2020) *Brexitland: Identity, Diversity and the Reshaping of British Politics*. Cambridge: Cambridge University Press.

Solanki, S., and Choudhury, B. (2024) 'Exclusive Interview with Rishi Sunak: "My Faith Drives me to Serve Britain"', *Eastern Eye*, https://www.easterneye.biz/rishi-sunak-exclusive-interviuew-hindu-faith/, accessed 9 Dec. 2024.

Sudan, R. (2024) 'Keir Starmer Doesn't Care About Black People', *Voice Online*, https://www.voice-online.co.uk/news/uk-news/2024/02/01/keir-starmer-doesnt-care-about-black-people/, accessed 9 Dec. 2024.

Thomas, P. (2024) 'Faiza Shaheen Alleges Labour has "Problem with Black and Brown People"', *Eastern Eye*, https://www.easterneye.biz/faiza-shaheen-alleges-labour-has-problem-with-black-and-brown-people/, accessed 9 Dec. 2024.

UK in a Changing Europe (2024) *Minorities Report: The Attitudes of Britain's Ethnic Minority Population*.

Waitzman, E. (2024) *Windrush Scandal and Compensation Scheme*. House of Lords Library, https://lordslibrary.parliament.uk/windrush-scandal-and-compensation-scheme/, accessed 9 Dec. 2024.

Waraich, A. (2024) 'Compassion, Integrity, Independence!, Vote Dr Ammar for Edgbaston', https://ammar.vote/, accessed 9 Dec. 2024.

White, N. (2022) 'Black Labour Staff Suffer Under Party's "Hierarchy of Racism"', Forde Report Finds', *The Independent*, https://www.independent.co.uk/news/uk/politics/forde-report-labour-party-racism-b2126627.html, accessed 9 Dec. 2024.

YouGov (2024) 'Ethnic Minority Britons at the 2024 General Election,' *YouGov*, https://yougov.co.uk/politics/articles/49877-ethnic-minority-britons-at-the-2024-general-election, accessed 9 Dec. 2024.

Tax, trip-ups, and transgressions: Reporting the 2024 UK General Election

David Deacon[1,*], David Smith[2], and Dominic Wring[1]

[1]Department of Communication and Media, Loughborough University, Epinal Way, Loughborough, Leicestershire, LE11 3TU, UK
[2]School of Arts, Media and Communication, University of Leicester, University Road, Leicester, LE1 7RH, UK

*Correspondence: d.n.deacon@lboro.ac.uk

This contribution examines British mainstream news reporting of the 2024 UK General Election. The analysis shows the two main parties' share of coverage exceeded their actual vote share by some margin, the first time this has occurred in the last seven campaigns. Levels of policy content was also low compared with previous elections and the substantive agenda was disconnected from voter priorities. Analysis of GB News, a new television channel that has positioned itself as a broadcasting alternative, revealed editorial patterns that aligned closely with those found in newspaper reporting. In national press coverage, criticism of the incumbent Conservative government was counterbalanced by negativity towards Labour. The 2024 campaign saw a dealignment rather than a realignment in press partisanship.

'Change' was the political watchword of the Labour Party's 2024 General Election strategy. It was also a recurrent theme in news commentary about the possible dynamics of the communication of the campaign. Interest was particularly focused on the new digital phenomenon, TikTok, which barely registered as an information source in the 2019 General Election but by 2024 was outstripping more established social media platforms, particularly among younger voters. To select a few examples from an abundance of news reports during the campaign, the Telegraph offered its readers a view 'Inside the First TikTok Election' (Titcomb 2024). The BBC later considered 'How social media is making young people accidental election influencers' (Spring 2024), while the *Guardian's* media editor speculated 'is this the first post-mainstream-media election?' (Waterson 2024).

Whilst the communication environment of electioneering is changing, and journalists are always inclined to horizon-scan for new trends, there is a need to be cautious about disregarding the continuities in election mediation. Specifically, there is a need to avoid simplistic assumptions about the growing irrelevance of mainstream news organizations in today's high-choice media environment. For example, the decades' long decline in the circulation figures of the UK printed press is often assumed to demonstrate their diminishing political voice. The figures alone indicate this: since the 2010 General Election daily national press circulation has decreased by 74%. This reduction has undermined significant revenue streams and hit profit margins, but we must not confuse a crisis of *resource* with a crisis in *reach* (Deacon et al., 2024).

If we recognize that legacy news providers are brands that exist online and offline, then their public reputation and profile remain very significant. Ofcom's (2024a) most recent news consumption survey is instructive on this point. Although described as heralding a 'generational shift' in citizens' news consumptions, the details of its findings provide testimony to the enduring importance of established news providers. For example, traditional platforms are still deemed more accurate, trustworthy, and impartial than online competitors, and TV news remains the dominant news platform, gaining importance as we track upwards through the age groupings (the demographic groups, incidentally, that are most likely to vote). It is also the case that the Ofcom research identifies a 'significant reduction' in the reach of print and online newspapers from 2023, but this will in part be explained by several titles introducing content quotas or exclusions from content for non-subscribers in the last year (something that is not mentioned in the report summary). Furthermore, when the 2024 General Election was called, the ten most popular digital sources of news were overwhelmingly legacy brands (Newman et al., 2024). Significantly, the list was dominated by outlets that still publish newspapers, with the print versions offering a useful distillation of their online content including campaign-related material.

Furthermore, to state that most people now get their news from social media raises a question rather than answers it. Social media are platforms not publishers, which has been key to their defence against statutory regulation. To gain a fuller insight, there is a need to consider which information sources people access when using these platforms. Research confirms that legacy news brands have a very large footprint across social media, and even on those platforms where 'celebrities/ influencers/ ordinary people' are more frequently cited as news sources than professional news creators, the basis for this opinion-leading is often framed by information derived from legacy news sources.[1] This is because journalists remain key intermediaries within our political system due to their sanctioned and privileged access to leading politicians both in front of the house and behind the scenes.

Another surprising omission in debates about the decline of established media is the failure to acknowledge the precarity of many of their digital competitors. For example, in the last year, X/Twitter lost 30% of its active users in the UK, with disengagement most evident among 'political progressives' (Kelly 2024). In 2023, Buzzfeed News shut down and Vice Media commenced bankruptcy proceedings. Many of the alternative news sites that excited much commentary during the 2017 General Election have since hit significant political and economic headwinds and are far less influential than they were at what proved to be the high-water mark of Jeremy Corbyn's leadership of the Labour party. Legacy news brands may be battered and bruised, but they continually demonstrate greater grip and resilience than the constituents of the ever-shifting online-only landscape. The recent furores about who gets to own the *Telegraph, Observer,* and *Spectator* demonstrate there are many powerful interests in the UK and beyond who recognize significant value in the mastheads of legacy news brands.

This is not to say that all is stable in the configuration of the traditional media landscape in the UK. The most notable difference in the broadcasting environment since the previous election lies in the arrival of GB News as a free-to-air TV channel in 2021, the first of its kind since Rupert Murdoch established Sky News 30 years previously. After inauspicious beginnings, with technical mishaps and the early departure of Andrew Neil as presenter/chairman seeming to mar the channel's bold mission to become Britain's biggest news broadcaster by 2028 (Mance 2024), GB News has increasingly attracted a mixture of significant public figures from the media and political sphere and has slowly cultivated a committed and growing audience whether online or on TV (Press Gazette 2024b). The channel's reliance on the politically affiliated hosts of primetime debate and interview-based programming has garnered controversy since the channel's inauguration. But it has mainly been the channel's viewpoint diversity, rather than its appointment of Conservative and Reform-affiliated hosts necessarily, which has elicited occasional regulatory rebuke or investigation from Ofcom (Adu 2023). Indeed, Ofcom continues to pursue multiple investigations and has ruled on several breaches of broadcast rules, but the channel has so far avoided significant censure.

---

[1] A prominent 'research note' in Ofcom's (2024a) recent survey concedes 'Please bear in mind that when a respondent indicates that they use online or social media platform for news, they may be referring to content or posts by traditional news publishers such as the BBC, posts by journalists, or content posted/ shared by friends and family, etc.' (2024, p. 4).

Changes in the party-political environment in 2024 also presented challenges to journalists and news editors in reporting the campaign. The renaming of the Brexit Party to Reform UK following the previous general election campaign, and in particular Nigel Farage's dramatic surprise return to the party's leadership role and announcement of his candidacy for Parliament at the start of the formal campaign for Clacton also represented a continuity with the identity of UKIP prior to the Brexit referendum and negotiations in the mid-to-latter 2010s. Whether the party would be handled as an upstart or not, the prospect of a shake-up in the media and political landscapes hinted at the potential for a 'change' election in more ways than one.

1. About this research

In this piece, we analyse UK national media reporting of the 2024 General Election campaign, comparing press and TV coverage. The findings are the latest in a series of UK General Election news audits conducted by Loughborough University's Centre for Research in Culture and Communication that commenced with the 1992 campaign. As in previous campaigns, we conducted a thematic content analysis of election-related news broadcast or published on weekdays between 31st May and 3rd July 2024. The media titles sampled were (Television) BBC1 10 p.m. news, ITN 10 p.m. news, C4 7 p.m. news, C5 Five News Tonight, Sky News 7–8 p.m., and GB News 7–8 p.m., (Newspaper) *The Guardian, The Daily Express, The Daily Mail, The Daily Mirror, The Daily Star, The Daily Telegraph, The Financial Times, The Guardian, The i, The Times*, and *The Sun*. All election-related items in the TV bulletins were coded. For the press, the analysis focused on the printed versions, where we coded all relevant items that appeared on the front page, the first two pages of the domestic news section, the first two pages of any specialist section assigned to the coverage of the campaign, and the pages containing and facing papers' leader editorials. Intercoder reliability tests were conducted throughout the analysis, which was conducted in 'real time' (i.e., findings were reported periodically as the campaign was evolving).[2]

---

[2]We adopted a two-stage approach to intercoder reliability: (1) comparing daily the consistency with which coders were using coding options, to identify any outlying practices; (2) conducting daily formal ICR tests on co-coded material on a cumulative basis as the election unfolded. The overall average pairwise Cohen's kappa results were: Actor1 (92.78%), Actor2 (69.68%), Actor3 (71.99%), Actor4 (58.17%), Theme1 (80.56%), Theme2 (87.08%), Theme3 (62.2%), Conservative evaluation (75.42%), Labour evaluation (73.75%), Liberal Democrat evaluation (92.2%), Green evaluation (94.44%), SNP (97.78%), and Reform UK (88.89%).

In the discussion that follows we present findings in three sections. The first examines overall trends in the reporting of the 2024 General Election, drawing comparisons with previous campaigns where relevant. The second provides a granular examination of the main TV channels' reporting of the election including GB News's output during the campaign. The final section explores the nuances of newspaper partisanship in the 2024 election and assesses the extent to which there was a significant realignment in press support.

2. Overall trends in General Election 2024 news reporting

The foundational measure for any assessment of media performance in a campaign is the amount of coverage given to the parties competing for office. Media exposure alone does not necessarily indicate political advantage, as it can contain a significant quotient of negative coverage. Nevertheless, political parties need to establish a presence in the news agenda to have any hope of influencing it and thereby the broader parameters of public discourse. Furthermore, asking 'who is news' in a campaign offers a basis for assessing the degree of fit between the editorial priorities of news organizations and eventual voting choices.

Table 14.1 compares the overall media share of the parties in 2024 electoral coverage with distributions identified in six previous election campaign studies undertaken by Loughborough CRCC. The results show that in the most recent

Table 14.1. Proportion of news presence of political parties across all news media 2001–24

	2001	2005	2010	2015	2017	2019	2024
Conservative	34.9	36.1	33.4	35.9	44.4	38.0	41.2
Labour	49.0	43.7	40.2	31.4	36.1	40.6	40.1
Liberal Democrats	10.2	17.2	22.4	10.8	7.8	7.4	3.9
SNP	1.0	0.8	0.7	9.4	3.2	2.9	1.7
UKIP/Brexit/Reform	0.1	0.3	0.5	8.5	3.6	5.6	9.3
Plaid Cymru	0.2	0.5	0.6	0.7	0.7	0.6	0.5
Green Party	0.2	0.5	0.7	1.3	1.4	1.1	1.2
Other	4.4	1.0	1.6	1.9	2.8	3.8	2.2

Notes: Percentages = ((number of party representatives featured in election items/ total number of party-political actors featured in election items) * 100). For each election item, up to five news actors could be coded. To be included, the party actor had to have an active status within the item, i.e. they were directly quoted and/or pictured/ reported by the journalist as engaging in a political action/ activity. Sample periods varied slightly across campaigns but media sources analysed were consistent. GB News is excluded from the 2024 count.

campaign, the combined media dominance of Labour and the Conservative voices increased from 2019 and attained levels only exceeded in the 2001 campaign. Beyond this two-party squeeze, Reform UK was the next most newsworthy party by a considerable margin, receiving nearly the same amount of news coverage as all remaining parties combined. Their presence also outperformed levels achieved by UKIP in 2015, which at the time marked a remarkable vault in that party's national media profile. The Liberal Democrats by comparison have witnessed a dramatic collapse in their national media profile overall since 2010 and despite all the hijinks photo-opportunities undertaken by their leader Ed Davey, recorded their lowest media presence in 2024 relative to earlier campaigns.

Fig. 14.1 differentiates the combined presence of Labour and Conservative actors in TV and press since 2001 and compares these distributions with the actual vote share achieved by the two main parties for each election. The results show that TV coverage consistently apportions less coverage to Labour and Conservative sources than press outlets in all campaigns, revealing the regulatory requirements on broadcasters to give 'due weight' to all parties and provide 'the appropriate level of coverage based on their past and/or current electoral support' (Ofcom 2024b). This is not an easy calibration to make, not least because actual vote share is imponderable at the time these judgements are applied. For this reason, one would expect to see a degree of lag in apportioned distributions, which seemed most evident in the reporting of the 2015 campaign, where five years of

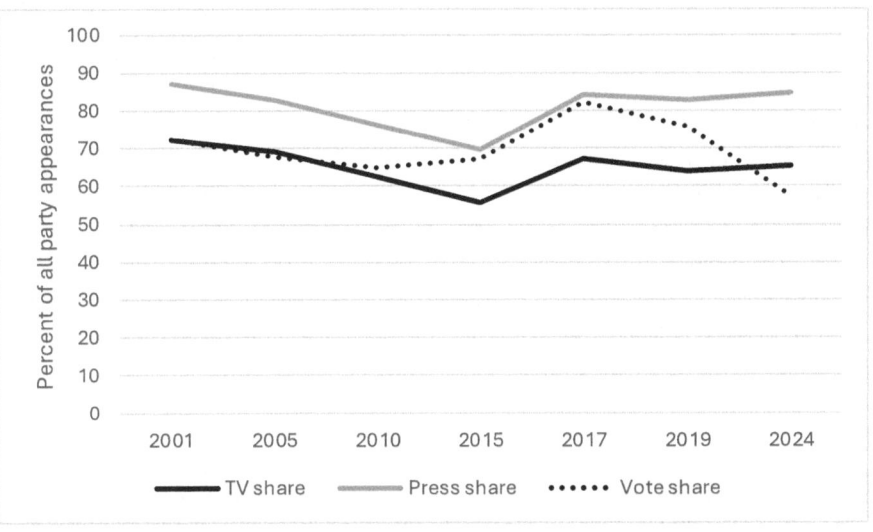

Figure 14.1. Labour and Conservative TV share, press share, and vote share 2001–24

Coalition government produced an atypical multipolarity in news reporting that was confounded by the eventual election result.

What is clear from the temporal comparison is that the 2024 campaign was the first time in recent campaigns where both TV and newspapers overreported the leading parties relative to their actual vote share. Apart from the SNP, the 'other parties' had remarkable successes in 2024, with the Greens and Plaid Cymru achieving their highest-ever levels of electoral support, Reform UK recording the third highest amounts of votes, and the Liberal Democrats winning the highest number of seats since the Liberal Party in 1923. In contrast, Labour's thumping majority was achieved with the lowest vote share of any winning party since 1945 and the Conservatives recorded their worst electoral performance both in terms of vote share and seats since 1832 (Cracknell and Baker 2024). From this evidence, it appears the mainstream news media failed to anticipate a significant resurgence in multi-party electoral politics in this campaign.

Table 14.2 presents data on the interpretative dimensions of the formal campaign, i.e. 'what was the election mainly seen to be about'? It is not unusual for coverage of the 'electoral process' to dominate the last weeks of campaigning, which was certainly the case in 2024. 'Electoral process' is a category that captures speculation as to who is winning the campaign, opinion poll projections, the parties' campaigning strategies, political mishaps or missteps by candidates,

Table 14.2. Top ten issues in the 2024 and 2019 media campaigns

	All		TV		Press	
	2024 %	(2019) %	2024 %	(2019) %	2024 %	(2019) %
Electoral process	37	(31)	36	(32)	37	(31)
Taxation	10	(5)	9	(6)	10	(4)
Standards/corruption/scandals/sleaze	7	(7)	10	(6)	6	(7)
Immigration/border/controls	6	(2)	5	(2)	5	(2)
Economy/business/trade	6	(8)	7	(6)	5	(9)
Health and NHS provision	5	(7)	4	(7)	5	(7)
Minority groups	5	(4)	3	(4)	5	(4)
Defence/military/security/terrorism	3	(4)	2	(3)	3	(4)
Environment including climate change	2	(3)	3	(4)	2	(2)
Brexit and European Union relations	2	(13)	2	(18)	2	(11)
All other issues	17	(16)	19	(12)	20	(19)

Notes: Percentages = (frequency of issue/total number of issues coded) × 100. A maximum of three issue responses could be coded per item. To be coded, an issue needed to occupy more than 10 seconds of TV coverage or two sentences. The most prominent issues were coded when more than three were present. Percentages are rounded. GB News is not included in the 2024 sample.

etc. Regarding the latter, there was no shortage of material in the 2024 election, particularly for the incumbent party. The unseasonal shower that dampened Rishi Sunak's surprise election campaign outside Number 10 presaged a litany of missteps for the Conservatives, the most notorious of which involved the Prime Minister's decision to stand up veterans and assorted international leaders on the commemoration of D-Day to make a prearranged interview scheduled with Paul Brand of ITV. Opinion polls also received substantially more coverage than in previous campaigns, as journalists sought to assess if the campaign was shifting the political dial or to estimate the scale of Labour's widely anticipated landslide. Journalists have had their fingers burned in previous elections, by over-reliance on inaccurate polling projections, and the underperformance of the polls in aggregate terms in 2024, particularly in the overestimation of Labour's lead over the Conservatives, cannot have helped editorial calibration of party presence (Whiteley 2024). Table 14.2 also demonstrates the prominence of coverage of 'standards/ corruption/ scandals/ sleaze in coverage', particularly in TV reporting, the bulk of which concerned allegations about Conservative candidates' betting on the timing of the election and exposés of the sexist and racist conduct of several Reform UK campaigners and candidates.

When coverage of scandals and the electoral process are combined, these results suggest that barely half of all coverage addressed substantive manifesto/ policy commitments and differences. Moreover, these levels considerably exceeded those found in the previous election. Taxation was the most prominent substantive issue, particularly during the first few weeks of the campaign, with 'immigration/ border/ controls' the next most frequently addressed. Both these topics were far more prominent than in 2019, whereas most of the other top ten issues were broadly consistent with their previous levels of media attention. The one major exception was coverage of 'Brexit and European Relations', which dominated the 2019 campaign but was signally side-lined on this occasion.

What is striking about this mainstream media issue agenda is its distinctiveness from what issues voters deemed most important in the lead-up to the vote (e.g. Ipsos 2024a; Smith 2024). According to this evidence, the UK public was more concerned about 'the cost of living', 'the economy', 'housing', 'social care', 'healthcare', 'the environment', and even 'Brexit/ European relations' than journalists. 'Taxation', on the other hand, appeared to be of more peripheral public concern.

3. The television campaign

Analysis of general distributions in news coverage is of value for assessing the overall tone and tenor of the media campaign, however, they can mask important variations within media sectors. In the next two sections, we provide a disaggregated analysis of TV and press reporting during the campaign to assess the extent to which specific news outlets varied in their coverage.

As discussed, the campaign saw the debut of GB News, a controversial new entrant which had been launched in 2021. Just prior to the calling of the election the UK public was asked to list the television news channels they used (Redfield and Wilton 2024). Although GB News was ranked seventh, it was mentioned by 10% of respondents, a steady start given its third birthday occurred during the campaign. By comparison, the BBC came top of the same list with nearly two-thirds (62%) selecting the broadcaster while the three ITN services—airing on ITV, Channel 4, and Channel 5—were second (40%), fourth (19%), and sixth (11%), respectively. While the category 'I do not use the television for news' was fifth, it scored a relatively modest 13% given the widespread commentary surrounding the supposedly fragmenting media landscape.

The electoral coverage of the GB News channel has not been included in any of our television analysis to this juncture, because to do so would produce inconsistencies in the cross-election comparisons. Moreover, there is a need to establish whether there was any atypicality in the form and focus of its reporting. One of the principal aims of this section is to establish whether this was the case.

Table 14.3 shows the top ten campaign themes disaggregated by broadcaster. As expected, the electoral process was the primary focus across all channels, particularly Channel 5 and Sky. Interestingly, the other topic not specifically orientated towards policy concerns, 'standards/ corruption/ scandals/ sleaze', was far less prominent in GB News output relative to all the others (at a mere 2% of its coverage). There are potential party-political implications to this editorial distinction, as coverage in this category principally concerned allegations about the misconduct of Conservative and Reform UK candidates and activists. A further effect of this marginalization was that GB News' coverage was more policy-focused than all other channels.

This greater overall attention to policy issues might be deemed a creditable aspect of its coverage, but it must also be acknowledged that GB News used interview/discussion formats much more frequently than other broadcasters, at almost two-thirds of its electoral coverage in our sample. This practice gives more space to address substantive topics.[3]

All broadcasters gave most coverage to 'taxation', especially GB News, followed by economy/business. Thereafter, the ordering and relative prominence of themes differed quite significantly. GB News apportioned the highest levels to

---

[3] This compares with only one-fifth of the BBC's coverage, and between three- and four-tenths of the other broadcasters' output.

Table 14.3. Issue balance per TV channel—top ten themes

Theme	BBC1	ITV1	C4	C5	Sky	GBN	Total
Electoral process	34% (1)	35% (1)	33% (1)	39% (1)	43% (1)	37% (1)	36.3%
Taxation	9% (2)	10% (2)	7% (4=)	8% (3)	9% (3=)	12% (2)	9.2%
Standards/corruption/scandals/sleaze	7% (4)	9% (3)	8% (2)	15% (2)	10% (2)	2% (10=)	8.1%
Economy/business/trade	5% (5)	6% (5)	7% (3)	5% (4)	9% (3=)	7% (4)	6.6%
Immigration/border controls	4% (6)	7% (4)	7% (4=)	2% (10)	4% (5)	9% (3)	5.8%
Health and NHS provision	8% (3)	4% (6=)	3% (10=)	4% (7=)	2% (10=)	5% (5)	4.3%
Environment including climate change	3% (9)	3% (9=)	3% (7=)	5% (5)	2% (10=)	2% (14)	2.8%
Minority groups	1% (19=)	4% (6=)	5% (6)	1% (18=)	2% (8=)	3% (7=)	2.8%
Scotland/Scottish independence	4% (7=)	4% (8)	3% (9)	4% (7=)	2% (10=)	0% (24=)	2.5%
Defence/military/security/terrorism	1% (16=)	3% (9=)	3% (10=)	1% (18=)	3% (6=)	2% (10=)	2.1%

Note: Percentages are rounded. Ranks per channel are provided in brackets.

'Immigration/ border controls'. For Channel 4, the issues of taxation, economy, and immigration were relatively balanced as foremost issues, but among other outlets, there was a clear division between the pre-eminent policy issue(s), and those further down the order. None of the broadcasters gave much airtime to Scottish independence, but GB News was the most conspicuously uninterested of them all.

Table 14.4 shows the quotation time for the political parties (and their leaders) disaggregated by broadcaster for news items only.[4] Here, there is some discrepancy between the broadcasters in the allocation of most quotations to either the Conservatives or Labour, but an equal number privileged one versus the other. The combined share of quotation time for Labour and the Conservatives among the established broadcasters ranged between 54% (BBC) and 66% (ITV), but for

---

[4] This attempts to recognize that soundbites in hard news items may be many times more contracted than the more expansive contributions afforded to participants of discussion and interview pieces, skewing our appreciation within the context of news format differences of which parties and leaders are afforded more or less news access than others.

Table 14.4. Quotation time in news items only

	BBC	ITV	C4	C5	Sky	GBN	Total
Cons	26% (16%)	37% (25%)	30% (8%)	34% (19%)	45% (34%)	43% (14%)	34% (18%)
Labour	27% (18%)	30% (21%)	34% (15%)	21% (19%)	19% (16%)	46% (20%)	30% (17%)
Lib Dems	8% (4%)	5% (4%)	12% (9%)	5% (3%)	6% (4%)	5% (0%)	8% (5%)
Reform	10% (8%)	12% (10%)	11% (4%)	2% (1%)	17% (15%)	6% (2%)	10% (7%)
Green	5% (4%)	4% (2%)	2% (2%)	18% (16%)	6% (4%)	0% (0%)	5% (4%)
SNP	12% (10%)	7% (5%)	2% (1%)	5% (5%)	3% (2%)	0% (0%)	5% (4%)
Plaid	4% (3%)	0% (0%)	3% (2%)	3% (3%)	3% (3%)	0% (0%)	2% (2%)
Other	8%	13%	5%	12%	2%	1%	5%
N items	112	99	93	74	82	54	514

Note: Leader percentages are in brackets. Percentages are rounded.

GB News this combined share was 89%. The only other parties who amassed any significant coverage in GB News coverage were the Liberal Democrats (5%) and Reform UK (6%). The other parties received no quotation in news items on GB News, representing a nearly unique degree of inattention to their campaigns.[5]

As noted, one of the significant challenges faced by broadcasters in this campaign came in the form of which party to afford third largest party status to: the SNP, Reform UK, and the Liberal Democrats could all lay claim to this mantle depending on broadcasters' interpretation of past electoral performance and polling. Ultimately, the ranking in quotation terms placed Reform UK in third overall, but this ranking was more starkly evident on ITV and Sky's output than on GB News's.

Despite GB News's well-documented controversies concerning the party-political diversity of their programme hosts and guests, the findings shown here suggest that—to a point—there is some degree of party-political viewpoint diversity in the broadcaster's output. The Labour Party and the Liberal Democrats, whether in comfortable editorial circumstances or not, obtained some share of GB News quotation, and the Conservatives and Reform UK, despite the affiliation of several

---

[5] This was also the case in interview items on GB News, in which 45% of speaking time was allocated to the Conservatives, 29% to Labour, 17% to the Liberal Democrats and 9% to Reform UK.

party representatives, did not completely dominate speaking time. But beyond these parties, the broadcaster provided no quotation time *at all* to the other parties.

As demonstrated in the issues domain, GB News dealt with policy issues in the campaign to a higher degree than other channels, mainly due to its marked lack of engagement with the political scandals that compromised the Conservative and Reform UK campaigns. The broadcaster broadly conformed with its competitors in its allocation of relative prominence to policy issues, albeit with greater emphasis on taxation, immigration, and EU relations. It provided space for Conservative, Labour, Liberal Democrat, and Reform UK politicians across its output to air their views, but its disregard for smaller parties is a notable departure from practices of due party-political impartiality among more established broadcasters. These patterns suggest that the channel has forged a path as a tabloid-style debate outlet, with less weight given to due impartiality and more editorial distinction in process and policy emphases compared with more established competitors.

4. The election in print

As noted, newspapers in the UK are in serious decline if measured by the stark fall in the circulations of the major print titles over the last few years. To give more detail on recent reductions: average sales of dailies fell to only 2.5 million during this election, a considerable reduction from 4.5 million in the previous campaign of 2019 (see Table 14.5). But as has also been discussed, the same publications retain an online presence that sustains a considerable public reach. From an audience perspective, those most likely to vote continued to belong to the older generations who were also the most loyal and enduring readers of newspapers (Ipsos 2024b).

The political influence of the printed press endures in other ways, such as intra-media agenda setting. British broadcasters are legally obliged to provide impartial coverage during an election in marked contrast to their press counterparts. But this has not prevented editors responsible for the major opinion-forming television and radio news from giving prominence to newspaper-originated content in their programming. This reporting includes covering the ritual whereby the final editorial declarations are made by newspapers in their leader columns, usually around the eve of polling day. Table 14.5 summarizes the way the major paid-for dailies 'voted' in this election based on the statement accompanying their formal editorial declaration. Significantly each preference is also characterized by the strength of its expression, which is an important qualification that enhances understanding as to the depth of support forthcoming from a particular outlet (Deacon and Wring 2002).

Half of the main dailies endorsed Labour in a significant reversal of what happened in 2019 when only two had. Conversely, the five titles that had backed the

Table 14.5. Daily newspapers' 2024 partisanship with circulations (hard copy in 000s) (with 2019 equivalent partisanships and circulations in brackets)

Title	2024 (2019)	2024 (2019)	Circulation loss 2019–24
Daily Mirror	**Very Strong Labour** (Strong Labour)	**226** (455)	–50%
Daily Express	**Strong Conservative** (Very Strong Conservative)	**140** (298)	–53%
Daily Star	**Moderate Labour** (None)	**127** (289)	–56%
The Sun	**Weak Labour** (Very Strong Conservative)	**700*** (1,217)	–45%
Daily Mail	**Strong Conservative** (Very Strong Conservative)	**689** (1,133)	–39%
Daily Telegraph	**Strong Conservative** (Very Strong Conservative)	**190*** (309)	–39%
The Guardian	**Moderate Labour** (Weak Labour)	**60*** (129)	–53%
The Times	**None** (Strong Conservative)	**180*** (365)	–51%
The i	**None** (None)	**125** (220)	–43%
Financial Times	**Weak Labour** (Very Weak Liberal Democrat)	**109** (163)	–33%
Totals	**Share of endorsements by circulation %** (2019) Con **40%** (72) Lab **48%** (13) LibDem **0%** (4) None **12%** (11)	**2,546** (4,578)	–44%

Source: Press Gazette (2024a) (Audit Bureau of Circulation figures), May 2024 (November 2019); figures marked * are *Press Gazette* estimates.

Conservatives were reduced to three. The headline story here was the decision of *The Sun* to declare for Labour on its front page after months of speculation. No other party received a newspaper endorsement, and only *The Times* and *The i* did not declare for any party.

The *Mirror* was the only title to give Labour enthusiastic support (see Table 14.5) although *The Guardian* was more fulsome in its praise than was the case in the last election. Two very different newspapers, the *Daily Star* and *Financial Times*, declared for the party with statements that were motivated by the same reasoning used in *The Sun* (albeit without the football analogy). As the *Star* opined 'New start is needed', so the *FT* headlined its equivalent declaration 'Britain needs a fresh start'. While the *FT* had supported Labour in the past, the move by the *Star* was perhaps more noteworthy given the endorsement signalled an end to its partisan

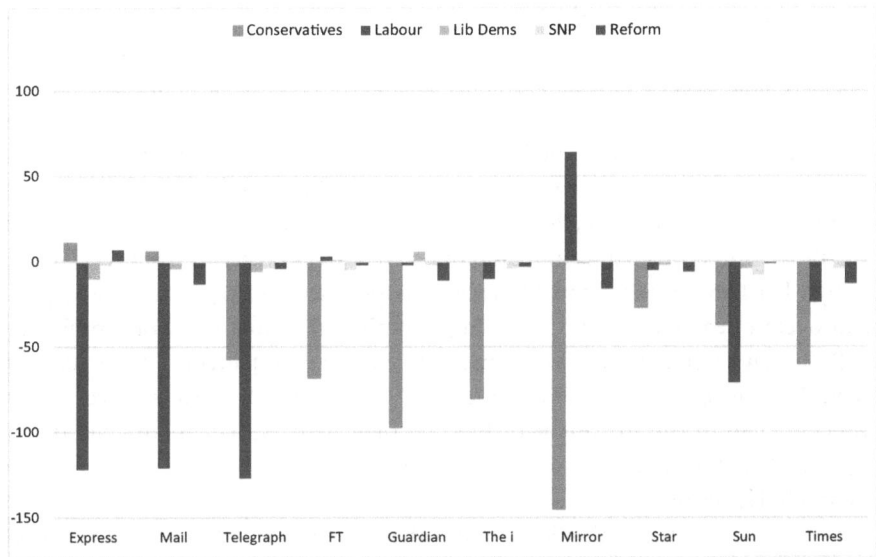

Figure 14.2. Proportion of positive to negative coverage of political parties by newspaper title

neutrality, a position it had reiterated earlier during the campaign. This change of allegiance was perhaps not so surprising given the paper's relatively recent and hugely successful political intervention: the comparing of the wilting premiership of Liz Truss with a lettuce, the latter of which went on to have a longer shelf life.

Given that final editorial declarations are often presented as considered and settled verdicts on weeks of intensive campaigning, one might expect them to be compromised by caveats, particularly among the less partisan titles. To gain insight into the wider evaluative responses of the press, we also tracked the extent to which election items emphasized positive or negative issues for the respective parties across the entire campaign.[6] Fig. 14.2 provides a tally of the extent to which positive coverage exceeded negative coverage for each party (or vice versa) for each national newspaper title.

The results show that of the three newspapers that 'voted' for the Conservatives, only the *Mail* and *Express* recorded a marginal surplus of positive Conservative stories to negative. *The Telegraph*, by comparison, heaped comparable levels of negativity alongside a considerable deficit in their reporting of their preferred party.

---

[6] For each item, we assessed whether the information or commentary contained within it had positive or negative implications for each political party. If an item mainly or solely focused on positive matters for a party, it was given a value of + 1. If it mainly/solely focused on negative matters for a party, it was assigned a value of −1. Items where there was (a) no clear evaluation, (b) contained positive and negative issues in broadly equal measure, or (c) no mention of the party was made, were coded as zero. Items where no reference was made to the party were excluded from the calculation.

The findings also highlight the tenuity of the *Sun's* support for Labour, with negativity to Labour in routine coverage exceeding that found for the Conservatives. Of the papers that declared for Labour, only the *Mirror* recorded a significant surplus of pro-Labour items. For the remainder, it was varying levels of negative reporting of the Conservatives that defined their coverage. These patterns provided a notable contrast with equivalent comparisons made for the preceding two UK General Elections (see Deacon et al., 2021: 381–2). In 2017, Conservative party divisions over Brexit and a misfiring campaign distracted press criticism from the Jeremy Corbyn-led Labour party considerably. This produced an equivocal and equivalent overall negativity in the reporting of both parties that was not repeated in 2019. In that campaign, the pro-Conservative press was strident in their support for Boris Johnson and detestation of Jeremy Corbyn, which delivered a very wide evaluative gap in the treatment of the two main parties, to Labour's disadvantage. In 2024, both main parties received comparable levels of press opprobrium in cumulative terms.

By comparison, the evaluations of the other parties fluctuate around the break-even point. This is primarily a measure of the far lower levels of press engagement with their policies and electioneering and the tendency for coverage to be more descriptive in tone. The one exception was in the reporting of Reform UK, where evaluative aspects were more consistently identified but often cancelled each other out. That said, only the *Express* recorded more positive to negative stories on Reform UK across the campaign and even here this was only a modest difference.

The distribution of coverage overall shows that newspaper disaffection with the Conservatives was not accompanied by significant positivity towards Labour. In short, print coverage overall was characterized more by disorientation than reorientation which, in partisan terms, translates into a case of press dealignment rather than realignment.

5. Conclusion

The mainstream news media in the UK still play a vital role in the shaping of public debate in the country, through their enduring reach and reputation and the 'two-step flow' of influence they exert via social media. Recognition of this, despite the advent of new digital intermediaries, is necessary as it ensures we retain focus on their democratic performance during periods of critical political importance. This audit of national news during the UK General Election of 2024 suggests three areas for consideration relating to the overall media agenda, broadcasters—new and old, and the role of the press.

First, the findings highlight an apparent disconnection between the reporting of the election and public preferences and concerns. For the first time, the media share of the two main parties exceeded their actual vote share, even among broadcasters expected to give due weight to all parties. Tracking earlier trends, the 2024 election remained a bi-partisan media campaign that correlated poorly with the multi-polar outcome. Furthermore, the media coverage was conspicuously light on policy content compared with previous elections: the substantive agenda, such as it was, seemed disconnected from the principal concerns of the voting public. The foregrounding of 'taxation' in particular may have reflected the agenda-setting power of the two main parties, but it was not of paramount public concern. Major issues of public import such as the cost of living, housing, and the environment were marginalized.

Second, the 2024 election saw the arrival of GB News, a television channel that has self-consciously positioned itself as an alternative seemingly prepared to challenge broadcast orthodoxy as well as the longstanding regulatory system. Our comparative analysis of this new player's performance in the general election suggests that, while it did not prove to be as dramatic an outlier as some had assumed, there were notable departures in its coverage of the campaign. Unlike other broadcasters, it provided negligible airtime to the gaffes and scandals that disrupted the Conservative and Reform UK campaigns. GB News also deployed a distinctive format in its coverage, providing a higher quotient of interviews and commentary than formal news reporting. The two main parties dominated the speaking time in the latter (Labour's direct quotation exceeding that of the Conservatives), with all the other parties side-lined. To our reading, these editorial patterns seemed to align more with those found in newspaper reporting.

Finally, although the conventional press may be diminished in terms of their hard copy sales, the related brands continue to play a role in the General Election following their successful transition to digital journalism. Together, familiar titles like the *Guardian, Sun, Mirror,* and *Mail,* still account for a significant part of the contemporary UK news market. Unlike their broadcast counterparts, they can and do exercise their editorial freedom to offer idiosyncratic if not downright partisan coverage of elections and 2024 was no exception. If the print coverage of the Conservatives was unprecedently negative, there was also plenty of criticism of Labour albeit mostly from the few remaining members of the 'Tory press' but also from the nominally supportive *Sun*. The other parties received markedly less attention and what they did receive was not so evaluative. Given this negligible interest, the approach of the newspapers to the campaign might be best characterized as 'a plague on both your houses'.

Acknowledgements

We wish to acknowledge the contribution of our co-researchers in developing this analysis (Brendan Lawson, Jilly Kay, and Nathan Ritchie), and the coding team in gathering the data (Hannah Bruce, Magnus Hamann, Alistair Kidd, Ella Muncie, Thomas Quinlan, Reuben Shapland, Benji Simpson, Mian Tiao, Roman Winkelhahn, and Caspar Wort).

Funding

This research was supported by a British Academy/ Leverhulme Small Grant (SRG23\231976) and Loughborough University.

References

Adu, A. (2023) 'GB News broke impartiality rules when Tory MPs interviewed Hunt, Ofcom finds', *The Guardian*. https://www.theguardian.com/media/2023/sep/18/gb-news-broke-impartiality-rules-when-tory-mps-interviewed-jeremy-hunt, accessed 12 Oct. 2024.

Cracknell, R. and Baker, C. (2024) 'General Election 2024: results and analysis', House of Commons Library, https://researchbriefings.files.parliament.uk/documents/CBP-10009/CBP-10009.pdf, accessed 12 Oct. 2024.

Deacon, D., Smith, D. and Wring, D. (2021) 'Enduring Brands: The Press'. In: R. Ford, T. Bale, W. Jennings and P. Surridge, *The British General Election of 2019*, pp. 347–85. Basingstoke: Palgrave Macmillan.

Deacon, D., Smith, D. and Wring, D. (2024) 'Why Mainstream News Media Still Matter', *Media, Culture & Society*, 46: 874–85.

Deacon, D. and Wring, D. (2002) 'Partisan De-alignment and the British Press'. In: J. Bartle, I. Crewe and B. Gosschalk (eds.), *Political Communications: The General Election of 2001*, pp. 197–211. London: Frank Cass.

Ipsos (2024a) 'Ipsos Issues Index', https://www.ipsos.com/sites/default/files/ct/news/documents/2024-06/Issues%20Index_June_v1_PUBLIC.pdf, accessed 12 Oct. 2024.

Ipsos (2024b) 'How the Voters Voted in the 2024 Election' https://www.ipsos.com/sites/default/files/ct/news/documents/2024-07/Ipsos%20July%202024_How%20Britain%20voted_GE2024_PUBLIC.pdf, accessed 14 Oct. 2024.

Kelly, J. (2024) 'With Blue Sky, the Social Media Echo Chamber is Back in Vogue', *Financial Times*, https://www.ft.com/content/65961fec-a5ab-4c71-b1c8-265be3583a93, accessed 12 Oct. 2024.

Mance, H. (2024) 'Why GB News is Angrier than Ever', *Financial Times*, https://www.ft.com/content/31600209-c8dc-4cf9-bcf3-9afdc10781ff, accessed 12 Oct. 2024.

Newman, N. et al. (2024) 'Reuters Institute Digital News Report 2024'. Reuters Institute for the Study of Journalism, https://reutersinstitute.politics.ox.ac.uk/sites/default/files/2024-06/RISJ_DNR_2024_Digital_v10%20lr.pdf, accessed 05 Aug. 2025.

Ofcom (2024a) 'News Consumption in the UK: 2024', *Ofcom*, https://www.ofcom.org.uk/siteassets/resources/documents/research-and-data/tv-radio-and-on-demand-research/tv-research/news/news-consumption-2024/news-consumption-in-the-uk-2024-report.pdf?v=379621, accessed 12 Oct. 2024.

Ofcom (2024b) 'Ofcom's Role in the General Election—What You Need to Know', *Ofcom*, https://www.ofcom.org.uk/about-ofcom/what-we-do/ofcoms-role-in-a-general-election--what-you-need-to-know/, accessed 12 Oct. 2024.

Press Gazette (2024a) 'Newspaper ABCs', *Press Gazette*, https://pressgazette.co.uk/media-audience-and-business-data/media_metrics/most-popular-newspapers-uk-abc-monthly-circulation-figures-2/, accessed 14 Oct. 2024.

Press Gazette (2024b) 'Top 50 UK News Websites in August: Guardian Rises above Sun and Mail as UK's Biggest Commercial News Site', *Press Gazette*, https://pressgazette.co.uk/media-audience-and-business-data/media_metrics/most-popular-websites-news-uk-monthly-2/, accessed 12 Oct. 2024.

Redfield and Wilton. (2024) 'Who Watches GB News', *Redfield and Wilton Strategies*, https://redfieldandwiltonstrategies.com/who-watches-gb-news/, accessed 11 Dec. 2024.

Smith, M. (2024) 'General Election 2024: What are the Most Important Issues for Voters?', *YouGov*, https://yougov.co.uk/politics/articles/49594-general-election-2024-what-are-the-most-important-issues-for-voters, accessed 12 Oct. 2024.

Spring, M. (2024) 'How Social Media is Making Young People Accidental Election Influencers', *BBC News*, https://www.bbc.co.uk/news/articles/cd1rl6p5p32o, accessed 11 Oct. 2024.

Titcomb, J. (2024) 'Inside the First TikTok Election', *Daily Telegraph*, https://www.telegraph.co.uk/business/2024/05/27/inside-first-tiktok-election/, accessed 11 Oct. 2024.

Waterson, J. (2024) '"There's a Lot Less Sharing": How News Consumption has Changed Since Last UK Election', *The Guardian*, https://www.theguardian.com/politics/article/2024/jun/24/news-mainstream-social-media-consumption-changes-uk-election, accessed 11 Oct. 2024.

Whiteley, P. (2024) 'Election 2024 Polls were Wide of the Mark on Labour's Margin of Victory—This is What may have Happened', *The Conversation*, https://theconversation.com/election-2024-polls-were-wide-of-the-mark-on-labours-margin-of-victory-this-is-what-may-have-happened-234485, accessed 12 Oct. 2024.

Breweries, bricklaying, and bungee jumping: Understanding the 2024 campaign trail

Alia Middleton[1,*] and David Cutts[2]

[1]Department of Politics and International Relations, University of Surrey, Austin Pearce Building, Guildford, GU2 7XH, UK
[2]Department of Political Science and International Studies, University of Birmingham, Muirhead Tower, Birmingham, B15 2TT, UK

*Correspondence: a.middleton@surrey.ac.uk

1. Introduction

Leaders' visits are now a 'staple diet' of British general election campaigns. Accompanied by a media scrum of national and local media, leaders' visits are often shown live on 24-hour news, fill the front page of national newspapers, become the subject of podcasts, blogs, and critical online scrutiny and are increasingly viewed widely by the public, with 'bite-size' footage commonly appearing on a plethora of social media platforms. As the electorate becomes less loyal and more volatile, voters increasingly turn to leaders' images and political messaging to make up their minds. For parties, visits are the settings through which leaders get their key messages across in the 'hustle and bustle' of the campaign. On the campaign trail, leaders are able to pitch policy positions in 'bite-size' chunks which simultaneously provide cues for voters while reducing their costs of acquiring political information necessary to make an informed choice. Visits are chosen to relay targeted policies to specific voters, highlight issues salient in the local electoral fight and to deliver core 'strapline' messages to the national audience. Increasingly though, leaders' visits give us a clear insight into a party's electoral strategy, its key messages, the tactics and targeting approach of the national 'air campaign' and the trajectory of the election. The 2024 election was no different. In this contribution, we detail the number of visits and how they varied weekly throughout the campaign and why. We examine where leaders went and why, the type of visits and how they differed by leader. We also compare how each party's strategy and approach varied from five years ago.

2. 2024 leader visits: how many and weekly frequency

Over the six-week campaign, 168 individual constituencies were visited in England, Wales and Scotland by the three main party leaders[1], five fewer than five years ago. In total, there were 184 visits with both Sunak and Davey undertaking multiple visits to the same constituency during the campaign. In 2019, then-Labour leader Jeremy Corbyn visited fifteen more seats than Conservative leader Boris Johnson. The reverse was true in 2024, with Sunak visiting six more seats than Starmer. Indeed, the Conservative leader visited only one more seat than Johnson in 2019 but Starmer visited twenty fewer seats than Corbyn. The major difference from 2019 though was the visibility of the Liberal Democrats. Davey only made three fewer constituency visits than Starmer and sixteen more visits than Swinson did five years ago.

In 2024, there were twenty-two crossover seats (where the same constituency is visited by two or more of the party leaders during the election), one fewer than in 2019. Fourteen seats were visited by both Sunak and Starmer while Sunak and Davey both visited eight seats. Five years ago, Corbyn and Swinson both visited seven seats. Tellingly, in 2024, no constituency was visited by both Starmer and Davey reiterating how both parties were laser-focused on targeting the Conservatives rather than each other. Since 2019, the Liberal Democrats have abandoned equidistance and politically positioned themselves as anti-Conservative. Likewise, Starmer had diluted the hostile rhetoric towards the Liberal Democrats which emanated from their coalition with the Conservatives and their complicity in the introduction of austerity measures. Under Corbyn, Labour labelled the Liberal Democrats as 'Yellow Conservatives' but Starmer noticeably avoided attacking the party thereby giving Labour supporters the 'go ahead' to lend their vote to the Liberal Democrats where they were the main challengers to the Conservatives. Of the ninety-eight seats where the Liberal Democrats were in second place, eighty-five were held by the Conservatives. Outside of Sheffield

---

[1]This article focuses on the national leaders of the Conservatives, Labour, and Liberal Democrats. We do not cover Nigel Farage's campaign trail as he became Reform UK leader on 3rd June, after the campaign had begun. We also collected data for the leaders of the Scottish Conservatives, Scottish Labour, Scottish Liberal Democrats, and the Scottish National Party. There are key differences in the Scottish campaign trail which require a more focused analysis than we can cover here. For instance, all four leaders were also Members of the Scottish Parliament and the election took place when for the most part Holyrood was sitting (dissolved on 28th June). This would have shaped how the leaders engaged with the campaign trail. And with the Scottish leaders contesting only 57 constituencies it was more feasible to conduct a wide-ranging trail.

Hallam, which Davey did visit, there were very few battleground seats against Labour which the Liberal Democrats had a reasonable prospect of winning. Labour were confident of defending these seats, so a Starmer visit was unlikely.

Campaigns are increasingly longer in duration which can make it difficult for parties to sustain momentum and public attention. However, the frequency of visits at different points during the campaign provides some insight into party tactics and whether and when they were gaining impetus or not. In 2024, like 2019, the frequency of visits over the six-week period fluctuated week by week and varied by party. Two major events occurred during the campaign—the D-Day commemorations and the G7 summit in week three and four respectively—which particularly impacted the frequency of Sunak's visits, albeit the fallout from his controversial early departure from D-Day events to record an interview with ITV may also have contributed to the fewer number of visits in week four. Three other observations are evident from the data. Firstly, the Conservative goal was clearly to try and build early momentum. Arguably, Sunak's surprise announcement did take the other parties, particularly Labour, off-guard. Sunak visited seventeen seats in the first week of the campaign (Starmer only visited ten seats) and after two weeks Sunak was visibly far more active than both his main opponents. At the end of week two, Sunak had visited more than 40% of all the seats he eventually visited during the election.

Secondly, as is consistent with previous elections, the number of visits increased considerably as polling day neared. In the final week of the campaign, there were actually more leaders visits in 2024 than in 2019. The frequency of visits in the final week and how they vary by leader though provides some insight into the state of the race and the trajectory of the campaign momentum of the respective parties. For instance, Starmer made fewer visits than his opponents and considerably fewer than Corbyn did five years previously. The reverse was true for Sunak who visited more seats in the final week than Johnson in 2019. Sunak's tour of the four nations occurred in week one with no equivalent in the final week. However, of the three leaders, it was Davey who visited the most seats in the final two weeks of the campaign, including a two-nation (England and Scotland) tour of nineteen seats in the week leading to polling day. Davey was clearly on the offensive. Excluding Edinburgh West, the other eighteen seats visited by Davey were where the Liberal Democrats were challenging the incumbent Scottish National Party in Scotland and the Conservatives in England. And the Liberal Democrats won them all in the 2024 election.

Lastly, the final day of campaigning proved to be untypical of past campaigns and ultimately fairly lacklustre. Usually, the last day of the campaign entails a frantic tour of multiple constituencies with leaders criss-crossing different nations of the United Kingdom in a final push for votes. In 2019, Johnson and Corbyn visited six seats while Swinson visited three resulting in disparaging remarks from the press about her dedication to the campaign. However, the final day of the 2024 campaign was comparatively quiet—all three leaders each visited three constituencies. Starmer's final day was most typical, holding activist rallies in Scotland, Wales and England whereas Davey's final day tour through three ultra-safe Conservative-held constituencies reflected the expansionist ambitions of the party. Yet Sunak's final day campaigning proved to be a 'damp squib' confined to ultra-safe Conservative-held seats in the South East of England. His penultimate day of campaigning had a far more typical 'final day' feel, with an early start at an Ocado distribution centre, followed by a stop at a service station, a visit to a supermarket, a visit to a food distribution business, ending with an evening rally in Central London. As such, Sunak's final day of the campaign, with two small activist rallies, a school visit and some leafleting was rather anticlimactic, and gave the sense of the Conservatives running out of steam. The party's campaign also showed the contraction of their ambition. While Sunak had completed visits in all four nations on the first full day of campaigning, the Conservative campaign trail increasingly focused on England. In the final ten days of the campaign, Sunak did not visit a constituency outside England.

3. 2024 leader visits: where did they go?

Evidence from the United States suggests that presidential visits during mid-term elections or the presidential election itself are determined by the competitiveness of the race in a particular state (Herrnson and Morris 2007; Eshbaugh-Soha, and Nicholson-Crotty 2009; Mellen, and Searles 2013). In the UK, early evidence suggested that competitiveness or the marginality of the seat was a decisive factor in whether a leader visits or not (Middleton 2018, 2021). More recent work suggests that leaders do visit seats that are more competitive but not exclusively so and that this differs by party and the electoral context (Middleton 2021; Cutts and Middleton 2024). Visit tactics are now more complex with parties adopting dual targeting strategies, both defending marginally held seats and going on the offensive visiting competitive seats held by opponents within an election (Cutts and Middleton 2024). Fig. 15.1 details which parliamentary constituencies each leader visited by marginality. Simply put, visits reflected the electoral context, with Labour and the Liberal Democrats operating strongly offensive targeting strategies in non-held seats while the Conservatives were heavily defensive, focusing primarily on their incumbent seats. More than 80% of Sunak visits were in seats the party held going into the 2024 election with 50% in constituencies the party held by 20% or more. In terms of battleground status, 55% of Sunak visits were where the Conservatives were defending from Labour. By contrast, 85% of Starmer visits were to target seats where Labour was challenging the incumbent with nearly 50% visits to constituencies where opponents enjoyed a 20% or more advantage

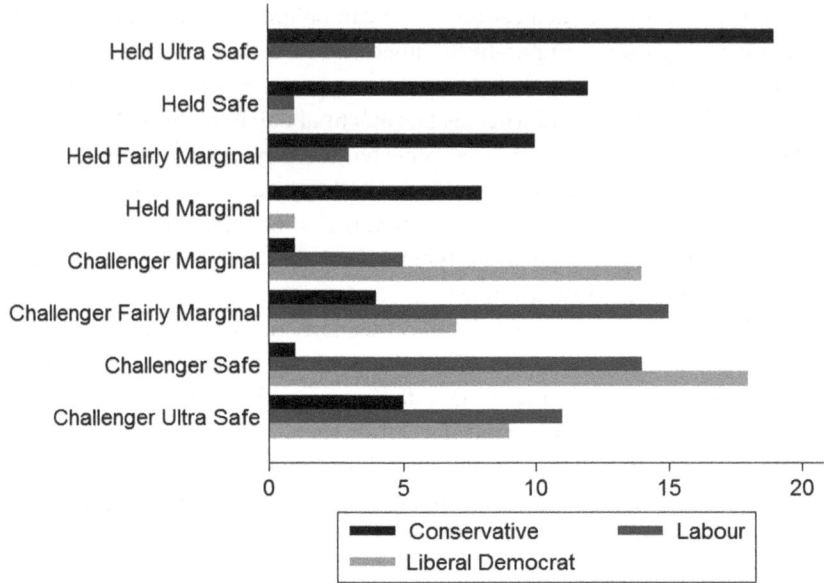

Figure 15.1. 2024 party leader visits by electoral competitiveness
Key: marginal = 0-9.99%; fairly marginal = 10-9.99% safe = 20-9.99%; ultra safe = 30% or more.

going into the election. Of those seats visited by Starmer, 70% were Conservative-Labour battlegrounds. Reflecting the low starting point for the Liberal Democrats, nearly all of Davey's visits were to seats held by their opponents. Like Labour, the Liberal Democrats aggressively targeted Conservative safe seats with 53% of Davey's visits to seats where their opponents held a 20% majority. Moreover, nearly a fifth of seats visited by the Liberal Democrat leader were to Conservative ultra-safe seats which before the election had a notional majority of in excess of 30%. Strikingly, 80% of Davey's visits were in seats where the Conservatives were the incumbents while only 27% of Sunak visits occurred in Conservative-Liberal Democrat contests.

But did the Conservative visit strategy become more defensive as the election campaign got closer to polling day? And is the reverse true for Labour? Broadly speaking, as Fig. 15.2 suggests, the answer is yes. In the final week, thirteen of Sunak's nineteen visits were to seats with a 2019 notional majority of 20% or more. It is worth noting though that roughly 50% of Sunak's visits in the first week were to notionally safe or ultra-safe Conservative seats so it was clear from the offset that the Conservative visit strategy was heavily defensive. Our evidence does suggest a slight shift in strategy during week two to more marginal incumbent Conservative seats before reorienting to safer seats in the middle of the campaign. For instance, across week three and four combined, more than 70% of Sunak's

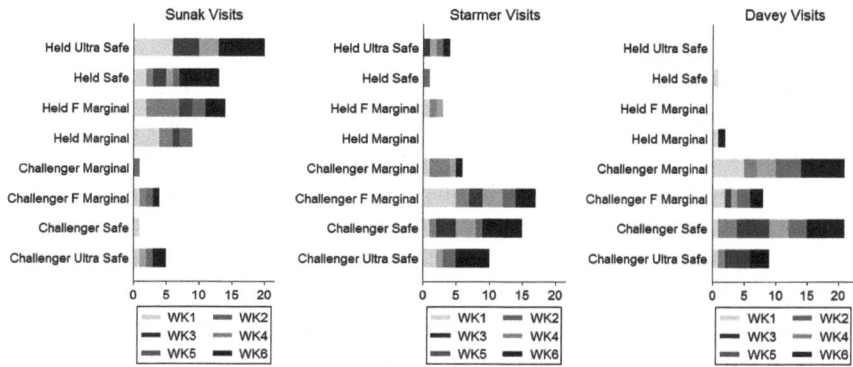

Figure 15.2. 2024 weekly leader visits by electoral competitiveness
Note: Graph is all visits including where the leader visited more than once.

visits were to seats with a 20% majority or more. The Labour strategy, by contrast, was more cautious in the first few weeks with Starmer primarily visiting more marginal Conservative and Scottish National Party held seats and those with a notional majority of less than 20%. However, as the campaign proceeded, Starmer increasingly started to visit safer, predominantly Conservative, seats. In the final week, nearly 80% of Starmer's visits were to safe or ultra-safe Conservative (and one Scottish National Party) notionally held seats. Aside from week three, when Davey principally visited very safe Conservative-Liberal Democrat battlegrounds, generally speaking, the Liberal Democrat visit strategy did not change very much throughout the campaign. Even during the final week, Davey visited Scottish National Party and chiefly Conservative-held seats irrespective of electoral competitiveness, with both extremely marginal and safe target seats on the itinerary.

During the election campaign, 'Red Wall' Conservative candidates accused party strategists of abandoning them and complained that Sunak's visits were focused on defending seats in the South of England (The Guardian 2024). Our evidence suggests that there is some truth to these claims. Sunak visited 35 constituencies in southern England, compared to ten across the North of England including Yorkshire and Humberside. Five years ago, the Conservatives' success in the 'Red Wall' was instrumental in Johnson's landslide victory. In 2024, the Conservatives' retreat from the 'Red Wall' was typified by Sunak's reluctance to visit these seats. The Conservative leader only visited nine 'Red Wall' seats in total (although he visited Redcar twice), five in the final three weeks of the campaign, which was roughly 15% of all visits during this period. Moreover, more than half of 'Red Wall' seats (Conservative and Labour held) were marginal, yet only three of these nine Conservative incumbent seats Sunak visited had notional majorities of less than 10%. Simply put, when Sunak did visit the 'Red Wall' they tended to be notionally safer Conservative-held seats.

Sunak though was not the only party leader to spend little time in these 'Red Wall' seats. Starmer surprisingly only visited six of these seats, all notionally Conservative-held, and actually went to fewer seats across the North of England than Sunak. Instead, a key part of Starmer's visit strategy focused on the Midlands, a key electoral battleground, where more than a quarter of all his leader visits took place and he was noticeably more visible than Sunak. Tellingly, more than 85% of Starmer's visits in the Midlands were to safe seats with majorities of 25% or more. These tactics paid off with Labour making forty-five gains in 2024 across this region including every seat visited by Starmer.

Unsurprisingly given Labour's landslide, Labour won all but two of the seats Starmer visited during the election campaign. Aside from Brighton Pavilion which remained Green, Labour also failed to win the new Caerfyrddin seat in West Wales which while notionally held by the Conservatives actually fell to Plaid Cymru. The Liberal Democrats won forty-four of the fifty seats visited by Davey which included forty from the Conservatives. While Davey primarily visited seats which the party had held in the past, seventeen of these successes visited by the Liberal Democrat leader were seats captured by the party for the first time. Of the seats visited by Sunak, the Conservatives lost forty-seven, thirty-four to Labour and thirteen to the Liberal Democrats. Predictably, just over 60% of the seats held by the Conservatives where Sunak visited had 2019 notional majorities of more than 30% with only one (Harrow East) below 20%. Even so many of these ultra-safe seats (roughly 65%) visited by Sunak fell to opposition parties reflecting the limitations of the Conservatives' defensive campaign.

4. Classifying visits: Sunak and Starmer

In order to understand the campaign trail and interpret party strategy, it is vital to explore the locations within constituencies where leaders go, the tasks they accomplish there, if the actions undertaken by the visiting leader provide opportunities for voter interaction, the extent to which the backdrop of the visit symbolizes a leader's commitment to a particular policy area and who their audiences are. Using the typology derived by Middleton (2021), it is possible to disaggregate these visits into different types by exploring not only the locations visited but also the actions undertaken by party leaders and specifically whether the leaders portray themselves as a winner, campaigner, policymaker or cheerleader. Different types of visits and leaders' engagements with their audiences tell us how they wish to be perceived. Leaders trying to portray themselves as winners will habitually be in front of a background, often relaying the party message, giving a set-piece speech, sometimes flanked by party activists or senior figures. There may be limited questions from the press, but it is chiefly a top-down style of communication. Those leaders who portray themselves as campaigners will adopt the guise of a local candidate during their visit to a constituency, posting leaflets and speaking to voters on the doorstep; although the downside is the risks associated with unstructured encounters with the public. Visits where the leader is showing their commitment to policy areas, will show the leader engaging with employees, perhaps in a question-and-answer session, before touring the location and observing or participating in activities. Lastly, leaders as cheerleaders will use their visit to mobilize the local activist base, by holding rallies and local events.

In 2024, both Sunak and Starmer used some of their visits to perform more than one activity. Sunak performed the most 'dual purpose' visits—for example, on 11th June he launched the Conservative manifesto at Silverstone racetrack before visiting a nearby technical college. Visiting multiple locations within the same constituency has seldom taken place in previous elections. More than 60% of Sunak's visits can be classified as policy-making, where he would highlight specific policy areas by visiting a location, touring its facilities, meeting with workers and occasionally engaging in a question-and-answer session. These were not without controversy. On the first full day of the campaign, Sunak made his way to a biscuit distribution centre in Erewash, an ultra-safe Conservative-held constituency. After touring the facilities, he stood in the warehouse encircled by employees, many of whom were wearing company-branded high-vis jackets. It later emerged that two of the 'employees' were Conservative councillors. Later that same day, in a visit by the teetotal Sunak to a brewery in the Vale of Glamorgan, he sat down with workers after touring the facilities. As part of their conversation, Sunak asked whether they were looking forward to the Euro Football tournament; an unfortunate question, considering that Wales had not qualified. Sunak also engaged in a sizeable number of campaigner-style visits compared to the other two leaders, which are arguably riskier due to the potential for casual encounters with voters. However, Sunak's campaigning style visits were little publicized—two on 23rd June were not picked up by the press, only meriting a single post on Sunak's X. All his campaigner visits were also made during weekends, when media coverage of the campaign was quieter. Activist rallies were a regular feature of Sunak's campaign from the very start (his first event of the campaign was a rally on the evening of the election announcement), occurring approximately once a week. However, he held five in the final week of the campaign, including on the penultimate day, where Johnson made an appearance. While Sunak's policy visits represent a similar proportion to Johnson's in 2019 (62 as opposed to 68% respectively), Sunak spent more time engaging with activists and doing campaigner-style visits. Johnson spent more time positioning himself as a winner.

Including dual-purpose visits, nearly 60% of Starmer's visits were policy-themed, including visits to pubs, ports, hospitals and farms. This is a substantial increase from the 18.3% of Corbyn's visits in 2019 that were policy related and presented a return to a pattern more typical of previous Labour leaders and leaders of the other parties. Whereas the majority of Corbyn's visits in 2019 were focused on engaging local activists, they comprise 32.8% of Starmer's visits; his second largest category. For Starmer, six of the eight local football ground visits he made were activist rallies (plus one cricket ground and one basketball arena). Indeed, Starmer's first visit in the election was to Gillingham football club. While Sunak also held a rally at a football ground, the frequency of Starmer's visits to such locations needs further consideration.

Prior to the election campaign, visiting non-league and league football grounds has been a core feature of Labour's strategy of re-connecting with local communities through listening to grassroots concerns and reaching local people with policy proposals and ideas. As a keen football fan, someone who regularly plays and is known to be an obsessive observer of the game, Starmer spearheaded this approach, drawing on this authentic appeal to build community attachments and spread the party message. His presence in such central community locations symbolically represented the party's commitment to the local area, assisted by multiple large signs on the stands giving the town's name. Using non-league and league stadia also has practical advantages. The election campaign took place in the closed season so the grounds were empty and available for use. Many venues are in a fairly central location to the community, with good access routes. Moreover, they represented safe options, closed from outside streets with locked gates, significantly reducing the risk of Starmer spontaneously encountering an angry member of the public. Unstructured encounters with the public are typically safer to hold in seats amenable to the party (hence Corbyn's large-scale open-air meetings in safe Labour seats), but Starmer's sports ground visits were all held in traditionally safe Conservative areas which in 2024 were battleground seats.

Starmer spent the most time out of the three leaders conducting grandstanding visits designed to showcase him as a national leader, fitting with polling expectations. Both Starmer and Sunak showed some caution in their engagements with the public, with question-and-answer sessions at workplaces the most typical encounter. Such scenarios are structured—sometimes employers or the campaign team will screen questions first, and employees are bound by workplace behavioural norms, with managers watching. The 2024 election mirrored other campaigns whereby retaining control over who leaders encountered became the primary focus. As such, the slow death of the traditional unstructured walkabout among members of the public continued.

5. Classifying visits: the Davey factor

From wheelbarrow racing in Yeovil, falling into the water live on ITV news when attempting to complete a floating assault course in Stratford-on-Avon, to bungee jumping from a crane shouting 'Do something you've never done before' in Eastbourne, Ed Davey's exploits 'tore up' the conventional approach to leaders' visits. Even when compared to Johnson's 2019 election antics of driving a bulldozer into a brick wall spelling out 'Get Brexit Done', delivering milk in Pudsey and taking his 'oven ready Brexit Beef and Ale pie' out of the oven in Derby, Davey's approach appeared to be on another level. On the one hand, when talking to the media after doing an aqua-aerobics class in Cheltenham or hula hooping in Edinburgh West, Davey was not shy to say he was having fun and not taking himself too seriously. Unsurprisingly Davey drew criticism from commentators on the right of the political spectrum with claims that the use of stunts was 'deeply cynical' (Unherd, 13th June 2024) while Quentin Letts in the *Daily Mail* described Davey's speech and manifesto launch as "emotively manipulative pieces of saccharine hucksterism" before questioning the visit to Thorpe Park for photo opportunities (The *Daily Mail*, 10th June 2024). But to characterize Davey's campaign as a 'six week jolly' demeans what proved to be carefully thought through and ultimately successful electoral strategy.

Throughout the late 1990s and 2000s, the Liberal Democrats often made headway during the election campaign as their leaders and policies got more exposure. This enhanced credibility with exposure contributing to the party converting votes into seats which then led to significant representation in Westminster. To replicate these previous strong electoral performances, the Liberal Democrats knew that it was imperative that the party gained maximum exposure in the 'six week' 2024 campaign window in order to cut-through and convince voters they were a credible alternative to the Conservatives in key battlegrounds.

Yet after going into coalition with the Conservatives in 2010, the Liberal Democrats suffered near electoral annihilation with subsequent attempts to revive the party to the levels of representation achieved during the mid-2000s proving highly unsuccessful. Post-2019, with few Westminster MPs, little airtime and Brexit decided (thereby neutering an issue where the Liberal Democrats had policy recognition) the path forward appeared unclear. However with the Liberal Democrats' electoral fortunes not lying in their own hands but instead dependent on the failure of one the mainstream parties, the party was about to get a political lifeline (Cutts, Russell, and Townsley 2023). With the Conservatives in a downward spiral, the Liberal Democrats started to make electoral progress both at the local level and through a series of significant by-election successes. And the party, with Davey at the forefront, began to use stunts to celebrate these wins and publicize their growing electoral credibility. For instance, following their success in the Chesham and Amersham by-election, live on the BBC, Davey used an orange hammer to knock down a wall of blue cardboard boxes to signify that the Liberal Democrats were starting to smash through the 'blue wall' of traditional Conservative strongholds. Then later in the Parliament after winning Glastonbury and Somerton from the Conservatives, Davey stood beside a mock circus cannon emblazoned with the phrase 'Get these clowns out of No 10!' as it fired yellow confetti to celebrate the by-election success.

With credibility the key to Liberal Democrat success, it was no surprise to see similar tactics used during the general election campaign – knocking down blue dominos in Taunton and Wellington and a game of political Jenga in Eastleigh. Yet after the game of political Jenga, Davey used the media interviews to highlight the party's manifesto pledges to clamp down on sewage dumping water companies by recruiting 100 new water quality inspectors, setting up a new regulator to replace Ofwat and various policies to reduce pollution in rivers, lakes and seas. Amidst the fun and frolics, Davey argued that such stunts came with a serious message. This example typified the Liberal Democrats' leader visit strategy. Simply put, the visits fused stunts with salient issues to which Davey himself and the party would get exposure and recognition through the promotion of party policy. It put Davey in the spotlight, which given the perceived dullness of the two main leaders and the marmite figure of Nigel Farage, seemed a political gamble worth taking. Moreover, it also tackled head-on public criticisms about the party's identity and where it stood on policy.

Davey's visits are therefore particularly difficult to classify compared to the two other leaders. As noted above, the Liberal Democrat leader's campaign trail was characterized by a series of stunts more akin to the party's celebrations after by-election victories than their usual campaign trail. There was a sole leader as winner visit, held in North London, with Ed Davey speaking in front of some of the party's candidates. There was also a sole campaigner visit as Davey went canvassing in Bath on 29th May. Davey engaged with activists for a quarter of his visits, which is comparable to Swinson in 2019. Most of these were open-air activist rallies, but also included dog walks with candidates and playing giant Jenga in front of activists. However, 60% of his visits can be classified broadly as policy focused which included typical visit locations, such as schools, care homes and farms. Many, however, were designed for the newsworthiness, with Davey throwing himself into a variety of activities such as aqua-aerobics, completing an assault course or enthusiastically participating in old-fashioned swing dancing. Whereas some of these can be understood in the context of existing categories (falling repeatedly into the water at an aqua assault course can nonetheless be understood as a visit to a business and using its facilities), some are too outside the norms of the campaign trail to classify as anything other than stunts. What is notable is that many of the visits Davey paid to the more conventional locations conveyed a very different tone than Sunak and Starmer's visits—more hands on and more humorous.

Whereas Starmer visited a hospital, chatted to staff and spoke to patients in their beds, Davey washed an ambulance or performed CPR on a dummy. This echoes some of the tone of Johnson's campaign in 2019. Unlike Swinson in 2019, Davey openly conceded he was extremely unlikely to be a candidate for Prime Minister. As such, while Sunak and Starmer had to appear prime ministerial, Davey had more freedom to attract attention to his party's campaign.

6. Policy-themed visits

Disaggregating policy-focused visits into particular themes reveals much about the policy priorities of a leader's campaign. The inherent symbolism of the backdrop that is chosen matters as it speedily communicates to those encountering images of the visit. Using Middleton's (2021) classification of business, healthcare, education and community visits as a template, it is clear that the majority of policy-related visits by all three leaders follow the convention that business receives the greatest proportion of visits (see Fig. 15.3). Roughly 63% of Starmer's policy-related visits were to businesses including farms and builders' yards, compared to just 29% for Corbyn in 2019. This highlights how unconventional Corbyn's visit strategy was. Sunak made 47 visits that related to policy, including four that were coupled with cheerleading or campaigning activities. Of these forty-seven policy visits, three saw Sunak visit two different policy locations in

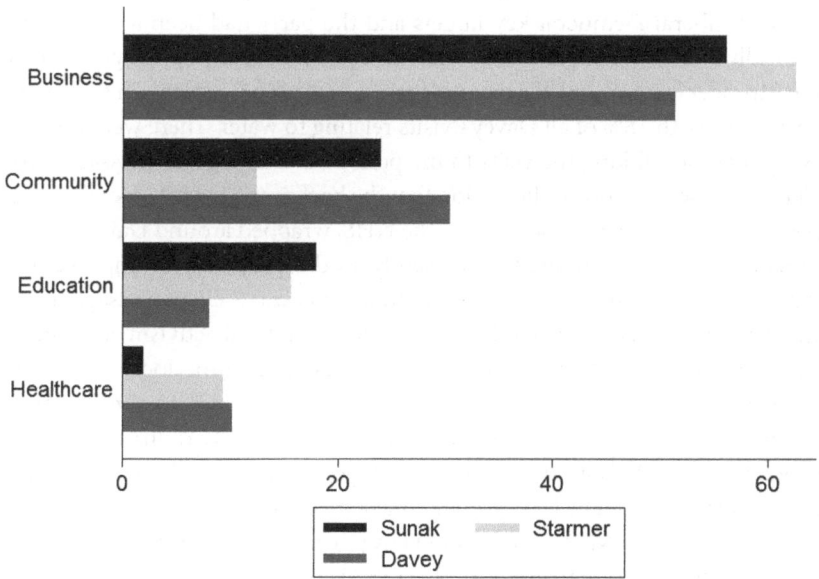

Figure 15.3. 2024 Campaign trail: policy-themed visits (%)

the same seat; for example, on 30th June he visited a synagogue and a bakery in Finchley and Golders Green. More than half of these policy visits saw Sunak visit business premises, including several visits to food outlets to buy provisions for the journalists accompanying him on the battle bus. Davey made fewer visits to educational establishments than the other two leaders. Compared to Johnson, Sunak visited businesses less frequently and community organizations (such as religious establishments) more frequently.

There is one notable difference in Sunak's policy-related visits compared not only to the other leaders in 2024, but also to their counterparts in 2019. Healthcare is a key issue in British politics—during the 2024 campaign it competed and sometimes headed the economy as the most important issue for voters (Ipsos 2024). Healthcare-related visits primarily encompass visits to NHS facilities such as hospitals, GP practices or other service-facing locations such as care homes or medical schools. Starmer and Davey spent almost 10% of their policy-themed visits in exactly these types of healthcare settings. Yet, despite speaking of the pride he had in being the son of a GP and a pharmacist, Sunak made only one healthcare-related visit over the course of the entire campaign. It was not to a pharmacy or a hospital but to a privately owned pharmaceutical distribution warehouse. All other leaders in 2024 and 2019 visited multiple healthcare sites, including Johnson who managed to visit four such locations. This clear disconnect between Sunak's visit locations and the policy priorities of the British public foreshadows the Conservative defeat.

Policies to deter sewage dumping and prevent water pollution were salient in a number of Liberal Democrat key targets and the party had been at the vanguard both locally and nationally over the electoral cycle mounting campaigns and advocating stronger action and deterrents against water companies. This provided a thematic cue, with 18% of all Davey's visits relating to water. There were no accompanying speeches linking the visits to the policy but the targeted message through media interviews reinforced the notion that the backdrops to visits are symbolically chosen. The party's flagship policies on the NHS, wrapped around Davey's personal experiences as a carer, featured prominently, as did proposals to improve mental health, education, farming and rural life. In most cases, the key message from the stunt-issue-policy visit matched the location based on local activism and data from the visit setting. So, policy messages could be tailored to the local contest while the broader national message was aimed at influencing voters in similar constituencies who share related concerns. Davey's stunts seemingly didn't do the Liberal Democrats harm. With around two weeks to go to election, a YouGov poll found that more Britons thought Davey would make a better Prime Minister than Sunak (YouGov 2024a). And when asked about Davey's campaign style, voters were slightly more favourable (26%) than unfavourable (23%), although crucially he was the only leader to get a net positive rating from voters (YouGov 2024b).

7. Conclusion

Where leaders go on the campaign trail, why they go there and what they do can tell us a lot about a party's strategy during the election campaign. By comparing visits over time we can also determine whether changes in the campaign trail are contextual or reflect discernible trends in how leaders campaign. Broadly speaking, our key findings show that the Conservatives and Labour leaders' 2024 campaign trails mirrored the national electoral context. Sunak ran a highly defensive campaign with nearly 60% of seats visited located in the South of England, irking many of his 'Red Wall' MPs. Despite starting the campaign at a pace, the frequency of Sunak's visits faded quickly as the dire electoral reality dawned. For Starmer, the campaign trail was all about showing the public he and Labour was ready for government. Visits were overwhelmingly expansionist, targeting Conservative and to a certain extent Scottish National Party seats, but they were carefully stage-managed, cautious in scope and like visits by leaders in recent elections, very conventional. Davey's stunts provided the main gear change in the campaign trail and largely stole the show. He made the Liberal Democrats visible on the issues that mattered to their target audience and crucially these were focused in seats that they needed to win to return to the top table of British politics. And it worked handsomely for the party.

Despite clear contextual differences and changes in leadership, there are some parallels between 2024 and 2019. Visits are now mostly closed-door affairs, with unstructured walkabouts and encounters with the public increasingly rare. Policy-related visits to businesses remained popular with leaders from all parties but Sunak's avoidance of hospitals and NHS primary care practices on the campaign trail is a notable anomaly. Theresa May was the only other sitting Prime Minister who has failed to visit the NHS during a campaign. The use of lower league football grounds as a setting for visits proved to be a novel development although these were carefully choreographed to avoid wider public encounters. Fundamentally though, of the three leaders, and in marked contrast to Corbyn in 2019, it was Starmer who was most likely to conduct grandstanding visits designed to showcase him as a national leader and a winner.

But do leader visits impact electoral outcomes? Previous evidence suggests they do although the effects are modest (Middleton 2021; Cutts and Middleton 2024). Further work is needed to determine whether this holds in 2024 but with parties increasingly looking to influence not only the outcome in the seats visited but those nearby and the leaders' campaign trail not only relayed on mainstream media but also through a plethora of social media platforms, the salience of the leader on electoral outcomes, part of which is through campaign visits, may be more impactful than we think.

References

Cutts, D. and Middleton, A. (2024) 'Where do they go and Why, How do they Vary and what is Their Impact: Assessing Leaders' Campaign Visits in England 2010-19', *Political Studies*, 73: 657–81.

Cutts, D., Russell, A. and Townsley, J. (2023) *The Liberal Democrats: From Hope to Despair to Where?* Manchester: Manchester University Press.

Daily Mail (2024) 'The Lib Dems' launch was one of the most emotively manipulative pieces of saccharine hucksterism I've had thrust down my gullet', https://www.dailymail.co.uk/debate/article-13515065/QUENTIN-LETTS-Lib-Dem-manifesto-general-election.html, accessed 10 Sept. 2024.

Eshbaugh-Soha, M. and Nicholson-Crotty, S. (2009) 'Presidential Campaigning During Midterm Elections', *American Review of Politics*, 30: 35–50.

Guardian (2024) "'Red Wall' Tory candidates lament lack of party support amid focus on southern England', https://www.theguardian.com/politics/article/2024/jun/19/red-wall-tory-candidates-lament-lack-of-party-support-as-it-focuses-on-south, accessed 8 Aug. 2024.

Herrnson, P. and Morris, I. (2007) 'Presidential Campaigning in the 2002 Congressional Elections', *Legislative Studies Quarterly*, 32: 629–48.

Ipsos (2024) 'Ipsos Issues Index', https://www.ipsos.com/sites/default/files/ct/news/documents/2024-06/Issues%20Index_June_v1_PUBLIC.pdf, accessed 10 Sept. 2024.

Mellen, R. and Searles, K. (2013) 'Predicting Presidential Appearances During Midterm Elections: The President and House Candidates, 1982-2010', *American Politics Research*, 41: 328–47.

Middleton, A. (2018) 'For the Many, Not the Few': Strategising the Campaign Trail at the 2017 Election', *Parliamentary Affairs*, 72: 501–21.

Middleton, A. (2021) *Communicating and Strategising Leadership in British Elections: Follow the Leader?* Cham, Switzerland: Palgrave Macmillan.

Unherd (2024) 'Ed Davey's stunt campaign is deeply cynical', https://unherd.com/newsroom/ed-daveys-stunt-campaign-is-deeply-cynical/, accessed 10 Sept. 2024.

YouGov (2024a) 'General Election: Britons say Ed Davey would be a better PM than Rishi Sunak', https://yougov.co.uk/politics/articles/49805-general-election-britons-say-ed-davey-would-be-better-pm-than-rishi-sunak, accessed 8 Aug. 2024.

YouGov (2024b) 'How well did Ed Davey's campaign go down?' https://yougov.co.uk/politics/articles/49958-how-well-did-ed-daveys-campaign-go-down, accessed 8 Aug. 2024.

An inexperienced parliament

Philip Cowley*

School of Politics and International Relations, Queen Mary University of London, 1 Westfield Way, Bethnal Green, London, E1 4PD, UK

*Correspondence: p.cowley@qmul.ac.uk

When Labour MPs gathered for their first meeting after the general election, there was no room of sufficient size in the Palace of Westminster to house them all. Instead, they crowded into the General Synod's room in Church House, just up the road, where they were addressed by the Chief Whip. The number of new MPs was so great that he began by noting that while normally he would ask how they were, this time he felt he needed to ask: 'who are you'? That was in 1997, the last time Labour entered government, and it is easy to see 2024 as 1997 *redux*. Elected after a prolonged period in opposition, the Parliamentary Labour Party (PLP) then was of record-breaking size—albeit based on what historically would not have been a massive share of the electorate; many accounts of the 1997 General Election focussed on the extent to which it had been an anti-Conservative event, with relatively little enthusiasm for Labour. Across the chamber, they faced a shattered Conservative parliamentary party, who sat on the opposition benches alongside resurgent Liberal Democrats. The new government's manifesto had been marked by its cautious nature; in terms of parliamentary reform, it promised House of Lords reform and a committee to modernize parliament.

Another key feature of the 1997 General Election was the very high degree of parliamentary turnover. Some 40% of MPs then elected were new to the Commons, breaking all post-war records back to 1945; on the government benches the figure reached 44% (Criddle 1997: 186). In 2024 when the PLP crowded back into the same room in Church House (again, no room in the Commons was big enough), every word of the above applied—just more so. The 2024 General Election brought in 335 new MPs to the Commons, more than half the House. (The figure is sometimes quoted as 350, but this includes the fifteen Labour and Liberal Democrat

© The Author(s) 2025. Published by Oxford University Press on behalf of the Hansard Society. All rights reserved. For commercial re-use, please contact reprints@oup.com for reprints and translation rights for reprints. All other permissions can be obtained through our RightsLink service via the Permissions link on the article page on our site—for further information please contact journals.permissions@oup.com.

'retreads', MPs in a previous parliament now returning to the Commons again). Just as in 1997, the government benches were even more inexperienced: a full 56% of MPs sitting on the Labour benches were elected for the first time in 2024. This record number of newbies was the result of a very high level of retirements prior to, combined with an extremely high level of defeats at, the general election. A total of 132 incumbent MPs had chosen not to stand again; prior to 2024, the post-war (median) average was seventy-four. The number of retirements in 2024 was higher even than the comparable figures for 1997 (117) or 1945 (129), albeit slightly lower than the post-war record seen in 2010 following the expenses scandal (149) (Criddle 2010: 307).

On top of the retirements, however, were the 218 sitting MPs who lost their seats. This figure topped every election back until 1931. There had previously only been two post-war elections in which more than 100 MPs had lost their seats (1945 and 1979); no post-war contest had seen more than 200 fall. Combined, the total of 350 departures was the greatest of any election back to, and including, 1918. In itself, this level of turnover was remarkable. The Commons normally changes membership gradually, a smallish cohort of new MPs arriving in the House alongside a mass of returning Members. The other demographic changes to the Commons seen in 2024—as discussed elsewhere in this volume—may be more obviously visible, but the turnover in membership may be at least as, if not more, consequential.

And if anything these headline figures understate the levels of inexperience in the new House of Commons. Because even among those who were *re*-elected in 2024, the amount of parliamentary experience was not great. This reflects the turmoil of recent years—multiple elections, many seeing dramatic results—as well as a more general sense that parliamentary careers are speeding up, with MPs choosing to serve in the Commons for shorter periods of time (Cowley 2022).[1] Even of the MPs elected in 2024 who *had* previously sat in the House of Commons, more than half had under a decade's experience in parliament.

Table 16.1 illustrates this in more detail. It shows the levels of parliamentary experience of the MPs in the Commons after the election, broken down by the era of entry and by whether the MPs sit on the government or opposition side of the House. Just a handful of MPs date back to 1983, including the Father of the House, Sir Edward Leigh. The Mother of the House, Diane Abbott, was first elected in 1987. But these are the outliers. Just 2% of MPs entered parliament before the Blair landslide of 1997 and just over one in ten MPs were in parliament during the Blair/

---

[1] As part of this phenomenon, we might note that the new Prime Minister first became leader of his party after a mere five years in the Commons. The new Leader of the Opposition, chosen by her party in late-2024, had just seven years under her belt, in which time she had managed to take part in *two* leadership contests. This is far from the post-war norm.

Table 16.1. Parliamentary experience of MPs, 2024

Era of entry	Labour		Opposition		Total	
	N	%	N	%	N	%
Con (1983–97)	5	1.2	10	4.2	15	2.3
Lab (1997–2010)	33	8.0	20	8.4	53	8.2
Con (2010–24)	142	34.5	105	43.9	247	38.0
Lab (2024–)	231	56.2	104	43.5	335	51.5
Total	411	100.0	239	100.0	650	100.0

Source: adapted from the data in Cracknell and Baker (2024).

Brown years or earlier. Almost 90% of MPs have not been in parliament during a Labour government.

Almost 40% of MPs were elected under the Conservative or Conservative-led governments from 2010 onwards and a full 80% were first elected in 2017 or after. The vast majority of the House of Commons has at most seven years of parliamentary experience; almost all the government MPs have never experienced government before; most of the opposition MPs have no experience of opposition.[2]

This chapter discusses the possible consequences of these changes in the parliamentary landscape—albeit with the caveat that prediction is very difficult, as Niels Bohr is believed to have said, 'especially about the future'. In some areas, there are obvious lessons to be learnt from previous parliaments. Yet even when the similarities are obvious, as with 1997, there are plenty of differences as well.

1. The fragmentation of the opposition

One reason why it may be difficult to read too many lessons from the past into current events is that what we see in the Commons today differs from most of the recent past in multiple ways. It is not just that this level of parliamentary turnover is way above the norm. The 2024 election also saw a government with a clear working majority replaced by another with a clear working majority. It was the first time that this had happened since the election of 1970—which had been the only previous occasion in post-war history. The new government's formal majority of 172 was also extremely large and almost identical to the record-breaking

---

[2]Similarly, among the Liberal Democrats, there are just four who were in the Commons before 2010—that is, the last time the party was the third largest party and in opposition.

majority achieved by Tony Blair in 1997 (then 179, but with a slightly larger House of Commons).[3] Majorities of this scale are also very rare.

Yet this does not tell the full story either. Also important is the balance on the opposition benches, which is now significantly different from any other parliament for a century. The 121 Conservative MPs elected in 2024 constituted a record low dating back to 1832. They sit on the opposition benches alongside a total of 118 other MPs who are not Conservative. This is yet another post-war record. The Conservatives, in other words, make up a bare majority (51%) of the Opposition.

Compare that to 1997; there were then seventy-five non-Conservative opposition MPs and 165 Tories. In 2001, the figures were eighty and 166. And in 2005—which until this election held the post-war record for the parliament with the largest number of MPs not from the two main parties—there were ninety-two, compared to 198 Conservatives. In other words, in each of these cases, the main opposition party outnumbered other opposition MPs by 2:1. That is no longer true. Relatedly, the third party is now much closer in size to the second; there are now fewer than two Tory MPs for every Liberal Democrat. Overall, this is a parliamentary layout much more like it would have been in the 1920s. It is not a parliament with which anyone alive today has any experience.

This presents a series of issues. It is a problem for the House of Commons in terms of the adequate representation of the diverse voices of the Opposition. The Commons is essentially set up to represent the Government and Opposition. It privileges the main opposition party, at the expense of the other opposition parties (Thompson 2020: 36). This is at its most obvious at Prime Minister's Questions, where the Leader of the Opposition gets six questions per week, the leader of the third party just two, but it also manifests itself repeatedly elsewhere. This is much more easily justified when the second party has, say, ten times or more the number of MPs of the third party; it is harder to justify when the ratio dips below 2:1.

The reduced Conservative rump will also cause a problem merely for the Official Opposition to function properly. Reflecting on his own experience of trying to form an opposition frontbench from a much diminished Conservative Party in 1997, William Hague noted: 'once I had excluded all those who were too new, too old, too mad or too opposed to the leadership, there weren't many more from whom to choose' (Hague 2024).[4] Hague limited his frontbench to what he thought was a bare minimum of around 70 MPs, but even then he found it difficult

---

[3] In this, and all that follows, I use the figures for MPs as elected on election night. In practice the numbers are often slightly different—the Sinn Féin MPs do not take their seats; MPs will lose the whip; the Deputy Speakers do not vote; by-elections will change the composition of the House—and so de facto figures will differ and anyway will vary across the parliament. But for comparability, it is best to discuss the raw numbers.
[4] As someone who experienced the sharp end of opposition after 1997, Hague's article is very good on the many other problems that come from such a lopsided House.

to find the right MPs—and he had around one-third more MPs to choose from than Kemi Badenoch. It was notable that even in her much-reduced frontbench every single member of the 2024 Conservative intake was given a job.[5] This is a problem for the management of the Conservatives as a party, but it should also cause a concern about the quality of scrutiny that will be offered by such a reduced opposition.

The fragmentation on the opposition benches will also prove an even more direct benefit for the government. The government's nominal majority may have been be around 170 at the election, but in practice it is frequently much higher. In the first ninety-one whipped votes it averaged 238 and only fell below 200 on thirty-six occasions. It is difficult to find issues around which the varied interests and beliefs of the opposition parties will coalesce, ones that will unite the disparate aims of the Liberal Democrats, the Greens, Reform UK and the Conservatives. It will happen, but such votes will be rare, and on day-to-day issues, the run-of-the-mill stuff that makes parliament function, the government will enjoy a much larger majority than it appears to have on paper. There may occasionally be issues for the government whips in knowing what each party is doing but for the most part, things will be fairly straightforward in terms of winning votes in the Commons. Keir Starmer's de jure majority may be marginally smaller than that enjoyed by Tony Blair, but in practice, it will almost certainly be the largest since 1945. While this may be good news for the government, it is also probably less good news for the quality of parliamentary scrutiny of legislation.[6]

Moreover, if anything, we might expect further fragmentation as the parliament goes on. One of the other distinguishing features of recent years has been the willingness of party leaderships to remove the whip from MPs. What used to be a nuclear option—to be used extremely rarely—has now become almost routine, with the whip being removed for both deviations from the party line in the voting lobbies on a scale that would have been unrecognizable previously but also for the wider behaviour of parliamentarians. Already, at the time of writing, less than six months after the election, the "independents" have become the fourth largest grouping in the House, comprising more MPs than the SNP.

---

[5]They can't all be that good.

[6]The only caveat to this is that once it becomes obvious to Labour MPs that the majorities are, in practice, so much larger than on paper, some will—just as happened after 1997—begin to resent being asked to stay late for votes when they might have other demands on their time. But if attendance in divisions begins to be seen as optional, it becomes a problem for the whips when one of the more crucial votes comes along. But these can be described as first world whipping problems.

2.Promotions and patronage

If Kemi Badenoch's problem is that she does not have a full pack of cards from which to draw, Keir Starmer's is that he has too many. The amount of patronage that is available to the party managers does not grow in proportion to the size of the parliamentary party. More MPs automatically means more disappointed and disgruntled MPs. As one party insider put it in 1997, despairingly shrugging his shoulders, with so many MPs 'what the fuck do you do?' (Cowley 2002: 11).

Not all of the new MPs will be ambitious for office, but most will be. If left on the backbenches for too long, that ambition could easily generate bitterness and discontent. But promoting them quickly just causes other problems. Because when the new MPs are promoted that in turn just generates bitterness from others—from those who have been passed over or who have to make way for them. This is not a problem peculiar to this government—it is a problem of party management that all governments have faced—but it is especially stark this time, both because of the size of the parliamentary party and because the intakes are so lopsided.

Immediately after the election six of the new intake were promoted directly to the frontbench. Such speedy promotion had not been seen since the young Harold Wilson was made a minister in 1945. Other new MPs were immediately made parliamentary private secretaries (PPSs). In part, this was a recognition of the talents of the new ministers and a recognition that among the new intake, there were some very able MPs.[7] But it put some noses out of joint, especially among longer-serving MPs who had done the hard yards of opposition and had expected to be rewarded for their service. Several found themselves with lesser or in some cases no jobs, scant reward for the unglamorous work of opposition. Even some of the other new MPs found themselves wondering why those particular six were chosen. Within the next few years, many more of the other 225 new MPs will need promoting and there will be a lot more of the older MPs who see their ministerial careers ending earlier than they might think justified.

In return, several members of the new intake put themselves forward to be chairs of the Commons departmental select committees despite having only been in parliament for several weeks. Only one was successful—Patricia Ferguson becoming chair of the Scottish Affairs Committee, and in a case where her competition was also from the 2024 intake—but rather like Dr Johnson's dog walking on its hind legs, it was more surprising that it was being done at all. Again, some noses were put out by this; their candidacies, according to one report, had gone down 'like a bucket of cold sick'.[8] But it was an example of the problems that such a large new intake will cause.

---

[7] Alistair Carns, Miatta Fahnbulleh, Hamish Falconer, Georgia Gould, Kirsty McNeill and Sarah Sackman.
[8] The source is Stacey (2024), drawing on a Politico report. But it was not difficult to find MPs rolling their eyes at the candidacies.

There are no easy answers to any of this. To expand the scope of patronage, the government have tried appointing people to (what some see as) Potemkin jobs – 'mission leads' and 'regional leads' – but there is a limit to how many of these can be created or how much good they will do. It all requires delicate handling. If people are good enough, why shouldn't they be promoted? And just because MPs served on the frontbench in opposition, when there were fewer MPs, why should that guarantee them a job when in government once more MPs are available to choose from? Perhaps ministerial promotion – or chairing a select committee – should not just be Buggins' turn. But party management also involves some *realpolitik*. Hundreds of MPs who feel disappointed and hard done by become a serious problem for party management. Disgruntled ex-ministers, who know all the tricks of government, and can act as the catalysts for discontent, can be especially damaging. One more experienced MP suspected this may be what eventually starts to cause serious backbench difficulties: 'Disappointment will be more of a driver than ideology'.[9]

3. Intra-party dissent

The relationship between the front and backbench has been a problem for every Labour administration—and a problem that has been getting worse. Every period of the Labour government since the Second World War saw more backbench rebellions than the one before. Between 1945 and 1951, there were eighty-four occasions when at least one Labour MP defied their whip; that rose to 110 between 1964 and 1970 and hit 317 between 1974 and 1979 (Norton 1975, 1980). The Blair/Brown years then saw over 700 rebellions; the 2005 Parliament alone witnessed more Labour revolts than the 1974-79 period (Cowley 2005; Cowley and Stuart 2014).

In part, this is reflective of a more general increasing willingness by MPs to be independent-minded. It is not just Labour MPs who have been willing to defy their whips; every recent Conservative Chief Whip has the scars to prove that. The high point of parliamentary cohesion came in the 1950s—there were two whole sessions when not a single government MP voted against the party line (Norton 1975)—since when life has been getting tougher for the whips of all parties.

The good news for Labour's whips is that there are several factors which should militate against backbench dissent being too serious, at least in the short term. For one, the party is coming out of an extended period in opposition. Few things focus the mind as much as a spell out of government. In 1997, for example, it had the effect of installing in many Labour MPs a desire not to rock the boat, well

---

[9] Any unsourced quotations are from MPs to the author.

aware of the damage that indiscipline and the appearance of division can do to a party's prospects. Plus, to begin with, the party will be implementing a manifesto on which it secured its election victory, and this carries weight with MPs. Victory alone normally means some MPs are more trusting of the leadership, especially those who might well feel they owe the leadership their seats. 'If it wasn't for Tony, you wouldn't be here', some MPs were told in 1997 (Cowley 2002).

The size of the new intake will be an important part of this, at least initially. New MPs tend to be less rebellious and more willing to toe the party line. They have their careers ahead of them; they can be less cynical about the workings of parliament and politics in general; they are more trusting of ministers. And while in 1997 the large new intake brought in many MPs who had not been rigorously vetted by the party leadership—dismissed by one insider at the time as 'flotsam and jetsam'—another crucial difference with today is that because the scale of the 2024 landslide was more widely expected, Labour had this time engaged in far more rigorous (and ruthless) ideological vetting of would-be candidates. There were relatively few surprises in the new intake and almost none who we can easily identify as obvious trouble-makers for the leadership.

Yet none of this is a Get Out of Jail Free card for the government, and even a cursory knowledge of the election of 2024 suggests that these factors may not be quite as positive for the government as we might normally expect. In the medium-term, as noted above, the sheer size of the new intake presents problems in terms of managing their careers and those of the more well-established MPs. The coattail effect also never lasts all that long; it was less than a year after the 2019 election that Boris Johnson was complaining to the Chair of the 1922 Committee about the behaviour of many of the MPs elected in 2019 (Brady 2024: 191). And the evidence that Labour MPs owe their seats to Keir Starmer may not be self-evident to all of them; many may feel they owe Rishi Sunak rather more.

Moreover, while the shallow nature of Labour's electoral victory, discussed by Eunice Goes in this volume, will not have a massive impact on day-to-day workings in the Commons—the votes of MPs elected with slim majorities or on a small minority of the vote count in the division lobbies as much as anyone else—Labour MPs are mostly aware of the electoral realities behind their victory. Labour MPs elected in 1997 worried primarily about the Conservatives. Today, in addition to the Conservatives, many of them are also variously concerned about Reform UK, the Greens, or a potential independent challenge.[10] 'Nobody wants to be the next Jonathan Ashworth', as one put it. The nature of this threat varies from MP to MP and from seat to seat; some will have no fears of being the next Jonathan Ashworth, but they will not want to be the next Thangam Debbonaire; others will be very aware of the possible threat from Reform UK, either directly in seats where

---

[10]But not especially the Liberal Democrats.

Reform UK are in second place or more generally in terms of a coalescence of right-of-centre vote. As one MP put it: 'Everyone's got a bogeyman'. This will not be a huge issue immediately, but when governments become unpopular (as they always do), MPs in the more marginal seats can be tempted to vote against their party whip, as an exercise in differentiating themselves from their party, to curry favour with voters. There is little evidence this works electorally (see for example Umit and Cowley 2023), but that does not usually stop them.

Indeed, the signs that Labour could face backbench difficulties began very early, with unease over the King's Speech. An SNP amendment criticizing the maintenance of the two-person benefit cap attracted support on the Labour benches. The government took a hard line, and when seven Labour MPs voted against it, they had the whip removed.[11] This was a significant ramping up of disciplinary practice. Similar threats were made on a later amendment about the removal of winter fuel payments in September 2024.[12] Again, there were dire warnings of MPs having the whip removed from them if they voted against it. In the event, just one Labour MP voted against it (while keeping the whip), although many others are believed to have abstained.

The concern of the party managers will not have been the fate of votes this early in the parliament because they know they can and will win those easily.[13] The concern is more about what happens in the future. Rebellion is habit-forming. It often starts with a principled vote on an issue of deep concern but it never ends there. The approach taken was about keeping the number of rebels as small as possible for as long as possible, trying to inculcate a culture of cohesion rather than allowing the habit of rebellion to spread.

In the short-term (as of the time of writing), it does appear to have worked. Both votes saw far fewer backbench rebels than might otherwise have been expected—none of them from the new intake. But it must be more doubtful that it will work in the medium or long-term, which is where it matters. All the evidence from recent parliaments is that threats can only go so far. Indeed, one problem with taking such a hard line this early in the parliament is that it can store up problems for later on. The problem is not just those who have been suspended (or, if it comes to it, expelled); there will also be a problem with those MPs, larger in

---

[11]The seven were suspended, with the suspension being widely reported as being for six months. In fact, it was for a *minimum* of six months, after which it would be reviewed, which is rather different.
[12]In many ways, this vote was a tougher test for the whips. This policy had not been in the manifesto and unlike the vote on the King's Speech vote the amendment was not merely declaratory but would have had direct policy impact.
[13]For example, the SNP amendment was defeated by 363 MPs to 103, the winter fuel payment by 348 votes to 228.

number, who have reluctantly toed the line and feel resentful about it, especially if they get grief from constituents or (even worse) local activists. They may bite their tongue now, but it may not last.

4. Parliamentary reform

Another of the direct parallels with 1997 was the manifesto commitment to establish a Modernisation Committee, to reform the Commons, 'tasked with reforming House of Commons procedures, driving up standards, and improving working practices'. The composition of the new Committee is itself a sign of the growing inexperience in the Commons. The equivalent committee established in 1997 consisted of MPs with an average of fifteen years in parliament each; nine of them had sat for twenty or more years; and the Chair had first entered the Commons in 1974.[14] In the committee established after 2024, the average experience was five years; just three MPs had been in the Commons for more than ten. Six came from the 2024 intake.

This is an area where some may see the relative inexperience of the new House—and the Committee—as an advantage. With smaller new intakes, it is relatively easy for the incoming MPs to be socialised into existing practices.[15] With so many new MPs, however, there could develop a critical mass eager for parliamentary reform. It became clear soon after the election that many of the new intake were frustrated with the way parliament functioned and were eager for change.

Still, it is worth being a bit sceptical here. For one thing, there will be pushback from some of the more established MPs. 'They tell me they want to change it all. Good luck with that!', as one MP put it. Or: 'Maybe you should try being here for a while before you start trying to change it', as another complained.

Perhaps more significantly, while there may well be reform, there will be questions about its nature. The story of Commons modernisation in the Blair and Brown governments was distinctly mixed. The Modernisation Committee certainly achieved reform (Fleming, and Kelly 2024). More debatable was what that reform achieved. Part of the problem then – and it will be true now – was that the word modernization was meaningless. As Richard Rose pointed out in 2001, the term 'shows a preference for what is new rather than what is old, and for change against the status quo. But it did not identify what direction change should take'

---

[14] Calculated from the date of first entry into the Commons. In a handful of cases there was some periods of broken service.

[15] This is also seen in the repeated difficulties some members of the new intake appear to have to master fairly basic aspects of parliamentary practice and procedure—presumably because there are fewer older hands to put them right.

(Rose 2001: 228). Modernisation meant different things to different people, and partly because of this, the record of the committee was patchy.

The Committee's work was variously criticized for detracting from the ability of the Commons to hold the government to account, for being too piecemeal, and for lacking coherence. This was an especial problem early on, where far too few of the reports contained proposals to help enhance the power of the Commons in relation to the executive. Other proposals were designed for cosmetic or tidying up purposes, or for the convenience of Members.

A lot depended on the attitude of the Leader of the House, especially important in this case as (unusually for a select committee) they chaired it. Robin Cook and Jack Straw both used their role to try to bring in changes that enabled better scrutiny of government. Yet others were more executive-minded. It is not yet clear how the new Leader of the House, Lucy Powell, sees the role. She made many of the right noises in opposition, but then that is what parties do in opposition. The same applies to the Commons Speaker, Lindsay Hoyle, who is much less reform-minded than his predecessor, John Bercow.

The Committee's initial consultation exercise attracted many suggestions for reform, but it was striking (and perhaps depressing) that many of those reported as being raised by new MPs were in fact about making their lives easier, rather than making the life of the government harder. These variously included making it easier to know who was taking part in debates, reforming sitting hours, a return to digital voting and changing the dress code (Webber 2024). Each of these ideas may have some merit (or not); each is debateable as an idea. But it was very difficult to see any sense in which they would help address the structural weaknesses in the Commons when it comes to scrutinizing the government.

5. Conclusion

It is common to talk about relations between government and parliament—but parliament is not a monolith. Different parts within it act independently and with different consequences. Or, as Tony King put it in a landmark article in 1976, parliament operates in a series of different modes. It was, he argued, usually misleading to speak of executive–legislative relations; instead, 'if we wish to understand the phenomena subsumed under this general heading, we need to identify and consider separately a number of quite distinct political relationships' (King 1976: 11).

The most public of these was what he called the 'opposition mode'—that is, the relationship between the government and those MPs sitting on the other side of the House. It is the one around which the House is formally organized and the one on which much media coverage focusses, but King argued it was usually of relatively little importance, not least because a government with a secure majority had little to worry about from the opposition. About all the opposition had was the power of their arguments and the ability to stall and delay. The Blair Government of 1997 took away the latter when it introduced programme motions and it is not too cynical to say that the former will do little against a majority of over 170. For the most part, to quote the former Labour MP Austin Mitchell, all that the opposition will be able to do is to 'heckle the steamroller'.

The House of Lords—where the government does not have a majority—will continue to play a role in scrutiny, and can, at times, be a serious irritant to government. But still, given all of the above, the opposition mode in the Commons is probably even less important now than it had been at most points in the post-war era.

More important was what King called the intra-party mode—which he argued was the key relationship in parliament. If a government with a majority in the Commons can keep its own backbenchers onside, then it can govern. Its problems begin when it starts to lose its own MPs. Here too, there are far more factors that will help the government, at least initially. A large majority, with a large new intake, needs careful handling—but it is still easier to handle than no majority. And initially at least that new intake will be relatively acquiescent.

It has been a long time since we had a government with such a solid position in parliament. The large majority after 2019 was neither as big nor as stable. The position after 2015 and 2017 was self-evidently more fragile. While the Coalition from 2010 to 2015 enjoyed a sizeable majority once you combined the two parties, there was the ever-present risk of it collapsing. The Brown Government had a smaller majority, with lots of MPs who had acquired the habit of rebellion. Even late-Blair, with landslide majorities, found himself facing record levels of backbench dissent and winning some votes narrowly.

Keir Starmer is not Tony Blair, and this is not 1997. The political and economic landscape are very different. But in terms of its parliamentary strength, this is a government in a very similar position to Blair's first term, in some ways even more powerful. We have got very used over the last two decades to almost perpetual parliamentary dramas—narrow votes, huge rebellions, make-or-break moments. There will no doubt be some excitement in the 2024 Parliament. Even Blair in his pomp faced backbench criticism and had to engage with his critics rather more than was obvious on the surface. But it seems much more likely that in parliamentary terms, the next four years may be rather stable, perhaps even a bit boring.

References

Brady, G. (2024) *Kingmaker: Secrets, Lies and the Truth about Five Prime Ministers.* London: Ithaka.

Cowley, P. (2002) *Revolts and Rebellions: Parliamentary Voting Under Blair.* London: Politico's.

Cowley, P. (2005) *The Rebels: How Blair Mislaid His Majority*. London: Politico's.

Cowley, P. (2022) 'Too much, too young?', *The House Magazine*, 3 May 2022.

Cowley, P. and Stuart, M. (2014) 'In the Brown Stuff?: Labour Backbench Dissent Under Gordon Brown, 2007–10', *Contemporary British History*, 28: 1–23.

Cracknell, R., and Baker, C. (2024) *General election 2024: Results and analysis, Research Briefing*. London: House of Commons Library.

Criddle, B. (1997) 'MPs and Candidates' In: D. Butler and D. Kavanagh (eds) *The British General Election of 1997*. London: Macmillan.

Criddle, B. (2010) 'More Diverse, Yet More Uniform: MPs and Candidates' In: D. Kavanagh and P. Cowley (eds) *The British General Election of 2010*. London: Palgrave.

Fleming, T., and Kelly, H. (2024) *Delivering House of Commons Reform: What Works?* London: Constitution Unit.

Hague, W. (2024) 'A tiny opposition is a danger to democracy', *The Times*, 17 June 2024.

King, A. (1976) 'Modes of Executive–Legislative Relations: Great Britain, France and West Germany', *Legislative Studies Quarterly*, 1: 11–36.

Norton, P. (1975) *Dissension in the House of Commons, 1945–1974*. London: Macmillan.

Norton, P. (1980) *Dissension in the House of Commons, 1974-1979*. Oxford: Oxford University Press.

Rose, R. (2001) *The Prime Minister in a Shrinking World*. London: Blackwell Publishers.

Stacey, K. (2024) 'Newly elected MP defends decision to run for select committee chair', *The Guardian*, 10 September 2024.

Thompson, L. (2020) *The End of the Small Party? Change UK and the Challenges of Parliamentary Politics*. Manchester: Manchester University Press.

Umit, R. and Cowley, P. (2023) 'Legislator Dissent Does Not Affect Electoral Outcomes', *British Journal of Political Science*, 53: 789–95.

Webber, E. (2024) 'Britain's new MPs rage at parliament's old traditions', *Politico*, https://www.politico.eu/article/britain-mp-parliament-old-traditions-uk-fresh-labour-government-westminister/, accessed 7 Aug. 2025.

Conclusion: A time to take stock

Stuart Wilks-Heeg[1], Alistair Clark[2,*], and Louise Thompson[3]

[1]Department of Politics, University of Liverpool, 8-11 Abercromby Square, Liverpool, L69 7WZ, UK
[2]School of Geography, Politics, and Sociology, Newcastle University, Newcastle upon Tyne, NE1 7RU, UK
[3]Department of Politics, School of Social Sciences, University of Manchester, Arthur Lewis Building, Oxford Road, Manchester, M13 9PL, UK

*Correspondence: Alistair.clark@ncl.ac.uk

For all that the overall outcome of the 2024 General Election was widely expected, it was none the less dramatic. A sizeable Labour majority and a Conservative collapse resulted after five turbulent years of Conservative majority government, and an overall fourteen years of Conservative (or Conservative-led) administrations. Smaller parties and independents also made significant breakthroughs. 'Change' was Labour's campaign slogan; change was certainly what the electorate delivered. As we noted in the introduction to this volume, it was an election that rewrote the record books.

The previous chapters have detailed the campaign and election outcome in considerable detail. In addition to highlighting some key themes from the election, in this conclusion, we also address a range of other issues which have, to date, received insufficient attention in post-election analysis. Indeed, there are various causes for concern in the UK's electoral process which have been highlighted by the 2024 General Election. Many of these have been building over several years, with only intermittent, if any, focus from government or parliament. If these issues are not to go on to impact British electoral democracy further, we argue that serious and sustained attention must be paid to them in advance of the next general election, expected in 2028–9.

The discussion proceeds in three main sections. The first section highlights some key thematic takeaways from the 2024 General Election. The second section moves on to discuss several causes for concern which, taken together, contribute to a perception that the electoral process in the UK is struggling to deal with

© The Author(s) 2025. Published by Oxford University Press on behalf of the Hansard Society. All rights reserved. For commercial re-use, please contact reprints@oup.com for reprints and translation rights for reprints. All other permissions can be obtained through our RightsLink service via the Permissions link on the article page on our site—for further information please contact journals.permissions@oup.com.

unprecedented challenges. We discuss what, if anything, might be done to address these issues. In the third section, we draw out what the chapters in this book suggest about the likely politics of the next general election.

1. Valence rules OK

After the excitement of the 2017 and 2019 'snap' Brexit elections, the 2024 contest seemed like a return to previous election practices. Although there was some doubt over when Rishi Sunak would call the election, it had been well-trailed as happening in the second half of 2024. The uncertainty was caused by the repeal of the Fixed-term Parliaments Act 2011, which put the power over election timing back in the hands of the Prime Minister. The result was continual, at times almost feverish, speculation over election timing, and which meant that the Conservative government had a 'lame duck' feeling about it. This was exacerbated by the excessive turnover of Conservative party leaders, with three different prime ministers residing in Number 10 during 2022 alone. There was a sense of finality throughout the second half of the 2019 Parliament, as though Liz Truss and Rishi Sunak were shepherding the party through to the inevitable election.

A key theme that emerges in several chapters is that 2024 was a general election that focussed voters' attentions on issues of relative competence. Consistent with valence theories of voting, the core considerations for many voters related to which of the two main parties, and which of their respective leaders, appeared most able to tackle the most pressing issues, such as the economy, inflation, health care, and law and order. The salience of these valence issues owed much to the cost of living crisis which had accelerated with the Ukraine war and the economic policies associated with the short-lived Truss premiership. But the issue agenda was also a consequence of crumbling public services, underfunding of and the ever-expanding demand on the National Health Service (NHS), the economic consequences of leaving the European Union (EU), and myriad other failures in economic and public policy, many of which had developed over a long period. From scenes of ambulances queued outside hospitals, unable to discharge their patients due to a lack of beds, to schools closing due to serious concerns that buildings containing RAAC (reinforced autoclaved aerated concrete) could collapse, an overwhelming sense developed that 'nothing works anymore'.

Put differently, it was a bad election to be an incumbent. Both the Conservatives and the Scottish National Party (SNP) suffered major defeats. The Conservatives' spectacular losses are comprehensively explained by Sam Power, Tim Bale, and Paul Webb with reference to the dramatic deterioration in how the public perceived the party's record on key issues. Likewise, as Ailsa Henderson and James Mitchell set out, the SNP's fifteen point drop in its vote share and loss of thirty-nine seats reflected a longer-term decline, but there can be no doubt that a significant factor was public dissatisfaction with how the SNP had been governing Scotland. With Scottish voters also prioritizing the removal of a Conservative government at Westminster, Labour's return to dominance of Scotland's Westminster representation was secured, albeit on a vote share well below that achieved in 2010, the last time Labour won the majority of Scottish seats. Only Welsh Labour seemed to buck the anti-incumbent trend, at least in terms of seats, but Labour in Wales still experienced a four point decline in vote share.

2. Did the campaign matter?

The received wisdom is that, with the exception of 2017, general election campaigns at the national level make limited difference to the eventual result. Given the modest movements in the polls during the 2024 campaign, it might be tempting to assume that national-level campaign effects were small. The two main parties ran very different campaigns. Labour's approach was cautious, designed to protect a longstanding poll lead. As Hannah Bunting documents, the party's twenty-five point lead was nonetheless eaten into over the course of the campaign, but the election result was never in doubt. By contrast, the Conservative campaign commenced energetically. Alia Middleton and David Cutts note that Rishi Sunak visited seventeen constituencies in the first week alone, in a blitz of activity designed to get the Conservatives back in contention. Yet, even armed with an array of high-profile policy announcements, Sunak's efforts did not seem to move the dial. The Conservatives quickly began to worry more about the risk of being overtaken by Reform UK than about their chances of catching Labour.

However, it would be misleading to assume that limited movements in headline voting intentions for the two main parties are proof that campaigns are not consequential. Timing certainly matters. Theresa May's mislaying of a majority in 2017 serves as a reminder that trying to wrongfoot your opponents by calling a snap election can be less of an advantage than it seems. Sunak's control over election planning was so tight that even senior Cabinet Ministers seemed caught out by his announcement of the date (although some members of the inner circle who did know the date were then found to have placed bets on it). If Sunak thought his chief weapon was surprise, there was no sign that his rivals feared it. Labour, in particular, were well prepared. As Eunice Goes notes in her chapter, Labour candidates in 150 battleground seats posted videos on social media right as Sunak announced the election date. Meanwhile, Sunak's decision not to wait until the Autumn likely proved consequential in drawing Nigel Farage into the race. Farage had previously said he would not be standing, as he planned to be in the USA in October, campaigning for Donald Trump.

The 2024 election provided for some notable contrasts in campaign approaches and offers pause for thought with respect to digital campaigning. Contributors to this book find grounds to dispute the efficacy of digital-first electioneering, despite the hype and large sums of money associated with it. Filip Biały and Rachel Gibson suggest that in many ways it was a 'no change' election in terms of digital campaigning. The use of TikTok grabbed attention, but claims about its significance were over-inflated, partly because parties were largely starting from scratch. Similarly the use of generative artificial intelligence featured less in the election than anticipated. The scale of party spending on digital campaigning was clearly substantial, albeit with very large variations but, overall, Bialy and Gibson find that digital forms of contact still reached fewer voters than more traditional methods. By contrast, some of the strongest evidence offered for the impact of campaigning relates to non-digital approaches. Justin Fisher underlines that the Liberal Democrats eschewed digital campaigning, wherever possible, opting instead for a paper-first strategy.

The Liberal Democrat campaign strategy differed from the two largest parties in other important ways. David Cutts and Andrew Russell note how the Liberal Democrats' geographically targeted campaign emphasized issues such as health, social care, and water quality. These were national issues with strong local relevance in target seats. Ed Davey's campaign stunts succeeded in securing media attention for him, with that coverage frequently used to highlight social care as an issue, where Davey was also able to relate his personal stories and experiences in a credible way. Meanwhile, for the Greens, the long-term targeting of seats paid off, as Lynn Bennie and Anders Widfeldt show. Traditional techniques, many borrowed from the Liberal Democrat playbook, were deployed in four target seats, identified from cumulative success in local elections, and which were the overwhelming focus for Green Party campaign resources. Bennie and Widfeldt suggest that this strategy paid dividends, particularly when contrasted to Reform UK's campaign. Built around Farage's late decision to lead the party, bolstered by a surge in donations and characterized by a national campaign focus, Reform UK's strategy served more to take votes from the Conservatives than deliver seats for Reform UK. In short, in the context of electoral volatility and heightened multi-party competition, how parties campaign is very likely to have made a difference, but with such a landslide national election, campaign effects were primarily evident at the constituency level.

3. Realignment reordered

A key reason why UK elections produced such tight outcomes from 2010 to 2017 was that support for the two main parties in England had become increasingly locked into two rival geographical blocks. Labour support was heavily concentrated in metropolitan areas and university towns, while an equivalent concentration of Conservative support was apparent in rural areas and constituencies dominated by small towns or suburbs. Underpinning these 'two Englands' (c.f. Jennings and Stoker 2016) was a bifurcation of support for the two main parties by age and education (Sobolewska and Ford 2020). A key consequence of this new electoral geography was that there were increasingly few Labour-Conservative marginals in play, creating a sort of electoral gridlock for most of the 2010s. As is well documented, the Conservative breakthrough in 2019 was enabled by the eventual collapse of Labour's 'red wall', a process that can be traced back to the mid-2000s.

However, talk of the 2019 result representing a stable realignment was seriously premature, as the outcome of the 2024 election demonstrates. Instead, the predominant mood of the 2024 election—to get the rascals out—drove new movements of support between the parties and enabled radical changes in the geography of that support. The most successful party campaigns went with the flow of those shifts, based on sophisticated geographical targeting and a recognition that a tide of tactical voting was likely unstoppable in many constituencies. As John Curtice details in his chapter, Labour's support increased where it needed to make gains, especially in Scotland, and was either static elsewhere or even fell, significantly so in its safest seats. Alongside Labour's tendency to win where turnouts are low, these shifts in support meant there were far fewer 'wasted votes' for Labour than at previous elections. By contrast, the Liberal Democrats' haul of seventy-two seats was a product of its vote becoming far more geographically concentrated. Winning 11.1% of the seats on 12.2% of the votes was a remarkably proportional result for the Liberal Democrats and, as Cutts and Russell argue, vindicated its targeted approach. Liberal Democrat success came overwhelmingly in southern England, especially in the South West and the South East.

Psephological hindsight is always more powerful after a general election. It seems clear now that the defining feature of UK general elections over the past decade and more has been volatility, not realignment. This volatility has been a long time in building and was boosted by two referendums, the 2014 Scottish Independence referendum and the 2016 EU referendum. In England, there is no doubt that patterns of socio-economic and cultural change have forged two rival camps of voters, described by Sobolewska and Ford (2020) as 'identity liberals' and 'identity conservatives', respectively. However, it would be a mistake to regard this development as one leading to a stable realignment of voters behind the two main parties. Voters may well be clustering around two poles but they have also moved in complex and unstable patterns between multiple parties. In 2024, it remained the case that Labour voters were typically younger than Conservative voters and that they were also significantly more likely to be educated to degree level or above. However, the starkest demographic divides were between the 2 million voters for the Greens and the 4 million voters for Reform UK. In Scotland, the post-IndyRef bubble for the SNP at Westminster has clearly burst. Whether this necessarily benefits Labour in Scottish elections remains uncertain; Scottish voters have proved adept in the past at voting in different ways for devolved and UK-wide institutions, and may well do so again. We return to the theme of electoral volatility below, suggesting that its persistence should be seen as a cause for concern.

4. Five causes for concern

General elections provide an important health check for any democracy. In a year of elections globally, the 2024 UK General Election was in many ways an exemplar of the democratic process. The election ran smoothly, with no notable or credible allegations of fraud. The result was accepted by both sides and there was an orderly transfer of power. Despite this general clean bill of health, however, there were five features of the 2024 election that we suggest should be seen as causes for concern. We would also argue that these issues, some of which are longstanding, carry important implications for government, parliament, political parties, election officials, the media, and other organizations engaged in the electoral process.

The first, and most pressing, area of concern is the extent to which candidates suffered from intimidation during the 2024 General Election. The Electoral Commission (2024) has reported that there was an 'alarming rise' in such instances. A record number of candidates standing for election in 2024 may seem to suggest that this did not deter would-be MPs from contesting the election. Yet this interpretation would be a mistake. Intimidation has a considerable democratic impact. More than half of the candidates reported forms of abuse that led them to avoid some campaign activities. Reports of intimidation were more frequent among female and ethnic minority candidates. Some would-be candidates were deterred from taking their interest further. These concerns are not new and they are not to be dismissed lightly. The issue was investigated by the Committee on Standards in Public Life in 2017 and by the Joint Committee on Human Rights in 2019. It scarcely seems necessary to underline that two MPs, Jo Cox and Sir David Amess, have been murdered since 2016 while conducting their duties as representatives of the people. Nor are issues of intimidation and abuse unique to parliamentary candidates. Both the Electoral Commission (2024) and the Local Government Association (2024) have reported serious concerns that candidates in devolved and local elections also routinely face such behaviour during election campaigns. The establishment by the House of Commons of a Speaker's Conference to examine threats against MPs and to examine what arrangements are necessary to secure the appropriate protection of election candidates is to be welcomed. Academics have also proposed a wider research agenda around the security of politicians (Matthews and Haughey 2024). It goes without saying that elections free from intimidation and abuse are a fundamental prerequisite of the democratic process and we cannot afford for abusive behaviour to be normalized in future election campaigns.

A second key concern is that turnout fell by 7.5 points, to 59.8%, the second lowest since 1945 and only just above the record low of 59.4%, recorded in 2001. As Hannah Bunting underlines, turnout was down almost everywhere, although the decline was especially marked in Wales and London. There were fifty-eight constituencies in which fewer than half of the registered electors turned out to vote. There has been little discussion of this sharp drop in electoral participation and the factors responsible for it. By contrast, falling turnouts in 1997 and 2001 prompted political concern, research, and inquiries into the causes and were responsible for a rush of government initiatives to try to boost engagement. Some of these, such as plans for e-voting, fell by the wayside but others, notably the introduction of postal voting on demand, are still with us.

There has been no equivalent political response this time around, despite the fact that none of the seven general elections since 1997 have seen turnouts reach 70%. Although administrators have highlighted many technical issues that might be addressed (Association of Electoral Administrators 2025), to the extent there has been a UK government response to 2024's decline, it has seemed underwhelming and lacking in urgency. In a letter to electoral administrators on 15th October 2024, the MHCLG Minister responsible for elections, Alex Norris, did not use the word 'turnout' once, but spoke about participation (Norris 2024). Instead, extending the vote to 16-17-year-olds, a manifesto commitment, was proposed, alongside tweaks to voter identification and a yet further review of electoral registration, something which there has been several parliamentary and Electoral Commission enquiries into in recent years. This response hardly seems adequate to the task, when more than 40% of voters decide to stay at home. The problem looks even worse when those of voting age but not registered, the so-called 'missing millions', are included (Patel and Valgarosson 2024).

Polling data suggest that the drop in turnout is more acute among some social groups than others. It is estimated that only 37% of 18–24s voted in 2024, a far cry from the talk of a 'youthquake' in 2017. Voter identification at polling stations evidently had at least some suppressive effect on turnout. Moreover, Nicole Martin cites evidence to suggest that this impact may have been greater in communities with large ethnic minority populations and higher levels of deprivation. Yet, it would be a huge mistake to return to a framing in which the ease, or otherwise, of voting is seen as the primary consideration. Grappling with the factors driving popular discontent with politics is almost certainly where the focus needs to be.

We regard the disproportionality of the election result in 2024 as a third concern. It should be stressed that the electoral system for UK general elections is not designed to produce proportional outcomes, although it generally did so during the peak of the two-party system in the 1950s and 1960s. However, even staunch supporters of first-past-the-post will struggle to defend its operation in 2024. With Labour securing two-thirds of parliamentary representation on one-third of the votes cast, the longstanding disproportionality of UK general election outcomes hit new heights. As John Curtice notes in his chapter, this level of disproportionately is not just unprecedented in the UK, but in the history of electoral democracy. With record numbers of voters opting for parties other than Labour or Conservative, multi-party politics is clearly here to stay, yet parliamentary representation is still characterized by a near-duopoly. Electoral reform should be on the agenda. Inevitably, it is not. As with previous cycles of debate within the party, Labour's interest in alternative electoral systems appears to have diminished greatly after winning handsomely under the existing one. Meanwhile, the Liberal Democrats, who have consistently suffered the most from the electoral system, and campaigned hardest for its replacement, achieved a remarkably proportional result this time around. The greatest pressure for a new electoral system could well now come from Reform UK, representing a significant shift from the liberal-left sentiments that have dominated debates about electoral reform for over four decades. Other parties, such as the Greens, Liberal Democrats, SNP, and Plaid Cymru, have also called for a fairer electoral system. A non-partisan approach to electoral reform is unimaginable, but meaningful cross-party dialogue on electoral reform has happened before and we would urge that it is attempted again.

The increased volatility of UK general elections is the fourth concern we identify. Arguably, the one consistent feature of elections since 2010 is that voters have switched in unprecedented numbers between rival political parties. The standard measure of electoral volatility, the Pedersen Index, confirms that the three most volatile UK general elections since 1945 have all taken place over the past decade: in 2015, 2017, and 2024. It should be stressed that volatility is not automatically a concerning development. Some landmark elections with high levels of volatility represent moments of significant realignment, ushering in a period of relative stability thereafter. However, for three elections in quick succession to evidence such high levels of volatility represents something else entirely. Set alongside a declining faith in politics, recent electoral volatility is a symptom of deeper democratic problems, not an indicator of electoral readjustment or dynamic democratic change. Sustained volatility is simply instability. We recognize, of course, that the current electoral system greatly reduces the extent to which volatility in vote shares results in volatility in party representation in parliament. However, we are far from convinced that suppressing the impact of electoral volatility can ever deal with its underlying causes. It is also worth underlining that even first-past-the-post has been unable to prevent an enormous turnover in MPs in 2024, as Philip Cowley's chapter sets out.

Our final area of concern relates to polling. Opinion polling is an essential component of modern elections, but its growing influence has also rendered it more controversial. Greater volatility and lower turnouts have become major challenges for the polling industry. Pollsters are having to grapple with volatility not just between elections, but also during election campaigns. Simultaneously, growing uncertainty about who will actually vote has become a major bugbear for those who try to estimate electoral outcomes. Overall, pollsters can claim to have had a relatively good campaign, in the sense that they universally pointed to a clear Labour victory and rarely waivered from that position. Meanwhile, the proliferation of Multi-Level Regression and Post-Stratification (MRP) polls, estimating the number of seats each party will win, rather than vote shares, demonstrated that these have become a mainstay of polling agency activity in contemporary election campaigns. Yet, there was variation in polling company performance underneath this broader picture, indicating that the industry still has issues it needs to resolve in addressing the new, more complex, environment. Questions have thus inevitably been raised about the role and reliability of polling once again. Labour's vote share was clearly over-estimated, although there was a recognition that it was falling as polling day approached. Speculation about Conservative-Reform UK 'crossover' in the polls almost certainly drove political analysis and even party strategy more than it should have done. MRP estimates were frequently wide of the mark and were also used, all too often, in media coverage to predict which senior Conservatives might lose their seats. Indeed, the extent to which polling drove campaign coverage in 'horse-race' style, while not a new concern, has been compounded by the proliferation of MRPs and remains a major issue since it clearly crowds out necessary policy debate during the campaign. There will clearly be lessons to be learned ahead of the next election, especially if the result is expected to be much closer.

5. The future

What, then, for the politics of the next general election? Despite the scale of their victory, there are plenty of warnings in this volume for Labour. The efficiency of Labour's victory in 2024 carries obvious dangers for the party. As John Curtice demonstrates, Labour's landslide victory was built on minimizing wasted votes, but the corollary of this is that remarkably few of its MPs are protected by large majorities. This was a landslide that provides surprisingly weak foundations for a second term. As Eunice Goes highlights, a number of Labour MPs, including frontbenchers like Wes Streeting, have very thin majorities and the party faces challengers in all directions. Lynn Bennie and Anders Widfeldt remind us that the Greens claimed forty second places in 2024 and, having built a stronger organization base, could be in a position to challenge Labour in some areas at the next election. Elsewhere, as Goes stresses, Reform UK came a close second in eighty-nine of Labour's seats, representing an entirely different sort of threat. In their analysis of the results in Scotland, Ailsa Henderson and James Mitchell stress that a fifth of voters said they voted tactically, either against the Conservatives or the SNP. These were ideal circumstances for Labour in 2024 but, as Henderson and Mitchell suggest, victories built on tactical voting are not a sustainable basis for the party's recovery north of the border.

However, none of this makes the Conservatives' task any easier. Labour have a hatful of seats to lose, but the Conservatives have many more that they need to win. While it would be foolish to rule anything out in an era of such electoral volatility, the route for the Conservative to return to power is very difficult to discern. Sam Power, Tim Bale, and Paul Webb suggest that a Conservative recovery over the next four to five years is not impossible but that it will require a fundamental reappraisal of the party's image and positioning. Such moments are challenging for any party but the new realities of multi-party competition add extra jeopardy for the Conservatives. David Cutts and Andrew Russell propose that, while the Liberal Democrats will struggle to advance further at the next election, it is a realistic aim for them to defend most, if not all, of the seats they won in 2024. They indicate that this alone would seriously limit the routes for a return to power for the Conservatives. Meanwhile, the Conservatives must also grapple with how to respond to Reform UK, whose key impact in 2024 was to split the right-of-centre vote. As Power et al. argue, those in the Conservative party urging a further shift to the right to challenge Reform UK are almost certainly very wide of the mark. Taking the fight to Reform UK might well enable the Conservatives to win back some ground, but it is highly unlikely to reinvent the Conservatives as an election-winning machine.

6. Conclusion: a multi-party politics struggling to get out

The idea that the electoral system has suppressed wider party system developments originating from voters' preferences is not a new one. However, it has taken on increased urgency in the aftermath of the 2024 General Election. The effective number of electoral parties (ENEP), a key measure of party fragmentation stands at 4.76, its highest post-war measurement, while the effective number of parliamentary parties (ENPP) remains at 2.24. The party system seems to be demonstrating both centripetal and centrifugal tendencies at the same time, thereby contributing to volatility. Labour have moved to and are governing from the centre, but with pressures to both their left and right, while the Conservatives are finding it hard to resist the siren call to their right from Reform UK.

Aggregating and articulating interests are two key functions of political parties. It is in the tension between these two issues that a key difficulty lies, and which contributes directly to volatility, fragmentation, and low participation. The main parties' efforts at aggregating interests are very clearly not what many people, whether voters or non-voters, want articulated. In other words, potential voters feel that their interests are not being heard by the two main parties. They feel disempowered as a consequence. What many seem to want is an indication that politicians understand their lives, their challenges, and pressures and that distant and centralized authority and responsibility, whether political or economic, offers communities very little sense of agency. Parties have long been said to be adaptive organizations. The difficulty now is that change and volatility are outpacing the more established parties' ability to adapt successfully to myriad complex challenges, including those beyond the nation-state, while at the same time remaining coherent in the offer they make to electors.

The adaptive nature of electoral democracy has always been argued to be a benefit in democratic societies. If parties and policies need to adapt, so too does electoral democracy and the institutions that it empowers—chiefly parliament and government. Addressing issues of disproportionality through some form of electoral reform is clearly necessary, in addition to measures to increase participation. But also making parliamentary procedure more accessible would go some way to opening up the political process. Similarly, instead of increased centralization, a genuine form of localism and devolution, which is not dependent on central government, is necessary. The potential list of reforms is long. Institutions will also need to adapt if the more established parties are not to succumb to the challenges that the 2024 General Election has so very clearly thrown up. To paraphrase a line from a historical novel, 'if we want things to stay as they are, things will have to change' (Tomasi di Lampedusa 2007). The same applies to British politics post-2024.

References

Association of Electoral Administrators (2025) *New Blueprint for a Modern Electoral Landscape: How to Bring Resilience and Capacity to UK Democracy*. Stafford: AEA.

Electoral Commission (2024) 'Research Reveals Unacceptable Abuse and Intimidation Towards Election Candidates', https://www.electoralcommission.org.uk/media-centre/research-reveals-unacceptable-abuse-and-intimidation-towards-election-candidates-3, accessed 22 Jan. 2025.

Jennings, W., and Stoker, G. (2016) 'The Bifurcation of Politics: Two Englands', *The Political Quarterly*, 87: 372–82.

Local Government Association (2024) 'Calls for Respect in Local Elections Amid Rising Levels of Abuse', https://www.local.gov.uk/about/news/

calls-respect-local-elections-amid-rising-levels-abuse#:~:text=Recent%20LGA%20 research%20found%20that,the%202023%20local%20election%20campaign, accessed 22 Jan. 2025.

Matthews, N., and Haughey, S. (2024) 'The Security of Politicians: Towards a Research Agenda', *Parliamentary Affairs*, 78: 227–56.

Norris, A. (2024) *Democratic Participation: Open Letter to the Electoral Sector*, https://assets.publishing.service.gov.uk/media/670ce64b92bb81fcdbe7b750/Alex_Norris_letter_to_electoral_sector.pdf, accessed 27 Jan. 2025.

Patel, P., and Valgarðsson, V. (2024) *Half of Us: Turnout Patterns at the 2024 General Election*. London: IPPR.

Sobolewska, M., and Ford, R. (2020) *Brexitland*. Cambridge: Cambridge University Press.

Tomasi di Lampedusa, G. (2007) *The Leopard*. London: Vintage.

Page intentionally left blank

Page intentionally left blank

Page intentionally left blank